Jesus and Myth

Jesus and Myth

The Gospel Account's Two Patterns

PETER JOHN BARBER

PICKWICK *Publications* · Eugene, Oregon

JESUS AND MYTH
The Gospel Account's Two Patterns

Pickwick Publications
An Imprint of Wipf and Stock Publishers
199 W. 8th Ave., Suite 3
Eugene, OR 97401

www.wipfandstock.com

PAPERBACK ISBN: 978-1-7252-5394-0
HARDCOVER ISBN: 978-1-7252-5395-7
EBOOK ISBN: 978-1-7252-5396-4

Cataloguing-in-Publication data:

Names: Barber, Peter John.

Title: Jesus and Myth : The Gospel Account's Two Patterns / Peter John Barber.

Description: Eugene, OR: Pickwick Publications, 2021 | Includes bibliographical references.

Identifiers: ISBN 978-1-7252-5394-0 (paperback) | ISBN 978-1-7252-5395-7 (hardcover) | ISBN 978-1-7252-5396-4 (ebook)

Subjects: LCSH: Bible. Mark—Criticism, interpretation, etc. | Mythology. | Jesus Christ—History of doctrines—Early church, ca. 30–600. | Girard, René, 1923–2015. | Narration (Rhetoric) | Malina, Bruce J. | Bible. Mark—Social scientific criticism.

Classification: BS2585.52 B37 2021 (paperback) |BS2585.52 (ebook)

02/09/21

"Commit thy works unto the Lord,
and thy thoughts shall be established."
(Proverbs 16:3)

"Commit thy way unto the Lord,
trust also in Him;
and He shall bring it to pass."
(Psalm 37:5)

יְהוָה
אֵלֶיךָ גּוֹיִם יָבֹאוּ מֵאַפְסֵי־אָרֶץ וְיֹאמְרוּ
אַךְ־שֶׁקֶר נָחֲלוּ אֲבוֹתֵינוּ
הֶבֶל וְאֵין־בָּם מוֹעִיל:
הֲיַעֲשֶׂה־לּוֹ אָדָם אֱלֹהִים
וְהֵמָּה לֹא אֱלֹהִים
(Jeremiah 16:19b–20)

εἴ γε αὐτὸν ἠκούσατε
καὶ ἐν αὐτῷ ἐδιδάχθητε
καθώς ἐστιν
ἀλήθεια ἐν τῷ Ἰησοῦ
(Ephesians 4:21)

Barber:
NIHILO NISI CRUCE

Hopkins:
Heb Dhuw Heb Ddim, Duw a Digon

Contents

Acknowledgments

I would like to thank the supervisor of my doctoral studies, Revd. Dr. Stephen Finamore, Principal of Bristol Baptist College, for making the completion of the dissertation form of this work a possibility, and all his invaluable guidance and support. And many thanks to my examiners, Dr. James G. Williams and Dr. Helen Paynter, for their helpful advice and encouragement. Thank you to all the faculty and staff at Bristol Baptist College and Trinity College Bristol, as well as the University of Aberdeen, for much valued support and assistance. I am also thankful to the late Dr. Dietmar Neufeld for his valued guidance and supervision over the years, and the other faculty and staff of the Classical, Near Eastern and Religious Studies department at the University of British Columbia (Vancouver).

On a more personal note, I am so thankful to my dear wife Amanda for supporting me in this work, and all that it entails, for so long. My joy throughout has been our four children, Abigail, Simeon, Taliah, and Emeth. Their patience is undeserved. To my parents, Calvin and Melony Barber, for teaching me faith in Jesus Christ the LORD and standing in His grace, modeling the pattern of Jesus in their walk in His Spirit, and for their unflagging support, I give thanks. I also give thanks for the prayers of the Church. But above all, I thank the LORD Jesus, "who loved me and gave Himself for me" (Gal 2:20). All thanks and praise to Him are due.

Abbreviations

AD	Anno Domini (Year of the Lord)
BC	Before Christ
COD	Canadian Oxford Dictionary
BDB	Hebrew-English Lexicon by Brown, Driver, and Briggs
LXX	Third-Century BC Greek translation of the Hebrew Bible
NASB	New American Standard Bible (English Translation)
OGL	Oxford Greek-English Lexicon by Liddell and Scott
OT	Old Testament (Hebrew Bible)

PART 1

Are the Gospels Mythological?

1

Introduction

The Gospels, Myth, and Culture

"For we did not follow cleverly devised myths
when we made known to you
the power and coming of our LORD Jesus Christ,
but we were eyewitnesses of His majesty."
(2 PETER 1:16)[1]

THE GOSPELS AND MYTH

From the outset in the mid-first century AD, the Gospels of Jesus Christ, the accounts of Matthew, Mark, Luke, and John that begin the New Testament, were recognized as displaying a close relation to myth. The nature of that relationship then, as now, was hotly debated. Today, many view myth as an umbrella under which the Gospels naturally belong, along with so many cultural stories of the ancient past. The earliest suggestions that events occurring in the Gospel accounts are not factual were proposed by persons recorded in those historical accounts. Included in making such statements were members of the Pharisaic (purity) sect of Judaism and the religious elders (chief priests and members of the ruling council or Sanhedrin), who were

1. Author's translation.

propagating disbelief in the resurrection of Jesus (e.g., Matt 27:62–64; 28:11–15). Most significantly, however, Jesus' disciples themselves are recorded as refusing to believe (initially) that Jesus actually rose from the dead (e.g., Matt 28:17; but more clearly in Mark 16:11, 13–14;[2] Luke 24:11, 25–27, 44–48; John 20:24–27). As Luke recounts, "But these words appeared in their sight as nonsense, and they would not believe them" (24:11).[3]

The essential miraculousness of Jesus and His conception, works, and resurrection, is at issue already in the Gospel accounts themselves. This scandal is not only central for the enemies of Jesus, but His disciples, His friends. Then, just as today, the presence of miracles in the Gospel accounts causes hearers and readers to reject Jesus and the Gospels as mythological. But are miracles mythological? What are miracles anyway? For the answers to these questions, see appendix 3. The presence of miracles in the Gospel accounts has nothing to do with the question of whether they are mythological or not, because miracles of creation and providence are actually the substance of everyday life. Morris writes, "There can be no doubt that miracles are possible. The God who established the cosmos in its framework of basic law and its three-dimensional structure of natural processes is clearly transcendent thereto and thus can intervene when and how He will. Such interventions we call 'miracles.'"[4] As such, the matter of the miraculousness of Jesus and the Gospels is not the subject of this book because, perhaps unexpectedly, it is not directly related to the question of Jesus and myth. However, Jesus' unique identity will have bearing on this question.

The central question is actually the similarity of the Gospels to myth, in the sense of the combat myth (hero pattern),[5] found globally in many versions and variants from most ancient times.[6] This similarity was first acknowledged in the New

---

2. The so-called "long-ending" of Mark's account (16:9–20) is considered unoriginal to the account by most biblical scholars today (e.g., Evans, *Mark*, 550). However, it is clearly demonstrable that it is in fact original, despite the witness of codices Sinai (א) and Vatican (B), which omit them (Burgon, *Last Twelve Verses*, 22, 36; Cooper, *Authenticity*, 1:72–3). Prior to the transcription of those two copies in perhaps the fourth century, many early Church Fathers quote, allude to, and discuss Mark 16:9–20. These include Papias (ca. AD 60–130) (Eusebius, *Ecclesiastical History*, 3:39); Justin Martyr (ca. AD 151) (*First Apology*, 1:45); Irenaeus (ca. AD 180) (*Against Heresies*, 3:10); and Hippolytus (ca. AD 190) (frag. Περὶ Χαρισμάτων; *Apostolic Constitutions*, 3:1). I discuss the authenticity of Mark 16:9–20 further in appendix 2. In my analysis of Mark's account, these final twelve verses make up the final twelfth motif of the patterns that I propose exist in the Gospel account.

3. Citations of Scripture are from the NASB unless noted otherwise. However, words and phrases from the Received Text have been restored where missing or altered. These restorations include at least those noted by G. W. and D. E. Anderson, but their list is not exhaustive (*Textual Key*, 1). All text within quotations of Mark that is within brackets is restored from the Received Text.

4. Morris, *Biblical Basis*, 68.

5. The relation between the Gospel accounts and the combat myth or hero pattern has been observed and analyzed to varying extents by a number of modern scholars (e.g., MacDonald, *Mythologizing Jesus*, 1–6; Segal, *Myth*, xxviii–xxxi; Forsyth, *Old Enemy*, 285–306; Dundes, "Hero Pattern," 179–216).

6. Cohn, *Cosmos*, foreword; Fontenrose, *Python*, 6.

Testament itself, and was perceived then by the Apostles as an actual attack on the Gospel message. According to the text,[7] Apostle Peter wrote, "For we did not follow cleverly devised myths [μῦθοι] when we made known to you the power and coming of our LORD Jesus Christ, but we were eyewitnesses of His majesty" (2 Pet 1:16).[8] Apostle Peter goes on to give an example of a miraculous event, the voice of the Father God speaking audibly as Jesus was revealed in His heavenly form, which Peter being present claims to have seen and heard (2 Pet 1:17–18; see Matt 17:1–6; Mark 9:1–7; Luke 9:28–35; and perhaps John 1:14).

Apostle Peter does not specify which myths in particular he and the other eyewitnesses were apparently being accused of having followed. A number of scholars today, and interlocuters of the apostles and early church fathers in the past, have claimed that there are parallels between Jesus and various contemporaneous myths, and mystery religions associated with them, in the Greco-Roman myth-culture.[9] It is fair to say that at first glance there are broad similarities between Jesus' life and actions and those of culturally foundational combat myth hero-gods and villain-gods. These myths were well-known to the peoples of the AD first-century Mediterranean world,[10] and the similarities were evidently apparent to early Gospel hearers and believers. Apostle Paul was ready to acknowledge, and use to his advantage in evangelism, such similarities (Acts 17:22–23, 28).

Certainly, keen awareness of this relation is evidenced in the writing of the Early Church Fathers. Justin Martyr (ca. AD 110–165), for example, soon wrote with specificity regarding combat myths that were evidently perceived to bear relation to the Gospel accounts.[11] He refers to known combat myth variants and their heroes as appearing to be similar, while ultimately being antithetical to Jesus in various key

---

7. The authorship of 2 Peter is disputed, with many biblical scholars today considering the work to be pseudepigraphical (e.g., Brown, *Introduction*, 767; Childs, *New Testament*, 468). However, as with the long-ending of Mark, again, in addition to the Bible's own witness (which for the believer is more than sufficient), we can be confident that 2 Peter is genuine. Among others, perhaps the strongest confirming evidence is the discovery of a fragment of this very letter amongst the Dead Sea Scrolls. The fragment (7Q10) was initially ascertained in all probability to be a piece of 2 Peter 1:15 by DSS staff epigraphist José O'Callaghan (*Papiros Griegos*). This identification is affirmed by Carsten Peter Thiede (*Earliest Gospel Manuscript*, 46–47; Cooper, *Authenticity*, 2:48–49).

8. Author's translation. Ca. AD 64–67. This date is based on the date of Apostle Peter's death as *terminus ante quem* (Robinson, *Redating the New Testament*, 150).

9. House, "Tongues and Mystery Religions," 135. Scholarly discussions of these similarities include Geden, *Mithraism*; Clemen, *Religions*; Pahl, "Mystery Religions"; Schweitzer, *Paul*; Heussi, *Kompendium*; Metzger, "Methodology of Mystery Religions."

10. "There were a number of versions of the combat myth in circulation in the first century CE and they had a common pattern" (Trebilco, *Early Christians*, 395n179). See also Yarbro Collins, *Combat Myth*, 57–100.

11. Similarly, a well-known example of the Early Church Fathers' debates with pagan apologists over whether the Gospels are dependent upon or related to pagan combat myths is Origen's response to Celsus (ca. AD 185–254) (*Origen Against Celsus* 6.42–43).

respects.[12] Justin included in his comparative analysis of myth and the Gospels Jupiter (Jove or Zeus) and his many sons, who engage in combat with and conquer various chaos-monsters that threaten cosmos (world order). He writes:

> And when we say also that the Word, who is the first-birth of God, was produced without sexual union, and that He, Jesus Christ, our Teacher, was crucified and died, and rose again, and ascended into heaven, we propound nothing different from what you believe regarding those whom you esteem sons of Jupiter: . . . Mercury . . . Aesculapius . . . Bacchus . . . Hercules . . . the sons of Leda . . . and Perseus . . . and Bellerophon. . . . And what of the emperors who die among yourselves, and whom you deem worthy of deification. . . . And what kind of deeds are recorded of each of these reputed sons of Jupiter . . . for all reckon it an honorable thing to imitate the gods.[13]

Among other things, it is noteworthy that Justin observes how the gods are regarded culturally as worthy of imitation. That is, he affirms that his contemporaries belonged to a myth-culture: believing in, worshiping and patterning their lives upon the mythical lives of their gods. And what pattern of life did these gods model? Justin Martyr's early and thorough treatment of our present subject, the Gospels' relation to myth and Jesus' relation to the gods of myth, remains highly relevant today. As our analysis proceeds, we will find that the pattern of myth-culture believed and practiced then is actually continuous with our modern culture.

Some nineteen hundred years on after Justin Martyr, and especially in the last two centuries, the debate over Jesus' relation to myth-culture may be said to have been reopened and reinvigorated.[14] While Justin and many since have made important contributions,[15] precision and clarity as to the relation between the Gospels and myth, in particular between Jesus and mythological gods, has eluded us.[16] Many prominent scholars today continue to view the structure, content and values expressed (that is,

12. Justin, *First Apology*, 21–68.

13. Justin, *First Apology*, 21.

14. The recounting of this resurgence often begins with Reimarus, *Apologie oder Schutzschrift für die vernünftigen Verehrer Gottes* [*Apology or Defense for the Reasonable/Rational Worshipper of God*] (1768), who advocated a determined materialist and humanist approach, denial of divine revelation, and rejection of the supernatural origin of Christianity (Gilman et al., "Reimarus"). The champion of this movement in its heyday was Albert Schweitzer, who referred back to Reimarus as originator and wrote the seminal work for the beginning of the modern scholarly search for an historical Jesus, *Geschichte der Leben-Jesu-Forschung* [*The Quest of the Historical Jesus*] (1906). Such a "quest" implies of course that the accounts of the eyewitnesses are untrustworthy.

15. As mentioned, a century after Justin Martyr, early Church father Origen would contend with the pagan apologist Celsus over the same questions. See Origen, *Origen Against Celsus* (ca. AD 248); Celsus, *On the True Doctrine* (ca. AD 176).

16. Despite all that has been written to date, it is still "open season" on the nature of this relation. Many scholars have looked at this question. See, e.g., Alexander, "What Is a Gospel?," 13–30; Culpepper, *Anatomy of Fourth Gospel*, 76–84; Brewer, "Gospels and Folktale," 37–52; Frye, *Anatomy of Criticism*, 158–239.

the whole) of the Gospels as ultimately just another reflection upon and iteration of the combat myth or hero pattern,[17] and/or of the cultures that both composed and were themselves defined by such myths.[18] It is the purpose of this work to demonstrate the inaccuracy of the view that there is any equivalence between Jesus and the gods of myth, between the Gospel accounts and combat myths, or between Jesus and myth-culture.

Nevertheless, the Gospels clearly resemble myth at first glance, and the sort of myth apparent in the Gospels is the kind termed the combat myth or hero pattern. This resemblance is perceived today by a great many scholars (see note 5). Beyond this observation, the precise nature of the relation between the Gospels and combat myth has been more difficult for scholars to ascertain (see note 16 for a number of inconclusive discussions). The Gospel accounts may appear initially to conform to the pattern of episodes and motifs typical of the hero pattern. However, these accounts simultaneously present striking antitheses in terms of the identity, actions and words of Jesus Christ Himself when compared with those of the gods and monsters of myth. What is needed, and so conducted here, is a thorough analysis of the similarities and differences in the structure and significance of the persons and events recorded. Such an analysis leads to a conclusive answer on the relation between the Gospels and myth, Jesus and the gods.

MYTH AND CULTURE

In close connection with the question of the Gospels' relation to myth is myth's relation to culture. Myth and culture are deeply interrelated, as has already been mentioned. As such I use these terms in close association throughout this study. That all human culture[19] has myth at its core is well recognized. For example, Bruce J. Malina

---

17. E.g., MacDonald, *Mythologizing Jesus*, 1–2.

18. E.g., Malina, *New Testament World*, 1–8. Dennis R. MacDonald, from a literary viewpoint, writes: "Ancient Christians told similar stories [to the Homeric poet(s)] about Jesus, their primary super-hero. A Jewish teacher named Jesus actually existed, but within a short period of time, his followers wrote fictions about him, claiming that his father was none other than the god [*sic*] of the Jews" (*Mythologizing Jesus*, 1–2). Similarly, from a social-scientific viewpoint, Bruce J. Malina states, "I submit that [the question of meaning] can only be answered in terms of cultural story. . . . The question we might put to [Bible readers] is whether such meaning comes from *their* cultural story or the cultural story of the people who produced the texts. . . . Jesus condemned divorce, people in our society get divorced, so Jesus must be condemning that sort of behavior in our society . . . [but] do marriage and divorce mean the same thing when Jesus speaks of them and when we speak of them?" (*New Testament World*, 11). From his perspective, Malina seems to assert that the Gospel accounts of Jesus' actions and (most of his) words are mere cultural products, as in mainly unhistorical fabrications or myths. In saying this, I am not implying that all cultural products are mythological.

19. All ancient cultures have myth at their core, that is, with the exception of one nation, ancient Israel (Num 23:8–10; Deut 32:8–18). However, Israel also tended to prefer to adopt the myths and cultures of Gentiles instead of that which God ordained for Israel through Moses. And after the Church's birth, with the rise of Christianized nations, we can speak of partially Christianized cultures. And yet,

asserts that when he says culture, he means the social outworking of shared "cultural stories," in other words, myths:

> Cultures symbol [sic] people, things, and events in such a way that all persons in the group share the *patterns of meaningfulness* that derive from this symboling process. These patterns are assimilated and learnt in the enculturation process, much as we all learn and assimilate the patterns of speech common to our group. For purposes of understanding, *cultural stories* might be broken down into the cultural cues that people assimilate. Such cues include those of perception, feeling, acting, believing, admiring, and striving.[20]

Note that Malina states that culture is governed by "cultural stories" that pre-determine "patterns of meaningfulness." Neither myth nor culture is prior; rather they generate one another. At the same time, while myth and culture are deeply interrelated, it is clear that not all of culture is mythological (see note 19). But it is critical to observe the deep interrelation of the two.

It is helpful to view this relation between myth and culture in terms of the so-called "three pillars" of religion and culture: myth, ritual and law.[21] René Girard asserts that every culture is founded upon scapegoating[22] and upheld by these "three pillars": "[There are] great legal, mythical and sacrificial principles at the basis of every culture."[23] The three religious pillars of law (prohibitions), myth (group narrative), and sacrifice (ritual) define every human culture, and may be best considered in terms of a Venn diagram, where they all overlay in the center. And the center is where the scapegoat lies, at the convergence of law, myth and sacrifice.

There was a time when ritual and myth theorists debated which was prior, ritual or myth, without reaching consensus.[24] This failure appears to be due to presupposing sequential development, whereas the "three pillars" of human culture (human law, myth, and ritual) originate together with scapegoating (Gen 4:1–24),[25] and sustain each other thereafter. It is apparent that it is best to speak of myth-culture (with

---

myth-culture persists in nations and societies, and it battles with Christianization. Yet Israel's prophets spoke of a day when all other nations would abandon their myths and myth-cultures for Israel's God: "O LORD . . . to you shall the nations come / from the ends of the earth and say; / 'Our fathers have inherited nothing but lies, / worthless things in which there is no profit. / Can man make for himself gods? Such are not gods!'" (Jer 16:19–20 ESV).

20. Malina, *New Testament World*, 26 (italics mine).

21. Theissen, "Theory of Christian Religion," 49–51. Theissen writes: "Religion is a cultural sign language which promises a gain in life by corresponding to an ultimate reality" (49). He adds that culture, to the extent that it is a religious sign system, "is characterized by the combination of the three forms of expression that are thus combined only in religion: myth, rites, and ethics" (49).

22. For Girard's view of scapegoating's centrality in myth-culture, see note 35.

23. Girard, *Things Hidden*, 250.

24. See Segal, *Myth*, 61–78.

25. Girard, *Things Hidden*, 99–100, 250.

culture consisting of at least the laws and rituals of a group, based on myth), given this essential interrelationship.

So, culture is myth in action. People act out their story (the "why"), and their story describes and explains their actions. Colloquially this reality is so well understood today that, as an example, news reports and academic papers frequently talk about "changing the narrative" (the myth) of society, or some part of it, in attempts to rectify perceived shortcomings of cultural stories (myths) that have caused or are causing perceived negative impacts on the actual behaviors (laws and rituals) of the group(s)/culture(s) involved in acting them out.

MYTH AND COMBAT MYTH FOR GIRARD AND MALINA

Prior to the analysis of the structure and content of the Gospels, which is the means by which we may better ascertain the relation between the Gospels and myth, Jesus and the gods, some groundwork needs to be established. First, further discussion of myth itself is needed, as we must establish the nature of the category to which we are to compare the Gospels. Secondly, we must have a sense of the current direction of scholarship on the matter. For the purposes of this analysis, I employ two principal representatives of scholarship on the Gospels and myth who work from social-scientific (though also literary) perspectives: René Girard and Bruce J. Malina. These two together display what I think are broadly representative views of myth, as well as of the Gospels' relation to it, amongst a major contingent of biblical and New Testament scholarship. Additionally, their respective views nicely place each other's in relief, forming "reciprocal illumination," which juxtaposition is an aid to the reader's own reflection on the subject.[26]

Girard's and Malina's views are briefly introduced separately here, and then compared and contrasted. Each will also receive a dedicated chapter that fully lays out their readings of the Gospel accounts, prior to our engagement in an analysis of the Gospel text. Before a brief recital of Girard's and Malina's definitions of myth, however, a colloquial baseline is helpful. When we use the term myth today, we usually mean one of six things:

> 1. A traditional narrative usu. involving supernatural or imaginary persons and embodying popular ideas on natural or social phenomena, etc. 2. such narratives collectively. 3. a widely held but false notion. 4. a fictitious person, thing, or idea. 5. an idealized version of the past, esp. as embodying significant cultural realities. 6. an allegory (*the Platonic myth*).[27]

By myth, then, people tend to mean narratives concerning the past that are usually collectively (culturally) formed and shared, but which they tend to view as largely

26. Sharma, *Religious Studies*, 35.

27. COD 1027.

unhistorical and/or immaterial, yet which nevertheless give shape to the present and influence the future.

Some scholars prefer to refer to the Gospel accounts of Jesus Christ as "true myth." Karl Barth preferred the term "saga" for the purportedly mythical portions of Scripture and the Gospels.[28] C. S. Lewis chose to divide true history from fanciful tales within the word myth itself, and so he viewed the Gospels as "true myth."[29] As Young writes, "[Lewis] came to accept the Gospels as, in a sense, myth—but true myth, myth that had actually happened."[30] However, while the term "myth" is simply the trans-literation of the Greek word μῦθος, meaning "story," the Bible itself signals the need to reject this term when referring to Jesus, the Gospels, and the Bible as a whole. We saw this with Apostle Peter's statement already (2 Pet 1:16). We find it again in four statements of Apostle Paul (1 Tim 1:4, 4:7; 2 Tim 4:4; Titus 1:14). These five instances are the only occurrences of the word "myth" in the Bible, and they are all disparaging of the term and what it represents. We can be sure, then, that to the apostles, "myth" is no fit term to describe Jesus, the Gospels, or the Bible.

For this reason, it seems, until about two hundred and fifty years ago, as evi-denced for example in Samuel Johnson's *Dictionary of the English Language* (1768), the Bible including the Gospels was not categorized as "myth," despite myth being defined similarly to the above dictionary definition at that time.[31] Since then, an extra-biblical system of thought has arisen and predominated in the West, which has vari-ously been described as secular, post-modern or neo-pagan in nature (as in departing from the biblical Christian worldview).[32] As a consequence, biblical scholarship today has returned to the sort of debate in which the Apostles Peter and Paul, and Early Church Fathers like Justin Martyr, were engaged, in their distinguishing of Jesus and myth. Oddly however, few scholars have engaged the discussion as thoroughly as the subject deserves, especially given the continued vagueness on the relation, with the claim that Jesus and the Gospels are myth. We now have a colloquial (dictionary) definition of myth, to which we will add the working scholarly definitions of René Girard and Bruce J. Malina.

René Girard's view of myth is something that he spent half a century in formulat-ing, a history that I will not recount in detail here. A number of others have done so

---

28. Barth, *Church Dogmatics*, 1:327.

29. Lewis, *God in the Dock*, 65–67.

30. Young, "Lewis on the Gospels," 1.

31. In Johnson's *Dictionary* we find the following definitions: "*Mythology* . . . a system of fables"; "*Mythologist* . . . a relator or expositor of the ancient fables of the heathens"; and "*To Mythologize* . . . to relate or explain the fabulous history of the heathens." Clearly, the Bible, the Gospels, and Jesus were definitely not myth to English people of the eighteenth century.

32. Of course, this tendency of thought grew with the development of the "enlightenment" critique of Christianity (e.g., Wilson and Reill, *Encyclopedia*, 26, 148).

admirably.[33] Girard's first major treatment of the subject of myth is in *La Violence et le Sacré* (1972), first translated into English in 1977 as *Violence and the Sacred*:

> The generative violence constitutes at least the indirect origin of all those things that men hold most dear and that they strive most ardently to preserve. This notion is affirmed, though in a veiled and transfigured manner, by the many etiological myths that deal with the murder of one mythological character by other mythological characters. That event is conceived as the origin of the cultural order; the dead divinity becomes the source not only of sacred rites but also of matrimonial regulations and proscriptions of every kind; in short, of all cultural forms.[34]

As you can see, Girard's description of myth (and myth-culture) is consistent with the colloquial dictionary definition provided, while adding greater perspective on its origin and nature. He additionally notes that the combat myth is typical of all world mythologies, which involve "the murder of one mythological character by other mythological characters," which he describes as a cultural cycle, re-enacted through ritual sacrifice, that is necessary for the vitality of the community.[35]

This combat myth or hero pattern is in fact considered the arch-myth-type,[36] preceding and encompassing all myth.[37] Ancient cosmogonies, or cultural records of

33. Finamore, *God, Order, and Chaos*, 59–94. For other excellent overviews of Girard's thought, see Golsan, *René Girard and Myth*; Williams, *Girard Reader*.

34. Girard, *Violence and the Sacred*, 93.

35. Girard, *Violence and the Sacred*, 93. Girard asserts that we must read ancient myths such as these in the same way that we read witch-hunting texts of the Middle Ages today (*Scapegoat*, 1–11). In both cases the killing in the accounts is real, but the presentation of the killing and the surrounding events, especially (but not only) with respect to the responsibility of the victim for the troubles afflicting the community, is to be viewed as suspect. The account is suspect in its characterization of the guilt of the victim because it is a product of the lynch mob, the group that slew the victim and wrote the account. Girard calls such accounts "persecution texts": "By [persecution texts] I mean accounts of real violence, often collective, told from the perspective of the persecutors, and therefore influenced by characteristic distortions" (*Scapegoat*, 9). Therefore, the victim in myth is a scapegoat, not a villain or chaos-monster, though usually presented as such. The ability to understand this truth, Girard argues, is an effect of the Gospels themselves on the tribes of the earth, an effect of the Cross (Girard, "Scapegoat," 32–34; Baillie, *Violence Unveiled*).

36. As Joseph Fontenrose concludes, "We have found that the Apollo-Python myth and the Zeus-Typhon myth are two closely related expressions of a single antecedent myth, itself a member of a myth family that ranged over most of Europe and Asia" (*Python*, 465). And he describes his method, saying, "My method of [combat] myth study is thematic. . . . It is a kind of structural method. . . . A single theme may appear spontaneously in several places; a pattern of themes must have a single origin" (*Python*, v). The combat myth pattern, which Nietzsche called "the eternal recurrence" of culture *via* sacrifice of the other (see aphorism 125 in Nietzsche, *Gay Science*), is the myth *par excellence*. It is this mythological world (*inter alia*) that the LORD God conquers as recorded in the Gospels.

37. Fontenrose, *Python*, v, 465; Frye, *Anatomy of Criticism*, 192. There have been many celebrated treatments of this arch-myth-type, the combat myth or hero pattern. See, e.g., Campbell, *Hero*; Rank, *Myth*; Raglan, *Hero*; Propp, *Morphology of the Folktale*.

the genesis of worlds, are consistently of the combat myth type. That is, all except one well-known and unique exception, the biblical creation account of Genesis 1–2.[38]

Bruce J. Malina also articulates a view of myth commensurate with the aforementioned colloquial definition, though he prefers to use the term "cultural story" (see the first quotation of Malina on p. 5). He later writes:

> I began with the observation that human meaning-building is a process of socially contriving lines in the shapeless stuff of the human environment, thus producing definition, socially shared meaning. Human groups draw lines through and around time . . . and space. . . . They also mark off persons with social roles and statuses, things with norms of ownership, and God as a unique being controlling the whole human scene. . . . Humans the world over are born into systems [cultures] of lines that mark off, delimit, and define nearly all significant human experiences.[39]

Malina's definition of myth, or "cultural story," is clearly consonant with the colloquial (dictionary) definition provided. But he certainly moves beyond it to further detail the ways in which myth is formed, maintained and enforced in cultures, in myth-cultures.

The views of both Girard and Malina on the subject of myth are found to be consonant with the colloquial definition given above, yet naturally adding nuance and specificity to common usage. The differences between these two scholars lie not in their views of myth *per se*, but in how each scholar then relates the Gospels to myth. Like Girard, Malina moves beyond our common associations with the term "myth" to offer a more robust sense of the subject, albeit with a different emphasis than Girard.[40] Whereas Girard chooses to analyze the significance of the violent center of

---

38. Some scholars assert that the Genesis creation account exhibits a divine opposition to and pacification of chaos (e.g., McKane, *Jeremiah*, 106–7; Childs, *Myth and Reality*, 42, 76), and therefore that biblical creation also has a cosmos versus chaos (combat myth) element. This view, however, has no basis in the text (see Tsumura, *Creation and Destruction*, 28–33). As Tsumura demonstrates, it is read into the text at Genesis 1:2 by the presupposition of mimetic intertextuality with pagan cosmogonies by falsely assuming a relation between etymologies and source-texts.

39. Malina, *New Testament World*, 152.

40. Girard and Malina also have a critical difference of approach in terms of their use of structural anthropology (which is studying social systems in terms of binary oppositions, recognizing that mythology describes culture in terms of passage from chaos to cosmos, disorder to order). Structural anthropology was pioneered in the work of Levi-Strauss (*Structural Anthropology* [1958]; see Girard, "Disorder and Order," 80). Whereas Girard takes a diachronic view of the structure of culture and myth (Finamore, *God, Order, and Chaos*, 60n5), developing over time and space, Malina works within a synchronic view of the structure of culture and "cultural story" (Malina, *New Testament World*, 19–20), asserting that such structures are treatable only in terms of the particular time and space of a given culture. This difference relates to how Malina speaks of taking a "still picture" of a culture, while Girard speaks of a cycle of recurring events that a culture goes through over a period of time. In keeping with his diachronic approach, Girard views the Bible as a "fantastic battle ground between the two great conceptions of the divine" ("Scapegoat," 19), the societal/cultural and the transcendent/divine. John N. Oswalt also affirms the genuine and unique transcendence of the Bible (*Bible Among Myths*, 185), which distinguishes it from myth.

cultural stories, which is scapegoating, Malina elects to draw attention to the stories' socially fabricated nature. Girard in fact discusses the fictitiousness of myth as well, principally in considering the collective self-deception of cultures' myths, which he alludes to above with the words "veiled and transfigured." Malina, for his part, makes reference to the violent and combative nature of myths, concerning both the social lines formed and maintained by groups (e.g., "clean and unclean"),[41] and pointing out that these socially-formed differences are formed and maintained at the expense of the Other ("limited good").[42] These interpretive models of Girard and Malina are discussed further in the following methodology chapter, and seen in action in their respective treatments of the Gospels.

Both Girard and Malina offer more nuanced understandings of myth than commonly held. Their differing emphases on myth and culture together form a fuller picture, which will be of help in the analysis of myth's relation to the Gospel account. It is their respective readings of the Gospel accounts that diverge most sharply, forming a "reciprocal illumination"[43] that aids in comprehension of how the Gospel account relates to the combat myth. As we shall see, Girard finds the Gospels paradoxically both to conform to and simultaneously contradict myth. We shall see that Malina, on the other hand, views the Gospels as essentially consistent in nature with all "cultural stories," and therefore fitting within the category of myth. This study will show that Malina is right that all those around Jesus belong to myth-culture, but wrong to include Jesus among them. Girard, on the other hand, sees the two patterns. But both provide helpful aids in seeing the two patterns in the Gospel accounts.

MYTH AND GOSPEL GENRE

In the broader, consistently inconclusive discussions attempting to determine the genre[44] of the Gospels, the question of the Gospels' relation to myth is an avenue often explored. Some of the best studies seeking to ascertain Gospel genre look to literary

---

41. Malina, *New Testament World*, 149–83.

42. Malina, *New Testament World*, 90–115.

43. Sharma, *Religious Studies*.

44. There have been many scholarly proposals for the structure of the Gospel accounts, which consideration has direct bearing on the question of genre. A good summary of these proposals is Stanton, *Gospels and Jesus*, 13–36. Examples of such proposals include the Gospels as biography (e.g., Aune, *New Testament*; Burridge, *What are the Gospels?*); as source-collections (e.g., Bellinzoni, *Two-Source Hypothesis*; Kloppenborg, *Formation of Q*); as proclamation-collections (e.g., Taylor, *Formation*; Bultmann and Jaspers, *Myth and Christianity*); as authorial redactions (e.g., Bornkamm, "Stilling of the Storm"); and/or as stories/narratives (e.g., Rhoads and Michie, *Mark as Story*). My intention is not to add another to the heap but to answer a different question—that of the Gospels' relation to myth. In the process of investigation, I have discovered a significant aspect of their structure (I do not assume it to be the only organizational principle of the accounts). This structural discovery has resulted in a greater understanding of Gospel genre.

considerations of myth, including folklore criticism, for answers. Recently one scholar concluded:

> How are we to regard the literary nature of the canonical Gospels today? The genre debate continues as to the nature and contents of a "gospel" or "the Gospels." . . . The literary approach has set the NT Gospels squarely within the concept of "story," with all its implications, including genre. The genre of a piece of literature, then, takes on a very critical role to help determine meaning and understanding for the reader. Recently, more and more scholars have investigated the Gospels as literary documents, comparing them to each other and to other ancient texts. The challenge of clearly identifying the "Gospel genre" presses on.[45]

Every scholar concerned with Gospel genre that I have encountered reaches the same ambiguous conclusion.[46] It seems the greatest success toward finding an answer has been in the realm of literary criticism of myth. The best treatment of Gospel genre in the field of literary criticism that the author has found is in the now classic *Anatomy of Criticism* by Northrop Frye (1971).

Throughout his work, Frye compares the recurrent hero pattern or combat myth with Jesus and the Gospels. As for the Apostles Peter and Paul, and the early Church Father Justin Martyr, to Frye it seems the obvious similarities of the Gospels and myth are not surprising and not problematic in and of themselves. What is interesting is the *nature* of the relation between the two; that is the key. Frye concedes his reading is only an "essay,"[47] and his aim in any case was never to answer the question that we are posing here. He does not reach a conclusion, but does make a significant observation. In his "essay," Frye discusses the Gospels and the Bible generally in relation to myth, involving exploring the mythological cycle: "*mythoi* . . . are these structures of imagery in movement. . . . The meaning of a poem, its structure of imagery, is a static pattern. . . . Narrative involves movement from one structure to another."[48] Frye argues that *mythoi* are "generic plots,"[49] and asserts, "I recognize six phases of each *mythos*."[50]

Frye's observations support the argument here that the combat myth cycle consistently has six phases or episodes,[51] and that the Gospel accounts do as well. I also observe six episodes in the Gospel account by viewing a Gospel account in the light of combat myth scholarship's twelve motifs[52] compared with René Girard's observation

---

45. Diehl, "What Is a 'Gospel'?," 184, 196.

46. Alexander, "What Is a Gospel?," 13–33; Stanton, *Gospels and Jesus*, 13–36.

47. Frye, *Anatomy of Criticism*, 3.

48. Frye, *Anatomy of Criticism*, 140, 158.

49. Frye, *Anatomy of Criticism*, 162.

50. Frye, *Anatomy of Criticism*, 177.

51. Frye, *Anatomy of Criticism*, 177, 198.

52. Forsyth's twelve motifs are listed in table A.

of the three-phase scapegoat cycle of all myth-culture[53] (see table A). This comparison has led me also to the observation of a six-phase structure, enveloping the three and the twelve. Frye never names the six phases, or rather, views them more fluidly than I, but he insists that all *mythoi* (of which he believes there are four types) are structured by them: "The four *mythoi* that we are dealing with, comedy, romance, tragedy, and irony, may now be seen as four aspects of a central unifying myth."[54]

Frye views the six phases as occurring always in two sets of three with varying tones (comic, romantic, tragic and ironic), but possessing consistent basic content. He regularly refers to the Gospel accounts to illustrate each phase or episode, and his description of the typical contents and meaning of the six phases tend to complement the terms and definitions that I offer for them below.[55] That the Gospels and myth both appear to possess these six typical episodes is very significant. It is the trail-head of the path to the answer. The relation between Girard's, Forsyth's, and my own observations on the phases of the pattern of myth is displayed in the following table:

Girard	Forsyth	Barber
1) CHAOS	1) Lack/Villainy	1) SAMENESS
	2) Hero Emerges	
	3) Donor/Council	2) SCANDAL
	4) Journey	
2) SCAPEGOAT	5) Battle	3) SNARE OF STRIVING
	6) Defeat	
	7) Enemy Ascendant	4) SCAPEGOAT
	8) Hero Recovers	
3) COSMOS	9) Battle Rejoined	5) SATIATION
	10) Victory	
	11) Enemy Punished	6) SEGREGATION
	12) Triumph	
TABLE A: Mythological Pattern Models		

GOSPEL GENRE AND THE BIBLICAL REFLECTION STORY

Some Gospel scholars have begun to wonder if the answer to the question of Gospel genre is found in their reception of the Old Testament (or Hebrew Bible), which consists of the Law (תּוֹרָה; Tôrâh), the Prophets (נְבִיאִים; Nĕbîʼîm) and the Writings (כְּתוּבִים; Kĕtûbîm): "But what may be unique is the particular form this tradition [of

53. Girard, *Things Hidden*, 142.

54. Frye, *Anatomy of Criticism*, 192.

55. René Girard has also noted Frye's keen observations of the relation between the Gospels and myth with respect to Frye's identification of the significant role and nature of the scapegoat or *pharmakos* in *mythoi* (Girard, *Oedipus Unbound*, 100; Frye, *Anatomy of Criticism*, 41).

the Gospels] takes when it is written down, a form whose external shape is strongly reminiscent of the Greek *bios* but whose narrative mode and theological framework (connectives, narrative structure, use of direct speech, intertextuality) owe much more to the [Hebrew] Bible."[56] These two aspects, then, are both at play in the Gospel account: (1) biblical structure and (2) biography.

Jesus Himself said after His resurrection, "These are My words which I spoke to you while I was still with you, that all things which are written about Me in the Law of Moses and the Prophets and the Psalms must be fulfilled" (Luke 24:44). Significantly, the biblical view of the origin of myth—the Bible's description of the foundation of myth-culture, beginning in Genesis 3–4 and again in Genesis 10–11—as well as Jesus' fulfillment of much biblical messianic prophecy in the Gospels, directly relate to our question of Jesus' relation to myth, because they converge in the Gospel account. Jesus came, according to the Gospel accounts and the biblical prophecies to which they refer, to fulfill what was written of Him in the Old Testament, and thereby save the world (e.g., Matt 20:28; Mark 10:45; Luke 19:10; John 3:16–17). And we shall see that myth-culture itself constitutes a major portion of that from which Jesus became a man to save humanity. That is, from the biblical perspective: myth-culture is a product of humanity's rebellion against its Maker; humanity's Maker became a human to save us from our rebellion and its consequences. There is a biblical structure to this pattern of events, for which there is a well-known biblical nomenclature.

Myth, with its violent cycle of culture in literary form, that recounts the founding and aids in the maintaining of culture, has origins that coincide with humanity's first great rebellions against God, according to the biblical history to which Jesus refers in Luke 24. And the Bible possesses a particular grammatical-historical structure for the relationship between myth-culture and biblical history, an inversive and subversive structure. One set of nomenclature for this inversive and subversive structure of the Bible-myth relationship, which is "reflection story," has been offered by Yair Zakovitz and Omri Boehm.[57] Based upon Zakovitz's work, Boehm's insights into certain biblical accounts as "reflection stories," as in containing or referencing two opposing patterns, is critical. Yet this terminology does not fully convey the nature of the relation within the terms themselves. I have turned instead to the terminology of chiastic parallelism.

The Bible is full of the literary device termed chiastic parallelism.[58] Various expressions of this device are known to form the structure of many biblical verses, accounts, and books—even the entirety of the biblical canon, and so biblical History.[59]

56. Alexander, "What Is a Gospel?," 29.

57. Zakovitz, "Reflection Story"; Boehm, *Binding of Isaac*.

58. Berlin, *Biblical Parallelism*. Chiastic or cross-like parallelism is the A B || B1 A1 structure so common to biblical literature as well as being found in other ancient writings. There are a number of good descriptions of its basic nature as well as thorough-going bibliographies (e.g., Welch and McKinlay, *Chiasmus*; Berlin, *Biblical Parallelism*; Kugel, *Biblical Poetry*).

59. Genesis 1:1 to Revelation 22:21 forms a sequential chiasm on the largest possible scale: (A) Creation, (B) Fall, (C) Flood, (D) Warring Tribes, (C1) Savior, (B1) Salvation, (A1) Restoration. Hermann

I suggest that the relation between the Gospel account and the combat myth-culture is a concomitant chiastic parallelism, or what I term the chiastic bi-pattern, structuring the entire Gospel account. That is, there are two patterns in the Gospel account. These two patterns proceed simultaneously throughout, but have an inversive and subversive relation to one another.

A working definition of this narratological form or structure of the Gospel account (narratology will be discussed further in the following methodology chapter),[60] which goes to explaining the Gospels' genre, may most succinctly be stated by borrowing the words of David Cayley. In conversation with René Girard, Cayley summarizes Girard's view of the Gospels as, "A redemptive return to the pattern of myth, as well as its overcoming."[61] The proposed twelve motifs and six episodes of the Gospel account contain the pattern of myth-culture, but myth's pattern is systematically inverted and subverted by Jesus. This feature of the Gospel account's two patterns, that of Jesus and that of His opponents (myth-culture), is termed here the chiastic bi-pattern. The nature of this structure, which defines what I therefore refer to as the genre of biblical chiasm, will be explained in the following chapter on methodology.

CHIASTIC PARALLELISM AND REFLECTION STORY

Before we explore the chiastic bi-pattern of the biblical chiasm genre as found in the Gospel account, more must be said about the literary device known as chiastic parallelism.[62] It is most often considered at the level of the Hebrew verse, which in biblical

---

Gunkel has been famously summarized as referring to this overarching sequential parallelism of biblical history as, "Endzeit gleicht Urzeit," or "the end-time closely resembles the beginning-time," in his seminal work, *Schoepfung und Chaos in Urzeit und Endzeit* (1895). Gunkel focused on the clear relation between the Genesis creation account and Revelation's account of the final consummation. He did not actually state it in that formulaic way, but it is a fair summary of his thesis. He wrote, "Wie es zu dieser Übertragung der Mythen von der Urzeit in die Endzeit gekommen ist . . . nicht erklären [As to how this transfer of the myth of the beginning-time came in(to) the end-time is . . . not made clear]" (*Schoepfung und Chaos*, 99). Yet Gunkel affirms the clear parallelism, stating, "In der Endzeit wird sich wiederholen, was in der Urzeit gewesen ist [Itself will be repeated in the end-time, what in the beginning-time has been]" (*Schoepfung und Chaos*, 370). This notion is summed-up in the phrase "eschatology is protology."

60. Narratology is studying the structure of the content of a narrative account as well as how this structure effects the hearer's/reader's perception of its meaning. This approach is thought to begin with Aristotle (*Poetics*), although the term is taken from the work of Todorov (*Grammaire*). The approach drawn upon here is thought to begin in modern scholarship with Vladimir Propp (*Morphology of the Folktale*). For more on this subject see Prince, "Narratology," 524.

61. Cayley in Girard, "Scapegoat," 31.

62. A good overview of the nature of the device as well as a fairly recent bibliography is found in Welch and McKinlay, *Chiasmus*. A much more thorough treatment of chiastic parallelism at the verse-level is found in Berlin, *Biblical Parallelism*. The earliest modern scholar to recognize the significance of this feature of biblical literature and bring its consideration to a prominent place in biblical scholarship, was Robert Lowth, *Isaiah*, written in the eighteenth century.

poetry typically consists of parallel lines. As Robert Lowth stated in his introduction to *Isaiah*:

> The correspondence of one Verse, or Line, with another, I call Parallelism. When a proposition is delivered, and a second is subjoined to it, or drawn under it, equivalent, or contrasted with it, in Sense; or similar to it in the form of grammatical Construction; these I call Parallel lines; and the words or phrases answering one to another in the corresponding Lines Parallel terms.[63]

A generic biblical term for this structure of thought is מָשָׁל (māšāl),[64] meaning a parallel comparison, which is usually translated into English as "proverb" or "parable." However, the meaning of this term in biblical Hebrew is more literally "imitation, likeness or representation."[65] The poetic use of מָשָׁל at the verse level is the most commonly considered form. The parallelism can have various purposes. Lowth identified three types of comparison formed by the parallel lines of the מָשָׁל: synonymous, antithetic, and synthetic.[66] It is the antithetical type that especially concerns us here, in part because it helps form a mental picture of the relationship between the two patterns in the Gospel account, Jesus and myth-culture.

The chiastic parallel antithesis that we are studying between these two patterns in the Gospel account is not at the level of the verse, however. Some scholars have noted that entire accounts (e.g., the global flood account of Genesis 6–9),[67] and entire books of the Bible (e.g., Philippians,[68] and others), are written start to finish with this literary device.[69] Fewer scholars have noticed the type of parallelism that concerns us here, which is also at the account-level in its scope, that I call the chiastic bi-pattern. As mentioned, Omri Boehm has observed two opposing patterns of this sort in the Abraham account (Gen 11:10—25:10). While he does not use my terms, Boehm recognizes two opposing patterns there: that represented by Abraham the LORD's

---

63. Lowth, *Isaiah*, viii.

64. See Kugel's discussion in *Biblical Poetry*, 69.

65. BDB 605.

66. Berlin, *Biblical Parallelism*, 2. Various additional types have been proposed since by various scholars. See Breck, *Biblical Language*; Auffret, *Vos Yeux*; Lund, *Chiasmus*; Alter and Kermode, *Literary Guide*; Andersen, *Sentence*; Bullinger, *Figures of Speech*. For an extensive bibliography, see Welch and McKinlay, *Chiasmus*.

67. Wenham, "Flood Narrative," 336–48.

68. Luter and Lee, "Philippians as Chiasmus," 89–101.

69. Incidentally, the recognition of the extended use of this literary device of chiastic parallelism in biblical accounts by many scholars today has been a key factor in the widespread reconsideration and abandonment of the documentary hypothesis of historical criticism. As Blomberg states, "As it turns out, narrative criticism has regularly demonstrated the literary unity of passages that source, form or redaction criticism often parcelled out into competing stages of the tradition . . . [instead, a text] together probably form[s] a fairly detailed chiastic structure, suggesting that the [account] was a unity from the outset" (*Historical Reliability*, 89).

servant, and that which Boehm calls "the ancient near-eastern myth of child sacrifice." Again, Boehm refers to an account with such a structure as a "reflection story":

> Despite the crucial difference, it seems clear that the similarities between the traditions are more than mere coincidence. . . . What is the connection between the stories? . . . [It is] its motifs being "the same but opposite," the Abraham narrative would appear to be constructed as a "reflection story" of the ancient Near Eastern myth. As soon as we recognize the outline of the reflection, we will be able to examine the nature of the polemic more accurately.[70]

He goes on to state,

> "Reflection stories" are a well-known feature of the biblical narrative. As defined by Y. Zakowich, a reflection story is one in which we can find the same motifs as in another, different narrative, but in inverted form. Like an image and its reflection in a mirror, the inverted image and its movements become an antithesis of the original one. A reader who is able to trace the relation between such stories and understand it—in similarities but especially in differences—will be able to re-evaluate them; their participants, actions, and contents. . . . The dissimilarities . . . are not without meaning; they are "opposite parallels."[71]

Boehm's observations suggest that the structure of the Gospel account proposed here, of two concurrent opposing patterns, does not arise from a vacuum but proceeds from precedents in the Hebrew Bible (Old Testament).

It bears repeating that the literary device termed chiastic parallelism, which at times structures narrative-level chiastic "A B || B1 A1" sequences in biblical accounts, is not the biblical chiasm genre that I am proposing for the Gospel account. Rather, the biblical chiasm genre consists of a different sort of chiastic parallelism. It is a chiasm not of grammar and syntax *per se*, but of narrative content. It is a chiasm of sequences of both narratological motifs and social-scientific episodes, both unfolding in two concurrent patterns. And as we shall see, these two patterns in the Gospel account are: (1) the LORD Jesus and (2) everyone else.

THE GOSPEL FOR GIRARD AND MALINA

Girard, as has been seen, while recognizing significant continuity between the Gospels and myth-culture, views their differences as more important. He provocatively states, "[The Cross in the Gospels] utterly discredits the notion that Christianity is in any sense mythological. The world's myths do not reveal a way to interpret the Gospels,

---

70. Boehm, *Binding of Isaac*, 51.

71. Boehm, *Binding of Isaac*, 51–52; Zakovitz, "Reflection Story"; Levenson, *Death and Resurrection*, 115.

but exactly the reverse: the Gospels reveal to us the way to interpret myth."[72] This view that, despite (or perhaps in part due to) their interrelationship, the Gospels themselves possess the interpretive authority over myth is very counter-cultural academically.[73] Most scholars look to myth to understand the Gospels, not *vice-versa*. Girard's reasons and support for his view will be explored more fully in the following methodology chapter.

Not surprisingly then, Girard's view of the relation between myth-culture and the Gospels faces various scholarly challenges.[74] As expected, a primary criticism Girard faces is opposition to his assertion that the Gospels interpret myth. However, the objection to Girard's position is more cultural than substantive, as it merely reflects the anti-biblical mores of contemporary academic discourse, which tend to dismiss biblical Christian positions out of hand. If Girard can demonstrate his view with the textual and historical evidence at hand, his position is defensible.

In contrast with Girard, Malina views the Gospels as largely consistent with all other "cultural stories," that is, as belonging to the category of myth-culture:

> I submit that [the question of meaning] can only be answered in terms of cultural story. . . . The question we might put to [Bible readers] is whether such meaning comes from *their* cultural story or the cultural story of the people who produced the [Gospel] texts. . . . Jesus condemned divorce, people in our society get divorced, so Jesus must be condemning that sort of behavior in our society . . . [but] do marriage and divorce mean the same thing when Jesus speaks of them and when we speak of them? . . . For the believing Christian, the incarnation of the Word of God means the enculturation [*sic*] of God's Word. And the only way the Word of God, both in the New Testament writings and in the person of Jesus, can make sense to us today is by studying it within the larger frame of AD first-century Palestinian and Mediterranean culture.[75]

Malina argues that the myth-culture in which Jesus lived holds interpretive authority over the Gospel accounts and Jesus Himself. Jesus' identity and the meaning of His

---

72. Girard, "Are the Gospels Mythical?," 27.

73. Robert G. Hamerton-Kelly agrees with Girard's assessment, writing, "The gospel is a critical interpretation of culture because it discloses the victim. Gospel is the opposite of myth. . . . [Myth] portrays culture as arising from the victim's death and thus makes murder necessary and good. Myth justifies the murderers; gospel vindicates the victim. . . . The Gospel tells the truth about the [generative mimetic scapegoat mechanism] and offers the kingdom of God as an alternative" (*Gospel and Sacred*, 12). Hamerton-Kelly calls this "the gospel in the Gospels." I would add only that the conquest of myth-culture is but one facet of the victory won by Jesus Christ in the Gospel account. Myth-culture's conquest is subsumed under Jesus' larger victory over sin and death, which are the causes of myth-culture in the first place, from the perspective of biblical history.

74. A good summary of criticisms of Girard's thought is found in Hamerton-Kelly, *Sacred Violence*, 189–98. A helpful overview of the varied reception of Girard's work is in Stephen Finamore, *God, Order, and Chaos*, 95–130.

75. Malina, *New Testament World*, 11, 17–18.

actions and words, according to Malina, can only be understood through the lens of the writers' culture's story, or myth-culture. Malina concludes that the Gospels' entire structure and meaning is inextricably tied to the "cultural story," and so the Gospels cannot escape being essentially mythological:

> The question then is, What perspective did the author adopt in telling the story of Jesus? . . . [It] is not a process of uncovering objective facts and details of a life story, or what might be called historical truth. Rather . . . it is the production of an articulated narrative understanding of [a] life story refashioned at various times . . . a sort of updated, edited narrative truth.[76]

Malina asserts here that the Gospel account is not "historical truth" but mere "narrative truth," a "production" that has been "refashioned at various times." If they were accurate, Malina's demonstrably fallacious assertions concerning the Gospels' historicity would pose a serious problem for this study's pursuit of the relation between the Gospel account and myth-culture, between Jesus and the gods.[77] But thankfully, Malina's claims that the Gospel account's content and meaning consist of a fabricated narrative arising from the myth-culture of Jesus' social milieu is demonstrably false. And this study demonstrates that reality.

Another obvious and over-arching difficulty facing Malina's view of the relation between the Gospel account and myth-culture is that if, as he contends, the Gospels are consistent with "cultural story," why have scholars been as of yet unable to situate their genre amongst other myth and literature?[78] Malina has a case, even a sound treatment, insofar as Jesus' cultural milieu's harmony with myth-culture as presented in the Gospel accounts,[79] but his attempts to read Jesus' identity, actions and words

76. Malina, *New Testament World*, 198–99.

77. The historicity of the Gospel accounts and the life of Jesus, broadly speaking, is not questioned by most scholars today (Stanton, *Gospels and Jesus*, 145), for the simple reason that in addition to the New Testament witness itself, which is certainly sufficient for believers, there is abundant ancient extra-biblical evidence, both literary and archaeological, that puts the historical reality of the life of Jesus beyond any reasonable doubt.

78. A fair criticism of Malina's thought may be found in Bockmuehl, "Review."

79. Yet Israel did maintain certain distinctives in worldview in the AD first-century Mediterranean from its neighbor cultures and suffered for it. As Bockmuehl notes, in criticism of Malina's broad equation of Israel with surrounding cultures, "Exaggerated claims for a homogeneous and apparently timeless Mediterranean culture seriously compromise the anthropological and historical applicability of Malina's model to the highly specific and unusual context of religious first-century Palestinian Judaism" (Bockmuehl, "Review," para. 6). Despite this important caveat, there remains a certain continuity between the two that comes to the fore in considering the cultural cycle of sacrificial violence distinctive of myth-culture, which is the focus of this study. As noted before, AD first-century Israel was unable and truly unwilling to rebuff the influence of gentile myth-culture. But more than that, human nature has a homogeneity that results in consistent features across cultures. For example, the ambition and fears of the cultural leadership of Israel that drives their antagonism toward Jesus, along with others they perceive to be rivals and destabilizers of cosmos. We see it in the populist sentiment of the people at large who, while harboring messianic expectations of biblical origin, yet do not understand the nature of their fulfillment (as articulated in the New Testament) and so appear to

as expressive of the "cultural story" fall flat. As will be born out in the analysis, Jesus' identity, words and behaviors are demonstrably contradictory to the "cultural story" at every turn of events.

CONCLUSION

The next chapter will lay out the methodology developed and employed for answering the question of the Gospels' relation to myth, and myth-culture. As introduced here, the approach involves both narratological and social-scientific aspects. The narratological aspect involves studying the combat myth in relation to the Gospel account, while the social-scientific aspect involves studying two prominent scholars' interpretive models of myth-culture in relation to the Gospels.

Although the historicity of Jesus and the Gospel accounts is well evidenced today through historical and archaeological analysis (as far as these tools are able),[80] many scholars and much of the general public seem to be under the impression that much if not all of the Gospel accounts are essentially mythological, including Jesus Himself. Looking more closely at the relation between Jesus and myth-culture from narratological and social-scientific aspects will greatly aid our understanding of the Gospel's relation to myth, and Jesus' relation to the gods. After the methodology, chapters 3 and 4 lay out Girard's and Malina's respective readings of the four Gospel accounts. Then in chapter 5, we deploy the method developed here to demonstrate that Jesus is not a myth, and not a product of myth-culture, through a verse-by-verse study of Mark's account of the Gospel. And along with this demonstration that Jesus is not myth comes a stunning discovery, which is that everyone else *is* mythological. While that may seem like an extraordinary statement, its truth and the meaning of it for us today will become clear as we continue this study.

---

expect a fulfillment in keeping with the cyclical pattern with which they are familiar, the pattern of myth-culture. This pattern is typical of all culture, including the first-century Jewish one, despite its obvious and significant differences in other respects. Perhaps, given their inherited Scriptures, they could be expected to have perceived the atypical way in which the Messiah would appear and achieve God's purposes. Indeed, it appears that a number did accept the sort of Messiah Jesus was, and saw that He did indeed fulfill Scripture. Yet the paradoxical nature of the Gospel accounts is such that, had more people seen Jesus for Who He is, much Scriptural prophecy would not have been fulfilled.

80. See, for example, Wenham and Walton, *Exploring the New Testament*, 121–30; Pixner, *Paths of the Messiah*; Stanton, *Gospels and Jesus*, 143–63. For further discussion of external literary evidence for the historicity of the Gospel accounts, see VanVoorst, *Jesus Outside*. For further discussion of archaeological evidence for the historicity of the Gospel accounts, see McRay, *Archaeology*; Rousseau and Arav, *Jesus and His World*.

2

Methodology
Narratology and Social-Science

"And He was saying to them,
'You are from below, I am from above;
you are of this world, I am not of this world.'"
(JOHN 8:23)

THE CHIASTIC BI-PATTERN OF JESUS AND MYTH-CULTURE

The proposed answer to the question of the relation between the Gospels and myth, and in particular between Jesus and the gods, is an account-level criss-crossing of two patterns, the pattern of the combat myth-culture and the pattern of the biblical God incarnate, Jesus Christ. I call this proposed structure of the Gospel account the chiastic bi-pattern. What this entails will become clear as the methodology is laid down, and the study continues into the Gospel readings of Girard (chapter 3) and Malina (chapter 4) and the analysis of Mark's Gospel account that follows (chapter 5).

This chiastic bi-pattern that forms the overall sequence and significance of the Gospel account, both narratologically and social-scientifically, constitutes what I think is fittingly described as the biblical chiasm genre.[1] While I believe there are other

1. Genre is simply a term we use to classify general kinds or styles of literature and art. The Gospels' genre is still debated today, as while it appears to have affinities with a number of different genres, it is not

examples of accounts possessing this structure and so belonging to this genre, both within biblical literature as well as subsequent Christian literature,[2] only the Gospel according to Mark will be thoroughly analyzed for this structure in this study. Mark's account is briefest of the four Gospels, yet it contains the full sequence of episodes, as are also found in full in the other three Gospel accounts (see table c). Since we have room for the treatment of but one Gospel account here, it is sensible therefore to work with Mark.

NARRATOLOGY

Narratology is studying the structure of the content of a narrative account, as well as how this structure effects the hearer's/reader's perception of its meaning. This pursuit is thought to begin with Aristotle, who endeavored to understand (*inter alia*) "the structure of the plot/narrative" (πῶς δεῖ συνίστασθαι τούς μύθους).[3] The term, however, is taken from the early work of Tzvetan Todorov, in which he coined (in French) "narratologie" to mean the search for the basic structure of narrative.[4] I use the term narratology to refer to consideration of the narrative structure of the Gospel account in relation to the combat myth motifs. This aspect differs from consideration of the social-scientific structure of the account in relation to the social episodes of myth-culture in the account.

While there are various schools of narratological scholarship today, the sort of narratology utilized here descends from the work of Vladimir Propp (*Morphology of the Folktale*, first published in 1928 in Russian). The primary combat myth scholar employed in this study, Neil Forsyth (*The Old Enemy: Satan & The Combat Myth*), cites as his primary scholarly precedents Joseph Fontenrose (*Python: A Study of Delphic Myth and Its Origins*) and Vladimir Propp.[5] For his part, Fontenrose writes, "My method of myth study is thematic. . . . It is a kind of structural method. . . . A single

---

unequivocally of a particular type. Some have thus considered the four Gospels to be *sui generis* ("of their own kind," "unique" [e.g., Kuemmel, *Introduction*, 37]). I propose here that, while I do not think it is the only genre reflected in the Gospels, they are indeed of a uniquely biblical genre that I term biblical chiasm. Using a similar term to the literary device of chiastic parallelism aids in recognizing the continuity this genre has with earlier biblical thought. The biblical chiasm genre is defined by a particular structure of the sequence and significance of an entire account, featuring a "cross-stitching" of the two antithetical patterns, the LORD Jesus and myth-culture. This sort of genre as encountered in the Hebrew Bible (Old Testament) has been previously termed a mirror account or a "reflection story" (e.g., Boehm, *Binding of Isaac*, 51–52).

2. There are many examples of later Christian literature structured with this dual antithetical pattern, and so falling into the proposed genre of biblical chiasm, but a more recent example that I have identified is the hugely popular *Harry Potter* series (see Barber, "Combat Myth," 183–200).

3. See Aristotle, *Poetics* (ca. 335 BC).

4. Todorov, *Grammaire*.

5. Forsyth, *Old Enemy*, 441–52.

theme may appear spontaneously in several places; a pattern of themes must have a single origin."[6] Forsyth, in turn, writes:

> Because Fontenrose's various themes and plot components are unsystemati-
> cally derived and depend so heavily on the personal characteristics of the ac-
> tors (a limitation from which Propp's model is free), it is clear that we need a
> more rigorous but still flexible model for the ancient combat narratives, based
> on the event principle of Propp's functions.[7]

Taking, as it were, the best of Propp and Fontenrose, Forsyth identifies a twelve-motif sequence of events typical of combat myths around the globe from ancient times. He writes, "Each of the twelve features of the schema in the table[8] represents a significant incident in the plot structure of most ancient combat narratives."[9] Forsyth includes in his table (*inter alia*) the combat myths: Gilgamesh and Enkidu versus Huwawa, Baal and Anat versus Yamm and Mot, Ninurta versus Anzu, Bel-Marduk versus Tiamat, and Zeus versus Typhon.

These last two combat myths, Marduk vs. Tiamat and Zeus vs. Typhon, will be used as representatives for comparison with the Gospel account. Zeus vs. Typhon is contemporaneous (in terms of still being widely believed and followed, as described by Justin Martyr, for example) with the time and place of the Gospel accounts' events and composition. The myth of Marduk vs. Tiamat as preserved in the *Enuma Elish* was contemporaneous in composition with the writing of the Hebrew Bible (Old Testament), and the Old Testament is explicit background in the Gospel account, it being what Jesus became a man to fulfill (e.g., Matt 26:56). We noted in the introduction that Zeus and his sons were compared and contrasted to Jesus by Justin Martyr, demonstrating that early on an association was being made between them. The twelve sequential motifs of the combat myth identified by Forsyth, based on the work of Fontenrose and Propp, are (1) Lack/Villainy; (2) Hero Emerges; (3) Donor/Council; (4) Journey; (5) Battle; (6) Defeat; (7) Enemy Ascendant; (8) Hero Recovers; (9) Battle Rejoined; (10) Victory; (11) Enemy Punished; and (12) Triumph (see table A).[10]

The Twelve-Motif Hero Pattern of the Combat Myth

The Zeus-Typhon myth is quite contemporary in usage with the time of Jesus,[11] though Fontenrose considers it to predate Hesiod in composition, who was active

---

6. Fontenrose, *Python*, v.

7. Forsyth, *Old Enemy*, 444.

8. Forsyth, *Old Enemy*, 448–51.

9. Forsyth, *Old Enemy*, 446.

10. Forsyth, *Old Enemy*, 448–49.

11. In the introductory chapter I noted that this myth—and many others—were "living" in the AD first-century Mediterranean, being widely known and believed (Trebilco, *Early Christians*).

perhaps in the eighth century BC.[12] The Zeus-Typhon myth is understood by Hesiod,[13] one of its earliest extant bards, as well as modern combat myth scholarship[14] to show mimetic intertextuality. That is, the myth borrows from and develops earlier similar combat myths, and, within its narrative admits of being a successive cycle of sacrificial violence typical of human myth-culture. Zeus is a rebel god, purportedly establishing "order from chaos" by combating and destroying a previous rebel god (Kronos, Zeus's father), who himself supposedly established "cosmos from chaos," and so on back to the original rebel (see Isaiah 14:12–15).[15] The latest rebel-god is considered the hero-god of the myth, and the older rebel is considered the villain-god or chaos-monster.

The pattern in the Zeus-Typhon myth has been shown by Fontenrose and Forsyth to possess the same typical sequence of motifs as all other combat myths:[16]

1. Lack/Villainy: The birth of Typhoeus to Tartaros and Gaius, who then threatens to take heaven and control of earth, hurling flaming stones and belching fire;[17]

2. Hero Emerges: Zeus alone stands his ground;

3. Donor/Council: Hera warns Zeus of the threat;

4. Journey: The other gods flee to Egypt, while Zeus sees Typhon and takes his stand;

5. Battle: Zeus pelts Typhon with thunderbolts from a distance, then moves in with a sickle and wounds Typhon who flees, Zeus follows and grapples him;

6. Defeat: Typhon captures Zeus in his coils and takes Zeus's sickle, severs his sinews, and takes him to his cave;

7. Enemy Ascendant: Typhon hides Zeus's sinews in a bearskin and sets a dragoness to guard them;

8. Hero Recovers: Hermes and Aigipan recover the sinews for Zeus and restore them to him;

9. Battle Rejoined: Zeus renews battle, mounting his chariot and hurling thunderbolts at Typhon;

12. Fontenrose, *Python*, 74; West, *Hesiod*, 40.

13. E.g., Forsyth, *Old Enemy*, 85–86.

14. Forsyth, *Old Enemy*, 85; Fontenrose, *Python*, 73–74; Walcott, *Envy and the Greeks*, 15–26.

15. This line of mythological "hero gods" traces back to Nimrod, the first rebel after the global flood, who has been identified as Gilgamesh (Livingston, "Who was Nimrod?," 71) and Marduk (Morris, *Long War*, 250; *Genesis Record*, 264), the first post-flood imitator of that first rebel, Lucifer (Satan). Satan was the first to claim to be restoring order from chaos while truly exalting himself and subjugating others (Gen 3:1–4). As is typical of myth-culture, he was merely engaged in sameness with another, in this case, the one true God of order (Isa 14:12–15; Morris, *Revelation Record*, 166–67). We will study what "sameness" is in what follows.

16. Forsyth, *Old Enemy*, 448–49; Fontenrose, *Python*, 9–11.

17. As summarized by Fontenrose (*Python*, 70–76), based on the combined extant accounts of the myth as per Hesiod, Homer, Aeschylus, Pindar, Apollodorus (the earliest and fullest account; *Bibliotheca*, 1.6.3), Oppian, Nonnos, Strabo, Nicander, Ovid, Nigidius, and Ammon.

10. Victory: Typhon flees then stands to fight, Zeus casts Mount Etna upon him and pins him down;

11. Enemy Punished: Zeus imprisons Typhon in Tartarus under Mount Etna;

12. Triumph: Zeus recovers Olympus and rule of the world for himself and the other gods.

The order and meaning of the twelve motifs of the combat myth are clear in Zeus's combat with Typhon. The question is: Does Jesus conform to this pattern?

The Twelve Motifs of Jesus' Pattern

Narratologically, the Gospel account may appear at first glance to share the sequence and significance of the combat myth with its twelve typical motifs, with two motifs within each of the six social-scientific episodes (see table A), but through careful observation and right division between Jesus and those around Him in each motif, it becomes clear that each motif of the myth-pattern is inverted in sequence and subverted in significance by Jesus. That is, Jesus' motif-pattern "criss-crosses" its mythological parallel.[18] The pattern of the biblical God in Jesus Christ criss-crosses the pattern typical of the gods of myth within the Gospel account. As such, I argue that Jesus "fails" to conform to myth's pattern, or succeeds in being non-mythological. Concurrently, those around Jesus, who oppose Jesus in the Gospel account, adhere to the pattern of combat myth motifs in sequence and significance. So, it is everyone around Jesus who fail to be non-mythological. From this narratological aspect, then, that looks at the pattern of the twelve myth-motifs, the proposed relation between the twelve motifs of the combat myth and the twelve motifs of Jesus' pattern may be illustrated the following way:

Myth's Episodes	1	2	3	4	5	6
Myth's Motifs	1 2	3 4	5 6	7 8	9 10	11 12
	X	X	X	X	X	X
Jesus' Motifs	2 1	4 3	6 5	8 7	10 9	12 11
Jesus' Episodes	6	5	4	3	2	1
TABLE B: The Combat Myth Pattern + Jesus' Pattern = The Chiastic Bi-Pattern						

18. Interestingly, this term was originally written "Christ-cross" (the first syllable being pronounced like that of "Christmas"), and even earlier, "cros-cryst" (the mark of a cross written before the Alphabet in hornbooks). It was (is) used in the saying, "Christ-cross me speed" (May Christ's Cross give me success) before reciting the Alphabet. The term is of late fourteenth-century origin and began to be spelt phonetically as "criss-cross" circa 1818 (Harper, *Etymology*; COD 359). Colloquially, it denotes anything that traverses or consistently cuts across another thing, and that sense is active here.

SOCIAL-SCIENCE

Social-scientifically, the interpretive models of Girard and Malina together aid in perceiving the relation between the Gospels and myth-culture, Jesus and those who emulate the gods of this world (which are everyone else in the Gospel accounts, as we shall see). The social-scientific aspect of the method enables the reader to perceive the six episodes of the pattern of myth-culture in the Gospel account, which is lived by everyone else in the account except Jesus, as well as the six concurrent episodes of Jesus' pattern in the Gospel account that form the opposing parallel. At the same time, as mentioned, the narratological aspect of the method enables the reader to perceive the twelve motifs of the combat myth pattern in everyone except Jesus in the Gospel account, as well as the twelve concurrent motifs of Jesus that form the opposing parallel.

The social-scientific episodes and the narratological motifs are simply different aspects of the same pattern, as will be evident in the analysis in chapter 5. The combined methodological lenses of narratology and social-science form a more comprehensive picture of the Gospels' relation to myth, and Jesus' relation to myth-culture. There is considerable overlay between the work of Girard and Malina on the nature of myth-culture, as stated in the introduction, and also crucial disagreement at the point of application of these interpretive models to the Gospel accounts, and to Jesus in particular. Each scholar's approach will now be laid out separately. Thereafter, their approaches will be compared and contrasted.

Malina recognizes six principal social "models," or staple features defining AD first-century Mediterranean myth-culture. He has called these models: (1) honor-shame, which is really the primary lens, guiding or over-arching the others; (2) dyadism; (3) envy; (4) limited good; (5) purity-impurity; and, subsumed under that last in Malina's view, (6) marriage-kinship.[19] The model of purity-impurity is equated by Malina with culture's insider-outsider (or cosmos-chaos) mentality, and so (among other reasons) accounts for many scholars grouping Malina's social-scientific approach with social identity theory.[20]

In describing his understanding of honor-shame,[21] Malina asserts that conscience equals culture.[22] By this he means that a person's sense of right and wrong is determined by his social milieu, and there is no higher morality. Honor, shame, and dishonor are

---

19. Malina, *New Testament World*.

20. Horrell, "Social Sciences," 3–28.

21. "Honor means a person's (or group's) feeling of self-worth and the public, social acknowledgement of that worth. . . . The word 'shame' is a positive symbol. Positive shame means sensitivity about one's own reputation, sensitivity to the opinion of others" (Malina, *New Testament World*, 48–49). Malina summarizes honor, in a word, as "reputation" and shame as "concern for reputation" (*New Testament World*, 50).

22. Malina, *New Testament World*, 58.

only ever socially determined to Malina.[23] Ultimately then, the primary goal of a good person is to be well-thought of by other people, to be praised by humans.

In defining dyadism,[24] Malina asserts that persons in the AD first-century Mediterranean[25] only have identity in relation to the group or culture.[26] Together with this view, Malina asserts that God is a culturally-determined idea, a projection of the group-mind of society. In other words, *vox populi, vox dei* ("the voice of the people (is) the voice of god") as the Latin motto goes.[27]

Arising out of a dyadic social context is rampant envy. Malina draws on the thought of Aristotle to define the phenomenon of envy as pain at the success of the other,[28] precipitating all manner of ill-treatment of the other to gain the life of the other, at the expense of the other.

Limited good is the term Malina uses to summarize the worldview and practice of gaining life at the expense of the other. He asserts that first-century Mediterranean people think "good"—comprised of social position, prosperity, pleasure, power, prestige, and "progress"[29]—is limited. There is not enough to go around, and so sacrifice of others to ensure "progress" (and the other limited 'p's) for you and yours is necessary and good.[30] Malina writes, "[Limited good means] . . . individuals, alone or with their family, can improve their social position only at the expense of others."[31] Subsumed under this model is patron-client relations, or the view that since there is not enough, the socially "lowly" must grovel to the "uppity" to "improve" by unequal exchange of favors.[32]

The fifth model for Malina's social-scientific approach is purity-impurity,[33] which is the perception that the cultural milieu of Jesus' time and place was heavily

23. Malina tends to assert that the culture of the first-century Mediterranean is less "evolved" or simply different than twentieth-century Western culture, though he quite regularly equivocates on this view (*New Testament World*, 66–67).

24. "The 'dyadic' person is essentially a group-embedded and group-oriented person (some call such a person 'collectivity-oriented'). Such a group-embedded, dyadic personality is *one who simply needs another continually in order to know who he or she really is*" (Malina, *New Testament World*, 62 [italics mine]).

25. But not here today, in Malina's view, since he subscribes to the popular "modern" notion of imperial individualism (*New Testament World*, 61–62).

26. Malina, *New Testament World*, 58–80.

27. For this reason (and others), scholars like Peter Berger and John Milbank have concluded that social scientific approaches like those of Malina amount to "methodological atheism." See Horrell, "Social Sciences," 16; Porpora, "Methodological Atheism," 57–75; Berger, *Sacred Canopy*, 180.

28. Aristotle, *Rhetoric* 2.10.1–3; Malina, *New Testament World*, 111.

29. Summarizing the culture's "limited goods" in terms of 'p's are my words, not Malina's.

30. Malina, *New Testament World*, 89; Horrell, "Social-Scientific Interpretation," 13.

31. Malina, *New Testament World*, 89.

32. Malina, *New Testament World*, 95–97. Malina does not address the clear continuity between the "then and there" and the "here and now" of this cultural model or the others he describes.

33. "Now purity is specifically about the general cultural map of social time and space, about arrangements within the space thus defined, and *especially about the boundaries separating the inside*

concerned (at the leadership level mainly) with the preservation of social purity and religious hierarchy by boundaries for those deemed unclean by the insiders.[34] Clear walls of separation between insiders and outsiders are necessary to maintain culture; cosmos expels and bars chaos.

Malina's final model of marriage-kinship[35] is really a subset of purity-impurity, which in his view involved (*inter alia*) the practice of gender inequality in AD first-century Mediterranean culture. "Goods" are less if at all accessible to females than males, and there are cultural and institutional features that maintain this problem.[36]

While Malina does not observe that his "models" occur sequentially, Girard describes the typical social behaviors of myth-culture in terms of a pattern, a cyclical social-ordering system: "Archaic religions and their sacrificial systems are an economy of scapegoating that violently evacuates internal violence and, *through the endless repetition of ritual*, slowly generates cultural institutions."[37] The "endless repetition" is of the ritual of scapegoating, and the episodes that lead up to and follow it. Girard refers to these episodes, describing the repetition as following a discernible pattern: "In an enormous number of myths, we find a cluster of themes that, despite the extremely diverse variations they can undergo, always remain compatible with the pattern I have in mind, the pattern of a scapegoating delusion narrated from the standpoint of the deluded persecutors."[38] So, Girard states, "The periodicity of the . . . rhythmic . . . changes that occur in human relationships . . . have as their pivot the death of a sacrificial victim."[39] This pattern, with scapegoating at its center, makes up the pattern of myth-culture, from the social-scientific viewpoint. The global combat myth or hero pattern is the same pattern, viewed through the narratological lens.

Girard equates this pattern of myth-culture with the "eternal recurrence" observed by Nietzsche;[40] a cyclical recurrence of cosmos to chaos to cosmos *via* what Girard calls the scapegoat mechanism, or substitutionary single victim mechanism.[41] Therefore, Girard appears to recognize three basic phases of the "endless repetition":

---

from the outside" (Malina, *New Testament World*, 164 [italics mine]).

34. Malina, *New Testament World*, 161–73.

35. "Social norms . . . present the 'oughts' of a group. These are the cultural cues guiding people to perceive and evaluate the persons, things, and events of their experience. Kinship refers to patterns of such social norms that regulate human relationships" (Malina, *New Testament World*, 134).

36. Malina, *New Testament World*, 158–59.

37. Girard, "Violence Renounced," 318 (italics mine).

38. Girard, "Generative Scapegoating," 79.

39. Girard, *Violence and Sacred*, 255.

40. Girard, "Scapegoat," 45. Nietzsche's descriptions of the "eternal recurrence" are found, for example, in *The Gay Science* (aphorism 125) and *The Will to Power* (aphorism 1052). In aphorism 125, Girard explains, "Nietzsche defines in rigorous fashion the passage from disorder to the sacrificial order through the mediation of the collective murder and the rituals which spring from it. One cannot kill the gods, any gods, without engendering new ones . . . the philosophy of the eternal recurrence" (Girard, "Founding Murder," 241).

41. Girard, *Violence and Sacred*, 254–55; *Things Hidden*, 142.

chaos, scapegoating, cosmos (see table A). To Girard, the mythological world (culture) can be articulated in social-scientific terms as the periodic oscillation between differentiation (cosmos) and non-differentiation (chaos), a process that social groups attempt to control and institutionalize *via* sacrifice, myth and law, or the three religious pillars of every culture.[42]

Girard makes plain his view that all cultures are mythological, asserting, "Every culture in the world is based on a foundational murder," "all societies believe in witch-hunting," and "scapegoating is universal."[43] Girard does not lay out "the cluster of themes" that "always remain compatible with the pattern"[44] in every culture in the manner of Forsyth, Fontenrose or Propp. However, he does go beyond his three broad phases of "chaos, scapegoat, cosmos" to actually describing the various states of affairs in the process of development throughout this "pattern."[45]

Girard considers there to be a default state of affairs for this world, a constant potentiality, which is the basis of myth-culture itself, that always sets the stage for the pattern of episodes that follow. This basic and initial state, or "episode," is:

1. Humans desiring what others desire, so that desire is ever "borrowed desire"[46] in pursuit of metaphysical "being."[47] Humans do not simply desire what others have, we desire what others desire. We imitate the Other's desire, and this is "mimesis."[48]

42. Girard, "Disorder and Order," 84–86.

43. Girard, "Scapegoat," 25, 33, 12.

44. Girard in Hamerton-Kelly, "René Girard," 79.

45. Girard has also described this pattern of myth-culture in terms of a "mimetic mechanism": "The expression 'mimetic mechanism' covers a phenomelogical [*sic*] sequence which is quite broad. It describes the whole process, beginning with mimetic desire, which then becomes mimetic rivalry, eventually escalating to the stage of mimetic crisis and finally ending with the scapegoating resolution" (*Evolution*, 56).

46. By internal mediation, Girard means: "Desire is essentially borrowed desire. There is no such thing as natural desire, otherwise it would be instinct. If desire had a fixed object, it couldn't change, and it would be the same thing as animal instinct. Therefore, desire comes always from the other. Therefore, this other, if he is close enough socially or physically, will necessarily become our rival when we desire his object" (Girard, "Scapegoat," 2). This statement summarizes internally mediated desire, or mimesis with someone close to you, and the way this mimesis produces acquisitive mimesis. Acquisitive mimesis is the desire to "consume" the rival-other in order to acquire the shared object of desire. See also Girard, *Things Hidden*, 7–10.

47. "Metaphysical being": "Being, in the traditional sense, absolute being, is something I don't have in me. I don't feel it. I feel my emptiness. But the other always seems to have more [being] than I have" (Girard, "Scapegoat," 36); "It's everybody's tendency to feel that the other is more successful. It's also everybody's tendency to feel I am more successful, or I should be more successful. But anyway, the problem will be there because Man is essentially a dynamic individual, who wants to occupy the whole ground" (3). Here Girard is also describing the concern for social reputation, as Malina refers to it, the desire to "keep up with the Jones's," a pursuit of "metaphysical being." These are two different ways of expressing the same social phenomenon.

48. Girard, *Deceit*, 5–9. The term mimesis (a transliteration from Greek) has various usages and meanings. The basic meaning, as in Greek, is imitation. But it is not imitation *per se* that Girard means by it, but rather imitation of another's desire, so that by mimesis he means borrowed desire. A good

As a result, Girard describes the culture as a mimetic model:[49] everyone wanting what everyone else wants, and ultimately, what everyone else *is*, their "being"; a state of affairs that Girard terms interdividuality.[50] Interdividuality is a state that is always prone to what Girard calls "non-differentiation" or chaos.[51]

2. Girard talks about what naturally arises from this state of uncertainty, or passive chaos, which is "scandal," or active chaos. Out of "interdividuality" arises "scandal," where the model for one's desire, whose desire one imitates, the "double,"[52] frequently blocks one's desire so that he feels he must scapegoat and "devour" the model (metaphorically, usually). The scandalized person hangs the shared scandal around the rival's neck, as if the other is solely responsible, and drives him out for it, or worse kills the rival. All this is in order to gain the (illusory) social being the model has, or blocks, and one lacks.[53] So, Girard uses the term "scandal"[54] to mean the blocking of desire, and he states that this term and its meaning comes directly from the Bible.

3. Scandal eventually gives rise, according to Girard and as mentioned previously, to his second broad phase of "scapegoating."[55] Girard sometimes refers to this

---

discussion of mimesis and Girard's usage of the term is in Finamore, *God, Order, and Chaos*, a section entitled "Imitation and Representation: Mimesis," 61–63.

49. Girard, "Scapegoat," 37.

50. Girard, *I See Satan*, 137n2. Interdividuality means that a person has a sense of identity only through another: "Where does desire, that is to say, psychological movement, come from? Where does it get its energy? From the relation to the other. This relationship with the other seems to me so close and so fundamental that it should not be seen as merely a relation between two individuals, two subjects, but as a reciprocal movement of back and forth, carving out in each of its poles, by its very motion, an entity that can be designated as the 'self.' That is why Girard, Lefort, and I . . . named the psychology of this relationship 'interdividual psychology.' We intended by this to found a new psychology . . . that would no longer be a psychology of the individual or monadic subject" (Oughourlian, *Genesis of Desire*, 31–32). A human should not be considered as monadic or individual, but as *dyadic* (as Malina also states), as interdividual.

51. Girard, *Violence and Sacred*, 49.

52. Girard describes the social phenomenon of mimetic doubling in this way: "The marvelous paradox is that the closer you are, the more your goals will be the same. . . . You receive the command, imitate me, and at the same time there is another command which is, do not imitate me. So I think the perfect form of the double bind is found in mimetic desire. . . . There is a tendency never to express a double bind because, if you express it, you express the essential contradiction of living together, which is competition" (Girard, "Scapegoat," 3–4). The double-bind moment, or mimetic doubling (sameness), leads to scandal with each rival for the same desire blocking the other. Girard borrows the term double-bind from the work of Gregory Bateson on schizophrenia (Bateson, "Schizophrenia," 201–27).

53. Girard, "Scapegoat," 22.

54. Scandal means that: "Others encourage us to imitate their desires; but, as soon as we do, we find that they become competitors because now we want the same thing and are in each other's way. The Greek word that the New Testament [and the OT] uses for this feature of mimetic desire . . . is 'skandalon,' which means literally 'snare' or 'stumbling block.' . . . The skandalon is the model that becomes an obstacle, period" (Girard, "Scapegoat," 22).

55. Girard describes what scapegoating means the following way: "What Frazer did was to realize that all communities have practices of the same type and he called them scapegoat rituals.

period between initial scandal and scapegoating as "mimetic snowballing," an escalation toward a crisis that scapegoating resolves.[56]

4. Scapegoating itself would be the fourth feature, then. A unanimous, collective scapegoating of an innocent victim brings about a return to order, differentiation, cosmos. But there is another transitional event between the scapegoating and the re-established cosmos, and that is:

5. A collective consumption event, or feast. Girard describes this event as a recovery of life for the community through consumption, metaphorical or otherwise, of the scapegoat.[57] A part of this event is the divvying-up of the corpse of the victim, literally and/or metaphorically. It is this event that leads directly to the re-establishment of:

6. Differentiation, hierarchical order; cosmos. This reorganization naturally flows out of the divvying-up of the corpse of the victim, literally and/or figuratively.[58] Re-establishment of cosmos, or order, involves the entombing or containment of the victim, literally or metaphorically.

While Girard does not list the events of the myth-pattern as I have just done, we can see that he clearly does speak of these six episodes. He also asserts that they belong to a cyclical pattern. Individuals and groups in this world go round and round in this predictable pattern of thought and behavior, with always another scapegoat. Is there an escape?

Myth-Culture for Girard and Malina

The following observations reveal that Girard's approach is in general agreement with Malina's approach to the mythological features of AD first-century Mediterranean culture, the cultural milieu of Jesus. Girard agrees regarding the nature of social values and behaviors in myth-culture. But Girard asserts at least two additions. First, God and His activity as Jesus Christ are not subsumable under cultural milieu; the god of culture is not the same God of biblical Christianity.[59] For Girard, Jesus Christ is not a

---

He called them scapegoat rituals because there was already a tendency in our language, in our modern languages, to use the word 'scapegoat' for an innocent victim who is killed or chased out by everybody . . . what the [Israelites] were doing in the scapegoat ritual [Lev 16:20–28], and all other cultures in comparable rituals, was to systematize and ritualize a psychosocial mechanism which is part of daily life" (Girard, "Scapegoat," 12).

56. Girard, *Violence and Sacred*, 93–99.

57. Girard, *Violence and Sacred*, 277.

58. Girard, *I See Satan*, 82.

59. "Before, I made only a great separation between the archaic and the Christian. And that's necessary because the Christian God is still the monotheistic God, not a pagan god. And it's love that is divinized, not violence. But there is complete symmetry between the two. And, when there was no Judaeo-Christian revelation, archaic religions were the only thing Man had, the only contact with

product of mythological culture; the voice of the cosmic crowd is not the voice of the biblical God. Secondly, Girard views not only AD first-century Mediterranean culture but all culture as mythological in the six (plus) ways that Malina outlines.

Like Malina, Girard also describes the fundamental social features (or models) of culture, including AD first-century Mediterranean culture. Though he uses different terms, Girard's various descriptors are comparable to Malina's models (which can be gathered into a rough table, table D), so that several general equations can be made between Girard's and Malina's social-scientific readings of culture, which we have shown to be defining characteristics of myth-culture or cultural story. These features of culture, as Girard notes, occur in a typical pattern. The sequence of everyday social events is in fact the sequence of the combat myth, hero pattern, or eternal recurrence.

To describe the fundamental principle of culture, rather than Malina's language of honor-shame and dyadism, which implicitly refer to concern for what others think of oneself and a desire to please others (a *passive* social pressure), Girard talks about "borrowing desire," acquisitive mimesis, internal mediation in pursuit of metaphysical being (an *active* social pressure). Girard's interdividuality is akin to Malina's dyadism. Humans only know "being," or a sense of really living, through imitating the desire of another, and so feeling part of a cultural group. Similarly for Malina, a dyadic person's sense of identity is helplessly tied to his or her social group, the culture.

What is honorable in culture, Girard agrees with Malina, is whatever the cultural elites are doing. Those with the most metaphysical being (social life), due to possessing most of the cultural 'p's or limited goods, define honor and shame. What is dishonorable is being unable to gain that social being, that sense of really existing, that a member of the myth-culture always feels he or she lacks.

In desiring what the other desires, a person regularly finds himself in rivalry with, striving with, his neighbor for the same objects, the same goals, the same cultural 'p's or limited goods. Honor is found in attaining aspects of elite social life, dishonor is failing to do so. Shame is the constant anxiety of dyadic or interdividual people, worrying about how they look and "measure-up" to the group's elites. Malina views this shame as a positive motivator with good social and individual effects. Girard views this internal mediation as a deformed mimesis; a dysfunctionality and a prison.

Malina's "limited good" describes the fundamental cultural feature that Girard terms scandal and the need for striving (combat) with the model-obstacle and scapegoating. Similarly, Malina's model of limited good is the difficulty of accessing the cultural 'p's (prosperity, position, pleasure, power, prestige, and progress) due to the impediment of others, often involving oppressive hierarchies, in the culture. So, gains of these goods are always at an other's expense.

---

transcendence. . . . So this complete symmetry of the symbolism between Christianity and archaic religions, the fact that it's the same story, is extremely important and should be read, not only as separation between the two, but as union" (Girard, "Scapegoat," 31–32).

Social purity, Girard agrees with Malina, is differentiation, or cosmos (order, hierarchy) and impurity is non-differentiation (which Girard equates with tragedy, or the loss of clear distinction in the group between good and evil, hero/god and villain/chaos-monster). Impurity is when there is no privileged form of violence or sacrifice.[60] This is a plague on culture, when the society or cultural group disagrees as to whether it is "good" scapegoating we do when we destroy and "devour" the other for our own cultural advantage, or whether some "pure" (one or ones) have become chaos-monster(s) themselves, the violence being criminal and not sanctioned or pure.[61] Impurity is also anything kept outside the society/group due to culturally perceived unfitness. Girard groups such social accusations among "stereotypes of persecution."[62]

Finally, there is Girardian and Malinan agreement that oppressive marriage relationships and gender hierarchies are a part of the oppressive order of myth-culture, and stereotypes of persecution, into which females often fall more often than males, amongst the weak/infirm (infants and elders), and regularly dirty and/or bloody.[63] Female impurity also relates to their liability to "cause" scandal to male mimetic rivals who objectify women and quarrel over them bringing chaos to cosmos (obviously, this scandal goes both ways for the sexes, but male power in most cultures skews the "narrative" or cultural story). In myth-culture, women must be controlled, hidden, and covered to prevent scandal or impurity.

The third pillar of myth-culture, law or prohibition,[64] is the domain of cultural mores including kinship regulations, which preserve differentiation and delay the return to chaos. Concerning the fundamental social features of myth-culture, Girard and Malina appear to be in broad agreement (apart from the aforementioned difference that Malina speaks only of AD first-century Mediterranean culture while Girard speaks of all culture). Malina's six social-scientific models complement Girard's six social-scientific events (see table D).

The Six Social-Science Episodes of Myth-Culture

As we read through the Gospel account, we will see that the people and worldly powers around Jesus in the Gospel account adhere to both the twelve-motif pattern of the combat myth as perceived through the narratological lens, as well as the

---

60. Girard, "Scapegoat," 14, 35.

61. Girard, "Scapegoat," 14.

62. Girard, *Scapegoat*, 12–23. "Stereotypes of persecution" means "the victims are chosen not for the crimes they are accused of but for the victim's signs that they bear, for everything that suggests their guilty relationship with the crisis" (Girard, *Scapegoat*, 24). In short, the person looks guilty but is not, and is punished anyway.

63. Girard, *Scapegoat*, 18–19.

64. Girard, *Things Hidden*, 10–19.

six-episode pattern of myth-culture as perceived through the social-scientific lens (see table A). For ease of usage I have chosen to provide alliterative names for the six episodes of the pattern of myth-culture while, I hope, avoiding any loss of the sense of the episodes. They are: sameness, scandal, snare of striving, scapegoating, satiation and segregation:

1. Sameness: un-differentiation or the chaos of many rivals for authority, which tend to reduce into two.[65] They are doubles, though one is considered to be a hero of cosmos according to myth and the other a villain of chaos: the hero-god and the monster-god.

2. Scandal: the blocking of the other by each rival for authority in their shared striving for the object of their desire. This episode is sometimes described as a council or two opposing councils, where plans are laid to block the other.

3. Snare of striving: the setting in motion of the plan, the war-path to combat, the skirmishing and testing of the combatants, and striving to ensnare one another.

4. Scapegoating: the victory of the hero of the mythological community; they have their monster in hand.

5. Satiation: the grotesque sacrifice, dismemberment and shared consumption of the monster.

6. Segregation: the re-establishment of order, of cosmos, on the foundation of the corpse.[66] As such, the tomb is the foundation of myth-culture (Matt 23:27; Luke 11:44).[67]

The following table lays out the six social-science episodes of myth-culture, and terms and/or concepts that Girard and Malina employ for them:

---

65. Why two? "The whole tribe ultimately will kill one victim. Why? Because, as the mimesis works laterally, it will be cumulative, ultimately, and from its own accumulating weight will become more and more intense. For instance, you can see this in a civil war where you have several centers of trouble which tend to turn into two. Why turn into two? Because with mimetic rivalry . . . this process of substitution, or transference, is . . . what makes the mimesis cumulative and, ultimately, must gather the whole group against a single victim" (Girard, "Scapegoat," 6).

66. Regarding this transition from the scapegoat phase to the segregation (final return to cosmos) phase, *through* the satiation or ritual consumption/devouring event, Girard states the following (note that although he speaks in literal terms here, the point is equally relevant metaphorically or socially): "The eating of sacrificial flesh, whether animal or human, can be seen in the light of mimetic desire as a veritable cannibalism of the human spirit in which the violence of others is ritually devoured. Mimetic desire, once frustrated, seeks at once to destroy and to absorb the violence incarnated with the model-obstacle. This explains why cannibals are always eager for their victim to demonstrate by a show of courage that he is the incarnation of supreme violence. And, of course, the victim is eaten only after he has been killed, after the maleficent violence has been completely transformed into a beneficent substance, a source of peace, strength, and fecundity" (Girard, *Violence and Sacred*, 277).

67. Girard, "Evangelical Subversion," 39.

6 EPISODES	GIRARD	MALINA
SAMENESS	Desire Doubles	Dyadism
SCANDAL	Model-Obstacle	Envy
SNARE of STRIVING	Mimetic "Snowballing"	Agonism
SCAPEGOAT	All Against One	An Other's Expense
SATIATION	Collective Devouring	Sharing of Limited Goods
SEGREGATION	Artificial Hierarchy	Social Classification

TABLE D: The Six Social-Science Episodes of Myth-Culture

THE PATTERN OF MYTH-CULTURE IN THE BABYLONIAN COMBAT MYTH

As stated, for the narratological and social-scientific analysis of Mark's account in chapter 5, we will compare and contrast representative combat myths on the one hand, and Jesus and His opponents in the Gospel account on the other. First, it is critical to recognize that the combat myth pattern viewed narratologically, and the myth-culture's pattern viewed social-scientifically, are one and the same. To demonstrate this, we will now analyze the combat between Marduk and Tiamat. This myth evinces the presence of both the twelve-motif pattern of combat myth as viewed narratologically, and concurrently the six-episode pattern of myth-culture as viewed social-scientifically. In fact, we find that each of the six episodes consists of two of the motifs (see table A).

The earliest probable date of composition for the Babylonian Cosmogony or *Enuma Elish* is circa the twentieth century BC, in the recently established city-state of Babylon,[68] after the global flood (Gen 10:6–12). Such a date would be contemporaneous with biblical Abram (Gen 11:10–26). Despite the obvious mythicality of the Sumero-Akkadian gods and their actions, there is a psychic honesty regarding emotions and motives behind the actions described in the Babylonian Cosmogony. These motives make plain not only the sequence of events of the twelve sequential motifs of combat myth, but also the cause driving each of the six episodes of the pattern of myth-culture.

First, we look for the initial two narratological motifs, lack/villainy and hero emerges (see table A), in that order, all amid descriptions of social-scientific sameness, with its chaos of non-differentiation and the formation of rival doubles between two persons who will become known as god and monster. And from the very first lines of this epic poem of "creation" we have described a definite lack, with basic aspects of reality already in existence, though with no specified origin or cause, and these basic

---

68. Dalley, *Myths*, 229.

realities, including the sky and the earth, are "not yet named," "not formed," with "no gods," "no names," and "no destinies."[69] So, lack is clearly the first motif.

Immediately following, we encounter the second motif expected of myth, which is the hero's emergence: "He, Nudimmud [Ea], was superior to his forefathers. . . . He had no rival among his peers."[70] Nudimmud (or Ea) is the initial hero described, but he would soon become the father of Bel-Marduk, who will be the main hero of the myth. These two motifs, lack/villainy and hero emerges make up the first sameness episode.

The sameness theme of the first episode runs throughout these two motifs. For example:

> The gods of that generation [led by Ea] would meet together / And disturb Tiamat, and their clamour reverberated. / They stirred up Tiamat's belly, / They were annoying her by playing inside Anduruna. / Apsu could not quell their noise / And Tiamat became mute before them.[71]

This is the beginning of the chaos of sameness, the beginning of mimetic rivalry between Ea (Nudimmud) and his son Bel-Marduk (as we will soon see) on the one hand, and Apsu and Tiamat (the first god and goddess named) on the other. Ea becomes the rival-double of Apsu, and most significantly for the narrative arc of this myth, Marduk becomes the rival-double of Tiamat. So to summarize, we have seen that the first sameness episode of the combat myth of Marduk and Tiamat is made up of the lack/villainy motif followed by the hero emerges motif. This is the expected order, content and meaning of events in episode one of the pattern of myth-culture (see table A).

The second episode is scandal, made up of the third and fourth motifs, donor/council and journey, in that order. The third motif occurs as Apsu holds a council in which his vizier (Mummu) advises him to destroy Ea and the younger gods.[72] And the fourth motif that ends this second scandal episode immediately follows as the younger gods, having heard of Apsu's plot to destroy them, send their hero Ea on a journey to pre-emptively destroy Apsu.[73] The theme of scandal runs throughout both motifs that make up this second episode, from Apsu and Tiamat's scandal at the younger gods' actions, led by Ea, to the younger generation of gods' scandal at hearing of Apsu's plan to destroy them. Ea's pre-emptive expedition that results leads to the first violence of the myth: "[Ea] put Apsu to sleep . . . / He unfastened [Apsu's] belt, took off his crown, / Took away his mantle of radiance and put it on himself. / He held Apsu down and slew him."[74] Then, during this journey that closes the second scandal episode, Bel-Marduk, son of Ea, is born out of the corpse of Apsu. So to summarize,

69. Dalley, *Myths*, 233.

70. Dalley, *Myths*, 233.

71. Dalley, *Myths*, 233.

72. Dalley, *Myths*, 234.

73. Dalley, *Myths*, 234–36.

74. Dalley, *Myths*, 235.

the second scandal episode is comprised of donor/council and journey, in that order (see table A).

The third episode of the pattern of myth-culture, snare of striving, immediately follows, made up of the fifth and sixth motifs of combat myth, battle and defeat. Preparations for battle begin as Tiamat is enraged by Ea's murder of her consort Apsu, and she and her supporters prepare for war to destroy Ea, Bel-Marduk and their supporters.[75] Tiamat selects a general for her forces named Qingu. Meanwhile, Ea also prepares to battle Tiamat and Qingu. Ea and the younger gods give all authority to "Marduk the hero!" to lead them into battle against Tiamat.[76] Marduk's terms for agreeing to be the hero are that when he wins, he must be given all authority over the gods and the cosmos.[77] All the younger gods, those not with Tiamat, agree to give Bel-Marduk all authority over themselves and the cosmos, and they equip him with powerful weapons and an army to battle Tiamat and Qingu.

But the sixth defeat motif immediately follows, concluding the third snare of striving episode, as Marduk sets out on the road to battle and "set his face" toward Tiamat. As their armies meet, Marduk becomes confused and disoriented in the fray, and he and his forces seem to face defeat, about to crumble before Tiamat and Qingu.[78] The theme of the snare of striving (or striving to ensnare) runs through these two motifs, as the rival god and goddess, Marduk and Tiamat, seek ways and attempt means of capturing and destroying each other. So to summarize, the third snare of striving episode of the pattern of myth-culture consists of the fifth and sixth combat myth motifs, battle and defeat, in that order (see table A).

The fourth episode of the pattern of myth-culture is scapegoating, comprised of the seventh and eighth motifs of the combat myth, enemy ascendant and hero recovers. Tiamat, "the enemy," is immediately ascendant as Marduk quails and, for a moment, Tiamat appears indomitable, as though she, Qingu, and their forces are certain of victory.[79] But then all at once, Bel-Marduk finds courage, and the eighth motif that closes the fourth scapegoating episode occurs as Marduk the hero recovers.[80] Marduk's new-found "courage" derives from assigning all of the responsibility for the conflict onto Tiamat and her "false" co-regent Qingu, notably failing to mention Ea's role in the troubles. And this lie gives Marduk the confidence he needs to attack Tiamat. The theme of scapegoating runs throughout these two motifs as Tiamat is repeatedly assigned all the blame for the scandal and violence taking place amongst the gods, the myth claiming of Tiamat that, "In her lips she was holding falsehood, lies, (wheedling)," and Marduk saying to her, "you have compounded your wickedness

75. Dalley, *Myths*, 236–52.
76. Dalley, *Myths*, 242.
77. Dalley, *Myths*, 244–49.
78. Dalley, *Myths*, 252.
79. Dalley, *Myths*, 252.
80. Dalley, *Myths*, 252–53.

against the gods my fathers."[81] So to summarize, this fourth scapegoating episode of the pattern of myth-culture is made up of the seventh and eighth combat myth motifs, enemy ascendant and hero recovers, in that order (see table A).

The fifth satiation episode is comprised of the ninth and tenth motifs, battle rejoined and victory. Battle rejoined immediately ensues as Marduk then uses his weaponry and, in single combat with Tiamat, splits her open down the middle, throws down her corpse, and stands on top of her. He also slays her new consort Qingu, and all of their forces are captured or killed.[82] The tenth victory motif immediately follows as Marduk declares his defeated enemies his slaves. He then smashes and mutilates Tiamat's body, carving and dividing it up, and he makes, "the North Wind carry off [her blood] as good news."[83] Marduk's fathers, the younger gods, are all spectators for this mutilation of the body and dispersion of their scapegoat's blood, and they "were jubilant: they rejoiced, arranged to greet [Marduk] with presents, greetings gifts."[84] The theme of the fifth episode, satiation, runs throughout the two motifs that comprise it. Marduk is sated on his enemies, and the young gods are collectively sated on Tiamat's mutilation and scattering. So to summarize, this fifth satiation episode of the pattern of myth-culture consists of the ninth and tenth motifs, battle rejoined and victory, in that order (see table A).

The sixth and final segregation episode of the pattern of myth-culture is comprised of the final eleventh and twelfth combat myth motifs, enemy punished and triumph. The eleventh enemy punished motif immediately begins as Marduk takes his time in further carving up various parts of Tiamat's corpse, and fashioning them into the world, so that her body is entombed in the earth, and also divided up for the benefit of the whole world, her corpse forming the cosmos.[85] With half of her corpse he forms the sky. He then arranges her waters, and builds a temple (a ziggurat) for himself, and makes stands (plinths) for the other great gods (Anu, Ellil, Ea). He sets up the stars and marks out the times and seasons with them. He makes various other things out of Tiamat's corpse to fill the cosmos, and from her head and two eyes Marduk forms the springs of the rivers Tigris and Euphrates. He also took the defeated gods and paraded them before the younger gods, his fathers. He set up images of them at the door of his palace, Apsu, as a warning sign "that will never in future be forgotten!"[86]

The twelfth and final motif, triumph, that ends the final sixth episode, immediately follows[87] as the three great gods of the younger gods, Anu, Enlil and Ea, Bel-Marduk's fathers, bring him gifts. All the gods come before Marduk and kiss his feet,

---

81. Dalley, *Myths*, 252–53.

82. Dalley, *Myths*, 253–54.

83. Dalley, *Myths*, 254.

84. Dalley, *Myths*, 254.

85. Dalley, *Myths*, 254–57.

86. Dalley, *Myths*, 257.

87. Dalley, *Myths*, 258–74.

and their leaders declare to all the gods, "Previously Marduk was (just) our beloved son / But now he is your king. Take heed of his command."[88] Marduk (Nimrod) then establishes cosmic order by first creating Babel (Babylon), the center of the world and religion.[89] He declares, "Whenever you [gods] come down from the sky [and up from the Apsu] for an assembly, / Your night's resting place shall be in [Babylon]."[90] Marduk then makes humanity from the blood of slain Qingu, the rebel god, to "impose the toil of the gods on man and release the gods from it."[91] Marduk thus established an oppressive order and purpose for humanity, and then divided up and subjugated the gods into their places and roles. The myth concludes with all the gods giving Bel-Marduk glorious appellations, kingly titles. Among the appellations heaped upon Marduk are various other decrees regarding the order and cycles of the natural world and its governance in perpetuity.

The theme of the sixth episode of myth-culture, segregation, runs throughout its two combat myth motifs. The eleventh motif, enemy punished, consists of Marduk dividing up the corpse of his scapegoat, and oppressing his defeated enemies. The twelfth motif, triumph, consists of him dividing up his subject gods, humans, and other creatures into their allotted positions and roles under his absolute authority. Note that all Bel-Marduk's fathers are subjected to him as well (the subjection of the father to the hero-son is characteristic of myth), and all gods and beings are required to heap praise on Marduk. So to summarize, the final sixth segregation episode of the pattern of myth-culture consists of the final combat myth motifs, enemy punished and triumph, in that order (see table A).[92]

The Bible's Second, Superior Logic

Girard refers to this pattern of myth-culture, as just explored in the Babylonian cosmogony, as conforming to what he terms the Heraclitean logos,[93] or logic of violence.[94] He notes that the Bible uniquely presents a second type of logic, which he calls the Johannine logos, or loving logic.[95] The two types of logos are social ordering systems expressed by the two types of mimesis, internal and external,[96] that he

88. Dalley, *Myths*, 258.

89. Dalley, *Myths*, 259.

90. Dalley, *Myths*, 259.

91. Dalley, *Myths*, 261.

92. Hamerton-Kelly, in his commentary on the Gospel of Mark from a Girardian perspective, compares the Babylonian Cosmogony and notes that it is clearly a sacrificial combat myth antithetical to the Gospel accounts (Hamerton-Kelly, *Gospel and Sacred*, 64–68).

93. By "logos" Girard seems to mean (*inter alia*) a principle of social order.

94. Girard, *Things Hidden*, 263–70.

95. Girard, *Things Hidden*, 270–74.

96. Mimesis that is externally mediated is a form of imitation of desire that does not cause non-differentiation, rivalry, and all that follows in the pattern of the myth-culture. Girard describes it this

proposes. Girard's two *logoi* appear to be other terms for the Two Ways message of the Bible,[97] which I think is at the heart of what I am calling the genre of biblical chiasm, because each of the two opposing patterns embodies one of the two logics. Of the first type of logos, which is the logic of myth-culture, Girard writes, "It is the violence of the sacred [i.e., myth-culture] that inhibits the doubles from unleashing even greater violence. The Heraclitean Logos . . . is the Logos of all cultures to the extent that they are, and will always remain, founded upon unanimous violence."[98] So, this logos corresponds to the pattern of myth-culture.

Of the second type of logic that Girard perceives uniquely in the biblical text, he writes, "The Johannine Logos is foreign to any kind of violence; it is therefore forever expelled, an absent Logos that never has had any direct, determining influence over human cultures. . . . The Johannine Logos discloses the truth of violence by having itself expelled."[99] This logos corresponds to the unique pattern of Jesus. While I do not entirely agree with Girard on his description of the nature of the Johannine Logos, his observation of two antithetical logics juxtaposed in the pages of the Bible, and the Gospel account in particular, is a genuine insight. So, the chiastic bi-pattern can be described as consisting of the Johannine logic in relation to the Heraclitean logic; the Two Ways theme.

The Six Social-Science Episodes of Jesus in the Gospel Account

We will see that Jesus in the Gospel account inverts the sequence and subverts the significance of both the twelve-motif pattern of the combat myth (as perceived

---

way: "Internal mediation is essentially tragic; it's violence and death. Whereas external mediation is play-acting and games for children. Children imitate their parents . . . [but] It will not be serious. [The son] himself will know that there is no rivalry with his father. . . . You learn a type of desire which makes you part of your culture without creating rivalries" (Girard, "Scapegoat," 35). Girard also speaks of external mimesis in this way: "We are immersed in mimetism. Some are lucky enough to have had good models and to have been educated in the possibility of taking distance. Others have had the bad luck to have had poor models. We do not have the power to decide; the models make the decisions for us. One can be destroyed by one's model: imitation is always what makes us fail in identification. It is as if there was fatalism in our violent proximity to the other. The event [of external mediation of mimesis] is thus rare, and presupposes an education based on solid, transcendent models, what I call external mediation" (Girard, *Battling*, 100). Girard appears to view the relation of humanity to God through Jesus Christ as the only stable form of external mediation; a mimesis that never necessarily occasions conflict.

97. Explicit biblical mentions of the Two Ways are, for example, Deut 30:15–19; Prov 12:28; 14:12; Matt 10:39; 16:25; Gal 5:1–26. They form the structure of the entire *Didache* (ca. AD 35–90), or "The Teaching of the Twelve Apostles" (Ehrman, *Didache*, 405–43). Scholarly discussions of the Two Ways include Suggs, *Christian Two Ways*, 60–74; Seltzer, *Jewish People*, 292; Urbach, *Sages*, 472–75 (as two antithetical expressions of יֵצֶר [yetser], which means "inclination/desire"); Anderson, *Christology*, 210.

98. Girard, *Things Hidden*, 267.

99. Girard, *Things Hidden*, 271.

through the narratological aspect; see table B), as well as the six-episode pattern of myth-culture (as perceived through the social-scientific aspect; see figure 1).

The terms inversion and subversion are perhaps not the best due to the possible implication of a reactionary response, which may imply the myth as prior. Such a temporal and causal relation is not what is intended in using these terms. There are no indications that the Bible generally, or the Gospel accounts in particular, were written in response to myth.[100] The point here is that the relation between the pattern of myth-culture and Jesus' pattern, when presented together in the chiastic bi-pattern, is inversive and subversive. The two patterns mirror one another in the sense of being opposing parallels; their structures, sequences, or patterns (στοιχεῖα; stoicheia) are entirely, systematically antithetical.[101]

From the social-scientific aspect, just as the myth-culture's pattern consists of six episodes, Jesus' pattern consists of a parallel sequence of six concurrent episodes, forming the chiastic bi-pattern. For ease of reference, I alliterate the six episodes of the pattern of myth-culture with 'S' terms (as stated), and the six episodes of Jesus in the Gospel account with 'D' terms (see figure 1). The two types of pattern are antithetical mirrors of each other when compared. On their own, each is a sequence toward order and life. However, Jesus' sequence is order and life according to the Father God's will (e.g., Mark 14:36b), without the use of sin, lies, violence and death, while the myth-culture's sequence is order and life according to human will (e.g., Mark 7:8), necessarily involving sin, lies, violence and death.

In both the mythological (myth-culture) and evangelical (Jesus) patterns, the six episodes may be divided into two sets of three. In the mythological pattern there is the problem set (chaos) and then the solution set (scapegoating to restore cosmos). In the evangelical pattern of Jesus there is the preparation (prophecy) set followed by the filling out (fulfillment) set. The alliterative names for the six episodes of Jesus' unique pattern are: distinction, diffusion, deference, deliverance, dispersive display, and deification of believers (see figure 1). What each of these terms summarizes in Jesus' identity, words and behavior will become clear throughout Girard's, Malina's, and my own analyses in the next three chapters. I propose that Jesus' pattern criss-crosses the pattern of myth-culture in sequence and significance, forming the chiastic bi-pattern of the biblical chiasm genre. This reality demonstrates that Jesus "fails" to

---

100. This is not to say, however, that historical figures in the Bible were not engaged in polemics with myths and their gods (e.g., Baal). Israel's prophets, like Elijah and Elisha, certainly were, as well as the apostles Peter and Paul, as noted previously. But the books of the Bible do not indicate that the purpose of their composition was to contradict myths.

101. Stoicheia is a term used for these two patterns by the apostle Paul in Colossians 2:8. I think Paul refers to this mirror-effect to some extent, describing the Word as a mirror (2 Cor 3:3–18). Likewise in Colossians he writes, "Beware lest any man spoil you through philosophy and vain deceit, after the tradition of men, after the [pattern or sequence] of the [cosmos], and not after [the pattern] of Christ" (Col 2:8). The word that I translate pattern or sequence, στοιχεῖα, literally means just that in Greek (OGL 747; or "row, line, order, series, system"), though it is often translated "elements" or "rudiments."

conform to the pattern of myth-culture, and is therefore neither mythological nor a product of His culture, as are assumed by many scholars today. The following table lays out the six social-science episodes of Jesus as they appear to be viewed by Girard and Malina, using terms and/or concepts that they employ:

6 EPISODES	GIRARD	MALINA
DISTINCTION	Transcendent Deity	(Fictive Deity)
DIFFUSION	Love of Others	(Hidden Rivalry)
DEFERENCE	Faith/Trust in the Father	(Veiled Agonism)
DELIVERANCE	God Himself Saves	(Honor Saves)
DISPERSIVE DISPLAY	The Victorious Victim	(A Dishonored Victim)
DEIFICATION	Disciples' Eternal Life	(Restored Social Status)

TABLE E: The Six Social-Science Episodes of Jesus' Pattern

As will become clear through both Girard's and Malina's readings (chapters 3 and 4), as well as the analysis of the Gospel according to Mark in chapter 5, in Jesus' distinction episode we encounter neither the sameness (A) nor segregation (F) of the myth-culture. When compared with the pattern of myth-culture, Jesus' distinction may be written F_1 subverting A and inverting F of myth-culture (see figure 1). In Jesus' diffusion episode we encounter neither mythological scandal (B) nor satiation (E). When compared with the pattern of myth-culture, diffusion may be written E_1 subverting B and inverting E of myth. In Jesus' deference episode we encounter neither the snare of striving (C), nor the scapegoating (D) of myth. When compared with the pattern of myth-culture, it may be written D_1 subverting C and inverting D of myth.

As we move to the second part of the evangelical pattern in Jesus, the inversion into a chiasm continues, with a repetition or re-affirmation that also involves development or a filling-out. In Jesus' deliverance we encounter neither mythological scapegoating (D) nor the snare of striving (C). When compared with the pattern of myth-culture, it may be written C_1 subverting D and inverting C of myth (see figure 1). In Jesus' dispersive display we encounter neither the satiation (E) nor the scandal (B) of myth. When compared with the pattern of myth-culture, it may be written B_1 subverting E and inverting B of myth. And finally, in Jesus' deification of the disciples we encounter neither mythological segregation (F) nor sameness (A). When compared with the pattern of myth-culture, it may be written A_1 subverting F and inverting A of myth. This chiastic relationship of Jesus' episodes with myth-culture's episodes will become clear as we go into the analysis.

Throughout the sequence of events in the Gospel account, consisting of both of these patterns in tandem (the chiastic bi-pattern), Jesus' pattern causes a rupture in the efficacy of the myth-culture's pattern, undermining its success for culture formation and maintenance, and resulting in the out-of-character and out-of-order triumph of Jesus over the pattern of myth-culture. Jesus' unique pattern transcends our mythological world. From the social-scientific aspect, the following figure illustrates the proposed relation between the pattern of myth-culture and Jesus' pattern, which together form the chiastic bi-pattern of the Gospel account:

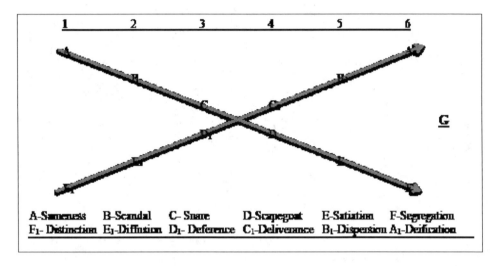

FIGURE 1: The Pattern of Myth-Culture + Jesus' Pattern = The Chiastic Bi-Pattern

CONCLUSION

We now have a working methodology for analyzing the Gospel account, to determine whether Jesus and the Gospels are mythological. We can now ascertain the answer to this question by going verse-by-verse through the Gospel account, examining it for the presence of the chiastic bi-pattern, the structure and therefore genre of biblical chiasm. If our proposal is correct:

(1) Narratologically, and unexpectedly from the viewpoint of the pattern of myth-culture, we expect Jesus instead to invert the sequence and subvert the significance of the twelve motifs of the myth-pattern in His identity, words and behaviors. Concurrently, we expect everyone around Jesus in the Gospel account, His opponents, to conform to the pattern of myth-culture, keeping both the sequence and significance of the myth-pattern in their identity, words and behaviors.

(2) Social-scientifically, and unexpectedly from the viewpoint of the myth-culture, we expect Jesus instead to invert the sequence and subvert the significance of the six episodes of the myth-pattern in His identity, words and behaviors. Concurrently, we expect Jesus' opponents in the account to conform to the pattern of myth-culture, keeping its sequence and significance, in their identity, words and actions.

While only Mark's account of the Gospel will be fully analyzed for the chiastic bi-pattern (in chapter 5), Girard's and Malina's readings (in chapters 3 and 4) consider the four canonical Gospel accounts together. The following table lays out the proposed divisions for the six episodes in the four Gospels. This table will be a useful reference while reading Girard's and Malina's analyses in the next two chapters, as well as for reading the verse-by-verse analysis of Mark's Gospel account in chapter 5:

6 EPISODES	MATTHEW	MARK	LUKE	JOHN
SAMENESS & DISTINCTION	1:1–4:17	1:1–15	1:1–4:44	1:1–34
SCANDAL & DIFFUSION	4:18–16:12	1:16—8:26	5:1–9:17	1:35–6:66
SNARE & DEFERENCE	16:13–21:32	8:27–11:33	9:18–20:8	6:67–12:43
SCAPEGOAT & DELIVERANCE	21:33–26:56	12:1–14:52	20:9–22:53	12:44–18:11
SATIATION & DISPERSION	26:57–27:56	14:53–15:41	22:54–23:49	18:12–19:37
SEGREGATION & DEIFICATION	27:57–28:20	15:42–16:20	23:50–24:53	19:38–21:25

TABLE C: The Six Chiastic Episodes of the Gospel Accounts

The transition points indicated in this table between the six episodes (and between the twelve motifs, for which see table F in chapter 5), are determined by comparing myth-culture's events and themes with Jesus' events and themes. We will discuss the distinguishing of these textual transition points as we encounter them in the text.

Finally, let me emphasize that in arguing that the Gospel accounts contain the pattern of myth-culture in the opponents of Jesus Christ, I am in no way claiming that the Gospels are in part mythological, in the sense of not being historically accurate. I believe the Gospel accounts are entirely historically accurate, and all the evidence confirms that fact. By myth-culture, I mean a pattern of human identity, thought, speech, and behavior that is entirely historical, and actually lived out everyday by humanity in all times and places since myth-culture began. However, the pattern of myth-culture is symptomatic of the sin-nature of Adam's race. This sin-nature is the very thing from which the LORD Jesus Christ became a man to save humanity, as recorded in the Gospel accounts.

3

René Girard's Reading of the Gospel Account

"But we speak the wisdom of God in a mystery,

the hidden wisdom which God ordained before the ages for our glory,

which none of the rulers of this age knew;

for had they known, they would not have crucified the Lord of glory."

(1 Cor 2:7–8 NKJV)

SAMENESS

René Girard has affirmed that the cyclical pattern of myth-culture begins with sameness, which he variously terms: non-differentiation, chaos, interdividuality, mimetic doubles, plague, impurity, or sacrificial crisis. Concerning this state of lost protective distinctions, or sameness, in *Violence and the Sacred* Girard writes, "A single principle is at work in primitive religion and classical tragedy alike, a principle implicit but fundamental. Order, peace, and fecundity depend on cultural distinctions; it is not these distinctions but the loss of them that gives birth to fierce rivalries and sets members of the same family or social group at one another's throats."[1] He later continues, "Ethnologists are not unaware that ritual impurity is linked to the dissolution

---

1. Girard, *Violence and Sacred*, 49.

of distinctions between individuals and institutions.[2] However, they fail to recognize the dangers inherent in this dissolution."[3] A few chapters later, regarding mimetic doubling amid sameness, Girard asserts that sameness of desire for the same object necessarily results in a "clash," and yet humanity routinely misses this fundamental cause of the loss of distinctions and ensuing conflict.[4] He observes:

> In human relationships words like *sameness* and *similarity* evoke an image of harmony. If we have the same tastes and like the same things, surely we are bound to get along. But what will happen when we share the same desires?[5]

Sameness of desire dissolves the distinctions that maintain peace and order in a relationship, and in a community.[6]

Concerning how such a dissolute context forms, Cayley summarizes Girard's argument in *Deceit, Desire, and the Novel* (1965), stating, "Cut off from any vital contact with God . . . 'men become gods' for one another, although always only fleetingly. Mimetic desire pursues an illusion, and this makes it at once urgent and insatiable. The race is intense, but there's no finish line."[7] Girard employs the old Latin motto, *vox populi, vox dei*, to summarize this phenomenon of humans as gods for one another:

> [Girard:] The . . . god of myth appears to the mob. He's the god of the mob. *Vox populi, vox dei*. He's the voice of the mob. [Cayley:] The mythological god embodies the entire community. He or she, quite literally, *is* that community in projected form . . . [Cayley:] . . . desire, in the last analysis, is metaphysical. What it seeks . . . is not the things others have but the other's very being. [Girard:] Being, in the traditional sense, absolute being, is something I don't have in me. I don't feel it. I feel my emptiness . . . the other always seems to have more [being] than I have . . . [people] . . . don't want to see the social aspect, the crowd as model, the culture.[8]

In *Things Hidden Since the Foundation of the World*, Girard names the three broad phases of the mimetic cycle characteristic of culture, the pattern of myth-culture, the first broad phase being this sameness, or passive chaos and uncertainty:

1. Dissolution in conflict, removal of the differences and hierarchies which constitute the community in its wholeness;[9]

---

2. See also Douglas, *Purity and Danger*. For further discussion of sameness, as in social dissolution, mimetic doubles, interdividuality (chaos), and the like, see Girard, "Plague," 136–54; Oughourlian, *Mimetic Brain*; Dostoevsky, *Double*; Durkheim, *Formes Élémentaire*; Callois, *Man and Sacred*.

3. Girard, *Violence and Sacred*, 55–56.

4. Girard, *Violence and Sacred*, 146.

5. Girard, *Violence and Sacred*, 146 (italics mine).

6. Williams, "Foreword," xi.

7. Girard, "Scapegoat," 36.

8. Girard, "Scapegoat," 26, 36–37.

9. Also see Girard's discussion of sameness in *I See Satan*, 10–12; "Scapegoat," 2–3, 6–7, 11, 18.

2. The *all against one* of the collective violence;

3. The development of interdictions and rituals.[10]

The first episode of the Gospel account is characterized in part by just such a situation of sameness.

Also note how this sameness is expressed in the opening two motifs of the combat myth or hero pattern, as seen in our examples of Zeus-Typhon and Marduk-Tiamat. The first "lack/villainy" and second "hero emerges" motifs articulate sameness, involving chaos and the formation of doubles, which lays the groundwork for the mythological cycle of the pattern of myth (see table A).

Girard discusses sameness occurring during the advent of Jesus in Matthew's account in the following way: "Everything is going to be fine [in Jesus' birth account]. But the next minute . . . Herod is killing all the babies in Bethlehem" (Matt 2:16–18).[11] Herod's jealous, rivalrous rage over the threat that this Baby King poses to his kingship drives him to shamelessly murder scores of baby boys. Herod perceives that someone, or a group, share his desire to rule, challenging his authority, and he deals with that sameness according to the typical pattern of myth-culture.

In addition, Girard comments on the presence of sameness near the end of Matthew's first episode in the form of Satan's contention with Jesus in the wilderness (Matt 4:1–11). He notes that Jesus' temptation by Satan indicates Satan's desire to take God's place as an object of worship, and as *the* model for behavior in thought, word and deed. Girard concludes that human imitation of Satan's desire ever results in the "false gods of violence and the sacred as long as men maintain the illusion."[12] His comments on Satan's attempted mimetic rivalry with God,[13] as exemplified in the account of Jesus' Temptation, apply equally to Mark's and Luke's accounts of the same event (Mark 1:13; Luke 4:1–13).

Hamerton-Kelly, in his commentary on the Gospel of Mark, also applies Girard's understanding of sameness to the first episode of Mark's account. He suggests that Jesus' command to "repent and believe in the Gospel" (Mark 1:14–15) that ends the first episode is a command to reject the practice of making oneself and others god(s), which is sameness and rivalry with God, and let God be God once again (distinction): "To 'repent and believe the gospel' means to think not as humans do but as God does, and so see the cross as the revelation of sacred violence and believe the gospel rather

10. Girard, *Things Hidden*, 142.

11. Girard, "Scapegoat," 41. This event in itself is an act of scapegoating. Herod the Great attempts to eliminate a perceived threat to his kingship, his cosmos, by murdering an entire class of people, little boys ages two and under, in the hope that the one boy that threatens him will be killed with the rest.

12. Girard, *Scapegoat*, 196–97.

13. Attempted rivalry with God is described throughout the Bible as including not only personal rivalries with God, but also collective religious and political establishments of nations, in addition to spiritual beings, being opposed to God and His Messiah, e.g., Pss 2:1–3; 76:8–12; 89:26–8; Isa 24:21; Luke 22:53; Eph 6:12; Col 1:16; 2:15; 1 Pet 3:22.

than the Sacred."[14] Hamerton-Kelly uses the term "sacred" for what I am calling the pattern of myth-culture.[15] This Girardian reading equally applies to the accounts of Jesus' command to repent and believe at the outset of His ministry as recorded in Matthew 4:17 and Luke 4:43.

Girard also discusses sameness as it is expressed in the Gospel of John's first episode. He distinguishes the logic opposing the incarnation of the Logos of God, and names it the Heraclitean logos, "the Logos of myth."[16] Girard cites John 1:5b, 10b, and 11b, as the sameness of the mythological world, contending with and rejecting Jesus, the Word of God, God incarnate.[17] The response of the people to Jesus' coming is one of incomprehension and expulsion, that is, according to the pattern of myth-culture. Jesus is treated like a mimetic rival, in keeping with the mold of sameness: "In the space of a few lines, the essence of the matter is repeated three times. The Logos came into the world, yet the world knew him not, his own people received him not. Mankind did not understand him."[18]

Regarding sameness in John's first episode, Girard concludes, "The illusion that there is difference within the heart of violence is the key to the sacrificial way of thinking."[19] That is, a world characterized by the combat myth is continually perceiving a hero-god and a villain-god, a god of cosmos and a chaos-monster, while all along the two are doubles. They are the same: "Everything is symmetrical on both sides, the two sides absolutely the same. But the rivals have to think of their relationship in terms of difference."[20] The symmetry of the rivals in the pattern of myth-culture goes unrecognized by its participants. Jesus, meanwhile, who is "not of this world" (Matt 4:8–9; Luke 4:5–6; John 8:23; 14:30; 18:36), is also perceived through the lens of myth as being a rival of the sort of myth-culture. As such, Jesus' opponents in the Gospel accounts have misjudged their mark.

The Gospel account presents Jesus as transcending the pattern of the myth-culture, and as a result, inverting and subverting the expected identity, thoughts, words and behavior of a mimetic rival-double. Jesus is presented as distinct, as recorded in John's first chapter (and the opening chapters of the other three Gospel accounts as well). The world, from its vantage of myth-culture, is unable to stop itself from attempting to press Jesus into its mold, labelling him a chaos-monster, and expelling him in the prescribed manner. But, since Jesus is the real biblical God according to the

14. Hamerton-Kelly, *Gospel and Sacred*, 64.

15. "The category of the Sacred designates the process by which differentiation is instituted on the basis of the difference between the victim and the mob. . . . The Sacred, in turn, provides the energy and structure of the social order through its primary manifestations of prohibition, ritual, and myth" (Hamerton-Kelly, *Gospel and Sacred*, 7).

16. Girard, *Things Hidden*, 264–74.

17. Girard, *Things Hidden*, 271.

18. Girard, *Things Hidden*, 271.

19. Girard, *Things Hidden*, 266.

20. Girard, "Scapegoat," 4.

Gospel account, it does not work this time. And John and the other accounts assert that we are not seeing another myth unfolding in the Gospels (2 Pet 1:16), but as it were, the judgment of myth, and its culture.

DISTINCTION

Therefore, in addition to sameness, René Girard affirms the presence of distinction in the first episode of the Gospel accounts. His specialized terminology for distinction includes referring to Jesus as having a non-chaotic, non-violent, non-mythological incarnation.[21] Girard also emphasizes how Jesus is the only stable external mediator of desire, the good mimetic model who does not make Himself a rival, which affirms His transcendent deity. Divine distinction in Jesus is subversive of mythological sameness, and inversive of mythological segregation.[22] Girard avers,

> Jesus is the only man to live on this earth in such a way that he can destroy single-handedly the kingdom of Satan. The kingdom of Satan rests upon the fact that ultimately we do his bidding. He says that the victim he offers us as a scapegoat is guilty, and we take him as guilty. And then we divinize that victim, and then we have order. But Jesus crushes that order forever *by refusing Satan's offer.* . . . The kingdom of Satan is autonomous in the sense that it's a circle of violence that is shut upon itself. Jesus opens it.[23]

Girard emphasizes the uniqueness of Jesus encountered in the first episode of the Gospels. His person and His behavior are not those typical of mythological heroes or villains, gods or monsters. While He is treated as such by others who do conform to those expectations, Jesus does not conform; He does not obey the laws of the world, the pattern of myth-culture. Girard goes on to say, "Jesus acts like God in the territory of Satan. In the territory of Satan, Jesus has to be expelled. He proves that He's God there. He demonstrates it."[24] Girard affirms that Jesus embodies a non-interdividual, non-dyadic, and so anti-sameness entity.

21. Girard, *Things Hidden*, 220. Girard notes critical features of the incarnation of God in Jesus that are antithetical to the expectation of the pattern of myth-culture, and demonstrates Jesus' prior transcendent deity: "The birth of the gods is always a kind of rape. . . . In every case we find the doubling effects . . . reciprocal violence and its method of working itself out. . . . Monstrous births provide mythology with a way of alluding to the violence which always haunts it. . . . To put its message across, no doubt the virgin birth of Jesus still resorts to the same 'code' as do the monstrous births of mythology. But precisely because the codes are parallel, we should be able to understand the message and appreciate what is unique to it—what makes it radically different from the messages of mythology. No relationship of violence exists between those who take part in the virgin birth" (Girard, *Things Hidden*, 220–21).

22. For further discussion of divine distinction, as in consistent external mimesis, non-violent beginning, and genuine divine transcendence, see Girard, *Things Hidden*, 220–23; Hamerton-Kelly, *Sacred Violence*, 171–82; Alison, *Joy*, 22–27, 186–210.

23. Girard, "Scapegoat," 28 (italics mine).

24. Girard, "Scapegoat," 32.

As mentioned, apart from accepting the plain description of Jesus' unique divinity in contrast with myth-culture in the first episode of the Gospels, Girard also notes a critical expression of this difference between the god of myth-culture and the God of the Bible in terms of patterns of imitation of desire, or Jesus' consistent external (good) mimesis versus the world's internal (evil) mimesis.[25] This difference is expressed in that as Jesus refuses Satan's offer, the offer that every other human accepts, He does not dispute Satan's claim that all worldly power is Satan's to give. Jesus distinguishes Himself here from the world, not participating in the Satanic imitation of desire. Jesus refuses to imitate Satan's desire; He has humbled Himself.

In Satan's kingdom of this world, he rules by "expelling himself," Girard says, by "repressing himself."[26] As the embodiment and principle of evil mimesis, Satan drives himself out by scapegoating the model-obstacle, the rival who desires the same thing. Girard describes it this way: "Our models pretend not to imitate anyone";[27] Satan's logic says to you:

> [Girard:] . . . imitate me because I don't imitate anyone. And this is total self-contradiction. All modern gurus tell you that. The individualistic guru says, imitate me insofar as I'm not an imitator. They put you in a double-bind.[28]

The "double-bind" is that Satan tempts us to become an imitator in order not to be an imitator. He says, "I am a rebel. I do whatever I want. Imitate my desire for rebellion." And of course, in imitating his desire, you are not distinguishing yourself at all. Once you imitate him, you are the same, finding that you do not get what you wanted, but are instead opposed and oppressed. Alternately, Jesus also calls for others to imitate His desire, but to imitate His imitation of the desire of His Father,[29] which sets men free.

Girard points out Jesus' clear distinction in the first episode of the Gospels in terms of how Jesus engages with Satan and mythological humans who would make Him their rival-double. Girard describes Jesus' response in social-scientific terms, and it is imitating the Father God instead of Satan:

> Jesus says if you don't want to be bothered by scandals, you have to imitate a model such as me who will not become your rival. That's why Paul is entitled to say the same thing, because he's a good imitator of Jesus who himself is a good imitator of the Father. And this chain of imitations is non-rivalrous.[30]

---

25. Girard, "Scapegoat," 22.

26. Girard, "Scapegoat," 22.

27. Girard, "Scapegoat," 23.

28. Girard, "Scapegoat," 23. Girard borrows this term from Gregory Bateson's work on schizophrenia, the "damned-if you-do, damned-if-you-don't," or "catch-22" scenario of sameness in the myth-culture. See Bateson, *Schizophrenia*.

29. Girard, "Scapegoat," 22–23.

30. Girard, "Scapegoat," 23.

Jesus makes a definitive break from the sin cycle of myth-culture in the first episode, the evil mimesis under Satan, and so positions Himself as the liberator of humanity from myth-culture: "[Cayley:] . . . only someone completely identified with God could have understood and undone the closed circle of violence in which humanity was trapped."[31]

In the opening episode of the Gospels, it is important to note the relation that divine distinction in Jesus has with respect to the initial two motifs of the combat myth pattern, the first "lack/villainy" and second "hero emerges" motifs (see table A). I claimed in the methodology that these two motifs are inverted in sequence and subverted in significance by Jesus in episode one of the Gospel account. At the outset, and so out of the mythological order, there is not the "emergence" of a mythological "hero-god," but the arrival of the biblical creator God in Jesus. Thereafter, in reverse order, is not "lack and/or villainy" of a chaos-monster but "lack" of acceptance of God's visitation to His people Israel, and "villainous" attempts to destroy Jesus and oppose His kingship. Jesus' unique divine distinction is clearly inverting and subverting—criss-crossing—mythological sameness in episode one of the Gospel accounts (see figure 1).

Hamerton-Kelly, working with Girard's approach to the Gospels, also notes distinction in Mark's first episode. He himself compares the beginning of the Gospels to the Babylonian Cosmogony, and asserts that Jesus and so the Gospels are clearly distinct from the sameness of myth.[32] As also mentioned above and in the methodology, Girard discusses the Gospel according to John's first chapter in terms of the presence of the two opposing λόγοι (logics), the biblical and the mythological.[33] The former is incarnated in Jesus in the opening verses of John's account, and then is rejected by the latter logos. So, Girard notes the biblical divine distinction being contrasted with the sameness of myth-culture in episode one of the Gospel account. He states:

> [Girard:] Before, I made only a great separation between the archaic and the Christian. And that's necessary because the Christian God is still the mono-theistic God, not a pagan god. And it's love that is divinized, not violence. But there is complete symmetry between the two. . . . So this complete symmetry of the symbolism between Christianity and archaic religions, the fact that it's the same story, is extremely important and should be read, not only as separation but as union. . . . [Cayley:] So Jesus takes his stand within this kingdom, submitting to it in order to lead people out of it.[34]

Divine distinction in Jesus, inverting and subverting mythological sameness, is the first social-science episode of the chiastic bi-pattern (the 'X').

31. Girard, "Scapegoat," 28.
32. Hamerton-Kelly, *Gospel and Sacred*, 66–67.
33. Girard, *Things Hidden*, 264–80.
34. Girard, "Scapegoat," 31–32.

SCANDAL

Girard affirms scandal as that which in the context of interdividuality or sameness (chaos), sets off the sequence of events leading to scapegoating and the temporary re-establishment of segregation, the peace and order of the world (cosmos). Girard states, "I define scandal as the obstacle which attracts you—the paradoxical obstacle. And it can only be the mimetic rival. But you deny this attraction. You want to think of the rival only in negative terms."[35] Mimetic rivals in a state of sameness, of undifferentiation of authority in an area, progress into a state of scandal. James G. Williams summarizes this event:

> "Scandal" translates words from both Hebrew and Greek that mean "stumbling block," something that people stumble over. . . . Girard means specifically a situation that comes about when a person or a group of persons feel themselves blocked or obstructed as they desire some specific object of power, prestige, or property that their model possesses or is imagined to possess. . . . When this kind of situation occurs often enough, there is an accumulation of scandals to the point that those involved must "let off steam" or the social fabric will burst.[36]

Girard elsewhere describes the social phenomenon saying, "The skandalon is the model that becomes an obstacle, period. The skandalon is Satan when he becomes the adversary. When you first imitate him, you think he's not going to be in the way. But then, suddenly, he's there as an obstacle."[37] And as Williams notes in the above quotation, scandal progresses at some point to what I call the snare of striving (or striving to ensnare the model-obstacle or scandalous person) in order to scapegoat that (or some substitutionary) person or persons.

Scandal is clearly seen in the two combat myth motifs of the second episode, the third "donor/council" motif and fourth "journey" motif (see table A). The model-obstacle to the hero's desire necessitates advice and/or equipping to overcome the scandal, as well as the setting out for refuge from and/or in order to engage with the scandal. All of these actions expressed in the two mythological motifs imply a model for desire that has transformed into an obstacle to be overcome.

Girard notes scandal's predominance in the second episode of the Gospel account. The demons and unclean spirits, as well as the religio-political leaders, begin to be scandalized by Jesus' actions and words. The accumulation of scandal over Jesus leads to the cosmic leaders coming down from Jerusalem and accusing Jesus of healing by the power of the prince of demons, Beelzebub or Satan (while Jesus was yet in

---

35. Girard, "Scapegoat," 4.

36. Williams, "Foreword," xi.

37. Girard, "Scapegoat," 22. A robust description of the phenomenon of scandal is given by Girard in *Violence and the Sacred* (145–48). For further discussion of scandal, see Girard, *When These Things Begin*, 11–18; Nordhofen, *Durch Das Opfer*, 148–55; Girard, *Things Hidden*, 416–31.

the Galilee; e.g., Matt 9:34; 10:25; 12:24–27; Mark 3:21–35). Jesus rejects the assertion that He Himself heals the demon-possessed by the power of Satan, but rather by the power of God, and warns them against denying the Spirit of God (e.g., Matt 12:31–32; Mark 3:29). But Jesus seems to affirm that Satan does operate in this manner of expelling himself, and explains the phenomenon before prophesying its approaching end, the end of the kingdom of Satan.

Concerning Jesus' teaching in response to the cosmic leaders' accusation in this second episode, Girard notes the technical tone of Jesus' question, "How can Satan expel Satan?" He observes that Jesus is highlighting the paradoxical nature of Satanic mimesis that we have been discussing, that "[Satan] is the principle of order [cosmos] as much as disorder [chaos]."[38] That is, Satan both causes mimetic rivalry and the chaos it brings, as well as providing his solution of scapegoating to restore the Satanic order.

The accusation of the agents of cosmos (the leaders from Jerusalem) against Jesus is highly ironic, and Jesus points out the irony. The very principle that they claim controls Jesus is the principle they themselves are controlled by and from which Jesus has come to liberate them. He declares this liberation when reading of Himself from the prophet Isaiah when He begins His ministry, asserting that the Scripture is being fulfilled in Himself (e.g., Luke 4:18; Isa 58:6). Girard's treatment of the text on Satan casting out Satan refers to events recounted in both Matthew and Mark's second episodes (Matt 12:26; Mark 3:23).

Hamerton-Kelly also applies a Girardian reading to the second episode of Mark's Gospel account. He comments on the accumulation of scandal, experienced by the religio-political authorities and many of the cosmic crowd, over Jesus' over-riding of their authority regarding various ritual observances (Mark 2:13–3:6).[39] Hamerton-Kelly concludes:

> Jesus is "angered and saddened by their hardness of heart" ([Mark] 3:5), a hardness that is precisely the attitude that serves the Sacred at all costs and sacrifices the human individual to the system. The climax of the section introduces the prospect of Jesus' death. . . . We meet . . . the two kinds of sacred authority that will contrive his death: the religious authority of the Pharisees and the state authority of the Herodians (3:6). From the Pharisees, [Jesus] is stealing the religiously enthralled of the synagogues and, from the Herodians, the prisoners of avarice and expediency in their toll booths.[40]

Jesus' running of the gamut of scandal against the religio-political authorities drives the pattern of myth-culture to its expected third episode, which is efforts to catch a scapegoat, or the snare of striving.

38. Girard, *I See Satan*, 34–35.
39. Hamerton-Kelly, *Gospel and Sacred*, 78–80.
40. Hamerton-Kelly, *Gospel and Sacred*, 80.

A key expression of scandal in the second episode as recorded in Luke is also discussed by Girard. It concerns Jesus' healing of a demon-possessed man near a town in the Decapolis called Gerasa (Luke 8:26–39; Matt 8:28–34; Mark 5:1–20). From the account we learn that the Gerasenes would intermittently chain up the demon-possessed man in town when a fit was coming on to keep him from wandering about amongst the tombs and hills assaulting people, but he would break free and they would have to repeat the process. Girard describes the scandal Jesus becomes to the Gerasenes by healing this man, which differs somewhat from the scandal he seemingly poses to the Jerusalem elite:

> The Gerasenes and their demoniac periodically repeat the same crisis in more or less the same fashion. . . . The repetitive character of these phenomena is somewhat ritualistic. . . . The Gerasenes are consternated at the idea of their being deprived of the suffering. They must gain some enjoyment from this drama and even feel the need of it since they beg Jesus to leave immediately and stop interfering in their affairs. Their request is paradoxical, given that Jesus had just succeeded, without any violence, in obtaining the result which they had professed to be aiming at with their chains and fetters but which, in reality, they did not want at all: the complete cure of the possessed man. . . . Jesus' presence reveals the truth of the hidden desires.[41]

Girard suggests that the scandal of Jesus for the Gerasenes is that he has blocked their desire to ritually scapegoat their pet "crazy." As all myth-cultures believe in scapegoating (*pace* Girard), every community in this world needs a laughing-stock,[42] a local idiot, someone to vent their collective maleficence upon for the cohesion and peace of the rest. The Gerasenes are so scandalized by Jesus' actions that they demand that he leave, and he obliges.

Jesus' miraculous healings that drove the Jerusalem leadership to such a state of scandal as to accuse Jesus of serving Satan, alternately also drove them to accuse him of blasphemy in his claims that he is equal with, even to be identified with, God (e.g., Mark 2:7; John 5:1–47). Jesus heals a man on the Sabbath day (e.g., Mark 3:1–6; John 5:8). It was not lawful, according to the Law of Moses, to work on the Sabbath (Lev 23:3; Jer 17:21–22). Jesus seems to override this command also using Scripture (Mark 2:25–27), asserting that human life is more sacred than the command not to work on the Sabbath (e.g., Mark 3:4). The religio-political leaders become so scandalized by Jesus in the second episode that they begin taking counsel together "as to how they might destroy Him" (Mark 3:6b).

---

41. Girard, *Scapegoat*, 169.

42. This was literally done in the past using stocks in town-squares, which may be exactly what was done in Gerasa to keep this demoniac "stock-still" during his fit (Luke 8:29).

DIFFUSION

The divine diffusion of scandal in the second episode of the Gospels is noted by René Girard (see figure 1). Jesus teaches and models divine diffusion of scandal. He does this by making room, providing space (and whatever is lacking) for even or especially for the antagonistic other, avoiding and dispelling scandal. All of this is in imitation of the way the Father God treats His creatures, the divine pattern criss-crossing the pattern of myth-culture. I claim in the methodology that divine diffusion subverts its opposite of mythological scandal, and inverts its chiastic opposite of mythological satiation.[43] Concerning Jesus' teaching and modelling of diffusion, Girard suggests that in contradistinction to Satan, what Jesus offers is freedom from the scandal that arises from sameness, through imitation of Jesus' desire. He argues that taking Jesus as the model for one's desires results in a non-rivalrous chain of imitation. The Father God is (almost) endlessly gracious to those who fail to acknowledge Him or be thankful, and even to those who deliberately and openly oppose Him.[44] And the Father is the One Whom Jesus imitates and calls humanity to imitate, saying, for example:

> But I say to you, love your enemies and pray for those who persecute you, so that you may be sons of your Father who is in heaven; for He causes His sun to rise on *the* evil and *the* good, and sends rain on *the* righteous and *the* unrighteous. For if you love those who love you, what reward do you have? Do not even the tax collectors do the same? (Matt 5:44–46)

In the second episode, therefore, Jesus teaches how to oppose scandal, and models it for His disciples. Girard discusses various examples of this.

It is once again helpful to consider how divine diffusion relates to the parallel combat myth motifs of the second scandal episode, which are the third "donor/council" and fourth "journey" motifs (table A). We noted that the actions these terms signify are, in the myth-culture, characteristic reactions of a person (hero) scandalized by a model-obstacle (villain). Jesus' teaching and behavior in response to this situation, however, do not conform to these motifs typical of the pattern of myth-culture.

Jesus' second episode does not begin with "counsellors" affirming His scandalized state over a model-obstacle for desire, and donating tools to Him for overcoming His obstacle. Rather, it begins with Jesus "journeying" about teaching against such a reaction when scandalized, and modelling diffusion. The second portion of Jesus' second episode is likewise not concluded with a "journey" to strive with and attempt to ensnare His model-obstacle, but rather Jesus Himself counsels *others* on how to reject scandal and *He gives to them* the tools to diffuse scandal (see figure 1).

---

43. For further discussion of diffusion, as in making room and provision for the other (grace and hospitality) in scandal-avoidance and imitation of the Father God, see Hamerton-Kelly, *Sacred Violence*, 161–70; Nygren, *Agape and Eros*, 70; D'Arcy, *Mind and Heart*, 36–47.

44. Girard, "Scapegoat," 23.

Girard notes examples of Jesus' divine diffusion in the second episode of the Gospel accounts. He observes Jesus' teaching on how to diffuse scandal in Matthew's account. Girard notes Jesus' command to "refuse the escalation when people provoke you,"[45] by "turning the other cheek" when someone strikes you (Matt 5:39; Luke 6:29), and "going the extra mile" when someone forces inconvenient and even harmful agendas upon you (Matt 5:41). Girard paraphrases Jesus' teaching from the second episode, found (for example) in Matthew 5:39, 44–8; 6:14–15, 22–34. In the last section listed (Matt 6:22–34), after Jesus discusses how diffusion is the path to being perfect like the Father God, and how a human cannot serve two masters (God and Satan), Jesus commands trusting in God for one's needs, believing that the Almighty will provide. This faith in God's provision also dispels scandal, preventing envy over the other's success. Other key examples of Jesus' teaching and modelling of diffusion in the second episode, to which Girard alludes, are Matthew 11:25–30 and 12:14–15.[46]

Mark's account features more modelling than teaching of diffusion by Jesus. Girard also refers to examples included in Mark's account including: Mark 2:16–17, 24–28; 3:1–7; 7:5–23.[47] Likewise, in Luke's second episode we find many of the same teachings and modelling of divine diffusion as in Matthew and Mark, to which Girard refers (e.g., Luke 6:27–40).[48] Girard's comments apply well to Jesus' divine diffusion in John's second episode also. Jesus goes the extra mile, turns the other cheek, gives not only His cloak but the shirt off His back, and demonstrates perfect imitation of the desire of Father God throughout the episode. Some key examples are John 2:1–8 and 5:19–24. Jesus' diffusion of the myth-culture's scandal continues the chiastic bi-pattern.

SNARE OF STRIVING

Girard talks about the third episode of the pattern of myth-culture, the snare of striving, or striving to ensnare the mimetic rival, in terms of the escalation of scandals, a "mimetic-snowballing" toward all-against-one. It is the transition period from scandal through to scapegoat.[49] Girard describes this snare of getting caught up in striving with the model-obstacle in various ways:

> [Cayley:] . . . once competition begins, Girard says, it will tend to be self-sustaining because the conflict itself will quickly become the main source of

45. Girard, "Scapegoat," 23.

46. Girard, *I See Satan*, 13–15.

47. Girard, *I See Satan*, 13–15.

48. Girard, *I See Satan*, 13–15.

49. For further discussion of the snare of striving, as in the escalation of mimetic scandals and rivalries involving striving to ensnare the model-obstacle, and the "snowballing" that eventually "requires" a scapegoat, see Girard, *Violence and Sacred*, 93–99; Hubert and Mauss, *Sacrifice*, 83; Delcourt, *Légendes et Cultes*, 102; Lienhardt, *Divinity and Experience*; Empedocles, *On Nature, Purifications*.

attraction. The competitor will become more interesting than the object of competition. Arguments provide an everyday example, wars a catastrophic one. In either case, the point of fact or pride that started the altercation is usually long forgotten by the time the struggle comes to an end. The obstacle itself is now what intrigues us.[50]

Girard also describes the nature of inurement or ensnarement in mimetic striving using the writing of Alexis de Tocqueville,[51] who describes the cultural shift that occurred in the Western world as monarchies and their rigid hierarchies were replaced by democracies. Tocqueville describes an unanticipated paradox: The loss of social hierarchy, rather than making men freer, actually brought about more obstacles to their desires, and so made men less free. Within the confines of a person's stratum in a monarchical and aristocratic culture, a person has one or two obstacles to overcome—one or two rivals for the same desire—for a marriage, or an occupation, *etcetera*. However, with the shift to a democratic culture, a person suddenly has dozens or even hundreds of rivals for the same desire:

> [Girard:] Each obstacle is smaller, but there are so many, because everybody has become an obstacle. . . . [Cayley:] people "encounter the competition of everyone." So desire is checked, even as it is encouraged to spread; and this contradiction . . . "torments and tires souls."[52]

Striving with other humans for the same desires is truly a snare that steals the good of life and brings despair, death and destruction. We see it clearly in the Gospel accounts in the words and behaviors of the people around Jesus, but we do not find it in Jesus' words and deeds, which consistently contradict the snare of striving, just as they opposed sameness and scandal. In humans of the myth-culture, "There is no longer any love without jealousy, any friendship without envy, any attraction without repulsion."[53] Girard concludes that the snare of striving, in which all the world always gets caught, is the very thing Shakespeare refers to in *Macbeth* as "full of sound and fury, signifying nothing."[54]

It is once again illuminating to consider the two combat myth motifs typical of this third episode, the snare of striving, which are the fifth "battle" and sixth "defeat" motifs (see table A). Jesus, once again, is a-typical of this pattern, beginning the

50. Girard, "Scapegoat," 4.

51. Tocqueville, *Democracy*.

52. Girard, "Scapegoat," 36.

53. Girard, "Scapegoat," 37. Girard also describes the phenomenon of the snare of striving in *Violence and the Sacred*, using an example from Sophocles's *Oedipus the King*: "Both parties in this tragic dialogue have recourse to the same tactics, use the same weapons, and strive for the same goal: destruction of the adversary. . . . Legitimate authority trembles on its pedestal, and the combatants finally assist in the downfall of the very order they strove to maintain" (Girard, *Violence and Sacred*, 48). See also Girard, *Violence and Sacred*, 127, 162–65; *I See Satan*, 22–23.

54. Girard, *I See Satan*, 25; Shakespeare, *Macbeth* 5.5.19–28.

episode by inversively and subversively declaring His approaching "defeat," and concluding the episode by inversively and subversively "battling" with His "enemies" by marching on Jerusalem, where He fully intends to submit Himself into their hands. Concurrently, Jesus' opponents (including His own disciples in many instances) do conform to the pattern of these two mythological motifs in the expected order and meaning. They "battle" with Jesus all the way from Galilee to Jerusalem, and then they themselves are "defeated." The disciples are unable to get Jesus to do their mythological bidding, and the religio-political leaders are unable to ensnare Jesus in His reasoning and discourse, or capture Him by subterfuge, but are themselves rendered mute before Him.

Girard notes the operation of the snare of striving in the third episode of the Gospel account. A key expression of the snare of striving is in the behavior of Simon Peter when he challenges Jesus' assertion that He is going to the Cross. Peter appears to view Jesus as a mythological hero and so cannot support Jesus' claim. Girard writes:

> When Jesus announces his passion for the first time, Peter says, No, Master, this will not happen to you. You're going to be successful. Don't think you're going to die. We'll all win the battle together.[55]

Jesus responds by calling Peter "Satan," and telling Satan to get behind Him. Then, Jesus seems to conclude that Peter's thinking is rooted not in God's pattern but humanity's pattern (e.g., Matt 16:23b), the pattern of myth-culture. Girard takes from this that Peter tempted Jesus to imitate a Satanic desire, but Jesus insisted on continuing to imitate His Father's desire instead.[56] This event in the Gospels happens early in the third episode (Matt 16:22–23; Mark 8:32–33). Simon Peter is clearly operating according to the logos of myth-culture, and attempts to get Jesus to be someone and something to which He is antithetical by definition, by nature.

The snare of striving is seen again in the disciples striving for the highest positions in the kingdom of God, as if God's kingdom operated according to the same logic as myth-culture. With respect to the event as recorded in Mark's account, Hamerton-Kelly writes:

> We are told explicitly that the disciples do not know what they are asking when they ask to be seated on the right and left hands of Jesus in his kingdom ([Mark] 10:37–38). They misunderstand the messianic power as the violence of the sacred. Their request provokes the anger of the other disciples and Jesus has to instruct them all about the peculiar nature of his power—the power to serve and to give one's life (10:41–45).[57]

---

55. Girard, "Scapegoat," 22.

56. Girard, "Scapegoat," 22.

57. Hamerton-Kelly, *Gospel and Sacred*, 71.

This event is recorded also in Matthew's and Luke's accounts (Matt 18:1; 20:20–21, 24; Luke 9:46). The snare of striving is condemned in no uncertain terms by Jesus in all of these examples.

Girard also notes the snare in John's third episode. The people around Jesus are caught up in the snare of striving, and Jesus reproves them of this behavior as imitation of Satan rather than of the Father God. The Judaeans express great pride of position as "Abraham's seed" (John 8:33), and never being in bondage to anyone. They take issue with Jesus' assertion that they are not free, but are near hopelessly enslaved, and will become free only if they believe on Jesus (John 8:31–32). These elites of the cosmos strive with Jesus as if He were an opponent from the myth-culture. Jesus responds saying, "Everyone who commits sin is the slave of sin" (John 8:34b), and explains that they are serving the Satan and not the Father God (John 8:42–44). Girard discusses the ensnarement of the people in this third episode and the nature of Jesus' analysis:

> Our contemporaries often condemn the text of John as superstitious and vindictive. What John does, however, is to define anew, abruptly indeed but also without hostility, the consequences for human beings of rivalristic imitation. These people have the devil for a father because it is the desires of the devil that they want to fulfill and not the desires of God. They take the devil as the *model* for their desires. . . . The sons of the devil are those who let themselves be taken into the circle of rivalristic desire. . . . If we do not imitate Jesus, our models become the living obstacles that we also become for them. We descend together on the infernal spiral . . . to the mimetic state of all against one.[58]

In the third episode of the Gospel account, scandals escalate in the snare of striving while Jesus distinguishes Himself from that mythological pattern, teaching against the snare and modelling its opposition in the form of divine deference, as we will discuss in the next section. Girard refers to the snare of striving, viewed in the actions and words of both Jesus' disciples and opponents, as "mimetic snowballing" that progresses toward scapegoating.[59]

DEFERENCE

Divine deference is the pre-occupation of Jesus in the third episode of the Gospel account, and this is affirmed by René Girard's reading. Deference is submitting oneself to the will of the Father God and the needs of the other, instead of being ensnared in striving against God and with other humans for personal interest (figure 1; table C). Jesus imitates the desire (submits to the will) of the Father God instead of the desire of Satan, and so loves and serves God and fellow humans created in the image of God. Deference is the subversion of the snare of striving, as well as the inversion of

---

58. Girard, *I See Satan*, 39–40.

59. Girard, *I See Satan*, 43, 124–25.

scapegoating.[60] Girard notes Jesus' teaching and modelling of deference in the third episode:

> [Cayley:] Jesus' teaching about the Kingdom of Heaven, in Girard's view, is not just generic wisdom, nor is it something that can be detached from Jesus' [crucifixion]. It's a teaching that quite specifically addresses the danger of escalating violence. . . . The injunction to love your enemy and the rest, Girard says, is neither an ideological blueprint nor some sort of impossibly exacting moral standard. . . . [Girard:] The precepts of the Kingdom of God point to certain crucial moments when others want you to collaborate with them in the game of violence. Therefore, they make outrageous demands upon you, and they secretly hope that you're going to reply in the same way. You're going to get mad and give them what they want which will be an opportunity to say the violence came from him, not from me. There are circumstances in which everything is at stake.[61]

That Jesus' teaching on and modelling of divine deference is eminently practical is fully recognized by Girard here, and directly connected to the path Jesus is deliberately walking toward the Cross. The Cross is the ultimate demonstration of deference, and Jesus offers this teaching on the rejection of the snare of striving, commanding whoever would come after Him to take up their crosses as well, even as He walks toward Calvary's Cross.

In comparing Jesus' deference in the third episode of the Gospels with the parallel combat myth motifs, the fifth "battle" and sixth "defeat" motifs, we do not see conformity but antithesis (table A). Within this third episode, Jesus inverts these motifs in sequence and subverts them in meaning, just as deference criss-crosses the larger structure of the pattern of myth-culture, inverting scapegoating and subverting the snare of striving. Focusing on the two expected motifs of combat myth, however, we see that Jesus embraces "defeat" at the outset, predicting it and preparing His followers for it while also prophesying His resurrection on the third day. Then Jesus engages in a "battle" of a very different sort, a battle against striving itself.

Hamerton-Kelly, applying Girard's social-science, notes key expressions of Jesus' deference in the face of His disciples' and the religio-political leaders' striving. Throughout this entire third episode, Jesus teaches and models the Way of the Cross, of deference to the desire/will of God (e.g., Mark 8:34–9:1, 12, 31; 10:33–34). Concerning these key passages Hamerton-Kelly writes:

> Through Peter the disciples acknowledge that Jesus is the Christ, and through Peter they refuse his definition of the role in terms of suffering and rejection

---

60. For further discussion of deference, as in submission to the desire (the will) of God to imitate the work of God, loving God, and loving the image of God in the Other, see Girard, *Things Hidden*, 205–20; *I See Satan*, 140; Alison, *Joy*, 53–62.

61. Girard, "Scapegoat," 24.

([Mark] 8:31–32). They represent Satan, the closed circle of violence in which Beelzebub casts out Beelzebub. They cannot conceive of any other way of controlling violence than by violence itself; for them, the Messiah cannot be weak. . . . In response, Jesus summons both the disciples and the crowd and teaches the way of the cross ([Mark] 8:34–9:1). . . . They are equally uncomprehending, and equally inclined to be ashamed of the Son of Man and his nonviolent way in this violent generation. The redefinition of the concept of the Messiah that is going on before the eyes of the reader is opaque to the participants in the narrative.[62]

Throughout this third episode, that immediately precedes the fourth scapegoating and divine deliverance episode, the most intense teaching and modelling of Godliness is occurring. Yet even the closest disciples of Jesus are too inured in the mythological frame of mind of myth-culture, too ensnared in the practice of striving, to receive Jesus' teaching.

SCAPEGOATING

René Girard affirms the presence of scapegoating in the fourth episode of the Gospel accounts. Scapegoating is the all-against-one phenomenon that occurs at the height of the mimetic crisis, or "snowballing" of scandal and striving. Responsibility for the crisis is placed entirely upon one person (or one sub-group), and then the victim is expelled or destroyed, carrying away the destructive violence with it.[63] Concerning the phenomenon of scapegoating Girard writes:

> The mimetic theory tells you that every culture in the world is based on a foundational murder. And Jesus says that this murder is being repeated constantly, because he says I'm going to die like all the prophets before me. He doesn't mean only the Jewish prophets, since the first one he mentions is Abel. He refers to that first culture and first murder. And the Gospel of John says Satan, the Devil was a murderer since *arche*, the beginning, the first culture. And in John he says, "And you are going to do it again."[64]

Girard is asserting here that scapegoating is the foundation and sustenance of human culture, operating at the heart of the cyclical pattern of myth-culture. Jesus has entered into this pattern and, though He rejects it and exposes it throughout, Jesus also willingly submits to it in fulfillment of Scripture, in order to lead humanity out of it. Scapegoating, to which Jesus willingly submits (though on His own terms), is the

---

62. Hamerton-Kelly, *Gospel and Sacred*, 103.

63. For further discussion of scapegoating, as in the sacrifice of the one person for the group, see Girard, *Violence and Sacred*, 101–3; *Scapegoat*; Hamerton-Kelly, *Sacred Violence*, 13–49; Finamore, *God, Order, and Chaos*, 69–75.

64. Girard, "Scapegoat," 25.

venting off of the myth-culture's accumulated, exasperated scandal and striving, on the back of an arbitrary victim. James G. Williams describes it this way:

> So sacrifice and scapegoating are two different expressions of the same reality, the victim mechanism by which human societies have typically operated. The mechanism is the origin of human culture, or "founding murder." A tremendous number of myths portray this founding murder, although the human reality is usually disguised and distorted. For example, in the ancient Babylonian myth of the origin of the world the god Marduk defeats Tiamat, the goddess of the salt water, splits her body, and places half of it over the sky and half under the earth. He kills Tiamat's consort, Kingu, and makes human beings out of his blood.[65]

Williams correlates the combat mythology with the cyclical behavior of culture, at the center of which is human sacrifice or scapegoating for the restoration of the order and peace of the world. It is always justified and disguised, however, in the mythological form of hero-god conquering villain-god, the god of cosmos vanquishing the chaos-monster.[66]

Let us compare this psycho-social phenomenon of scapegoating, which occupies the fourth episode of the Gospel accounts, to the two parallel combat myth motifs, the seventh "enemy ascendant" and eighth "hero recovers" motifs (table A). At the outset of the fourth episode, from the vantage of the elite of the myth-culture, it seems clear that Jesus is gaining in power and prominence amongst the people ("enemy ascendant"), so that they are clearly terrified by Him and seek to capture and destroy Him. The episode closes with these heroes of cosmos succeeding in capturing Jesus, getting their hands on their scapegoat, a great recovery for them that clearly leaves them in a state of elation ("hero recovers"). From Jesus' perspective and that of the Gospel writers (the divine pattern), however, the fourth episode is exactly the opposite in sequence and significance, as will be discussed in the next section concerning divine deliverance.

Girard discusses key expressions of scapegoating in the Gospel account's fourth episode. He notes the unanimity of the cosmic crowd, including Jesus' own disciples, at the critical moment of Jesus' scapegoating. This crucial unanimous moment, typical of all scapegoating, occurs in Matthew 26:56–57; Mark 14:48–52; Luke 22:52–53; and John 18:11. Of this all-against-one phenomenon, Girard writes:

> Jesus is presented to us as the innocent victim of a group in crisis, which, for a time at any rate, is united against him. All the subgroups and indeed all the individuals who are concerned with the life and trial of Jesus end up by giving their explicit or implicit assent to his death: the crowd in Jerusalem, the Jewish

---

65. Williams, "Foreword," xv–xvi.

66. For further discussion of the mimetic escalation toward the event of scapegoating, see Girard, *I See Satan*, 82, 94; "Scapegoat," 11–12, 24–26, 29.

religious authorities, the Roman political authorities, and even the disciples, since those who do not betray or deny Jesus actively take flight or remain passive.[67]

This is the moment of Jesus' scapegoating. At the precise moment of the "hero's recovery" in the combat myth pattern, Jesus is "finished"; His death a foregone conclusion. Therefore, Jesus is not a mythological hero. He defies the expected pattern of myth-culture. The heroes of myth in this critical moment of the Gospels' fourth episode are the religio-political leaders, the cosmic elites, not Jesus, not God.[68]

DELIVERANCE

René Girard's reading affirms that divine deliverance is what Jesus' actions and teaching consist of in the fourth episode of the Gospel accounts. Passively, deliverance involves trusting in God's salvation rather than one's own heroism, and rather than the solution of myth-culture that is scapegoating. Actively, deliverance is laying down one's life to save the lives of others. Continuing the chiastic bi-pattern, divine deliverance is the subversion of its parallel opposite of mythological scapegoating, and the inversion of its chiastic parallel of the mythological snare of the striving.[69] Girard describes deliverance in the following way:

> By resorting to the founding mechanism once again against Jesus (who had revealed the secret of their power, the founding murder), the powers of this world thought to stifle the Word of Truth for ever. They thought to triumph yet again by the method that had always allowed them to triumph in the past. What they failed to appreciate was that, in spite of the temporary consensus in which even the most faithful of the disciples cooperated, nothing like the usual mythological falsehood would appear in the Gospels. They would show, not the lie common to the religions of the entire planet, but the structural matrix in itself. Under the influence of the Spirit, the disciples perpetuated the memory of the event, not in the mythic form that ought to have triumphed once again, but in a form that reveals the innocence of the just man who has suffered martyrdom. Thus they avoid sacralizing the victim as the guilty party and prevented him from being held responsible for the purely human disorders that his death was supposed to end.[70]

---

67. Girard, *Things Hidden*, 167.

68. For other helpful discussions of scapegoating in the Gospels' fourth episode from a Girardian perspective, see Girard, *I See Satan*, 137; *Things Hidden*, 158–67; "Evangelical Subversion," 37–43; Hamerton-Kelly, *Gospel and Sacred*, 27–52.

69. For further discussion of divine deliverance, as in God's salvation rather than the mythological solution, see Schwager, *Scapegoats*, 200–214; Girard, *When These Things Begin*, 33–45; *I See Satan*, 137–53; *Scapegoat*, 100–11.

70. Girard, *Things Hidden*, 193–94.

Girard is describing here a key way in which Jesus' scapegoating, instead of serving its intended purpose for the restored transient peace of the world as the world gives it (John 14:27), actually serves an unintended purpose (though purposed by God; e.g., Mark 14:21, 24, 36, 49) of delivering humanity from the actual "chaos-monster" of sin (e.g., Mark 1:4–8; 2:10, 17) and the pattern of myth-culture itself, which appear in the moment to be succeeding once again.

Girard describes Jesus' fulfillment of His name, Savior/Deliverer from sin (e.g., Matt 1:21), in the following way:

> The Gospel Revelation . . . in order to come to completion . . . requires the good news that God himself accepts the role of the victim of the crowd so that he can save us all. This God who becomes a victim is not another mythic god but the one God, infinitely good, of the Old Testament.[71]

With this, Girard goes on to assert that unlike the scapegoating events of mythological cultures, Jesus' deity does not result from the "mimetic snowballing" from scandal to scapegoating that results in both the condemnation and exaltation of the victim to the status of deity by human decision. Rather, Jesus' deity is established prior to the scapegoating through the revelation of the truth that also reveals the lie of mythological culture. Ultimately, Girard claims, there is a clear distinction between the God that is Jesus by divine declaration, and the gods of myth-culture by human invention. This distinction is manifest in its fullest form, Girard suggests, when Jesus voluntarily submits to the role of single victim for the mythological mob.[72] Girard's understanding affirms Jesus' antithetical divine deliverance in the fourth episode of the Gospel account in comparison with the mythological solution of scapegoating.

The two combat myth motifs parallel to the fourth episode of the Gospel accounts, and that appear in proper sequence and significance in the words and actions of the people of the world around Jesus, are the seventh "enemy ascendant" and eighth "hero recovers" motifs (table A). As mentioned above however, Jesus' identity, words and deeds, by comparison, invert the order of these motifs and subvert the meaning of them. In the initial portion of episode four, Jesus wins His case before His trial, as it were, by explaining and exposing everything that is about to happen in the light of truth, and so silencing the cosmic authorities ("hero recovers"). Thereafter, Jesus allows the authorities to have their moment (Mark 14:41–42, 49; "enemy ascendant"), but it no longer means what they intend it to mean. The authorities of myth-culture are rendered "toothless."

Applying Girard's social-science, Hamerton-Kelly notes key expressions of deliverance in the fourth episode of the Gospel account. The first event that he notes

71. Girard, *I See Satan*, 130.

72. Girard, *I See Satan*, 130. For other elaborations on Jesus' deliverance of humanity in freely submitting to the mythological lynch-mob, see Girard, *Things Hidden*, 190–96; *I See Satan*, 82, 123, 130–32, 140–42, 151–53; Williams, "Foreword," xiv, xviii; Hamerton-Kelly, *Sacred Violence*, 85, 173–80.

is Jesus' telling of a parable that opens the fourth episode (Mark 12:1–11). Of this parable of Jesus that exposes the religio-political authorities, Hamerton-Kelly writes:

> The point of the parable is clear; the religious establishment is opposed to God, and it shows that opposition by killing his representatives. The sacrificial victims are the representatives of God! The issue is defined for us by the preceding question about two kinds of authority, from men and from heaven. The authority from men operates by expelling and killing; the authority from heaven operates by including and vindicating.[73]

With this parable Jesus inaugurates the fulfillment half of His ministry, and of His unique evangelical pattern. The three preparation episodes are complete. Jesus, according to the divine pattern, begins this final leg of His conquest of sin and death, and their myth-culture, by pre-empting the "solution" half of the pattern of myth by succinctly explaining all that has led up to this moment, and what the aftermath of it will be.

Hamerton-Kelly also notes a key event that concludes the fourth episode, Jesus' pre-emption of the satiation of the cosmic crowd on its victim (belonging to the fifth episode of the pattern of myth) in the Lord's Table (Mark 14:1–26). Hamerton-Kelly writes:

> At several points in the narrative, the powers have indicated a desire to apprehend Jesus; now they fulfill that desire. . . . By taking their money, Judas indicates that he sees Jesus as another victim of the sacrificial system to be killed behind a screen of substitution. . . . Once in the [upper] room, the talk turns to the "handing over" of Jesus as a sacrificial victim to the chief priests, who, like the patrons of the temple traders, have bought but not yet paid for him. . . . The institution of the Eucharist is an inversion of the temple sacrifices. The usual direction of the sacrificial offering is reversed; instead of the worshiper giving to the god, the god is giving to the worshiper. Jesus "gives" ($\delta i \delta \omega \mu \iota$) his body and blood, symbolized by bread and wine, instead of their giving their bodies and blood, symbolized by money, to the temple.[74]

Jesus, with this New Covenant (e.g., Mark 14:24; Jer 31:31), is (*inter alia*) replacing scapegoating with divine deliverance from it. God Himself is taking the place of the sacrifice, to end all such sacrifice. Jesus reveals the meaning of His approaching execution at His Table just prior to His scapegoating, a scapegoating in which even the disciples in the upper room will all participate.

---

73. Hamerton-Kelly, *Gospel and Sacred*, 27.

74. Hamerton-Kelly, *Gospel and Sacred*, 43–44.

SATIATION

René Girard affirms that mythological satiation predominates in the fifth episode of the Gospel account. The collective satisfaction of the cosmic crowd on their scapegoat is what we read of in Jesus' treatment by the myth-culture's authorities and people-general, even the reluctant participants in Jesus' disciples. The concept of satiation is derived from the collectively beneficial consumption or devouring of the sacrificial victim. With human sacrifice this has been known to occur literally (and with far greater frequency around the world than generally recognized), but is just as often, and more importantly for the vitality of the myth-culture, practiced metaphorically or symbolically.[75]

In the previous episode, Jesus anticipated satiation with His New Covenant at the Lord's Supper, even as the mythological mob was preparing to capture Him. He thus imbues the coming satiation episode with subverted and inverted meaning: "So Jesus said to them, 'Truly, truly, I say to you, unless you eat the flesh of the Son of Man and drink His blood, you have no life in yourselves. He who eats My flesh and drinks My blood has eternal life, and I will raise him up on the last day'" (John 6:53–54; 13:2–17, 34–35; Matt 26:26–29; Mark 14:22–25; Luke 22:15–20). In stark contrast to Jesus' statement here, in mythology the satiation of the cosmic crowd is a temporary rather than eternal participation in salvation. For the myth-culture there will be another cycle, with another victim, and another feast. Girard writes:

> The eating of sacrificial flesh, whether animal or human, can be seen in the light of mimetic desire as a veritable cannibalism of the human spirit in which the violence of others is ritually devoured. Mimetic desire, once frustrated, seeks at once to destroy and to absorb the violence incarnated with the model-obstacle.[76]

Girard here suggests that the scapegoat, being viewed and/or labelled as responsible for the chaos, must be killed to destroy the source of the trouble. Once dead, the scapegoat is no longer viewed as maleficent, but now beneficent, and so consumption of the scapegoat represents acquisition of the peace and order (cosmos) that the scapegoat formerly threatened.[77] Note that Jesus offers Himself to be eaten, metaphorically, *before* He has been sacrificed. Unlike in myth-culture, the real God is beneficial prior to His scapegoating, because He is good and pure without bloodshed, and that perfect shed blood of His washes away all our sins (Matt 26:28; Mark 1:4–8; 2:10; 14:24).

---

75. For further discussion of human sacrifice and collective (metaphorical) consumption, or satiation, for the benefit of the community, see Berthelot, "Jewish Views"; Harrill, "Cannibalistic Language"; Girard, "Evangelistic Subversion"; Lang, "This is My Body"; Chilton, "Eucharist."

76. Girard, *Violence and Sacred*, 277.

77. Girard, *Violence and Sacred*, 277.

The contrasting mythological, collective (semi-metaphorical) satiation on the scapegoat is expressed by the mythological mob in other ways too. Girard recounts other ritualistic grotesqueries of mythological satiation:

> Because it reproduces the founding event of all rituals, the Passion is connected with every ritual on the entire planet. There is not an incident in it that cannot be found in countless instances: the preliminary trial, the derisive crowd, the grotesque honors accorded to the victim, and the particular role played by chance, in the form of casting lots, which here affects not the choice of the victim but the way in which his clothing is disposed of. The final feature is the degrading punishment that takes place outside the holy city in order not to contaminate it.[78]

The authorities of the world conform again to the pattern of myth-culture in this fifth episode of the Gospel accounts, in ritual satiation. All these elements of satiation described by Girard are what we read of the mythological mob around Jesus as they crucify Him. James G. Williams describes the satiation episode of the combat myth of Marduk-Tiamat, which parallels the behavior of the mythological mob that has scapegoated Jesus:

> In the ancient Babylonian myth of the origin of the world the god Marduk defeats Tiamat, the goddess of the salt water, splits her body, and places half of it over the sky and half under the earth. He kills Tiamat's consort, Kingu, and makes human beings out of his blood.[79]

The grotesque splaying and divvying-up of the victim as spoils to be shared by the reconciled group is the expression of the reunification of a cosmos recently threatened by chaos.[80] But Jesus does not conform to the expected cultural pattern of myth in this fifth episode, but to His unique evangelical pattern instead.

The two combat myth motifs that parallel episode five of the Gospel account are the ninth "battle rejoined" and tenth "victory" motifs (table A). This pattern holds true for the religio-political opponents of Jesus, but not for Jesus Himself. The cosmic leadership is able to capture Jesus with a lynch-mob ("battle rejoined") and march Him back to their palace for trial, collective beating and ridicule, and eventual execution ("victory"). The fifth episode ends with an apparent victory for the religio-political establishment of the world, just as it "ought" to be according to the pattern of myth-culture.

Girard notes a key moment of satiation in this fifth episode of the Gospel account, the denials of the disciple, Simon Peter; Peter joins the cosmic crowd in sating themselves on their scapegoat. Girard writes:

78. Girard, *Things Hidden*, 167.

79. Williams, "Foreword," xvi.

80. For further discussion of satiation, see Girard, *Scapegoat*, 100–111, 112–24, 149–64; *I See Satan*, 124–25, 131–33; *Things Hidden*, 24–27.

> The companion of the Nazarene is behaving as if he were among his own, as if he belonged around this fire. . . . The best way not to be crucified, in the final analysis, is to do as everyone else and join in the crucifixion.[81]

Peter tries to keep himself from being numbered with Jesus by ingratiating himself to Jesus' enemies. He tries to pass himself off as one of them, but they do not accept him. In the attempt to make himself acceptable, he willingly joins in scapegoating Jesus by denying Him three times. The cosmic crowd is not sated, not satisfied, until everyone joins in ridiculing, abusing, and killing the scapegoat, sharing in His mutilation and divvying of spoils. Those that want to resist, like Peter, cannot bear the pressure. Peter himself cannot be satisfied until he has denied and ridiculed Jesus as well.

Hamerton-Kelly notes another key moment of satiation in the Gospel account's fifth episode, which is the derisive crowd at Jesus' crucifixion made up of all the disparate segments of the culture, united in sating themselves on their shared victim while He suffers in agony on the Cross. He writes:

> The soldiers' treatment of Jesus shows the essential solidarity of the Romans and the Jews in violence, for their mockery parallels the Sanhedrin's ([Mark] 14:65). The question that Pilate asks him, whether he is "king of the Jews," seems to have been answered in the ironic affirmative by his adversaries, for he is mocked as such by the soldiers and by those watching him on the cross. . . . The chief priests and the bandits join in this taunt [Mark 15:32]; they demand the only kind of proof they can understand, an act of violent self-affirmation. . . . The King of Israel to leap down from the Roman cross and lead the armed resistance. Jesus is not the Davidic Messiah of violence but the Son of God ([Mark 15:]39) and the suffering servant (Isa 53:9, 12).[82]

The gods of myth have their victory over their chaos-monster. But the gods of myth are not represented by Jesus here, but by the world's authorities. They attempt to make Jesus their chaos-monster, but He does not conform to that element of myth either. The imminent threat to cosmos seems over, and it is time, according to myth-culture's pattern, to tie things off and re-affirm order, as we will see in the final episode.

DISPERSIVE DISPLAY

René Girard affirms that in the fifth episode of the Gospel account, while mythological satiation is taking place at the hands of the cosmic authorities, the Word of God is dispersed abroad, His blood sprinkling many nations (Isa 52:15; Heb 12:24), and the light of God is broadly displayed in and through Jesus Christ (Isa 9:2; John 12:46; 2 Cor 4:6), putting Satan and his authorities with their pattern of myth-culture on full display. The divine dispersive display in Jesus' crucifixion subverts its parallel opposite

81. Girard, *Scapegoat*, 150–55.
82. Hamerton-Kelly, *Gospel and Sacred*, 56.

of mythological satiation, and inverts its chiastic opposite of mythological scandal (figure 1; table c).[83] Girard describes this dispersion of the biblical divine Seed, the light of the world, and its effect of putting evil on display, in the following way:

> [Cayley:] What makes the story unique is the fact that the victim is someone who stands completely outside of the violence of which everyone else is, without exception, a prisoner. . . . [Girard:] That violence is ugly and not heroic. The Bible reveals that violence is the birth of the community, the ugly birth of the community. If you look at the Cross, you can see it. . . . [Cayley:] Only someone completely identified with God could have undone the closed circle of violence in which humanity was trapped.[84]

Jesus is willing, though it is a battle for Him (e.g., Mark 14:36), to submit to the scapegoating of the Cross, in order to lead humanity out of the pattern of myth-culture. Girard describes here the dispersive display that Jesus performs while He is "devoured" and killed cruelly by the cosmic crowd. For this reason (*inter alia*) the Cross is the light to a world lost in darkness.

Another critical way in which Jesus, even as the world is satiated upon Him, engages in divine dispersive display of satiation and scandal is with His words in the moment. Jesus sows the Seed of His Word throughout His torment. One of His sayings in the fifth episode that Girard highlights in this regard is, "But Jesus was saying, 'Father, forgive them, for they do not know what they do'" (Luke 23:34). Of these words of Jesus Girard states:

> It means that the scapegoaters, literally, don't know what they are doing. They are unconscious. They believe the victim is guilty. They believe they are doing their duty. There is a sentence which corresponds to Jesus' statement from the Cross in the Acts of the Apostles. Peter, a few days after the cross, talks to the crowd of Jerusalem and tells them, you don't realize that you've killed the Son of God, the Messiah, but you're not as guilty as you might think, if you were to understand what you have done, because you were in ignorance. This has the same meaning as the sentence of Jesus. And I think it has to be interpreted in a technical way. The mimetic violence is unconscious: it doesn't know what it's doing. The mob is always innocent. Don't count on the mob to tell you what they've really done. They'll give you the myth of Oedipus. They'll say, there was this guy that had killed his father and married his mother, and we had to get rid of him. That's what they would say. We judged him, according to the rules, and we decided he had to be expelled.[85]

---

83. For further discussion of divine dispersive display, see Girard, *I See Satan*, 137–53; *Things Hidden*, 167–70; Hamerton-Kelly, *Sacred Violence*, 53–87.

84. Girard, "Scapegoat," 27–28.

85. Girard, "Scapegoat," 26.

Jesus' silent innocence before His accusers, combined with these words of affirmation (there are others as well) of the truth of what the cosmic crowd were actually doing throughout the mythological satiation, functions as a dispersive display of the pattern of myth-culture from which (*inter alia*) God saves humanity in that moment.[86]

Comparing the dispersive display of the fifth episode of the Gospel account with its parallel combat myth motifs, the ninth "battle rejoined" and tenth "victory" motifs (table A), also shows the chiastic bi-pattern of Jesus' actions and words in comparison with the actions and words of the authorities and their mythological mob toward Jesus. In the first half of the episode, during the "trial" ("battle rejoined") the myth-culture fails to find Jesus guilty of anything. They deny the truth of Jesus' identity, though Jesus explicitly declares it to them, and declares His victory (out of sequence and with subverted meaning) right then: "And Jesus said, 'I Am [ἐγώ εἰμι]: and you shall see the Son of Man sitting at the right hand of Power, and coming with the clouds of heaven'" (Mark 14:62). This "victory" inverts the mythological sequence of motifs and subverts their meaning since the "victory" of Jesus is not "of this world." Likewise thereafter, Jesus' "battle rejoined" is His combat with evil as they viciously destroy Him (myth's "victory"). Jesus shows He is still "battling" confidently by forgiving His persecutors as they hang Him on the cross and ridicule and revile Him. Again, the sequence is inverted and the meaning subverted compared with the expectations of myth-culture.

In addition to Girard's examples from the Gospel account, of Jesus' dispersive display of mythological satiation in the fifth episode, Hamerton-Kelly applies Girard's social-science to this matter as well:

> The trial before the Sanhedrin is the key to the passion narrative and one of the keys to the whole Gospel. Here the innocence of the victim is revealed. . . . The reference in [Mark] 15:10 to the envy (φθόνος) of the Sanhedrin underscores the unfairness of the trial and reveals the real, mimetic motivation of the priests. Jesus is the innocent victim of envy [scandal], and envy is the essence of mimetic violence; the verdict has been decided beforehand ([Mark] 14:55). . . . This court has all the impartiality of a "people's tribunal" in a revolution.[87]

Hamerton-Kelly shows how the trial in particular, instead of demonstrating the guilt of the sacrificial victim, serves to demonstrate the fraudulence of the pattern of myth-culture. Jesus is dragged into the pseudo-courtroom and dismantles the myth-culture's illogical sense of justice. Jesus disperses the light of truth, putting mythological satiation on display.

---

86. For further discussion of the divine dispersive display of mythological satiation and scandal, see Girard, *Things Hidden*, 191; *Scapegoat*, 100–11; *I See Satan*, 82, 137–53.

87. Hamerton-Kelly, *Gospel and Sacred*, 53.

SEGREGATION

René Girard affirms the presence of mythological segregation in the sixth and final episode of the Gospel account. It is the re-establishment of cosmos, of the world, out of the corpse of the scapegoat. The mythological mob has shared in being satiated by the flesh and blood of the victim, and now the carcass is employed to re-organize the cultural hierarchy, the oppressive order and peace as the world gives it.[88] Girard describes this final episode of the pattern of myth-culture in the following way:

> When we examine the great stories of origin and the founding myths, we notice that they themselves proclaim the fundamental and founding role of the single victim and his or her unanimous murder. The idea is present everywhere. In Sumerian mythology cultural institutions emerge from a single victim: Ea [Apsu?], Tiamat, Kingu. The same in India: the dismemberment of the primordial victim, Purusha, by a mob offering sacrifices produces the caste system. We find similar myths in Egypt, in China, among the Germanic peoples—everywhere. The creative power of this murder is often given concrete form in the value attributed to the fragments of the victim. Each of these is identified as producing a particular institution, a totemic clan, a territorial subdivision, or even the vegetable or animal that furnishes the community its primary food.[89]

From the corpse of the scapegoat the oppressive hierarchical order of all culture is established and organized, re-differentiated, pseudo-individuated. It is truly a cosmos, as in a fabricated artifice. It does not correspond to reality, but it seems necessary for sameness and scandal-inured humanity to function together, that is until Jesus ("Savior"). Girard describes the need in myth-culture for this forced differentiation for controlling the intrinsic sameness (or sin-nature; the "chaos-monster" that Jesus combats and defeats in the Gospel account; e.g., Mark 1:4–8) and preventing a recurrence of scandal and the entire cycle of sacrificial violence of the pattern of myth-culture:

> "Degree," or *gradus*, is the underlying principle of all order, natural and cultural. It permits individuals to find a place for themselves in society; it lends a meaning to things, arranging them in proper sequence within a hierarchy.... At the moment when differentiated unity is urgently needed ... the surrogate victim comes to the rescue.[90]

---

88. For further discussion of segregation, as in the re-establishment of cosmic order and hierarchy out of the corpse of the scapegoat, see Girard, *Things Hidden*, 48–83; "Generative Scapegoating," 95–103, 118–20; Lévi-Strauss, *Totemism*.

89. Girard, *I See Satan*, 82.

90. Girard, *Violence and Sacred*, 49–50, 307. For further discussion of mythological segregation, see Girard, "Scapegoat," 6–8, 26–27; *I See Satan*, 24, 28–30, 44, 186–89; *Violence and Sacred*, 255, 259, 266–73.

The scapegoat, and the community's satiation upon it, enables the restoration of differentiation that is always being threatened, and is routinely broken down, by the mimetic rivalry, the sameness, of the members of myth-culture.

Mythological re-segregation occurs in the final sixth episode of the Gospel account in the disciples' sin of unbelief in Jesus, and the actions and words of the religio-political authorities. Prior to Jesus' resurrection, the authorities believe they have completed the myth-culture's circle again; and they set about re-establishing and securing their control over their cosmos at the sacred center, Zion in Jerusalem (over which the Roman authority also has new "peace"). They do this, in part, by means of taking control of the corpse of their victim, Jesus.

The two combat myth motifs that parallel the mythological element of the sixth episode of the Gospel account are the eleventh "enemy punished" and twelfth "triumph" motifs (table A). As we saw, from the perspective of the religio-political leaders, these motifs, in this order, with this meaning, is what we read in the Gospel account. Jesus "the enemy" has been "punished," His death is confirmed. The cosmic leaders demand that His corpse be removed from the cross and buried, and guarded, so as not to spoil the high feast day, which will be an especially joyous one this year, a real "triumph" for the cultural elites at Jerusalem.

We can see the attempted re-segregation of the cosmos by the religio-political leaders in how they fuss over the corpse of Jesus, desperate to ensure it is entombed under the earth and remains there. They seek also to prevent Jesus' disciples from re-igniting opposition to the myth-culture's authority (Matt 27:62–66; 28:11–15). The disciples (the men at least) evidently hide in fear of the authorities. However, not only fear but unbelief in Jesus becomes explicit here. So, mythological segregation is apparent in the defeated state, continued ignorance, and unbelief of the disciples after Jesus' death, and how these factors drive them back into their "proper place" in the cosmic hierarchy of myth-culture (e.g., Mark 16:11b, 13b).

DEIFICATION

René Girard affirms divine deification in the sixth episode of the Gospel accounts. Girard regards this as true individuality rather than the pseudo-individuation of the mythological world. By using the term deification, I do not mean that Jesus becomes God due to His resurrection (He was prior to it), or that the disciples become gods *per se*. A Greek term for deification is "theosis," meaning likeness to or union with God. This transformation is by baptism with and the indwelling of the Holy Spirit in a person (e.g., Matt 3:11; Mark 1:8; 13:11; Luke 24:49; John 20:22). Deification, then, is through repentance from sin (e.g., Mark 1:4–8) and faith in Jesus (e.g., Mark 16:14–16; Luke 24:47), which among other things results in apprehension and declaration of the truth. Completing the chiastic bi-pattern, deification is the subversion of mythological segregation, and the inversion of mythological sameness.[91] Girard describes deification in the following way:

> [Cayley:] In the Gospel, he says, it is only those who have woken up and recognized what they have been doing who encounter the risen God. [Girard:] The resurrected Christ appears only to the people who, ultimately, have seceded from the mob. The resurrected god of myth appears to the mob. He's the god of the mob. . . . [Cayley:] The risen Christ is apparent only to a minority who have seceded. . . . [Girard:] In myth you never have a dissident minority. . . . In the Gospels you have an enormous majority who say, Jesus is a blasphemer. . . . At the beginning all the disciples are scattered. It takes the resurrection for them to say the truth. In other words, the anthropological truth, the judicial truth, that Jesus is obviously innocent, comes only through the Resurrection. That's what one has to see. And it affects only a few people.[92]

This initial effect, as Girard says, is performed by Jesus as well. Jesus has to come again and personally reveal and explain the truth, the reality, to the disciples, and to give them His Spirit to continue them in the truth. Girard continues describing this effect:

> [Cayley:] The Resurrection breaks the spell of unanimous opinion which Girard thinks is the basis of the old sense of the sacred. . . . [Girard:] To become a Christian is to become aware of oneself as a persecutor of Christ. . . . It is the revelation of what that violence is about, that that violence is untrue, is a lie. The violence of scapegoating in myth is reported as the guilt of the victim. If everybody believes in that guilt, if everybody can transfer their own guilt to the scapegoat, then they won't transfer against each other. Therefore, the misinterpretation of the collective murder is the peace of the world, the peace as the world gives it [John 14:27]. . . . Why is Satan the Prince of Darkness? Because his secret is hidden. The Cross reveals it.[93]

Recognition of the resurrection of Jesus Christ, by Jesus Christ's direct revelation, enables those who are beginning to believe to step outside the pattern of myth-culture, and to begin to see and speak the truth about the actual nature of "the sacred," the pattern of myth-culture. Jesus Himself, after His resurrection, imparts His Holy Spirit to the disciples, just as He declared the need to believe and be "baptized" in His Spirit (e.g., Luke 11:13; John 7:39; 14:17, 26; 15:26; 16:13; 20:22; Acts 1:4–5; 2:1–4). Deification, then, is the receiving of the Holy Spirit through belief in Jesus. Among other things, the Spirit wards against the inclination to the pattern of the myth-culture, the

---

91. For further discussion of divine deification, as in confession of persecuting Jesus and belief in Him, resulting in God's Spirit indwelling, see Girard, *I See Satan*, 189–93; *Scapegoat*, 206–12; Schwager, *Scapegoats*, 220–27; Burkhardt, *Biblical Doctrine*.

92. Girard, "Scapegoat," 26.

93. Girard, "Scapegoat," 27, 30, 32.

old sin-nature. Girard describes this effect on the disciples in the days following Jesus' resurrection and ascension:

> Where did they suddenly find the strength to oppose the crowd and the Je-
> rusalem authorities? . . . The Resurrection is not only a miracle. . . . It is the
> spectacular sign of the entrance into the world of a power superior to violent
> contagion. . . . What is this power that triumphs over mimetic violence? The
> Gospels respond that it is the Spirit of God, the third person of the Trinity,
> the Holy Spirit. The Spirit takes charge of everything. It would be false . . . to
> say the disciples "regained possession of themselves": it is the Spirit of God
> that possesses them and does not let them go. . . . The Resurrection empowers
> Peter and Paul, as well as all believers after them, to understand that all impris-
> onment in sacred violence is violence done to Christ. Humankind is never the
> victim of God; God is always the victim of humankind.[94]

Girard describes the gift of the Holy Spirit from the Father through Jesus and its effects on the disciples. The effect is their individual deification, their personal communion with God. This effect is certainly what we read in the sixth episode of the Gospel
account, and also thereafter in the Acts of the Apostles and the disciples' many letters
that follow in the remaining New Testament canon (and beyond).

The final two combat myth motifs that parallel the final episode of the Gospel
account are the eleventh "enemy punished" and twelfth "triumph" motifs (table A). As
we have seen, these motifs' sequence and meaning hold true for the actions and words
of the representatives of the myth-culture in the sixth episode of the Gospel, but not
for Jesus Christ. Jesus' "triumph," which is not a mythological "triumph," comes first,
His resurrection from death and the grave. Jesus' "enemy punished" comes second,
and it is the punishment of sin that Jesus performs here; sin that has until this moment
held humanity in the pattern of myth-culture (among other things). Jesus provides
His Spirit as a seal within each person that repents and believes, the seal of eternal life.

Key expressions of deification in the final sixth episode of the Gospel account are
noted by Girard (previous) and Hamerton-Kelly.[95] In the Gospel account, the resurrected Jesus appears to His disciples in the flesh, reveals the truth to them, and states
that belief in Him is necessary to be saved from eternal condemnation, and instead
live forever in His kingdom. Jesus promises to send the Holy Spirit to come upon the
apostles with power, and commands them to preach this Gospel of the kingdom to "all
creation" (Mark 16:15).

---

94. Girard, *I See Satan*, 189, 191.

95. Hamerton-Kelly, *Gospel and Sacred*, 57–59.

4

Bruce J. Malina's Reading of the Gospel Account

"But Jesus, on His part, was not entrusting Himself to them,

for He knew all men,

and because He did not need anyone to testify concerning man,

for He Himself knew what was in man."

(JOHN 2:24–25)

SAMENESS

Bruce J. Malina affirms the presence of sameness in the first episode of the Gospel account. Like Girard, he uses his own specialized social-scientific terminology to articulate it. For sameness, Malina uses terms including: dyadism, collectivistic personality, and group-embeddedness.[1] However, Malina attempts to confine such culture to what he calls the honor-shame cultures of the AD first-century Mediterranean. Malina writes:

> What sort of personality sees life nearly exclusively in terms of honor? For
> starters, such a person would always see himself or herself through the eyes of

1. For further discussion of sameness, as in dyadism and collectivistic personality, see Malina, "Mediterranean Self"; Pierce, *Conscience*; Triandis, "Cross-Cultural Studies."

others. After all, honor requires a grant of reputation by others. So what others tend to see is all-important. Further, such individuals need others for any sort of meaningful existence, since the image such persons have of themselves has to be indistinguishable from the image held and presented to them by their significant others in the family, tribe, village, city, or ethnic group.[2]

Malina goes on to say, "Respectability, in this social context, would be the characteristic of a person who needs other people in order to grasp his or her own identity."[3] So Malina's conception of sameness accords with Girard's, except that Girard attributes it to all persons in all times and places since culture began. Malina's conception also comports with what we see in the behavior of those around Jesus in the first episode of the Gospel account. However, Malina contends that Jesus Himself also conforms to the culture in this respect: "Jesus, too, is depicted as a man of honor . . . concerned about 'who . . . men say that I am.'"[4] Malina argues throughout his work that Jesus is in general conformity with the myth-culture. This reading by Malina, as exemplified by this interpretation of Mark 8:27, is a serious misrepresentation of the text,[5] taking this passage and the contextual meaning of Jesus' words out of context.

And yet, such misrepresentation is a consistent theme in Malina's writing on the Gospels, as we shall see. His presupposition that Jesus is a product of His culture results in misinterpretation of the entire account of the Gospel. This type of error is increasingly found in scholarship on the entire Bible today. When a reader gives the cultural milieu of a text's composition interpretive authority over that text, it necessarily results in misinterpretations and so misrepresentations of the text and what it is saying.[6] The author of the text must always be the primary and ultimate authority for the meaning (the interpretation) of his writing, and the Bible is no different. This means we must always read contextually.

Similarly, due to this basic interpretive blunder, Malina includes the biblical God, in general, in this category of myth-culture. As such, he asserts that God is a projection of the group-consciousness of the myth-culture:

> Since statements about God, like statements in the physical sciences, derive
> from analogies based on human behavior, it follows that biblical descriptions

---

2. Malina, *New Testament World*, 58.

3. Malina, *New Testament World*, 58–59. Note that Girard also recognizes "being," involving identity, as experienced *through* others.

4. Malina, *New Testament World*, 59.

5. When reading this verse in context, it is clear that Jesus is asking if men perceive His actual identity, which is from God's perspective, as the Messiah, not His reputation or identity among men.

6. Popular examples of this mistaken approach to interpretation of the Bible, in which the cultural milieu is given interpretive authority over the text of Scripture, are various N. T. Wright works, including, *Jesus and the Victory of God* and the *Christian Origins and the Question of God* series; and various John H. Walton works, including *The Lost World of Genesis One* and the *Lost World* series.

of how God functions will take the shape of analogies drawn from perceptions
of how human beings function.[7]

In other words, the culture's projected mythological god is declared by Malina to be
the God of the Bible. For many reasons, this view of Malina is quite surprising, as (*inter alia*) unlike the gods of myth, God in Jesus identifies with the victims of the crowd's
violence, the scapegoats of myth-culture, rather than with the mythological mob or
cosmic crowd of culture, as is observed by Nietzsche and Girard (e.g., Isa 52:13–53:12;
Matt 21:33–46; Mark 12:1–12; Luke 20:9–20; John 12:44–50; 15:1–27). Nevertheless,
Malina insists that "statements about God . . . [are] based on human behavior . . . [and]
perceptions of how human beings function."[8] According to Malina, God and Jesus are
beings made in our image, in the image of human groups: "This cultural model of
human makeup is applied analogically to God. God, too, gets described in terms of
these three zones."[9]

Leaving that critical error aside for the moment, positively we can see that myth-
culture's fundamental state of sameness is affirmed by Malina as present in the honor-
shame culture of the AD first-century Mediterranean, and in the first episode of the
Gospel account. The combination of honor-shame, dyadic relations and collectivistic
personality forms a myth-cultural context that naturally occasions envy or scandal;
the conflict of same desire. (Therefore, as we have seen, scandal is the episode that will
follow sameness in the pattern of myth-culture.)

The first two motifs of combat myth, the first "lack/villainy" and second "hero
emerges" motifs, conform to this phenomenon of sameness that Malina identifies (see
table A). The first phase of myth is a context of the perception of lack and villainy
(the Malinan term is "limited good"), as well as the felt need to be perceived as good
(honorable), as a hero of the group or culture, as someone devoid of lack and villainy.

Malina notes the presence of sameness in the outset of Matthew's first episode. In
their commentary, Malina and Rohrbaugh note King Herod the Great's terrible envy
of Jesus' kingship. They describe it as arising from this underlying context of dyadism

---

7. Malina, *New Testament World*, 72.

8. Malina, *New Testament World*, 72.

9. Malina, *New Testament World*, 76. The three zones to which Malina refers are "eyes-heart,"
"mouth-ears," and "hands-feet" (*New Testament World*, 68), and Malina goes on to say: "In sum, it
would seem that the distinctive post-Jesus group conception of God in terms of the Trinity has its
roots in the three-zone model of the human being typical of the culture we are considering. It is a sort
of replication—the application of the same pattern to another area—of the model of what constitutes
the human being applied to experience of God, undoubtedly due to the experience of Jesus. Further,
the conceptions of God in the Bible in general are likewise rooted in the three-zone model of human-
kind's makeup" (Malina, *New Testament World*, 75). In other words, as Girard says of the mythological
god and not the God of the Bible, to Malina, the God of the Bible is also a projection of the human
group. Of course, the very opposite is the viewpoint of Scripture, e.g., Gen 1:26–7; 9:6; Lev 26:1; Deut
4:25; Matt 19:4–6; Mark 10:5–9; Rom 1:23; 2 Cor 4:4; Col 1:15.

and concern for honor that gives rise to envy/scandal.[10] Malina and Rohrbaugh entitle this portion of Matthew (2:13–23), "God's Protection from Herod's Envy."[11]

Malina also notes sameness in Satan's temptation of Jesus (Matthew 4:1–11), entitling the event, "Testing Jesus' Status as God's Son."[12] He describes Jesus in terms of honor-shame, contending that Jesus is concerned about His reputation before humans (as noted). As there is no crowd, no humans at all, there to see that conflict between Jesus and the Devil to give the "necessary" grant of honor to Jesus, however, Malina has difficulty supporting his reading with the text.[13] Again, this is what happens when we do not read contextually, and instead force an extra-biblical interpretation upon the Scriptures. Actually, there is a logical break in the text of the first episode, an opposition of antithetical logics (Jesus' and myth's), as occurs throughout the Gospel account. A key corollary of the temptation event is that Jesus is not of the world, not under Satan's sway, not a product of the myth-culture despite attempts to read it that way. Jesus demonstrates this by rejecting Satan's offer of the world's prestige, power, and possessions, etc.; all its "limited goods" (Matt 4:8–11).

Malina and Rohrbaugh's comments on those events recorded in Matthew's first episode are equally applicable to the same events recorded in Mark's and Luke's first episode. Additionally however, Malina notes sameness—honor-shame concern amid dyadism—in Joseph and Mary's upset over Jesus' behavior when twelve years of age (Luke 2:48).[14] The twelve-year-old Jesus describes Himself as distinct from cultural categories, referring to Himself as God's Son and so needing to be in His Father's House, the Temple in Zion/Jerusalem (Luke 2:49). Malina claims that Jesus' view of Himself is "fictive,"[15] again refusing to acknowledge a clear antithesis formed in the Gospel account's first episode between mythological sameness and divine distinction in Jesus. Malina argues that Jesus' real social category is son of Joseph and Mary, and all that this entails regarding the culture's definition of Him. Obviously, the text does not support this reading.

Malina affirms the presence of sameness in the opening episode of John's Gospel also, noting the rivalry that arises from the context of sameness.[16] However, Malina asserts that the rivalry characteristic of mythological contenders—where both are defined by the same logic, desiring the same thing—applies to both the world's authorities named in John 1:1–34 *and* to Jesus. However, what we actually read in John

---

10. Malina and Rohrbaugh, *Synoptic Gospels*, 33–34.

11. Malina and Rohrbaugh, *Synoptic Gospels*, 34. The question must be asked, however, how can a god who is a projection of the culture protect anyone? Malina's approach becomes inconsistent with the text's claims when applied to it.

12. Malina and Rohrbaugh, *Synoptic Gospels*, 41–42.

13. Malina and Rohrbaugh, *Synoptic Gospels*, 41–42.

14. Malina and Rohrbaugh, *Synoptic Gospels*, 299.

15. Malina and Rohrbaugh, *Synoptic Gospels*, 299.

16. Malina and Rohrbaugh, *Gospel of John*, 30–31.

1:5b, 10b, and 11b, is not two equal-opposites, but rather two un-equals approaching each other in antithetical ways, with antithetical desires. In other words, Malina sees only sameness in John's first episode, while the text explicitly describes both sameness in the *people's* reception of Jesus, as well as distinction in the nature of *Jesus* and His reception of the world. In fact, the distinction element of the text of John's first episode far outweighs the sameness element.[17] While two contradictory social-science patterns are present, Malina acknowledges the presence of only one, that of myth-culture.

Regarding the myth-culture's leaders' interrogation of John the Baptist (John 1:19–28), Malina strangely accuses John the Baptist of hostility.[18] It is clear contextually that the leaders of Israel sent emissaries down from Jerusalem to assess the threat-level of John and Jesus, and to serve notice that they are watching. This fact clearly indicates that there is an oppressive and hostile authority over-shadowing John's ministry in the first episode. This plain reading is quickly affirmed with John's imprisonment and beheading by the religio-political authorities of the cosmos (John 3:24).[19] Positively, the myth-culture's sameness is affirmed by Malina in the first episode of the Gospel account, but sadly it is all he sees. The clear distinction articulated in opposition to sameness, in the text of episode one, is mischaracterized by Malina as one and the same.

DISTINCTION

Bruce J. Malina at times openly rejects the divine distinction of Jesus in the Gospels' first episode, as noted, and at other times appears to entertain the possibility in a highly contained and diminished form[20] compared with the plain sense of the account. In his specialized terminology, Malina characterizes Jesus' distinction that the Gospels' first episode expresses as "fictive" (as noted above), and Jesus' identity and behavior instead as in conformity with the pattern of the myth-culture. For Malina to be forced to comment in the negative, concerning an explicit claim of Jesus and of the Gospel account regarding who Jesus is, is tacit acknowledgement that there is in fact an anti-myth-cultural voice in the text of the Gospel account. Nevertheless, Malina presses on in his reading:

---

17. The two are indicated by color-coding the account of Mark's Gospel in appendix 1.

18. Malina and Rohrbaugh, *Gospel of John*, 46.

19. John the Baptist's imprisonment is noted in John's account, but not his beheading, as in the other three accounts. John's Gospel has been noted for assuming events recorded in the other three Gospels as having taken place, without explicitly mentioning them itself. See Barrett, *Essays on John*; Lightfoot, *St. John's Gospel*, 29.

20. An example of this temporary and moderated equivocation, in the face of biblical texts that clearly do not support his reading, is Malina's comments on the way Scripture compares God to man-made idols (Malina, *New Testament World*, 72–76).

Jesus, the Gospel authors and the persons referred to in their writings, Paul, the Pharisees, Sadducees, the early post-Jesus[21] group members—all these persons derived from and lived according to the *patterns of their societies*. Their behavior made sense; their interactions took place according to the *patterns of their culture*; their values were judged noble or ignoble in line with cues shared in the groups of the time. When they got angry at each other, they knew why. For the modern believing Christian, the incarnation of the word of God means the enculturation of God's word.[22]

Leaving aside the untenable equation of the early Church and the "patterns of their culture," as Malina does in the first two sentences of this quotation, that last sentence seems to jump out of nowhere. In it, Malina places his idiosyncratic equation of Jesus with the world with which He engaged (*contra textum*) into the hearts and minds of "modern believing Christians," who, it is safe to say, certainly do not equate Jesus with His cultural context in such unqualified terms. That is, the text presents Jesus not only as fully human, but also as fully God (e.g., Matt 16:16; Mark 1:1; 14:61–63; Luke 1:35; John 1:1, 14).

As mentioned, Malina does not simply attempt to equate Jesus with myth-culture and so distinguish Him from God, but goes on to include God as a product of culture as well:

No symbol can mean just anything. . . . The symbol gets its range of meanings from the available shared social expectations, that is, from the available shared social symbol system . . . the *symbolic model* . . . attached to objects that are socially valued. Such socially valued objects include the self, others, nature, time, space, and the All (God).[23]

This placing of God under the control and fabrication of human myth-culture effectively asserts that God is god, or mythological, and certainly not distinct as He is presented in the Gospel and the Bible as a whole. Rather, to Malina it would seem, God conforms to the pattern of sameness and the mythological cycle of culture. Despite the fact that Jesus clearly rejects viewing the other as a potential rival-double of desire, Malina expects and so concludes that Jesus conforms to the cultural model and is therefore a typical mythological rival-double with the religio-political leadership of Israel, and all His opponents.

21. This turn of phrase, "post-Jesus," is additionally telling. From the perspective of the Gospel writers and disciples of Jesus following the resurrection and ascension, is it textually bearable to characterize the Church as "post-Jesus"? Such a phrase implies rejection of the fundamental assertions of the text.

22. Malina, *New Testament World*, 16 (italics mine).

23. Malina, *New Testament World*, 22. This equation of the biblical creator God with His creation by referring to Him as "All" is an additional oddity in Malina's reading. Such a conflation of Creator with the created universe is an eminently unbiblical notion, and surprising in a scholar of religion who should know that this particular matter is a key distinguisher of the Bible and Christianity from other religions and their texts around the globe.

Let us now compare the initial two motifs of the combat myth pattern, the first "lack/villainy" and second "hero emerges" motifs, to Malina's sense of the first episode of the Gospels regarding divine distinction. If, as the Malinan reading explicitly contends, only the myth-culture's sameness is to be found in the first episode of the Gospel account, we would expect to encounter in Jesus the two motifs of the mythical pattern, un-inverted in sequence and un-subverted in significance. However, we do not! Contrary to Malina's claims, Jesus does not conform to the order or meaning of the "shared social expectations" of the myth-culture in His identity or behavior. This reality will be confirmed in detail when we turn to Mark's account in the next chapter. Since Malina views the first episode of the Gospel accounts as fully conforming to the pattern of myth-culture, including Jesus Himself, we cannot discuss in further detail how he reads the divine distinction described there, because he has ignored and/or misrepresented that content of the episode.

SCANDAL

Bruce Malina affirms the reality of scandal arising out of dyadic honor-shame contexts, or situations of sameness. He prefers to call scandal envy (which term Girard also uses at times to describe scandal). In dyadic honor-shame societies, the perception of limited goods always potentiates envy. Malina writes:

> Few readers consider the cause of Jesus' death to be something so relatively unimportant . . . as envy . . . "Through the devil's envy, death entered the world" (Wis 2:24). Philo [of Alexandria] . . . insisted that envy was "the most grievous of all evils" (*Special Laws* III.1.2). . . . It seems that the configuration of the perception of limited good and concern for honor and shame . . . produces preoccupation with envy.[24]

It is interesting that Malina cites the original source of envy, or scandal, in the world as "through the devil's envy," which certainly harmonizes with the account of its biblical origin. Malina cites two causes of envy in the world (which are symptomatic and exacerbate envy), honor-shame and limited good. While limited good would perhaps be better placed after envy in sequence, Malina does not consider his models sequentially. Notwithstanding this grouping of cause and symptom, we can see that Malina's model affirms scandal as the second episode.[25]

In supporting his reading, Malina quotes Aristotle's understanding of this social phenomenon, which I also provide here:

> It is equally clear for what reason, and of whom, and in what frame of mind, men are envious, if envy is a kind of pain at the sight of good fortune in regard

24. Malina, *New Testament World*, 108.

25. For further discussion of scandal, as in envy at the success of the other, see Foster, "Anatomy of Envy"; Walcott, *Envy and Greeks*; Malina, "Limited Good"; Hagedorn and Neyrey, "Out of Envy."

to the goods mentioned; in the case of those like themselves; and not for the sake of a man getting anything, but because of others possessing it. For those men will be envious of others who are or seem to be like them.[26]

Malina affirms that Aristotle has the grasp of it, and indeed we find in his words confirmation of sameness ("in the case of those *like* themselves" . . . "others who are or seem to be *like* them") giving rise to envy, or the phenomenon of the model-obstacle ("pain at the sight of good fortune . . . not for the sake of a man getting anything, but because of *others* possessing it"), all summable with the term scandal.

Once again it helps to now compare envy to the combat myth motifs typical of the second episode, the third "donor/council" and fourth "journey" motifs (table A). As with Girard's understanding of the event of scandal, as well as what we have read in the Gospel account, the activities of the "hero" and his allies represented in the mythological motifs are consonant with a situation of scandal, the felt threat of a contender for a shared desired object and what to do about it. This object may only feel like the whole world in everyday examples of scandal, but in combat mythology it is articulated as actually the whole world. Similarly, in the Gospel account the opponents of Jesus describe the object of scandal as the whole world, the cosmos that they want to possess and think others want to take from them (e.g., Matt 4:8–9; John 12:19). And yet, Jesus Himself counts the world as of no value; that is, in the mythological sense (e.g., Matt 4:10; Mark 8:36; Luke 9:25).

Malina reads the presence of envy, or scandal, in the second episode of Matthew's account. He and Rohrbaugh note that the religio-political leaders accuse Jesus of demon-possession, and/or blasphemy, out of envy (Matt 12:22–37).[27] They also note that the cosmic leaders justify their accusations by what Malina terms "deviance-labelling,"[28] which is what Girard calls "stereotypes of persecution."[29]

Regarding Mark's second episode, Malina also notes envy at work in the reception of Jesus. An example here is Jesus' family's felt shame, and fear of dishonor, due to the scandal caused by Jesus' words and deeds (Mark 3:20–30). Malina writes, "The comment about Jesus' family seeking to retrieve him suggests their perception that the honor of the family was indeed threatened."[30]

Malina also notes scandal in Luke's second episode, discussing an event also commented on by Girard, which is Jesus' healing of the Gerasene demoniac (Luke 8:26–39; Matt 8:28–34; Mark 5:1–20). Malina notes that the city of the Gerasenes had been engaging in "deviant labelling and abuse,"[31] and they are scandalized by Jesus' healing of the afflicted man, as well as His allowing thousands of their swine to die.

26. Aristotle, *Rhetoric* 2.10.1–3; Malina, *New Testament World*, 111.

27. Malina and Rohrbaugh, *Synoptic Gospels*, 97–98.

28. Malina and Rohrbaugh, *Synoptic Gospels*, 97.

29. Malina and Rohrbaugh, *Synoptic Gospels*, 97–98; Girard, *Scapegoat*, 12–23.

30. Malina and Rohrbaugh, *Synoptic Gospels*, 199.

31. Malina and Rohrbaugh, *Synoptic Gospels*, 337.

But Malina is thrown off the scent by the term "legion" and interprets the scandal as due to fear of Rome.[32] Again, Malina misinterprets the text due to his giving the cultural context interpretive authority over the textual context. It is clear from the text that the scandal is caused by Jesus, not by Rome.

Finally, Malina also notes scandal as predominant in John's second episode. In the same portion that draws Girard's attention, John 5:1–47, Malina notes Jesus' healing of a human on the Sabbath (as also occurs in the other three accounts): "This controversy between Jesus and the Judeans over lawbreaking (and later, over Jesus' claims of kinship with God) will eventually lead to Jesus' death."[33] Jesus makes such claims of being God just a few verses later (John 5:17–18). That Jesus makes this claim of being God is affirmed by how His audience receives it, which is as blasphemy deserving of execution. This scandal of the cosmic crowd over Jesus constitutes the second episode of the pattern of myth-culture in Jesus' opponents, but not in Jesus Himself.

DIFFUSION

As we saw with distinction, Malina at times openly rejects the text's assertion of Jesus' divine diffusion of scandal, and at other times seems to entertain Jesus' opposition to the pattern of mythological culture with respect to envy or scandal. Malina acknowledges what Girard also notes regarding myth-culture, which is that people deny that they envy. They imitate the desires of other humans, envying constantly due to their state of sameness (dyadism or interdividuality), but tend to hide this reality. Malina cites Plutarch's *On Envy and Hate* in support:

> [Plutarch] begins by observing that the source of the pain of persons who feel envy . . . is "the fortunate man." So envy is a typically human experience. . . . "Men deny that they envy as well; and if you show that they do, they allege any number of excuses and say they are angry with the fellow or fear or hate him, cloaking and concealing their envy . . . implying that among the disorders of the soul it alone is unmentionable."[34]

Girard also discusses this typical denial of conflictual imitation of desire, or scandal/envy, as noted above. Girard observes the significance of the tenth commandment in this regard ("You shall not covet your neighbor's . . . " [Exod 20:17]), and Jesus' reference to it in His teaching on diffusion of scandalous envy.[35]

32. Malina and Rohrbaugh, *Synoptic Gospels*, 208, 337. The demons afflicting the man themselves explain what they mean by "legion," which is "for we are many" (Mark 5:9). A legion consisted of several thousand soldiers and so is used here of a great occupying force, a natural metaphor for demon-possession. The numerical significance is affirmed when Jesus allows them to enter a herd of several thousand swine (Mark 5:13).

33. Malina and Rohrbaugh, *Gospel of John*, 112.

34. Malina, *New Testament World*, 128–29; Plutarch, *On Envy and Hate*, 537E.

35. Girard, *I See Satan*, 13.

Strangely, however, Malina views Jesus' clear opposition to envy—His teaching against it, and instead modelling emulation of the Father God's desire instead of other humans' desires—as nevertheless, simply operating according to the pattern of myth-culture:

> In ancient Mediterranean society interpersonal relations are characterized by competition, rivalries, and conflicts of opinion. In this limited-good world, where anything gained, whether new wealth, position, honor or whatever, was always believed to come at someone else's expense, one could never appear to be grasping or self-aggrandizing in public, . . . The much-discussed "messianic secret" motif . . . can be seen in this light. . . . Jesus could not claim to be anything more than a village artisan without being viewed as grasping in the extreme. . . . Jesus prefers concealment to ward off envy.[36]

This argument by Malina makes a false-equivalence of the antithetical tension between the pattern of myth-culture and the pattern of God manifest in Jesus Christ. It is a classic example of that logical error, that fallacy of ambiguity called equivocation. Contextually, we can see that Jesus certainly does avoid scandalizing others, in imitation of the Father God, but not out of desire to please or appease other humans. Rather, once again, Jesus avoids scandal out of a desire to please His Father and achieve His Father's purpose in due time and circumstance. Jesus is not secretly desiring the same object as those who make Him their rival. The motives and goals are antithetical, beyond any apparent similarity of method, and the context makes that plain.

In his reading, Malina appears to be unable to hold in tension the opposing logics clearly presented in the text. Malina expects to see and so concludes that Jesus is bound by envy, typical of the myth-culture, despite what the text says. He asserts that Jesus is engaged in hidden rivalry in the same way and of the same sort as the people around Him. In contradiction of the Gospel account, Malina reads Jesus' words and actions as conforming to the pattern of myth-culture despite clear evidence to the contrary. Since Malina views the second episode of the Gospel accounts as fully conforming to the pattern of myth-culture, including Jesus Himself, we cannot discuss in further detail how he reads the divine diffusion in Jesus described there, because he has ignored and/or misrepresented that content of the episode.

SNARE OF STRIVING

Bruce Malina recognizes the snare of striving in the third episode of the Gospel account. His terminology for this social phenomenon includes agonism and honor contests of challenge-response, viewing them as natural corollaries of envy (scandal) in dyadic honor-shame (sameness) contexts:[37]

36. Malina, *New Testament World*, 125.

37. For further discussion of the snare of striving, as in agonism and honor contests, see Neyrey,

> Challenge and response is a sort of constant tug of war, a game of social push and shove. . . . The challenge is a claim to enter the social space of another. . . . A positive reason for entering another's social space would be to gain some share in that space. . . . A negative reason would be to dislodge another from that person's social space. . . . Receivers of a challenge look on the action from the viewpoint of its potential to dishonor their self-esteem, their self-worth. . . . The challenge, then, is a threat to usurp the reputation of another, to deprive another of his reputation.[38]

Such honor contests are certainly what we expect of this third episode of the pattern of myth-culture, as seen in the Zeus-Typhon and Marduk-Tiamat myths. Malina recognizes this, providing as an example of this behavior the religio-political leaders' words and actions toward Jesus.[39]

Malina also comments on the escalatory nature of agonistic myth-culture, the way that envy accumulates into terrible acts of violence:

> Competitions could be as innocent as rivalry at plays, dances, and songs at festivals, or as deadly as quarreling, feuding, and warring. Hence, it is not surprising that "love of honor" in competitive contexts is translated by scholars as "rivalry" or "aspiration" or simply "ambition." . . . Envy differs from jealousy or zeal as well as from hate. It was of central concern in the ancient Mediterranean since all goods were considered limited, and the person expressing honor as well as the honor itself detracted from others. It took away something invariably at some other person's expense. Envious people demonstrated their envy by ostracism, gossip, negative challenges, litigation, or homicide.[40]

Malina nicely summarizes the nature of agonism here; the snare of striving.

It is interesting to note how this social-scientific language accords with the typical combat myth motifs of the third episode, which are "battle" and "defeat" (table A). Both the hero-god and the villain-god, the cosmic god and the chaos-monster, strive to ensnare the other using similar weaponry, in perfect symmetry. They strive for pride of place, for assertion of their authority and control over the other, just as Malina describes in the motives and actions of myth-cultural persons above. However, in the Gospel account, while we certainly see such motives and behavior in people around Jesus, we once again do not find it in Jesus Himself.

Malina notes instances of the snare of striving (agonism) in Matthew's third episode. Like Hamerton-Kelly, Malina sees it in the behavior of the disciples as they contend for pre-eminence in the kingdom of God (Matt 18:1–10).[41] Unexpectedly, Malina

---

World of Luke-Acts, 67–122; Malina, *Christian Origins*; Malina and Neyrey, *Calling Jesus Names*.

38. Malina, *New Testament World*, 33–35.

39. Malina, *New Testament World*, 35.

40. Malina, *New Testament World*, 112, 131.

41. Malina and Rohrbaugh, *Synoptic Gospels*, 116–17.

acknowledges that Jesus criticizes such a view, which clearly shows that Jesus contradicts the myth-culture.[42] Likewise concerning Mark's third episode, Malina notes (as did Girard) Simon Peter's agonistic rebuke of Jesus (Mark 8:32),[43] attempting to encourage Jesus to strive for the world, like the world, which Jesus rejects. Malina makes the same comments on the snare of striving in Luke's third episode (Luke 9:46).[44]

John's third episode, while differing at times in form and specifics, is harmonious with Matthew, Mark and Luke in structure and general content. As such, we see Malina noting the dominance of agonism or the snare of striving in John's third episode also. An example among many noted by Malina is Jesus' brothers' challenge to Jesus to strive with the world, like the world (John 7:1–9).[45] Jesus responds that He is not of the world and so will not be engaging it in the fashion His (half) brothers do, and would like Him to imitate. Jesus will not imitate their desire. Throughout Malina's analysis of the third episode of the Gospel account, he affirms that the snare of striving prevails in Jesus' opponents. Although he notes Jesus' refusals to operate according to the snare of striving expected of pattern of myth-culture, Malina is unable to explain Jesus' behavior outside of his pre-determined social-scientific articulation of the principles of myth-culture. We can see that this inability is, as stated, a direct result of his false, extra-biblical presuppositions about Jesus.

DEFERENCE

Concerning deference in the third episode of the Gospel account, and despite Malina's acknowledgement of Jesus' opposition to the snare of striving, he nevertheless attempts to assert that Jesus is inconsistent, also getting caught up in the snare of striving, just as do all the other humans around Him. Once again, at times Malina does appear to acknowledge that Jesus is doing something different than expected according to myth-culture, but he is conspicuously silent about what that might be. Malina fails to comment at all in his commentaries on the portions explicitly expressing Jesus' Way of the Cross in this third episode.[46] Malina contends that prior to the crucifixion, Jesus engaged in the same agonistic striving with humans that all people do,[47] though often in a hidden or secretive way,[48] and that *ex postfacto* Jesus' disciples also pitted Jesus agonistically over-against others.[49] Malina is determined to view Jesus as in conformity with the myth-culture regardless of the textual evidence to the contrary.

42. Malina, *New Testament World*, 117.

43. Malina and Rohrbaugh, *Synoptic Gospels*, 232.

44. Malina and Rohrbaugh, *Synoptic Gospels*, 344.

45. Malina and Rohrbaugh, *Gospel of John*, 141.

46. Malina and Rohrbaugh, *Synoptic Gospels*, 114.

47. Malina and Rohrbaugh, *Synoptic Gospels*, 42.

48. Malina, *New Testament World*, 125.

49. Malina, *New Testament World*, 36.

Concerning how Malina's reading of the third episode of the Gospel relates to the pattern of myth-culture, we can see that he essentially equates the two. Despite Jesus clearly not conforming to this pattern of myth, Malina presents Jesus as conforming, and he goes silent when the textual evidence is not supportive of his view. In short, once again, we are unable to look at examples of Malina's reading of divine deference in Jesus, as they do not exist.

SCAPEGOATING

Malina does note the definitive presence of scapegoating in the fourth episode of the Gospel account. With regard to the social phenomenon itself, Malina curiously (or perhaps expectedly) avoids talking about the event directly, but circles around it constantly with his preferred social-scientific terminology of limited good.[50] He describes scapegoating in the following way:

> The people presented in the pages of the New Testament would see their existence as determined and limited by the natural and social resources of their village . . . city, their immediate area and world . . . all the desired things in life, such as land, wealth, prestige, blood, health, semen, friendship and love, manliness, honor, respect and status, power and influence, security and safety—literally all goods in life—exist in finite, limited quantity. . . . Since all goods exist in limited amounts . . . it follows that individuals, alone or with their families, can improve their social positions *only at the expense of others* . . . improvement in someone's position with respect to any good in life is viewed as *a threat to the entire community*.[51]

What Malina is dancing around here is his clear awareness that the context of dyadism that he has affirmed constitutes human social life in the myth-culture (sameness), which produces envy (scandal), and which multiplies agonism and social strife (snare of striving), also eventuates sacrifice of others for the gain of oneself and/or one's family, subgroup, cosmos. Clearly, scapegoating is the phenomenon to which Malina points with the notion of limited good. I italicized key portions of Malina's description of limited good above to also show that he understands scapegoating of the other as operating at the level of the "entire community." That is, scapegoating is a unanimous collective act.

When he discusses the purpose of sacrifice, however, which he notes is the means for protecting and re-establishing the purity of the community by expelling

---

50. For further discussion of scapegoating, as in limited social good "requiring" sacrifice of the other, see Malina, "Limited Good"; Foster, "Anatomy of Envy"; Gregory, "Image of Limited Good"; Malina, "Mediterranean Sacrifice."

51. Malina, *New Testament World*, 89 (italics mine).

impurity (cosmos expelling chaos),[52] Malina acknowledges the entire community's benefit from human sacrifice and the other forms of sacrifice. He writes,

> For just as an offense against one's fellows that might result in lethal feuding requires reconciliation, so there was a range of purification and reconciliation sacrifices directed to God to keep life-threat away and to re-establish life-supportive relations. These sacrifices marked reconciliation and a new social start; they are often called *expiatory sacrifices*. . . . Sacrifice is a ritual transaction that affirms or celebrates the life of a kin group or polity, or that marks the restoration of life of a person or group deserving to forfeit life . . . *human or animal is killed*; flour is baked; wine is poured out. Then God receives a portion . . . *to be shared with the sacrificing circle.*[53]

Once again, Malina makes the astonishing, counter-textual, assertion that the God of the Bible is equivalent with pagan gods. And additionally bizarre, though to be expected when one falsely views the biblical God as the same as pagan gods, is that he claims that the Biblical God receives human sacrifices. It is apparent from Scripture, under the Law of Moses, that God accepts and even commands animal sacrifice during the period of the Gospel accounts, but He explicitly condemns human sacrifice (e.g., Lev 18:21; Jer 19:5).[54] Once again, despite that error, Malina here acknowledges that scapegoating, the sacrifice of a person or persons for the life of the group, is a key part of the pattern of myth-culture. While, as noted previously, Malina does not make the connection between cause and effect in the cyclical sequence of myth-culture, he does describe the social values and their practices typical of each episode.[55]

Malina's reading of scapegoating, which typifies the fourth episode of the Gospel accounts, complements the two motifs of the combat myth that are a part of its expression, "enemy ascendant" and "hero recovers" (table A). As seen with reference back to the example of Zeus-Typhon provided in the methodology, these two motifs are concerned with a tussle or tug-of-war over a particular limited good, a shared object of desire. In the Zeus-Typhon example, the limited good is Zeus's sinews which Typhon has stolen and hidden, and which Zeus must recover in order to have a chance to defeat his monster, and so recover the greater limited good at issue, control of the world. For Jesus' opponents in the Gospels, the limited good is the objectified people of Israel that are slipping away from the religio-political authorities into the hands of Jesus. In the heroes' dismay over Jesus' (their enemy's) apparent "ascendance," they declare "the world has gone after Him" (John 12:19).

---

52. Malina, *New Testament World*, 186.

53. Malina, *New Testament World*, 186–87 (italics mine).

54. Of course, this position is challenged by various scholars (e.g., Niditch, *Ancient Israelite Religion*).

55. For further discussion of limited good and scapegoating, see Malina, *New Testament World*, 113, 118–20, 166–67, 171–77, 210.

Malina notes key instances of limited good and scapegoating in the Gospel's fourth episode. In Matthew he notes Jesus' criticism of the myth-culture's elites' appropriation of widows' houses (Matt 23:1–39),[56] which is a gain for the group of elites at the expense of one socially vulnerable person or minority group. Malina also notes the religio-political leaders' decision to scapegoat Jesus out of envy, and Jesus' apparent control of the limited good of the people's affections (Matt 26:1–5).[57] Malina writes,

> The notice that the authorities were concerned about a "riot among the people" is another way of saying that at this point in the story the public perception of the honor status of Jesus was extremely high. It is precisely this perception that the process traditionally called "the passion and death of Jesus" will seek to undermine.[58]

Malina likewise notes similar expressions of limited good and scapegoating in the fourth episode of Mark's account (e.g., Mark 14:1–11),[59] Luke's account (Luke 22:1–38),[60] and John's account (John 15:18–16:4a; 18:1–11).[61]

DELIVERANCE

Bruce Malina does not describe or analyze the deliverance from scapegoating, sin and death performed by Jesus in the fourth episode of the Gospel account. He does point to the fact that the text appears to be indicating forgiveness of sins in Jesus' institution of the Eucharist, but Malina believes (*contra textum*) that sin is only against the group (as noted previously), against the myth-culture, and he believes that God is the myth-culture.[62] Malina emphasizes that the meal Jesus has with His disciples before His murder is another sacrificial meal typical of the myth-culture of the time.[63] He does note that the Church of Jesus Christ (what Malina refers to as "the Jesus Movement"), following His resurrection and ascension, understand Jesus to have changed fundamentally the way they perceive Israel's pre-Messiah operations,[64] because of the things Jesus says and does in these final chapters of the Gospel account.

However, as we will see in the final two episodes of the Gospel account, Malina views the new "Jesus Group(s)" as just another myth-cultural group, functioning

---

56. Malina and Rohrbaugh, *Synoptic Gospels*, 144–45.

57. Malina and Rohrbaugh, *Synoptic Gospels*, 152.

58. Malina and Rohrbaugh, *Synoptic Gospels*, 152.

59. Malina and Rohrbaugh, *Synoptic Gospels*, 264–66.

60. Malina and Rohrbaugh, *Synoptic Gospels*, 402.

61. Malina and Rohrbaugh, *Gospel of John*, 237–38, 249–51.

62. Malina, *New Testament World*, 58–60, 66.

63. Malina and Rohrbaugh, *Synoptic Gospels*, 155.

64. Malina, *New Testament World*, 187–96.

according to the same pattern of myth-culture.[65] He writes concerning the early Church of Jesus Christ, "irrespective of the culture involved, it seems that all human beings form groups in a similar, if not identical, way."[66] To Malina, what Jesus has achieved in the Gospel account is nothing new. There has been no real deliverance from the pattern of myth-culture after all, let alone a more fundamental deliverance from sin and death, in Malina's view.

So it is interesting again to see how Malina's reading of deliverance in the fourth episode once again comports with the pattern of myth-culture, despite all the textual evidence to the contrary. To Malina, despite what the text says, Jesus' words and deeds conform to the pattern of myth-culture. To Malina, Jesus is a sort of revolutionary "hero" (like Zeus or Marduk), correcting perceived shortcomings in a "villainous" (like Typhon or Tiamat) social system: "The Jesus movement group was a type of political action group, looking to societal change by God's intervention."[67] However, the text clearly shows that Jesus' actions and deeds are inversive of the myth-culture's pattern in the fourth episode, and subversive of their meaning, just as in the three previous episodes.

SATIATION

Bruce Malina affirms the presence of satiation dominating the fifth episode of the Gospel account, and views it as a predictable behavior of the dyadic honor-shame culture.[68] He writes,

> The first-century Mediterranean *civitas* or *polis* was really a large . . . central place. . . . The elite united to promote and defend their collective honor in face of the out-group. . . . The good things in life . . . [are] there to be divided and re-divided . . . only at the expense of others. Hence any apparent . . . improvement in someone's position with respect to any good in life is viewed as a threat to the entire community. . . . The one who is envious becomes negatively disposed towards the person with the singular possession and is often seized by the desire to deprive the other person of that possession—often in the name of the group. *It is right to cut down anyone standing above his/her status . . . [with] gossip and slander, feuding, litigation, and homicide. . . .* The same is true in Pilate's assessment of the high priests who want Jesus killed (Mark 15:10). . . . Sacrifice is a ritual transaction that affirms or celebrates the life of a kin group or polity, or that marks the restoration of life of a person or group . . . [so that

65. Malina, *New Testament World*, 198–217.

66. Malina, *New Testament World*, 201.

67. Malina, *New Testament World*, 214.

68. For further discussion of satiation, as in collectivistic sharing in the sacrifice of the scapegoat, and communal status-degradation rituals, see Malina, "Mediterranean Sacrifice"; Garfinkel, "Degradation Ceremonies"; McVann, "Rituals of Status Transformation"; Thérèse and Martin, "Shame, Scientist!"

> *a] human or animal is killed . . . to be shared with the sacrificing circle. . . .* It
> seems to be certainly the motive of the collectivistic persons who had Jesus put
> to death. *As regards Jesus' core group . . . they all abandoned Jesus.*[69]

As Malina observes, the community felt it had to "cut down" Jesus, this threatener of
the cosmic order. They had to make an example of Him for the mythological mob to
see and participate in, and share the spoils amongst its elites. In this case, the spoils
were mainly the restoration of their authority and control over the people, though
symbolized by Jesus' divided garments and their collective ridicule at His pain and
death, *etcetera*.

Once again, we can see that the expected combat myth motifs of this fifth satiation episode, "battle rejoined" and "victory" (table A), are precisely what we witness in
order and meaning in this episode of the Gospel account, as Malina affirms, but only
from the perspective of the mythological mob "devouring" Jesus. The perspective we
get from Jesus and the Gospel writers is antithetical to the voice of the mob; it is the
divine dispersive display of the evangelical pattern that Jesus epitomizes.

Malina considers key examples of satiation in the fifth episodes of the Gospel
account. In Matthew, he notes what he terms status-degradation rituals,[70] performed
by the religio-political elites upon Jesus. He writes,

> As Jesus is arrested and abandoned by his core group (Matthew 26:55–56),
> and then brought to the house of the high priest (26:57), the first of the deg-
> radation rituals that Matthew records takes place. Jesus is blindfolded, struck
> from behind, and mocked as a "prophet." He is reviled and insulted in other
> ways as well. By such humiliation in public . . . which he appears powerless to
> prevent, Jesus' lofty status in the eyes of the people begins to crumble. . . . In
> the end, the success of the degradation ritual made Pilate's "sentence" a mere
> recognition of the obvious.[71]

Malina clearly affirms the group satiation of the cosmic crowd upon their scapegoat
here. He also recognizes accounts of the same events in Mark and Luke's fifth episodes.[72] Likewise, Malina notes satiation in the fifth episode of John's Gospel account,
which essentially describes the same event in a similar way, according to the pattern
of myth-culture.[73]

---

69. Malina, *New Testament World*, 84, 89, 118, 187, 210 (italics mine).

70. Malina appears to borrow this term from the work of Garfinkel, "Conditions of Successful
Degradation Ceremonies."

71. Malina and Rohrbaugh, *Synoptic Gospels*, 159–60.

72. Malina and Rohrbaugh, *Synoptic Gospels*, 271–72, 406–8.

73. Malina and Rohrbaugh, *Gospel of John*, 253–65.

DISPERSIVE DISPLAY

Concerning Jesus' divine dispersive display in the fifth episode of the Gospel account, Bruce Malina once again equivocates over whether Jesus is conforming to the pattern of myth-culture or not. At times Malina says that Jesus' behavior is typical of myth-culture in this episode, and at times he appears to acknowledge significant differences. Malina views God's activity in Jesus Christ as not that at all, but a humanistic social-change movement, which, when Jesus was crucified, failed.[74] In other words, he agrees with the mythological mob, with the cosmic elites, that they have won as Jesus dies on the Cross.

Malina goes on to say that Jesus' apostles pick up the social movement thereafter, like a special-interest group, and function according to the pattern of myth-culture all over again, just as he believes Jesus did.[75] Malina offers a series of titles for his phases of group development to which he believes Jesus' so-called social movement conforms, as well as those of his followers after Jesus' death. And this cycle is the cyclical pattern of myth-culture, in fact. Malina thinks, once again, that Jesus conforms to the pattern of the world. Malina calls the phases of the special-interest group cycle: Forming, Storming, Norming, Performing, and Adjourning.[76]

We can see, when comparing Malina's reading of the fifth episode of the Gospel account, that he affirms the two parallel combat myth motifs, "battle rejoined" and victory' (table A), of the myth-culture that is crucifying Jesus. He does not notice the inversion and subversion of those motifs by Jesus, despite the clarity of the text. Concerning Matthew's account of it, Malina even goes so far as to argue that Peter's denial of Jesus in the moment of his satiation (Matt 26:69–75) was both expected culturally (true), and in no way wrong of him (untrue): "Lying to others about his relationship to Jesus would not be considered wrong."[77] The text of the Gospels clearly contradicts Malina's reading (see Jesus' rebuke of Peter's denials in John 21:15–19). Likewise, throughout his commentary on this fifth episode of the Gospels of Mark, Luke and John, Malina affirms the people's mythological actions and deeds while remaining conspicuously silent on Jesus' antithetical actions and deeds and their significance.[78]

74. Malina, *New Testament World*, 219.

75. Malina, *New Testament World*, 218–19.

76. Malina, *New Testament World*, 198–219.

77. Malina and Rohrbaugh, *Synoptic Gospels*, 160.

78. Malina and Rohrbaugh, *Synoptic Gospels*, 405–9; Malina and Rohrbaugh, *Gospel of John*, 252–75.

SEGREGATION

Bruce Malina affirms the presence of myth-culture's segregation in the sixth and final episode of the Gospel account. For segregation, Malina uses the terms purity-impurity and marriage-kinship.[79] He describes segregation in the following way:

> Human meaning building is a process of *socially contriving lines in the shapeless stuff of the human environment*, thus producing definition, socially shared meaning. Human groups draw lines. . . . Now, purity is specifically about the general cultural map of social time and space . . . and especially about *the boundaries separating the inside from the outside* . . . every culture patterns reality by means of such line making . . . we are enculturated to react with strong negative feelings toward certain anomalies, to view them as triggers of disgust or hate . . . *every culture has a classification system* . . . concerned with maintaining the wholeness or completeness of the social body. . . . Either the maintenance of life or the restoration of life is what sacrificers are concerned with. . . . Sacrifice is a ritual transaction that affirms or celebrates the life of a kin group or polity, or that marks the restoration of life of a person or group.[80]

Malina here describes how segregation is the "healthy" state of a functioning myth-culture, and it is maintained and restored *via* sacrifice, even and especially human sacrifice or scapegoating, as is (felt) necessary.

We noted that the two combat myth motifs that comprise the sixth episode of the myth-culture's share of the Gospel account are "enemy punished" and "triumph" (table A). These two motifs are affirmed by Malina as occurring in that order and with that significance for the cultural order that sacrifices Jesus to restore their purity, their cosmic peace and segregation. But does what Jesus says and does in this final episode of the Gospel account conform to the pattern and meaning of myth-culture? The answer is a resounding "no," and we will discuss that antithesis to myth-culture in Jesus below.

Malina cites key examples of segregation in the sixth and final episode of the Gospels. In Matthew, the chief priests and Pharisees send their own guards, with Pilate's permission, to keep watch over Jesus' tomb in order to ensure the peace they have won for their cultural order (Matthew 27:62–66).[81] Later in Matthew's sixth episode, after Jesus has risen, the religio-political leaders attempt a cover-up with bribery and a "smear-campaign," as Malina puts it, to keep control of their power and authority

---

79. For further discussion of segregation, in terms of purity-impurity and marriage-kinship, see Malina, "Mediterranean Sacrifice"; Neyrey, "Clean/Unclean," 80–104; Douglas, *Purity and Danger*; Jeremias, *Jerusalem*, 271; Todd, *Explanation of Ideology*.

80. Malina *New Testament World*, 164–66, 168–69, 186–87 (italics mine).

81. Malina and Rohrbaugh, *Synoptic Gospels*, 165.

(segregation) in the face of their scapegoat, Who has proven them wrong, unjust, and powerless by His rising from the dead (Matthew 28:11–15).[82]

Mark, Luke and John's accounts do not cover the explicit actions of the myth-culture's elites in re-segregating their cosmos, but rather the implied impact that their re-segregating has on the disciples of Jesus, who are hiding in terror or fleeing Jerusalem lest they share Jesus' demise. Apart from the fear of the religio-political leaders shown by the disciples of Jesus (John 20:19),[83] Malina is curiously silent on their (temporary) re-segregation into the myth-culture's oppressive order.

DEIFICATION

As with the five previous episodes of inversive and subversive divine identity, actions and words of the uniquely divine-human Jesus, in this sixth and final episode of the Gospel account, Malina is not clear in his social-scientific reading on Jesus' relation to His cultural context. To Malina, the relation is largely one of equivalence, with some radical social behaviors attempting to bring social change, but change that is entirely consistent with previous cycles of myth-culture (so, no change). While Malina well-describes the segregation of the world by the cultural elites in the sixth episode, he is again largely silent on the deification of the disciples by Jesus. The resurrected Jesus calls His disciples to belief in Him, and "baptism" in His Holy Spirit, and so into "partakers of the divine nature" (2 Pet 1:4), as Apostle Peter would later describe it.

Malina does note the odd behavior of Jesus' disciples, following His resurrection and ascension, in casting off much of the purity expectations of the myth-culture's cosmos. He writes,

> However, not long after the death and resurrection of Jesus, a notable group of Jesus followers rejected those purity arrangements for members of (the abominable) other ethnic groups who accepted Jesus as Messiah to come with power. . . . To accept Jesus as Messiah without Israel's purity arrangements clearly meant to spurn God's will . . . [they] considered Israelite purity rules as optional.[84]

This quotation shows how much Malina has selectively missed from the Gospel accounts. His interpretive social-scientific models, which incorrectly made the extra-biblical cultural context authoritative over the interpretation of the biblical text, have as a result only been able to account for the myth-culture in the text. Malina remains almost entirely silent on the antithesis of the pattern of myth-culture embodied by Jesus throughout the text. Malina concludes that Jesus' actions are a "social gospel,"

---

82. Malina and Rohrbaugh, *Synoptic Gospels*, 166.

83. Malina and Rohrbaugh, *Gospel of John*, 281.

84. Malina, *New Testament World*, 187.

that is, Jesus was a human only, who wanted Israel to be more "big-hearted" toward those who were formerly perceived as unclean/impure:

> His activity and teaching point to a new vision of priorities based on Jesus' own perception of God and God's will. The purity rules, while important, do not have precedence but are secondary to some other central concern . . . openness to all, openhanded, openhearted.[85]

This "gospel of tolerance" seems so enlightened, being open to all. The irony, however, is that this reading is, for some reason, not open to or tolerant of the identity, words and deeds of Jesus as presented in the Gospel account, or to the people who accept the text at face value.[86] This reading shows an intolerance of the explicit text of the Gospels. In the Malinan reading of the Gospel there is no deification, no salvation from sin, death, or the pattern of myth-culture. Instead, there is a widening of the circle of the sacred in an apparent attempt to include more people in a shared myth.

85. Malina, *New Testament World*, 189.

86. Malina refers to such people, and such readings, as childish. Real scholars, in his words, "outgrow their symbol of the ultimate 'really Real' [God] that served them so well in childhood" (*New Testament World*, 13–14). He asserts that an "adult, scholarly way" (*New Testament World*, 24) to read the Gospels is to reject the non-mythological majority-element of the text, which is Jesus Christ, the LORD.

PART 2

The Two Patterns in the Gospel of Mark

"For you have been called for this purpose,
since Christ also suffered for you,
leaving you an example for you to follow in His steps."
(1 PETER 2:21)

JESUS' PATTERN	MYTH-CULTURE	MARK'S 6 EPISODES	MARK'S 12 MOTIFS	COMBAT MYTH	JESUS' PATTERN[1]
Distinction	Sameness	1:1–15	1:1–12	Lack/Villainy	"Hero Emerges"
			1:13–15	Hero Emerges	"Lack/Villainy"
Diffusion	Scandal	1:16—8:26	1:16–3:6	Donor/Council	"Journey"
			3:7–8:26	Journey	"Donor/Council"
Deference	Striving	8:27–11:33	8:27–10:45	Battle	"Defeat"
			10:46–11:33	Defeat	"Battle"
Deliverance	Scapegoat	12:1–14:52	12:1–44	Enemy Ascends	"Hero Recovers"
			13:1–14:52	Hero Recovers	"Enemy Ascend"
Dispersion	Satiation	14:53–15:41	14:53–15:14	Battle Rejoined	"Victory"
			15:15–41	Victory	"Battle Rejoined"
Deification	Segregation	15:42–16:20	15:42–16:8	Enemy Punished	"Triumph"
			16:9–20	Triumph	"Enemy Punish"

TABLE F: Social-Scientific Episodes and Narratological Motifs in Mark

1. The placing of Jesus' motifs in quotation marks is to indicate that, not only does He invert the sequence of motifs in each episode as indicated, but His motifs are also subversive in significance. Jesus' motifs conform neither to the order nor the meaning of the motifs of the pattern of myth-culture.

5

Episode 1

Mark 1:1–15: Sameness and Distinction

Sameness	Distinction
"You said in your heart, 'I will ascend to heaven; I will raise my throne above the stars of God. . . . I will make myself like the Most High.'" (Isa 14:13–14)	"Let this mind be in you which was also in Christ Jesus, Who, being in the form of God, did not consider equality with God something to be grasped." (Phil 2:5–8)[2]

OVERVIEW

The initial sameness episode of myth-culture is, in the Gospel account, unexpectedly chiastically inverted and subverted by divine distinction in Jesus. Jesus' anti-myth-cultural pattern begins in the first verses of the Gospel account with the introduction of Jesus Christ to the world. This first episode continues up to the point when Jesus begins preaching that, "the kingdom of God is at hand" (Mark 1:1–15; refer to table C or F for the first and last verse of each episode). The first and last verses of each social-scientific episode are selected based upon their positions at the beginning and end of the content of each episode of the myth-culture's pattern (social-scientifically determined), as well as the transition points of the twelve sequential motifs of the combat myth pattern (narratologically determined). These two patterns, being fundamentally related as shown in the methodology, align so that each myth-culture episode contains

2. Author's translation.

two combat myth motifs. This alignment is itself a mark of the validity of the approach employed here, confirming the presence of the two patterns in the Gospel account.

The first two sequential motifs of the combat myth pattern, as seen in the combats of Zeus versus Typhon and Marduk versus Tiamat, for example, form the sameness episode of the pattern of myth. They are "lack/villainy" and then "hero emerges,"[3] in that order (refer to table A). However, what we see uniquely in the first episode of the Gospel account is the reversal of these two motifs as they pertain to Jesus. In other words, while both lack/villainy and a hero's emergence are present for Jesus, He, being the hero emerging, comes first, in the place of the lack/villain (chaos). Meanwhile, the cosmic establishment, who oppose God and so represent lack/villainy, appear second where we would expect the hero, according to myth-culture's pattern.[4] Additionally, not merely the sequence but also the significance of Jesus' motifs is fundamentally discordant with myth-culture's motifs in the Gospel account, as we shall see throughout the analysis.

Jesus' reversals, that is, from the vantage of myth-culture's expectations—the inversion of motifs with respect to sequence and their subversion with respect to meaning—form the chiastic bi-pattern of the LORD Jesus' unique evangelical pattern in relation to the mythological pattern of culture. Concurrently, the representatives of the myth-culture in the Gospel account, being found in opposition to Jesus almost immediately, conform to both the expected sequence and significance of the first two motifs of the pattern of myth-culture, as we will soon see. The two opposing patterns of Jesus and myth-culture run concurrently through the episode, forming a narratologically and social-scientifically discernible transversal, chiasm, or cross-structure.

The point at which the second of these two inverted and subverted myth motifs ends, as determined through the narratological lens, constitutes the transition point from the sameness-distinction episode into the scandal-diffusion episode, as discerned through the social-science lens. So identifying the two mythological motifs typical of each of the six myth-culture episodes aids in pinpointing the transitions between the six episodes. (For the specific transition verses, see table C.)[5] The proposed points of transition are argued in the course of the analysis below.

---

3. The meaning of these motifs is captured in their titles and seen by analogy in the examples from the Zeus-Typhon and Marduk-Tiamat myths as well as the many other culture-founding combat myths from around the world. It may be helpful to view the tabular breakdown of fifteen such combat myths in Forsyth, *Old Enemy*, 448–51.

4. The verses breakdown as follows in this respect (the two motifs are separated by a bold black line in table 1A): a part of the criss-crossing of the pattern of myth-culture with Jesus' unique pattern in this first episode is seen in the LORD Jesus' appearing in the place of the villainy or chaos-monster of myth (Mark 1:1–12), and in the arrival of the cosmos' leadership in the place of the hero's emergence (Mark 1:13–15). So in this reversal, we begin to see from the outset of the account that the logic governing Jesus' identity, actions and words is antithetical to the logic governing the world's identity, actions and words. This contradiction continues throughout the account, both at the structural level as well as in the details.

5. Once both "lack/villainy" and "hero's emergence" have taken place in the myth-pattern's first episode, and the opposite in Jesus' concurrent pattern, it is time to look for the next two motifs that

In the first episode of the account, looking through the social-science lens, we see that a primary contrast is formed between the world's leaders' (misplaced) concern over Jesus as a typical mythological rival-double (sameness),[6] and Jesus' actual identity being described as completely distinct from the world's definition *per* the myth-culture's pattern; thus His distinction. The Lord incarnate,[7] as a man in the world (Mark 1:2–3; Isa 40:3–5), declares that His kingdom has come in His own arrival.[8] We will establish and analyze the verse-by-verse breakdown of sameness and distinction, or the pattern of the myth-culture and the pattern of Jesus, as we read through Mark's Gospel account. This breakdown is also provided in tabular form for each episode and each motif. (For Episode 1, including the first two motifs, see table 1A just below).

The historical persons mentioned in the accounts have to sort through the question as to who truly has authority between the myth-culture's establishment and Jesus of Nazareth, and we see that unfolding. But the reader is never in doubt about who Jesus is asserted to be (whether or not the reader accepts Jesus' claim), and therefore who holds ultimate authority, from the viewpoint of the Gospel account. Unlike the chaos of non-differentiation and general disarray of the gods that characterize the pattern of myth-culture's opening lines, in the Gospel account the identity and purpose of Jesus is clear from the first verse. This initial certainty about Jesus also contrasts sharply with the confusion of the first episode of the myth-culture, and with the confusion of the world's powers in the Gospel's first episode.

GOSPEL According to MARK			
WORLD'S SAMENESS		**JESUS' DISTINCTION**	
Lack/Villainy		1:1–12	Hero Emerges
Hero Emerges	1:13a		Lack/Villainy
		1:13b	
	1:14a		
		1:14b–15	
TABLE 1A: Sameness and Distinction, Lack/Villainy and Hero Emerges			

correspond to the second episode. Scandal's mythological motifs are typically "donor/council" followed by "journey" motifs, in that order (table A). In Jesus' pattern these motifs begin, again in reverse order to myth-culture, at the division-point I have noted in table C.

6. In other words, the cosmic leaders see Jesus as a chaos-monster. And if Jesus were to conform to the pattern of myth-culture, we would expect Him to fit either the hero or villain profile, but He fits neither.

7. While Mark lacks an incarnation account as found in Matthew, Luke and John, Mark does state clearly that Jesus is born of Mary (see Mark 6:3; 15:40, 47; 16:1) and yet that Jesus is Lord (e.g., Mark 1:1–15; 14:61–64). A number of modern commentators assert that Jesus is clearly being equated with the Lord in Mark (e.g., Guelich, *Mark*, 11; Stein, *Mark*, 43).

8. Rhoads et al., *Mark as Story*, xiii.

MARK 1:1–12: JESUS' "HEROIC EMERGENCE"[9]

Narratology

The first twelve verses of Mark's Gospel make up the "hero emerges" motif for Jesus in the account. However, this seemingly mythological motif is out of sequence; it is inversive. We would expect it to come second, after "lack/villainy," as is the established pattern of the myth-culture (see table A). Also, the significance of Jesus' "heroic emergence" motif likewise fails to conform to the pattern of myth; it is subversive.

Jesus' "heroic emergence" is not like the typical "heroic emergence" of myth-culture exhibited by the hero-god: Immediately in the Gospel account, the type of divine being that is Jesus differs sharply from the hero-god of myth. The first verse of the Gospel according to Mark refers to Jesus (which means Savior) as the Christ (Messiah) and as "the Son of God" (υἱοῦ θεοῦ [Mark 1:1]), writing, "The beginning of the gospel of Jesus Christ, the Son of God" (1:1). So far, Jesus might possibly be equated with a son of Zeus. However, Mark then immediately quotes several passages from the Hebrew Bible (Old Testament), writing, "Behold, I send My messenger ahead of You, / Who will prepare Your way (Exod 23:20; Mal 3:1); / The voice of one crying in the wilderness, / 'Make ready the way of the LORD, / Make His paths straight' (Isa 40:3)" (1:2–3). By quoting (or paraphrasing) Exodus 23:20, Malachi 3:1, and Isaiah 40:3 as explicitly referring to Jesus and John the Baptist in these next two verses, Mark declares Jesus to be the LORD, the God of the Old Testament.

Robert A. Guelich, in his commentary on Mark's account of the Gospel,[10] writes that in Mark 1:1, we encounter Mark's announcement of the good news of Jesus Messiah's "word and works,"[11] and the proclamation that this "Jesus Messiah" is "the Son of God." Mark's proclamation of Jesus' identity as "the Son of God" is of "great importance," says Guelich, not least because Jesus' later affirmation of His divinity becomes the basis for His death sentence by the high priest and Sanhedrin (Mark 14:61–64).[12] He comments on Mark's quotations of the Old Testament (Hebrew Bible) in relation to Jesus and John, saying that the phrase "As it is written" (1:2a) refers to the preceding claims of verse one.[13]

---

9. For the full text of Mark's account of the Gospel, using italics to distinguish the two patterns—Jesus and myth—refer to appendix 1.

10. Guelich describes his approach to the Gospel according to Mark as belonging to "literary criticism," reading Mark as narrative (*Mark*, xxii–xxv): "The discussion has shifted [from form and redaction criticism] to the Gospel as a whole viewed as the literary product of the evangelist. Mark has again come to be seen as a narrative in its own right" (xxiii). He continues regarding his method, stating, "A broad look at two [literary] features, point of view and plot, reveals how the story is told and the broad strokes of the story line. Both features condition how we read the Gospel" (*Mark*, xxiii).

11. Guelich, *Mark*, 9.

12. Guelich, *Mark*, 10.

13. Guelich, *Mark*, 7, 10.

Although Guelich states that Mark claims that the events he now records as the beginning of the Gospel were prophesied by Isaiah (40:3), this is actually an error of the NU text of the New Testament. When we read the Received Text, we find that it accurately records Mark as quoting "the prophets," not only Isaiah as the evidently corrupted NU text has it. Clearly, as Guelich also observes, Mark also quotes from Moses (Exod 23:20) and Malachi (3:1).[14] So here in Mark 1:2, as in many other verses, the NU text is corrupted, and we must return to the Received Text for the correct, preserved text of Scripture. Sadly, most scholars today work with the NU text despite its despoiled state.[15]

Concerning the remainder of verse 2, Guelich states that it is clear that "My messenger" (Mark 1:2), while referring to Elijah in Malachi, also clearly refers to John the Baptist in Mark's Gospel, who will prepare the people's hearts for the LORD, according to Malachi 3:4–5.[16] Finally, Guelich makes the following significant observation: "Here 'before you' [1:2b] clearly refers to the 'LORD' of 1:3 whom 1:1–15 identifies as Jesus Messiah, Son of God. Though Jesus has not yet personally entered the scene, the evangelist assumes the reader understands Jesus to be the 'LORD' of 1:3 and thus the 'you' of 1:2b whose way is prepared by the following events in 1:4–8."[17] Guelich finds it plain, then, that in Mark's account, Jesus is immediately identified as the LORD God in the flesh. (He therefore dismisses the notion of a "messianic secret.")[18] Guelich goes on to state that "the way of the LORD" (1:3b) refers to, "Isaiah's call to make ready for a triumphal march to be led by God himself," meaning the LORD Jesus, according to Guelich.[19] It appears that Jesus' "triumphal march" is in fact the very unique pattern He is beginning to walk, in contradistinction to the pattern of myth-culture.

This occurrence, then, is the first time the term κύριος is used for Jesus in Mark's Gospel account, and it is a quotation of the Greek translation of יְהוָה (the LORD) in Isaiah 40:3 as explicitly referring to Jesus (Mark 1:3–9). As such, in the Gospel account Jesus is immediately identified as the LORD in human form, the biblical Almighty God

---

14. Guelich, *Mark*, 7.

15. The cause of the despoiled New Testament in the NU text is two-fold: (1) the addition of, followed by (2) the favoring of two clearly corrupt manuscripts, called Codex Sinaiticus (א) and Codex Vaticanus (B). These two manuscripts were rejected by the Church for centuries, and were only recently added and favored in the nineteenth century, beginning with the misguided work of B. F. Westcott and F. J. A. Hort (Watts, *The LORD Gave the Word*, 24–25; Cooper, *Authenticity*, 1:124–27).

16. Guelich, *Mark*, 11.

17. Guelich, *Mark*, 11.

18. Guelich, *Mark*, 11.

19. Guelich, *Mark*, 11. So, Jesus is directly equated with the LORD, the Greek of Mark 1:3 translating the vocalized (קְרָא; qārē') rather than the written כָּתַב; kātab) form of the Hebrew Tetragrammaton יהוה; YHWH), which is the unspeakable name of the God of the Hebrew Bible (Old Testament): "Make ready the way of the LORD"; ἑτοιμάσατε τὴν ὁδὸν κυρίου; פַּנּוּ דֶּרֶךְ יְהוָה—Mark 1:3; Isa 40:3b. The English translation of the Tetragrammaton in the Hebrew Bible is always LORD, in all capitals in order to capture in translation its special grammatical form, and to distinguish this LORD from other lords mentioned in the Old Testament.

come among humans. In the Old Testament, the LORD God is described as having no equal, no rival (e.g., Exod 15:11; 1 Kgs 8:23; Ps 89:6; Isa 40:18–28), so that by logical extension in the Gospel account, the LORD Jesus' power and authority is unquestioned and unequaled.[20] Whenever appropriate based upon the text and context, therefore, the term LORD is applied to Jesus in the Gospel account. At first, this divine identity, power and authority of Jesus is acknowledged most frequently in Mark's account by the demons whom Jesus casts out.

The Gospel account does not arise from a vacuum, but is explicitly based on the Hebrew Bible (Old Testament). This biblical God is referred to immediately in the first three verses of Mark's Gospel account, with direct quotations from the Hebrew Bible, as both the Father of Jesus (Mark 1:1), and Jesus as being the LORD Himself (1:3). As we see in the natures of Marduk and Zeus, the gods of myth are always much more like us than like the God of the Bible. The deities of myth are temporal (having a beginning), relatively powerful (can be defeated and permanently killed), and relatively knowledgeable (can be unaware and outwitted), *etcetera*.

Mark's immediate identification of Jesus as the distinctive, unique, God of the Bible in human form is important to our analysis because in the combat myth pattern, while the deity of the hero and villain is not typically in question, the type of deity and its relative power and authority is always in question. In other words, the deities of myth-culture do not conform to the biblical definition of deity. The LORD God of the Hebrew Bible is described as an eternal, all-powerful, all-knowing deity (e.g., Isa 40:26, 28); as the only real God, in other words: e.g., "I am the LORD, and there is no other; / Besides Me there is no God" (Isa 45:5a); "I am God, and there is no one like me, / Declaring the end from the beginning, / And from ancient times things which have not been done, / Saying, 'My purpose will be established, / And I will accomplish all My good pleasure'" (Isa 46:9b–10). As we will see, the distinctive identity of Jesus, as well as His purpose of fulfilling divine prophecy, has direct bearing on His unconformity to the sameness typical of the pattern of myth-culture, and is an explicit and central theme of the Gospel account from the first verse.

Mark 1:4–11 explains just how it is that John the Baptist and Jesus Christ fulfill the prophecies of Israelite Scripture that Mark cites in 1:2–3. The only opponent mentioned, in this first out-of-sequence "hero emerges" motif of Jesus, is sin. This sin is that from which John prepares the people to be set free by Jesus, ultimately through His death on the Cross (Mark 10:45; 14:24; Mic 7:19) and His baptism of humans in the Holy Spirit (Mark 1:4–8). It is sin from which Jesus comes to actually free the people (1:9–12), a mission inaugurated with Jesus' baptism by John in the Jordan river.

---

20. As Guelich observes, it is clear from the immediate context of Mark 1:1–11 that the prophecies quoted by Mark are understood by Mark to refer to John the Baptist and Jesus of Nazareth. The first prophecy's messenger is John, who prepares the way of Jesus the LORD. The second prophecy's voice in the wilderness, making ready the way, is John, and the LORD is Jesus.

Firstly, John the Baptist, the LORD Jesus' forerunner, is described: "John the Baptist appeared in the wilderness preaching a baptism of repentance for the forgiveness of sins" (Mark 1:4). Then, all the country of Judea is described as going out to John in the wilderness, along with all the people of Jerusalem, and they were being baptized by John in the Jordan river, "confessing their sins" (1:5).

The sin described in this first motif of the Gospel account (Mark 1:4–5) holds the first position, which is supposed to be occupied by the "lack/villainy" motif, as expected according to the pattern of myth-culture. However, the meaning of "lack/villainy" in myth is the depredations of a monstrous or villainous god who threatens with chaos the other gods, as well as the health and stability of the cosmos/world. Yet in this first motif of the Gospel account, it is the inured monstrous behavior of the people of Israel (and all nations), their sin and its cursed depredations, that appears to be the source of "lack/villainy" bringing chaos to Israel and all creation. So that in the Gospel account, the monstrous depredations threatening humanity are not the result of an individual or minority group who can be expelled or destroyed (scapegoated), thus saving the rest. Rather, the "monster" abides in every person, and "all the country" is going out to John in the wilderness to repent and be cleansed of the "chaos-monster" sin.

Mark describes John's appearance and diet, saying that John was clothed in camel's hair with a leather belt, and was eating locusts and wild honey (Mark 1:6). John speaks openly of himself as the forerunner of someone much greater than himself who is coming, and from whom John says that he is not fit to untie the thongs of his sandals (1:7). John says that he baptizes with water, but the greater one coming will baptize the people "with the Holy Spirit" (1:8). Jesus, the "emergent hero," is announced as coming not to destroy the people, the source of "lack/villainy" due to sin. Rather, Jesus comes to save the people from sin itself, which causes their "lack/villainy."[21] And Jesus will perform this salvation, says John, by (at least in part) baptizing the people in the Holy Spirit. In this, too, we see the subversive meaning of Jesus' first evangelical motif in relation to the myth-pattern's first motif.

Joel Marcus, in his commentary on the Gospel according to Mark,[22] affirms Guelich's reading noted above, writing that we immediately see Mark, in 1:4–8,

21. As will become clear, the socio-cultural pattern of myth itself is a feature of the sin from which Jesus is declared to be coming to defeat. In other words, the criss-crossing of the socio-cultural pattern of myth is a part of Jesus' conquest of sin.

22. Marcus describes his approach to the Gospel according to Mark as belonging to two types of criticism. In his comments on passages, Marcus first utilizes redaction criticism, making "an attempt to reconstruct [each passage's] redactional history (i.e., to separate Mark's own contribution from the tradition he has inherited)" (*Mark 1–8*, 81). While I do not accept the assumptions of redaction criticism, I have not space to address them here. Second, Marcus employs narrative criticism: "Mark has produced a narrative text . . . and he intended it for specific first-century readers, or, better, for specific first-century hearers" (*Mark 1–8*, 81). As a part of Marcus's narrative criticism, he considers something more central to our subject, which is what he calls "the cosmic battle" in "Mark's narrative" (*Mark 1–8*, 72). Marcus writes that in Mark, humans are subject to the "strong man" (Satan), and cannot save themselves, until the "Stronger One" (Jesus) arrives to save them (Mark 3:27; *Mark 1–8*,

bringing John the Baptist on the scene in fulfillment of the prophecies quoted in 1:2–3.[23] And, in keeping with the prophecies quoted by Mark, Marcus writes, "In the course of the passage, however, the focus shifts from John to Jesus, the 'coming one' whose way John prepares."[24] Marcus writes that John's preparation of the people to be set free from their sins through Jesus is the primary focus of this passage:

> The Markan context (1:6) suggests that both the baptism of the people and their confession of sin result from the same eschatological initiative of God that has brought "all Judaea and all the Jerusalemites" out to the wilderness. . . . The reader is left with the impression that a powerful action of God is taking place, one that expresses itself both in the baptism of myriads of people and in their being moved to confess their sins, which epitomizes their repentance . . . in *Mark's* understanding, John's baptism was only a proleptic cleansing from sinfulness, since the true remission resulted from Jesus' death as a "ransom for many" (10:45).[25]

This reading of Marcus comports well with our narratological analysis—which makes regular comparison with the pattern of myth—showing that in this first motif of the Gospel account, Jesus is an out-of-sequence and out-of-character "emergent hero" (in comparison with the pattern of myth), Who comes to save the people from an in-sequence though out-of-character form of "lack/villainy" in humanity's sins (in comparison with myth's pattern).

Marcus notes that Mark immediately follows John's prophecy about the "coming one" (Mark 1:7–8) with "the narrative of Jesus' own baptism and reception of the Spirit. . . . The Spirit is above all the divine power that enables Jesus and his followers to do battle with the *evil* spirits" and Jesus' "ability to rout the forces of Satan."[26] Marcus views Jesus as the "stronger one" whom Satan cannot resist (Mark 3:27).[27] This reading affirms our assertion that Jesus is not a typical hero of the sort expected in the pattern of myth. That is, Jesus does not battle an equal opponent; He is distinct rather than the same as His opponent, because (*inter alia*) Jesus' power is unassailable and His triumph assured. By contrast, in myth, the hero-god is supported by the narrator and reader/hearer but is not invincible or certain of triumph over the chaos-monster.

Then, in keeping with the sequence of events laid out by Mark's quotation of Israel's prophets, and as predicted by John as well, Jesus quickly succeeds John's ministry of water baptism: "And it came about in those days that Jesus came from Nazareth in Galilee, and was baptized by John in the Jordan" (Mark 1:9). During Jesus' baptism

---

72). He views even the human opposition to Jesus as an extension of the cosmic, Satanic (demonic) opposition to Jesus (*Mark 1–8*, 73).

23. Marcus, *Mark 1–8*, 153.

24. Marcus, *Mark 1–8*, 153.

25. Marcus, *Mark 1–8*, 156.

26. Marcus, *Mark 1–8*, 157–58.

27. Marcus, *Mark 1–8*, 72.

something astonishing happens. As Jesus rose out of the water, "He saw the heavens opening, and the Spirit like a dove descending upon Him; and a voice came out of the heavens: 'You are my beloved Son, in You I am well-pleased'" (1:10–11). Mark describes three persons or beings—the Father, the Son, and the Spirit—as all participating in this moment, with both the Spirit and the Father directing their attention and power and glory onto the Son, Jesus. An incredibly powerful "hero" has "emerged" from the waters of baptism, out-of-sequence with and without the meaning found in the combat myth pattern and myth-culture.

Regarding the focus turning fully onto the LORD Jesus the man in Mark 1:9–11, now that John has prepared His way, Marcus writes that there is an eschatological expression, "in those days," employed in the introductory phrase of Mark, "It came to pass in those days" (1:9a), which "alludes to the end-time in the OT [Old Testament] prophetic books (e.g., Jer 31:33; Joel 3:1; Zech 8:23) and the first two Gospels."[28] So that, "The cumulative effect is to suggest unmistakeably that Jesus is the coming eschatological figure to whom John pointed."[29]

Marcus sees in Jesus' baptism an echo of Isaiah the prophet (63:11–64:1): "Where is he that brought up from the sea the shepherd of his flock? / Where is he who put within him his Holy Spirit? . . . / O that you would rip the heavens apart and descend!"[30] Marcus affirms that in this first motif of the Gospel account, Jesus the "hero emerges," which is not what occurs in the first motif of the pattern of myth where "lack/villainy" occurs first. "Lack/villainy" does occur in this motif, but unexpectedly (from myth's perspective) it is the sins of humanity and their effects from which this atypical hero has come at the "wrong" time to deliver them. It is important to emphasize that Jesus has come at the moment "lack/villainy" is expected in the pattern of myth, because to the world's powers Jesus *is* the coming of "lack/villainy," as we will see, and their own "hero" (Satan/Accuser) is about to "emerge" in the mythically expected place in the sequence to oppose Jesus.

Mark 1:12 is the final verse of Jesus' first motif of the Gospel account. It concludes Jesus' inversive and subversive "heroic emergence" in comparison with the pattern of myth's initial "lack/villainy" motif. Mark 1:12 has Jesus carried away by the Holy Spirit into the wilderness immediately following His baptism by John in the Jordan. Regarding this event Marcus writes, "The Spirit, which Jesus has just received, now challenges Satan by hurling Jesus out into the wilderness, where the two will inevitably clash. . . . It is as though the Spirit, having finally found the human instrument through whom it can accomplish its ends, is now spoiling for a fight with the Adversary."[31] In other words, the first motif concludes with the LORD God in human form picking a fight

---

28. Marcus, *Mark 1–8*, 163.

29. Marcus, *Mark 1–8*, 163.

30. Marcus, *Mark 1–8*, 165.

31. Marcus, *Mark 1–8*, 168.

with the Evil One. It is not the order or meaning of the myth-pattern. There is combat but not myth, in other words.

This action by the Spirit of God in "impelling" Jesus out into the wilderness is the third statement regarding the relationship between Jesus and the Spirit in Jesus' opening "hero emerges" motif. First, Jesus will baptize the people in the Holy Spirit, says John (Mark 1:8); second, the Spirit descends on Jesus as a dove at His own baptism (1:10); and third, Jesus is driven by the Spirit on His way into combat (1:12). It is notable, likewise, that there are three statements regarding the Father God in relationship with Jesus in this first "hero emerges" motif as well. First, Jesus is declared the Son of God (1:1); second, the prophetic words of the Father God speaking directly to Jesus about John (the forerunning messenger) are quoted from Israel's prophets (1:2–3); and third, the Father's voice is audible from heaven at Jesus' baptism (1:11). Mark makes it emphatically clear that Jesus is being presented as distinctive here in His identity with the LORD God of the Bible, and therefore He is not like the gods of myth. Mark 1:1–12 consists entirely of Jesus' divine distinction, with no trace of the sameness of myth. To discuss this further, let us now look through the social-science lens at the sequence and significance of Jesus' unconformity to the order and meaning of myth-culture in this first motif.

Social-Science

The social-science lenses of Girard and Malina, each summarized separately in the preceding two chapters, aid us in further appreciating the meaning of Jesus' evangelical inversion and subversion of myth culture's pattern in the Gospel account. At this point in the pattern of myth-culture, we expect to see sameness preeminent in the interactions of the hero god and the villain god. However, Jesus does not conform to these mythological expectations. Jesus initiates the evangelical pattern with His divine distinction, which subverts the typical sameness meaning, and inverts the sequence of myth-culture's pattern. This inversion also results in a strong anti-segregation element in this first motif.

We can see that the first twelve "hero emerges" verses of Mark are solely expressive of divine distinction in Jesus. No agents of the pattern of myth-culture, of sameness, are mentioned here (unless we consider all people, that is, all sinners). The sin from which Jesus has come to deliver Israel and humanity does not conform to the mythological type of chaos-monster, nor can sin be said to be in a dyadic/mimetic double relation with Jesus. Neither is there any trace in Jesus, or in His forerunner John, of the sameness typical of the myth-pattern's first episode. However, there is a notable anti-mythological sort of "sameness" in the cooperative, equitable action of the Father, the Spirit, and Jesus the Son in this first motif. Also, there is a notable self-abasement of John in relation to Jesus (Mark 1:7), the very opposite sort of relation to what occurs between persons in the opening motif of myth.

The first instance of myth-culture's sameness in this first episode does not occur until the second motif, Jesus' "lack/villainy" and myth's "hero emerges," which begins at Mark 1:13. And there still, the sameness is found in Satan and the opponents of John, not in Jesus. In Mark 1:1–12, the "hero," Jesus, is not described as what could be termed a "desire double" (interdividual) or viewed as in a "dyadic" relation with others (see table D). However, in the typical pattern of myth's "lack/villainy" and "hero emerges" motifs, this dyadic social relation between the hero and others is always present, as seen in the examples of Zeus and Marduk. The mythological chaos of rival-doubles for ultimate authority is not found in Jesus, though it is found in the opponents of Jesus, as we will see. In other words, agents of evil in the Gospel accounts do conform to myth's pattern, while Jesus does not.

As mentioned, Jesus' divine distinction in this first motif is also inversive of the segregation of myth-culture's pattern. In myth-culture, segregation is the final episode of the cycle, and the final achievement of the hero-god that ends the pattern. The hero-god of myth-culture achieves segregation always *via* scapegoating/sacrifice of the monster-god. This mythological segregation involves re-establishment of a collapsed hierarchy amongst the gods, as well as in the cosmos. A part of this reformed hierarchy is the hero-god lording over and subjugating his father and everyone else, as we saw with Bel-Marduk. Here in the Gospel account, however, in the very first motif, the LORD Jesus is described as a faithful Son to His Father God, in whom His Father is very pleased (Mark 1:11). There is no mimetic chaos in the relation between the Father God, Jesus the Son, and the Spirit of God here, but rather concerted action against sin (1:4–9).

In contrast with myth-culture, Jesus already enjoys a superior form of "segregation," not *via* scapegoating/sacrifice, but simply as an extension of His identity in relation to His created universe. Rather than declaring His kingdom come at the end of the pattern, like Zeus and Bel-Marduk, Jesus declares His kingdom come at the outset of His pattern. Rather than being a part of the problem He has come to fix, Jesus transcends the problem from the beginning. Yet, although Jesus is declared to be the LORD, and so is above all, in the first verses of Mark, we see Him "coming down" and entering into the fray as a man, on behalf of sinners. Jesus' superiority is in place from the beginning. He does not need to establish it like the heroes of myth, yet He humbles Himself, allowing John to baptize Him, and entering into combat as a man. These actions of Jesus demonstrate His divine distinction, subverting and inverting both the sameness and the segregation of the myth pattern.

GOSPEL According to MARK			
WORLD'S SAMENESS		**JESUS' DISTINCTION**	
Lack/Villainy		1:1–12	Hero Emerges
Hero Emerges	1:13a		Lack/Villainy
		1:13b	
	1:14a		
		1:14b–15	
TABLE 1A: Sameness and Distinction, Lack/Villainy and Hero Emerges			

MARK 1:13–15: JESUS' "LACK/VILLAINY"[32]

Narratology

Sin and Satan, and the rulers of the world/cosmos (the myth-culture) are named as the sources of "lack/villainy" in this first episode of the Gospel account, in the first two motifs, but not in the mythological sense. Sin appeared in the first motif in the position of "lack/villainy," beginning the mythological pattern as Jesus appeared out of position as the "emerging hero." Here in the second motif (Mark 1:13–15), in the place where the hero of myth is expected to appear, Satan and the rulers of the world appear (those who put John in prison), and Jesus experiences His atypical pattern's "lack/villainy." We expect, according to the myth-pattern, "lack/villainy" to be the first motif in the sequence/pattern, but here in Jesus' pattern we find it in second position. And it also fails to conform to the meaning of "lack/villainy" as found in myth.

"Lack/villainy" here begins with Jesus "in the wilderness forty days being tempted by Satan" (Mark 1:13a), yet "He was with the wild beasts, and the angels were ministering to Him" (1:13b). The latter portion of the verse confirms that Jesus is the hero, with creation and Heaven on His side, and in His experience of "lack/villainy" He is comforted and strengthened. Adela Yarbro Collins, in her commentary on the Gospel according to Mark,[33] writes that in Mark 1:13, Jesus' forty-day temptation by Satan in the wilderness, "recalls the forty days that Moses spent on Mount Sinai (Exod 24:18; 34:28)," though she notes the contrast between Moses receiving revelation and

---

32. For the full text of Mark's account of the Gospel, using italics to distinguish the two patterns—Jesus and myth—refer to appendix 1.

33. Yarbro Collins describes her approach to the Gospel according to Mark as reading the Gospel as an "eschatological historical monograph" (*Mark*, 42). She approaches the text in this way because of how Mark refers to his account at the outset, which is as "good news," and because of how Mark defines what that is in the opening verses: "The good news is that the divine plan, foretold in Scripture, is about to be fulfilled" (42). Yarbro Collins asserts that the first verses of Mark are not to be considered an isolated fulfillment of a few particular verses of Scripture but rather as the beginning of a sequence of events all of which fulfill the divine plan laid out in the Scriptures (42–43).

instruction from the LORD while Jesus is here being tempted by Satan.[34] This contrast serves to highlight Jesus' experience of "lack/villainy" in this second motif.

Yarbro Collins reads the statement that "Jesus was *with* (μετά) the wild beasts" (1:13b) as describing Jesus in conflict with demons, so that Jesus would be in combat with the wild beasts who embody, support, or are possessed by demons of the wilderness.[35] She cites Psalm 91:11–13 in support of this reading. The text does not plainly support such a reading, either in grammar or contextual sense. Rather, and in keeping with both the prophecy-fulfillment context and Jesus' circumstance of temptation in the desert by Satan, more fitting Old Testament (Hebrew Bible) allusions are Job's temptation by Satan (Job 5:17–27, esp. 22–23), and continued messianic prophecy in Isaiah of the LORD God as the coming Savior (Isa 43:8–21, especially 19–20). In both of these Old Testament passages, the "wild beasts" are clearly described as *with* the tempted one (who is "reproved of God" and "disciplined of the Almighty"; Job 5:17) for comfort and support, and *with* the "Savior LORD" (Isa 43:11) glorifying Him and accompanying Him in the wilderness. These two allusions better fit the context in Mark, better support Yarbro Collins's "eschatological historical" reading, and also support Jesus' second anti-mythological "lack/villainy" motif in His subversive and inversive pattern. Jesus' authority over His creation, over "heaven and earth" represented by angels and wild beasts, meaning the created universe, is affirmed as unthreatened here despite the continued rebellion of Satan and sinners. Contrariwise, in the pattern of myth, the hero-god's authority and control *are* threatened, the future of the cosmos *is* uncertain, and wild beasts *do* array against him on the side of the chaos-monster.

Jesus is distinct from His opponent Satan, since Jesus is the hero yet not of the cosmos (world). Satan is the hero of the world, which is confirmed in the second expression of "lack/villainy" in the Gospel account's second motif: "Now . . . John had been taken into custody" (Mark 1:14a). This event shows that Satan and the rulers of the world are aligned, one attacking Jesus and the other attacking Jesus' forerunner and fellow minister of God's kingdom. These two events are the only instances of the sameness of the pattern of myth-culture found in the first episode (the first and second motifs) of Mark's account of the Gospel. And the sameness is one-sided, being Satan's and the world leaders' rivalry with God's messengers of salvation from sin. According to myth's pattern, we expected to see the hero emerge in this second motif. What we see is Satan emerge as the world's hero, in opposition to Jesus, and Jesus facing lack and villainy in the wilderness while combating Satan, though supported by Heaven and earth. And then suddenly, Jesus is "lacking" His forerunner John, who is put away in prison by the world's authorities.

Of John's imprisonment by the world's authorities (Mark 1:14a), Yarbro Collins writes that although Herod Antipas (worldly leader of that region of Israel in which John ministered [Mark 6:16–18]) is not absolved of responsibility for the act, John's

---

34. Yarbro Collins, *Mark*, 151.

35. Yarbro Collins, *Mark*, 151.

being "handed over" (taken into custody) is also of divine ordinance, just as Jesus' being "handed over" will be both an act of worldly opposition and divine will.[36] Yarbro Collins notes here that the same Greek term is used twice in Isaiah 53 (LXX) for the "Suffering Servant's" betrayal and death "for our sins." Her observation that the seizure of John and Jesus are both acts that fulfill the purposes of both sides, or both patterns, is significant here. That is, the pattern of myth-culture is allowed to have its way, even as the LORD Jesus' unique evangelical pattern proceeds unhindered simultaneously.

After John's imprisonment, writes Mark, "Jesus came into Galilee, preaching the Gospel [of the kingdom] of God" (Mark 1:14b). Jesus offers the good news to His people Israel that their real "lack and villainy," their sin (as established in the first motif), can now be over, because, says Jesus, "The time is fulfilled, and the kingdom of God is at hand" (1:15a), and the people must, "repent and believe in the gospel" (1:15b). Here again, Jesus' pattern is inversive of the sequence of myth, and His actions and preaching are subversive of the meaning of myth. Unlike in myth, the people's "lack/villainy" is their own sin, not some other "monster" whom they all accuse of being the problem and then scapegoating it. Jesus commands Israel to repent of their own sins and believe in His gospel, in order to enter His kingdom.

In relation to Jesus coming into Galilee and preaching the gospel of the kingdom of God (Mark 1:14b) *after* John's imprisonment, Yarbro Collins observes that the time of the eschatological fulfillment of Scripture (1:2–3) is clearly divided into periods. Both the times and the "qualities" (Mark 1:8) of John's and Jesus' ministries differ.[37] John's is a time of repentance and Jesus' is a time of good news and belief, though she notes that "the distinction is of course not absolute."[38] Regarding what Jesus says in His preaching, that "the time is fulfilled and the kingdom of God is at hand" (1:15a), Yarbro Collins writes that Jesus is announcing the beginning of "the end of days."[39] She asserts that this process of "the end of days" is only complete with the coming of the Son of Man, concerning which she cites Mark 9:1 and 13:24–27.

According to Yarbro Collins, in Mark 1:15 Jesus "associates the fulfillment of history with the kingship of God."[40] Finally, she writes that Jesus' command to "repent and believe in the gospel" (Mark 1:15b), "signifies a turning away from one's previous way of life, determined by particular sets of convictions, practices, and social affiliations and a turning to and acceptance of the new divine initiative through the agency of Jesus."[41] This reading affirms our assertion that in the Gospel account, Jesus is setting out a pattern of belief and behavior systematically opposed to the pattern of myth-culture explicitly practiced by the leadership and membership of the world round about Him.

36. Yarbro Collins, *Mark*, 153–54, 223–24.
37. Yarbro Collins, *Mark*, 154.
38. Yarbro Collins, *Mark*, 154.
39. Yarbro Collins, *Mark*, 154.
40. Yarbro Collins, *Mark*, 155.
41. Yarbro Collins, *Mark*, 155.

Jesus' preaching here has three parts: (1) the time is fulfilled (presumably for Hebrew Bible prophecies of the Christ's coming), (2) God's kingdom is come, and (3) the people of Israel must repent of their sins and believe in the Gospel (Mark 1:14b–15). These three statements are inversive in relation to the expected pattern of myth-culture. Firstly, there is fullness here instead of lack, in that (*inter alia*) the "fullness of time" has been reached for an ancient promise of salvation from sin to be realized. (This is seen both in the Hebrew prophecies quoted and John's explanation of what Jesus will do: Mark 1:2–3, 8.) The second statement, that the kingdom of God has come, is inversive of the myth-pattern, in that at this point in the myth-pattern the kingdom of the gods of myth is lost or seriously threatened by the chaos-monster. The reverse is true in the Gospel account. And the third statement is inversive of myth in that Jesus commands the people to give up their "lack/villainy," which is their sin, since sin occupies the place of "lack/villainy" in the Gospel's first episode. This "hero" requires His people Israel to take an active role in their salvation, repenting of their sins and believing the Gospel; though as we will see, Jesus Himself intends to do the lion's share. In fact, the account makes it abundantly clear that Jesus *must* do the lion's share of saving His people because they cannot possibly save themselves.

It is interesting that the people are told by the "hero" to repent (involving "re-thinking") of sin and believe (involving patterning one's thought after) something else instead, the Gospel. This last statement of the first episode confirms that our analysis is exegetical (arising out of the text itself). It speaks to the presence in the Gospel account of the two opposing patterns, the unique evangelical pattern of Jesus and the typical pattern of myth-culture (the chiastic bi-pattern). Jesus is explicitly declaring war on sin and offering another way. Sin involves following the pattern of myth-culture, with its "hero" Satan who came out in opposition of the "villain" Jesus. John prepared the way for Jesus' inversive and subversive pattern by preaching repentance from sin. Then Jesus appeared with an identity and activity that completely cut across the expected pattern of myth-culture, which all sinners follow (Mark 1:4–5, 15). That all sinners follow myth's pattern becomes clear by the end of the account, when everyone has abandoned Jesus to walk His own pattern alone.

In Jesus' second motif of this first episode, which in the myth-pattern comes first, is not the "lack/villainy" of a chaos-monster inflicted upon the world and its gods, but voluntary lack of Jesus' basic needs in the desert for forty days, as He overcomes the villainous temptations of Satan. While He is tempted by Satan, it is clear that Jesus does not succumb, in that the wild beasts and angels minister to Him and He goes forth to preach the Gospel of the Kingdom powerfully. Even in the desert, which is the very picture of lack, and in the presence of Satan, who is the very embodiment of villainy, Jesus has fullness and peace in the abundant company of ministering animals and angels. So rather than seeing the hero truly threatened, as in myth, Jesus has fullness in the least amenable circumstances.

While there is villainy and lack in these events, they are not of the sort found in myth. That Satan emerges here in the place that we expect to see the hero of myth is telling, as was Jesus emerging in the first motif in the place where we expected villainy and lack to take place. It is also telling of the close association of myth and Satan, that it is Satan and the world, and not Jesus, that follow the pattern of myth.

Social-Science

Once again, the social-science lenses of Girard and Malina aid us in better appreciating the inversive sequence and subversive meaning of Jesus' second out-of-sequence motif, "lack/villainy." At this point in the pattern of myth-culture, sameness continues to be preeminent in the interactions between the heroic god and the villainous god. Not so in Jesus' evangelical pattern, however. Jesus exhibits divine distinction that subverts the meaning of sameness, and inverts the sequence of the pattern of myth-culture, which also results in a strong anti-segregation element.

In these three verses, Mark 1:13–15, are a mixture of divine distinction exhibited by Jesus and His attendants, contrasted with mythological sameness exhibited by Satan in tempting Jesus, and the worldly powers that imprison John. By tempting Jesus, Satan presents himself as a rival-double of Jesus, in a state of sameness typical of myth-culture. Satan attempts to exalt himself to the same status of the Lord Jesus, making himself the rival of God. While there are contenders with Jesus in the Gospel account, they are not rival doubles *per se*. Satan, as a created being (Ezek 28:15),[42] is not an actual contender for power or authority with Jesus; certainly not of the sort we see in myth.[43] In myth, it is entirely possible that either double could be victorious. In the Gospel, the success of the Lord Jesus is never in doubt.

The divine distinction of Jesus continues in this second motif of the first episode. During and following His temptation by Satan, Jesus enjoys the company of the wild beasts as well as the ministrations of the angels (Mark 1:13b), who are the servants of the Lord. And despite John's imprisonment, Jesus forges ahead into Galilee, preaching the Gospel and making His three bold claims that are highly subversive of the sameness of myth-culture, and inversive of the oppressive segregation of myth-culture. Jesus' anti-sameness is readily clear in that He is so authoritative here. Sin is no contender with Jesus as He declares its time fulfilled/ended, inaugurates His kingdom on earth, and authoritatively issues the command to the people of Israel to repent of sin and believe in the Gospel (which is that the Messiah, the Christ, has come, and will do all that is written of Him [Mark 1:7–8; 8:27–31]).

---

42. Ryrie, *Basic Theology*, 161–63.

43. We do not find the concept of dualism (two equally powerful and opposed gods), which is typical of myth, in the Gospel account or in the Hebrew Bible (OT). In the Bible, the Lord Jesus is, with the other two persons of the Godhead, the Creator of the universe (e.g., John 1:1–3; Col 1:16), while Satan is a created angel, and the first rebel against his Maker (e.g., Isa 14:12–17).

Once again in this second motif as well, myth culture's segregation is inverted by Jesus' distinction. Rather than being the result of the hero's actions at the end of the myth-pattern, Jesus is clearly described as atop the hierarchy of things in this first episode, with angels ministering to Him and the wild creatures accompanying Him in the desert (Mark 1:13b). And as He moves onward into Galilee to really begin His work, Jesus exercises incredible authority in the declarations and commands He issues. Clearly Jesus does not need to re-establish segregation as in the pattern of myth-culture; Jesus is LORD already in the Gospel-pattern.[44] By contrast, as we saw, Marduk only becomes "lord" after he has slain and mutilated his rival.

More than that, though, rather than exalting and distancing Himself over and above His creation (including the humans who are usually described as far below and subjugated by the gods), as is done by the hero-gods in the segregation episode of the myth-pattern (e.g., Marduk, in imitation of Satan), Jesus has lowered Himself to be among His people Israel, as one of the people, even making Himself the servant of His people, and yet without losing His authority over the people. Jesus has proximity with the people inured in sin, and yet He exhibits neither sameness with them in the myth-culture's manner, nor segregation from them in the myth-culture's manner.

---

44. As the Christmas carol "Silent Night" puts it: "Jesus, LORD at Thy birth!"

6

Episode 2

Mark 1:16—8:26: Scandal and Diffusion

Scandal	Diffusion
"Woe to the world because of its scandals! . . . Woe to that man through whom the scandal comes!; . . . [He] said to Peter, 'Get behind me, Satan! You are a scandal to Me.'" (Matt 18:7; 16:23)[1]	"It is good not to . . . do anything by which your brother is scandalized; . . . I will not cause my brother to be scandalized." (Rom 14:21; 1 Cor 8:13)[143]

OVERVIEW

The second episode of the Gospel account begins with Jesus calling His disciples (Mark 1:16—8:26; see tables C and F). The focus clearly shifts away from a primarily sameness-distinction emphasis, as viewed through the social-science lens, to a primary emphasis on the myth-culture's scandal and Jesus' divine diffusion, which together continue the chiastic bi-pattern in episode two. In the Gospel account this second episode ends with Jesus miraculously feeding thousands of people in the wilderness. The episode is characterized by a contrast between the people—both leaders and commoners—becoming increasingly scandalized toward Jesus, and Jesus diffusing their gathering offence with His graciousness, creation of space, and generosity. The first and last verses of this second episode are determined by noting the positions of the beginning and end of the myth motifs of this episode. The two motifs that make up episode two in the combat myth pattern are "donor/council" and "journey," in that order (table A).

---

1. Author's translation.

Just as in the first sameness-distinction episode, the second scandal-diffusion episode of the Gospel account presents an uncharacteristic reversal of these two mythological motifs in Jesus' identity, actions and words. In the myth-pattern, Zeus is first counselled and then takes his journey, while in the Gospel account Jesus first journeys—with His peripatetic gathering of disciples and ministration of the Gospel of the kingdom—and thereafter comes Jesus' a-typical donor/council motif in the episode.

The "journey" motif, occurring out of typical mythological sequence in first position, is found in Mark 1:16—3:6. The "donor/council" motif, that brings us to the conclusion of this second episode, is found in Mark 3:7—8:26. The "donor/council" motif begins with Jesus summoning the twelve particular disciples that He had collected on His journey, and counselling them. This is another reversal, as in myth the hero receives, rather than gives, the counsel. Another council is held by the religio-political heroes of cosmos at about the same time (Mark 3:6), on how they might destroy Jesus, who to them is a chaos-monster threatening their cosmos. We see that it is not Jesus who behaves in accordance with mythological precedent, but the world around Him. Thereafter, continuing this inversion and subversion, Jesus receives a donation from a child to aid in His fight with sin, death, and the myth-culture, miraculously multiplying the food to feed the hungry in soul and body who are oppressed by the world. The feeding pericopae conclude the second episode.

These two motifs being concluded, we see the transition into the third episode of the Gospel account. So once again, comparison of the Gospel account contents to combat myth motifs enables us to distinguish the six episodes based upon both Jesus' a-typical motifs and the world's typical motifs, and thus derive the chapter and verse numbers for the transition points between motifs as well as episodes.

GOSPEL According to MARK			
WORLD'S SCANDAL		JESUS' DIFFUSION	
		1:16–23	
	1:24		
		1:25—2:5	
	2:6–7		
		2:8–15	
	2:16		
Donor/Council		2:17	Journey
	2:18		
		2:19–23	
	2:24		
		2:25—3:1	
	3:2		
		3:3–5	
	3:6		

Journey			Donor/Council
		3:7–10	
	3:11		
		3:12–20	
	3:21–22		
		3:23–30	
	3:31–32		
		3:33—4:3	
	4:4–7		
		4:8–38a	
	4:38b		
		4:39–40	
	4:41		
		5:1	
	5:2–7		
		5:8–13	
	5:14–17		
		5:18–34	
	5:35		
		5:36–39	
	5:40a		
		5:40b—6:2a	
	6:2b–3		
		6:4–13	
	6:14–28		
		6:29–37a	
	6:37b		
		6:38–48	
	6:49		
		6:50–51a	
	6:51b–52		
		6:53–56	
	7:1–5		
		7:6—8:3	
	8:4		
		8:5–10	
	8:11		
		8:12–15	
	8:16		
		8:17–26	

TABLE 1B: Scandal and Diffusion, Donor/Council and Journey

MARK 1:16–3:6: JESUS' "JOURNEY"[2]

Narratology

Narratologically, this section of the Gospel account is comprised of the "journey" motif for Jesus, but inversive in sequence and subversive in significance when compared with the pattern of myth-culture. The expected mythological motif of "donor/council" does predominate here in the people's leadership, the opposition to Jesus, but not in Jesus Himself. In Jesus' evangelical pattern we instead see the "journey" motif preeminent and in first position. Not only is the sequence of the motifs reversed, however, but their significance as well. Jesus' journey is not like the typical journey of myth-culture experienced by the hero-god there.

Jesus begins His out-of-order "journey" motif by walking along the shore of Galilee and calling Israelite fishermen there to be His followers (Mark 1:16–20). To two brothers, Simon and Andrew, Jesus says, "Follow Me, and I will make you become fishers of men" (Mark 1:17). They immediately leave their fishing nets and follow Jesus (1:18). Jesus keeps walking along the shore and sees two more fishermen, James and John the sons of Zebedee (1:19). Jesus calls them also, and they leave their father Zebedee, "with the hired servants, and go away to follow Jesus" (1:20). This portion of the Gospel account begins what is often referred to as Jesus' peripatetic ministry,[3] because He begins to continually travel about on foot as He preaches, teaches, heals, exorcises demons and performs various other miracles. Jesus' growing band of followers accompany Him on His "journey," learning to think, live and speak as He does, to trust and believe in Him, and to walk in His pattern.

Beginning at Capernaum on the shore of Galilee, Jesus starts teaching in the synagogue (Mark 1:21–22), notably teaching "with authority," out-teaching the scribes (a contingent of Jewish leadership). And Jesus begins casting out "unclean spirits" (1:23–28). The unclean spirit in one man in the synagogue (!) is scandalized by Jesus' interference in the demons' affairs, saying, "What business do we have with each other, Jesus of Nazareth? Have You come to destroy us? I know who You are—the Holy One of God!" (1:24). Jesus tells the demon to be quiet and to come out of the man (1:25), and it obeys, violently exiting the man with a scream (1:26). The result is that the people are amazed and spread the news of Jesus and His amazing teaching and authority over unclean spirits (1:27–28).

This scandalizing of the demons is the first of seven scandals that Jesus incites[4] and diffuses in Mark's third motif. Jesus has begun an expeditionary force against

---

2. For the complete text of Mark's third motif, please refer to appendix 1.

3. E.g., France, *Gospel of Mark*, 6.

4. It is critical to observe that Jesus is never the direct cause of the scandal. He is not "the man through whom scandal comes." Rather, the scandal arises from the agents of or those inured in the myth-culture. And it originates in the heart of a person, as Jesus teaches in Mark 7:20–2. Scandal does not come out of Jesus' heart, so that He is never the cause of scandal to others. Therefore, when others

sin, evil spirits, and their myth-culture, while building up His following for His kingdom. The people immediately perceive Jesus to be superior to their current leadership (the scribes, etc.; which will also lead to them being scandalized toward Jesus). R. T. France, in his commentary on the Gospel according to Mark,[5] comments on Jesus' ministry's inaugural acts at Capernaum, noting that Jesus is immediately perceived by the demons as coming to destroy them,[6] and by the people as coming to replace their current unauthoritative and feckless leadership.[7]

Then, Jesus begins to heal physical ailments at His disciples Simon's and Andrew's house in Capernaum (Mark 1:29–34), while continuing to cast out demons, so that "the whole city" gathers at Simon's house for healing of diseases and exorcism of demons (1:33). First, Jesus heals Simon's mother-in-law of a fever that has her "lying sick" (1:30). Jesus "came to her and raised her up, taking her by the hand," so that the fever left her, and "she waited on them" (1:31). As with the first exorcism at the synagogue, during these exorcisms Jesus commands the demons not to speak, "because they knew who He was" (1:34). This silencing of the demons shows that Jesus desires that His divine and messianic identity not be made public yet, evidently to control the spread of scandal until the opportune time (e.g., Mark 8:31; see Guelich's statement on this below, at Mark 3:12).

Jesus conducts all of this teaching, exorcising and healing at Capernaum within a single day, the Sabbath. Early the next morning He is already on the move again, continuing the "journey" motif, going out into "a secluded place" to pray (Mark 1:35). Simon and the other new disciples of Jesus seek Him out and find Him praying (1:36). They tell Jesus that "everyone is looking for You" (1:37). But Jesus says, "Let us go somewhere else to the towns nearby, so that I may preach there also; for that is what I came for" (1:38). So, Jesus begins leading His new disciples on a "journey" all over the Galilee region, preaching in the synagogues and casting out demons (1:39).

France comments that this difference of expectation between Jesus and His disciples—He expecting to continue an itinerant ministry to inaugurate His kingdom versus their expectation of Him continuing to grow His local popularity on home ground—begins a theme that continues throughout the Gospel account.[8] France writes, "[Jesus'] whole conception of how God's kingship is to be made effective is quite

---

are scandalized at what Jesus says or does, the scandal is arising from within the heart of the person scandalized. This reality is confirmed as we read through the account.

5. France describes his approach to the Gospel according to Mark as primarily exegetical of the text of Mark and decidedly not concerned with "theories of prehistory or the process of its composition" (France, *Gospel of Mark*, 1). His object is to understand and appreciate "Mark's text as we have it" (1) and to exegete the Greek text of Mark rather than exploring theories. He aims to read Mark as a narrative unity, considering literary and historical approaches, deploying "literary common sense with historical sensitivity" (2).

6. France, *Gospel of Mark*, 103.

7. France, *Gospel of Mark*, 102.

8. France, *Gospel of Mark*, 111.

different from theirs. While they would naturally pursue the normal human policy of taking advantage of popularity and building on success . . . Jesus' onward drive will lead to anything other than growing popularity and response."[9] France's observation highlights again that Jesus' pattern of behavior and perspective is extremely divergent from the pattern followed by His disciples. It becomes clear that the disciples' pattern remains that of the myth-culture, in keeping with the rest of the world around Jesus.

This expeditionary "journey" of Jesus, involving calling followers, praying, preaching, healing, and exorcising, continues until the end of this third motif (Mark 1:40–3:6). In addition to being out of sequence, throughout the motif the meaning of Jesus' "journey" in His evangelical pattern is clearly very different from its meaning in the pattern of myth-culture. While the "journey" in myth involves a setting out to engage in violent combat or to flee from it, Jesus' "journey" is to free people from possession by demons, to heal their diseases, pains, and sufferings, and to teach them the anti-myth-cultural way. Jesus' emphasis on teaching will be seen in the second part of episode two, the fourth motif. His way is one of freedom from scandal, lies and murders; freedom from sin.

Jesus next heals a leprous man who comes to Him, saying, "If You are willing, You can make me clean" (Mark 1:40). Jesus is "moved with compassion" and "stretched out His hand and touched him," saying, "I am willing; be cleansed" (1:41). Mark tells us that the leprosy immediately leaves the man (1:42). Jesus "sternly warns" the man to "say nothing to anyone," and sends him on his way to show himself to the priest and offer a sacrifice for his cleansing as Moses commanded in the Law, as a testimony to the religio-political leaders of Israel (1:43–44). But the man does not listen to Jesus' command to say nothing. He "proclaim(s) it freely" and "spread the news around" so that "Jesus could no longer publicly enter a city," but had to stay in the wilderness. Yet, people came out to Him "from everywhere" (1:45). Jesus seems to have two motivations for keeping His identity and some of His miracles quiet: (1) to enable Him to work without being stampeded by the crowds (as implied here); and (2) to diffuse (for the time being) the scandal to the Jewish leadership, which becomes clearer as this third motif progresses.

Regarding this passage on the cleansing of the leper, and of consequence for its effects on the progress of the two patterns, France writes that the scene sets up an "intriguing tension" moving forward, "as the controversies between Jesus and the scribes develop."[10] Quoting Sergeant,[11] France writes that there are "two currents of mounting trouble which combine to overwhelm the Galilean ministry: the opposition of the authorities, and the suffocating pressure of the crowds."[12] Jesus ministry is "ground to a halt between the upper and nether millstones of official opposition and overwhelming

9. France, *Gospel of Mark*, 111.

10. France, *Gospel of Mark*, 116.

11. Sergeant, *Lion Let Loose*, 44–45.

12. France, *Gospel of Mark*, 116.

popularity."[13] France's observation, citing Sergeant, confirms the reading of the beginning of scandal in this third motif of the second episode. With every miracle and teaching as He "journeys" about, Jesus' popularity grows, and His opposition from the religio-political leaders grows correspondingly; the scandal blossoms, or begins to "snowball."

After several days of "journeying" about Jesus returns to Capernaum, to Simon's house, and the people hear about it (Mark 2:1). Jesus teaches the people "the word" from the house, with "many . . . gathered together, so that there was no longer room, not even near the door" (2:2). Because of the crowds, four men remove the roof of Simon's house, dig a hole in the ceiling, and lower a paralytic on a pallet through the opening to Jesus for healing (2:3–4). Seeing the faith of the sick-man and his friends, Jesus says, "Son, your sins are forgiven" (2:5). While the demons have been scandalized at Jesus before this (1:24), and Jesus has anticipated Israel's religio-political leaders' scandal after the healing of the leper (1:43–4), this forgiving of the sins of the paralytic is the first time the Jewish leaders are described as being scandalized at Jesus. As noted above, the scandal begins in their hearts.

Mark tells us that after hearing Jesus' words, the Scribes reason in their hearts, "He is blaspheming; who can forgive sins but God alone" (Mark 2:6–7). Mark tells us that Jesus knows "by His spirit" what they say in their hearts, and openly questions them on it (2:8). Then Jesus demonstrates His authority to forgive sins by healing the paralyzed man, commanding him, "I say to you, get up, pick up your pallet and go home," and the man does just that (2:9, 11). Jesus tells the Scribes that He does this miracle to show that, "the Son of Man has authority on earth to forgive sins" (2:10), as a confirming miracle (attesting sign), clearly meaning that He is the Son of Man, that He has come from Heaven to earth and so is God, and that He therefore does not break the Law of Moses in Scripture against human blasphemy when He forgives sins. The paralytic got up and took his pallet and walked out "in the sight of everyone" so that "they were all amazed," the Scribes and all the people there, "and were glorifying God" (2:12). So, the gathering scandal over Jesus is diffused for the moment. Jesus then leaves again to "journey" along the shore of Galilee, and "all the people were coming to Him, and He was teaching them" (2:13).

Regarding Jesus forgiving the sins of the paralytic, and the scandal in the hearts of the Scribes at Jesus' forgiveness of sins, Robert H. Stein, in his commentary on the Gospel according to Mark,[14] writes, "The scribal conclusion, 'he is blaspheming' . . . indicates that Jesus's pronouncement of forgiveness in 2:5b was understood as a personal act of forgiveness on His part, not a divine passive. . . . He is exercising a

---

13. France, *Gospel of Mark*, 116.

14. In his commentary, Stein describes his "primary goal" as "not to construct a life of Jesus of Nazareth but to ascertain the meaning of Mark, that is, what the second evangelist sought to teach by his Gospel" (*Mark*, xiii). Stein approaches the Gospel according to Mark as, "essentially a historical biography/narrative of Jesus Christ, the Son of God, that focuses on his ministry, passion, and resurrection" (*Mark*, 23).

prerogative in forgiving sins that belongs exclusively to God (cf. John 10:33), no one but God alone."[15] It is this same supposed blasphemy according to Israel's leadership's unbelief in Jesus' LORDship and Messiahship that becomes their justification for ultimately condemning Jesus to death (Mark 14:64).

As Jesus continues His inversive and subversive "journey" motif, He calls another disciple in addition to the first four, a man named Levi (aka Matthew)[16] son of Alphaeus, a tax collector (Mark 2:14). Jesus brings Levi and his friends who were "tax collectors and sinners[17]" to eat with Jesus at "His house" (presumably Simon's in Capernaum; see Mark 1:29; 2:1), along with Jesus' other followers, who are now called "disciples" here (Mark 2:15). This results in the third explicit scandal noted by Mark in response to Jesus' behavior, with the "Scribes [and] the Pharisees" objecting to Jesus eating with such sinful people (2:16). Jesus explains to the scribes and Pharisees that He came to call sinners "[to repentance]," or rather those who know they are sinners, rather than the righteous (or self-righteous; 2:17). In other words, repentance—acknowledgement that one is a sinner in need of forgiveness—is needed to enter into the kingdom of God (see Mark 1:15).

This scandal is quickly followed by a fourth, which is John's disciples' and the Pharisees' scandal over Jesus' disciples not fasting as they do (Mark 2:18). Jesus explains His disciples' behavior using the allegory of the bridegroom's attendants not fasting while He is with them. Only after the bridegroom is gone do the attendants fast, and just so Jesus' disciples (2:19–20). With these words, Jesus also points to His future departure from His disciples (the "attendants"),[18] when He is "taken away," hinting at His coming arrest and murder.[19]

Jesus then concludes His teaching (both about fasting and eating with sinners) with a parable about the new not working with the old. Jesus uses the imagery of not using new cloth to patch an old garment, and not putting new wine into an old wineskin (Mark 2:21–22). He seems to be saying that He is deliberately working primarily with "new followers" in that they are not members in good standing of a recognized "righteous" sect of Judaism/Israel. He instead calls those who clearly know they are sinners, because they will not be too proud to receive His "new wine" (Jesus' New Testament/Covenant [Mark 14:24–25]), and His new "righteous clothes' patch" (faith in Jesus rather than works of the law [Mark 10:17–31]), that "the righteous" are usually too proud and scandalized to receive. While Jesus' teaching diffuses those

15. Stein, *Mark*, 119–20.

16. Stein, *Mark*, 126.

17. All men are sinners (e.g., Rom 3:9, 23; 5:12; etc.). The term in this context means Jews who do not keep the Law of Moses.

18. Notably, Jesus' disciples are not called "the bride," as some might expect. Rather, some other group of people is "the bride," and Jesus' disciples and followers are "the attendants."

19. Stein, *Mark*, 137–38.

back-to-back scandals, the reprieve is short-lived, as the scandals are increasing in frequency and continuing to "snowball."

While Jesus continues His anti-myth-cultural third "journey" motif through grain-fields on the Sabbath, His disciples following Him pick the heads of grain (Mark 2:23). In response, the legalistic Pharisees suffer the fifth scandal of the motif over Jesus' disciples unlawfully working on the Sabbath (2:24). Jesus offers yet another teaching in order to, in part, diffuse the gathering scandal. He reminds the Pharisees of what David did when he and his men were hungry (1 Sam 21:1–7; 22:18–23), how he went to the Tabernacle and, with the priest Ahimelech's permission, ate the holy showbread that is unlawful for any but the priests to eat (Mark 2:25–26). Jesus then makes the logical inference, with allusion to the creation account and the ten commandments (Gen 1–2; Exod 20), that the seventh day's rest was created for humanity's benefit; humanity was not created for the seventh day's benefit (2:27).

Stein comments, "Jesus did not seek to deprecate the Sabbath by this statement. He simply wanted to place it in perspective and demonstrate that humanity created in the image of God must be seen as more important than God's gift of the Sabbath to him."[20] Jesus concludes by affirming that He, the Son of Man (see Mark 2:10), is the LORD of the Sabbath (2:28). He appeals to consistent examples from Scripture, and to His own ultimate authority over the Sabbath day. Stein observes how audacious Jesus' statement concerning His own personal LORDship is to His hearers, the religio-political leadership as well as the people of Israel generally. Jesus calling himself Lord of the Sabbath is to call Himself LORD, of course.[21] And this fact is not lost on His opponents, as becomes very clear a few verses later in Mark 3:6.

As Jesus inversely and subversively continues His third "journey" motif, He enters a synagogue and there He sees a man with a withered hand (Mark 3:1). Mark tells us that "they," presumably the scribes and Pharisees who have contended with Jesus so far (and 3:6 confirms that "they" are the Pharisees), are watching Jesus closely to see if He will heal on the Sabbath, "so that they might accuse Him" (3:2). So, the leaders are scandalized before Jesus has even said or done anything. This degree of scandal is now very intense, and perhaps not surprising. Since they do not accept His claims about Himself as in Mark 2:28 just previous, they must view Jesus as a terrible blasphemer. Their behavior in collectively hounding and watching Him tells us that while Jesus has diffused the scandal of the leadership so far using Scripture, miracles and logic, their resentment has been building nonetheless. This fomenting scandal is

---

20. Stein, *Mark*, 148.

21. Stein writes: "In each instance 'so that' introduces a conclusion that is the result of the preceding statement. Consequently, we should interpret 2:28 as the logical result of 2:27." Also, we must not ignore "the 'also' (καί) of the statement. In this chapter of his Gospel, Mark has already demonstrated Jesus' Lordship in 2:10, so he is 'also' Lord in 2:28. . . . In the present text Mark, as well as Matthew and Luke, understood Jesus as saying that he, the Son of Man, was Lord of the Sabbath. . . . The audacity of this claim should not be missed, for in the OT God is the Lord of the Sabbath because he instituted and consecrated it (Gen 2:3; Exod 20:8–11; 31:12–17; Lev 23:3; etc.)" (*Mark*, 148).

also evidenced by the steadily increasing frequency of their verbal assaults on Jesus as the motif progresses.

Jesus then calls the diseased man forward, and asks the congregation, "Is it lawful to do good or to do harm on the Sabbath, to save life or to kill?"; but they are silent (Mark 3:3–4). Jesus' question clearly continues His Scripture-based logical argumentation from before. Jesus presupposes the Bible as the ultimate authority, and so bases His logical reasoning upon Scripture.[22] Here, Jesus asserts that saving and healing humanity takes precedence over Sabbath laws against work, because the Sabbath is of no benefit to dead men. As before, the Sabbath was established for humanity; humanity was not created for the Sabbath (Mark 2:27). Regarding Pharisaic and Rabbinic tradition concerning Sabbath work (which amplified the LORD's commands, like Exod 35:1–3, regarding Sabbath labor), James R. Edwards, in his commentary on the Gospel according to Mark,[23] writes, "The general rule of observance was not to begin a work that might extend over to the Sabbath, and not to do any work on the Sabbath that was not absolutely necessary—by 'necessary' meaning life endangering (*m. Yoma* 8:6). . . . Sabbath regulations could be overridden only in cases of endangerment to life (*m. Yoma* 8:6)."[24] So, Jesus' logical reasoning from Scripture was affirmed by Jewish "oral law" (the Mishna, etc.).

By asking His question, Jesus appears to attempt to diffuse His audience's scandal over what He is about to do, by reminding them rhetorically that human life trumps Sabbath law. However, they are silent, evidently more concerned about having more reason to hate Jesus than reason to accept Him. As Edwards writes, "Among the congregation some are not simply neutral and impartial observers. They are, rather, motivated "to accuse Jesus." Markan irony is again present: the authorities deny Jesus the right to do good on the Sabbath while they conspire to do evil on the Sabbath."[25] This contrast again shows the two patterns in the Gospel account, Jesus' unique divine pattern versus the pattern of myth-culture in His opponents. They do not care if He is right or wrong; they are unconcerned about truth and lies. Their motives are rooted in sameness and a scandalized heart.

22. This may surprise some readers since Jesus could simply refer to His own personal authority as God (see John 8:13–18). But here He does not. Jesus both (1) submits Himself to the Scriptures, His Word spoken before His incarnation, for how He lives as a man, and also (2) submits His thinking to the authority of Scripture. Jesus calls those to whom He ministers "the Word" to do the same, imitating His pattern.

23. Edwards describes his approach to the Gospel according to Mark in the following way: "My primary objective has been to concentrate on three aspects of the Gospel of Mark that in my judgment are essential to its proper understanding: its *historical* setting and narrative, its *literary* methods, and its *theological* purposes" (*Mark*, xiv).

24. Edwards, *Mark,* 94, 98. Here, Edwards cites Rabbinical law from the Mishna, Yoma 8:6, part of which translates, "Moreover, Rabbi Matya ben Charash said, If a person has a sore throat, it is permitted to put medicines into his mouth on the Sabbath, because of possible danger to his life, and whatever threatens to endanger life supercedes [the observance of] the Sabbath" (https://www.sefaria.org/Mishnah_Yoma.8?lang=bi). This Jewish "oral law" affirms Jesus' logical reasoning from Scripture in Mark 2:27 and 3:4, and the work He does to save life, both temporal and eternal.

25. Edwards, *Mark,* 98.

Mark tells us that Jesus looked at them "with anger, grieved at their hardness of heart"; He commanded the sick-man to stretch out his hand, and as he did so it "was restored [whole as the other]" (Mark 3:5). At that moment when Jesus heals the diseased man in the synagogue on the Sabbath day, the seventh scandal of Jesus' third "journey" motif occurs. The Pharisees' scandalized state drives them to make a significant move against Jesus. They go out of the synagogue immediately and take counsel with the Herodians against Jesus, "as to how they might destroy Him" (3:6). Jesus' third "journey" motif coincides, then, together with the third "donor/council" motif of the pattern of myth-culture that unfolds in the religio-political leadership of Israel opposed to Jesus. These two branches of worldly governance, the religious and the political, the Pharisees and the Herodians, take counsel together right on cue in the expected pattern of myth-culture.

The leaders of the people (Pharisees and Herodians) are the only entities here in this third motif that clearly engage in the "donor/council" motif of myth in the expected order/position of myth, and with the expected meaning of the myth-culture. Seven scandals are recorded in this third motif of Mark's Gospel account, and they involve increasingly united opposition to Jesus, and result finally in an organized council together against Jesus. Jesus' "journey" motif is inversive of Israel's leadership's mythological motif of "donor/council," and subversive of the mythological meaning of this motif. Israel's leadership fulfill the pattern of myth-culture, but Jesus consistently opposes the pattern of myth-culture, instead fulfilling His unique divine pattern that criss-crosses myth-culture's pattern.

Social-Science

Social-scientifically, this third motif is comprised of diffusion exhibited by Jesus, continuing His unique pattern, intermingled with scandal exhibited by both demons and the people, especially at the leadership level, that continue the myth-culture's pattern. The social-science lenses of Girard and Malina aid us in perceiving this chiastic bi-pattern. At this point in the pattern of myth-culture we typically see scandal preeminent. However, not so in the Gospel account due to the evangelical pattern here in Jesus Christ. Instead, Jesus exhibits diffusion of scandal. Jesus' diffusion subverts the scandalous meaning expected of this episode, and inverts the myth-sequence so that this episode also contains a strong anti-satiation element.[26]

As we saw, in His (third) "journey" motif in Mark's Gospel account, Jesus encounters seven scandalized responses to His words and deeds, all of which Jesus

---

26. As shown in the methodology, while the narratological chiasm is within each episode, involving the switching (inversions) of the two motifs and their meanings, the social-scientific chiasm involves the switching of the entire sequence of episodes and their meanings, inverting one and six, two and five, three and four. These two narratological and social-scientific aspects of the inversive and subversive chiastic relation of the evangelical and mythological patterns is confirmed as we go along.

successfully diffuses, despite it being clear that scandal is building or "snowballing" into intense resentment (harbored scandal) and hatred by the religio-political leadership of Israel. They progressively fulfill the expected myth-pattern here by holding a council together as to how to destroy Jesus. Jesus models divine diffusion of scandal throughout this motif, and also offers some important teaching on diffusion of scandal, though His teaching on diffusion of scandal only begins to predominate in His next (fourth) "donor/council" motif, which will conclude this second scandal-diffusion episode. As we will see, Jesus' teaching is a key aspect of His inversive and subversive relationship with the mythological "donor/council" motif.

As we have seen in the previous narratological analysis of this third motif, and will continue to see throughout this second scandal-diffusion episode, Jesus uses at least five methods to diffuse gathering scandal over who He is and what He says and does. Jesus: (1) refers to His authoritative Scripture (the Hebrew Bible/Old Testament), and so teaches with authority; (2) He performs miracles of exorcism and healing, which also demonstrate His divine authority; (3) He practices privacy, authoritatively commanding both exorcised demons and healed people not to reveal His identity; (4) He employs logical reasoning, always based upon Scripture, which helps dispel the irrational scandal of the religio-political leadership; and (5) He creates space, maintaining social distance, staying on the move and withdrawing to wilderness locations. These are the five ways we see Jesus diffusing the scandalized hearts of those inured in the myth-culture.

Nevertheless, both the demons and the Israel's leadership continue the expected pattern of myth-culture. They began in that default state for all of sinful humanity, which is sameness, here directed against Jesus and John. And that view of Jesus (and John) as a rival-double of theirs for power and control logically progresses in this third motif of the second episode to the expected state of scandal. Jesus is now perceived as a model-obstacle to their supposedly shared desire, and so they decide by the end of this motif that Jesus has to be destroyed. They have put John in prison, but that will not be enough to deal with Jesus. He must be discredited and killed.

Jesus, however, was not in a state of sameness with Satan or the religio-political leaders of Israel in the first episode. Rather, He is shown, and shows Himself, to be distinctive. Similarly, in this second episode, Jesus is not found to be in a state of scandal in relation to the demons or the religio-political leaders. Near the end of this third motif, when Jesus desires to heal the man with the withered hand in the synagogue on the Sabbath, we read that Jesus becomes "angry" with the leaders. But this emotion is not due to scandal. Mark tells us that Jesus is angry because He is "grieved at their hardness of heart." The demons and the leaders are described as opposing Jesus out of envy. For, as Jesus sets the people free from demonic possession and control, heals their diseases, and teaches the people in a way with which the scribes and Pharisees simply cannot compete, the people increasingly love Jesus and flock to Him, presumably to the neglect of their former leadership. The demons and leaders feel they have reason to be scandalized by Jesus, but only according to the twisted logic and pattern of myth-culture in which they have made themselves contenders for control of the cosmos/world. Jesus is not actually challenging them for their position or seeking to replace them; at least, not in the expected mythological way. He is doing something never seen before, that does not follow myth-culture's pattern at all.

Just as Jesus diffused the previous six scandals of this third motif, we will see that Jesus further diffuses this seventh scandal of the Pharisees and Herodians as well at the outset of the fourth motif, by "withdrawing to the sea with His disciples" (Mark 3:7). Jesus creates some space, diffusing the gathering scandal. Jesus does not seek to destroy the religio-political leadership as they do Him. He is not their rival in the myth-cultural sense. They are no obstacle to Him, and His purpose is not like theirs.

Jesus' unique pattern, here in the form of divine diffusion, is not only subversive of the scandal-meaning of this second episode, but inversive of the pattern of myth-culture's episodes as well, just as we saw in the first episode. As such, Jesus performs an anti-mythological satiation of the people of Israel here in the second episode. Satiation is the fifth episode of myth-culture, but Jesus is already satisfying the desires of the people here in the second episode, without the supposedly necessary human-sacrifice (scapegoating) that myth-culture requires for the people to be sated upon a victim. Throughout Jesus' "journey," and despite opposition from demons and religio-political leaders, He goes about unhindered, exorcising, healing, teaching, leading and comforting the people of Israel. Jesus pre-emptively provides a sort of satiation that the culture's myth-pattern cannot offer. He freely satisfies the deepest desires of their souls, hearts, minds, and bodies. This inversive satiation is a key element of Jesus' divine diffusion.

GOSPEL According to MARK		
WORLD'S SCANDAL		JESUS' DIFFUSION
		1:16–23
	1:24	
		1:25—2:5
	2:6–7	
		2:8–15
	2:16	
		2:17
Donor/Council	2:18	Journey
		2:19–23
	2:24	
		2:25—3:1
	3:2	
		3:3–5
	3:6	

Journey			Donor/Council
		3:7–10	
	3:11		
		3:12–20	
	3:21–22		
		3:23–30	
	3:31–32		
		3:33—4:3	
	4:4–7		
		4:8–38a	
	4:38b		
		4:39–40	
	4:41		
		5:1	
	5:2–7		
		5:8–13	
	5:14–17		
		5:18–34	
	5:35		
		5:36–39	
	5:40a		
		5:40b—6:2a	
	6:2b–3		
		6:4–13	
	6:14–28		
		6:29–37a	
	6:37b		
		6:38–48	
	6:49		
		6:50–51a	
	6:51b–52		
		6:53–56	
	7:1–5		
		7:6—8:3	
	8:4		
		8:5–10	
	8:11		
		8:12–15	
	8:16		
		8:17–26	

TABLE 1B: Scandal and Diffusion, Donor/Council and Journey

MARK 3:7—8:26: JESUS' "DONATIONS/COUNSEL"[27]

Narratology

Narratologically, this section of the Gospel account makes up the fourth "donor/council" motif for Jesus, but unexpectedly it is inversive in sequence and subversive in significance when compared with the pattern of myth-culture. The expected mythological motif of "journey" does predominate here in Israel's leadership, the opposition to Jesus, so that they continue in the pattern of myth-culture in opposition to Jesus' unique divine pattern.

It is notable, however, that in some ways the motifs of the pattern are cumulative, so that once a motif has begun, it continues throughout the remainder of the account. As such, in this fourth motif of "donor/council" Jesus continues to emerge as a "hero" to Israel, continues to experience "lack/villainy" and be accused of "lack/villainy," and continues to "journey" about ministering the Gospel of the kingdom. And now in addition, the fourth "donor/council" motif begins here for Jesus, and predominates in Jesus throughout this section.

The expected mythological "journey" motif predominates in this motif only in the religio-political leaders who oppose Jesus. The sequence of the motifs is inverted by Jesus, and He subverts their significance as well. Jesus' "donor/council" is not like the typical "donor/council" of myth-culture experienced by the hero-god there.

As mentioned at the end of the narratology section on the second motif, Jesus' first act here is to diffuse the gathering scandal of the Pharisees and Herodians, who have now begun taking counsel together as to how to destroy Him. Jesus further diffuses their scandal by creating distance, in that He "withdrew" with His disciples "to the sea" (Mark 3:7). Nevertheless, and no doubt to the dismay of the religio-political leaders, Mark tells us the people of Israel flock to Jesus from all over, a "great multitude" from Galilee, Judea, Jerusalem, Idumea, beyond the Jordan, and the vicinity of Tyre and Sidon. They come because they "heard of all that He was doing" (3:8).

With this unprecedented gathering of disciples and people of Israel around Jesus, He begins His "donor/council" motif. Instead of receiving donations like the heroes of myth-culture, Jesus is the donor to sinners all about Him. And instead of, like the heroes of myth, receiving counsel as to how to defeat the villainous god, Jesus is the giver of counsel to sinners as to how to be free from sin and death. So, not only is the sequence of motifs inverted by Jesus, but just as in the first episode, the meaning of the motifs is subverted by Jesus. Jesus' "donations" to the people are not weapons and powers of warfare as in myth-culture, but are exorcisms of demons and healings of diseases. Jesus' "counsels" are not information for overcoming a monstrous villain-god as in myth, but teaching against the sinful pattern of myth-culture itself, especially against scandal in this fourth motif of the second episode. Scandal, arising out

---

27. Please see appendix 1 for the entire fourth motif in Mark's account.

of the myth-culture's state of sameness, is the "match" that sets people "ablaze." Jesus counsels His disciples and the people to diffuse scandal, just as He has been modelling (see Jesus' five diffusive tactics used in the third motif, noted above).

While on the shore of Galilee, surrounded by many people, Jesus tells His disciples to have a boat ready for Him because of the great multitude, in case they crowd Him (Mark 3:9). Jesus has healed so many that the diseased and afflicted "pressed around Him in order to touch Him" (3:10). Mark tells us that whenever Jesus encountered a demon in the crowd as He "donated" healing and exorcism, the unclean spirit would "fall down before Him" and cry out, "You are the Son of God" (3:11). Jesus would respond by continuing His diffusive method of privacy, "earnestly warn(ing) [the demons] not to make Him known" (3:12). Jesus was determined that the demons not reveal His distinct identity, yet.

Guelich further explains Jesus' diffusive practice of privacy regarding His identity, which is evidently to delay public understanding of Jesus' identity, and its accompanying scandal, until the right time. As Guelich writes:

> The unclean spirits are subdued or forbidden to speak (1:34; 3:12), lest they, who know (1:34), make known who Jesus is (3:12). . . . Mark himself has made them the witnesses in 3:11 ("You are the Son of God," cf. 1:24; 5:7) . . . as supernatural beings they recognize Jesus and Mark has placed on their lips the correct identity of Jesus as "Son of God" . . . [but] their statement of who Jesus is came at an inappropriate time. Though the demons knew and understood who Jesus was, others could not. In fact, this understanding can only come in view of the cross and resurrection (cf. 9:9; 15:39). Thus . . . Mark's own "messianic secret" has to do with the timing and thus meaning of the proclamation of Jesus as Son of God.[28]

Guelich has previously stated, as noted above, that he does not accept the hypothesis of a messianic secret in Mark's account, and he continues that view here. Similarly, I propose an additional purpose for Jesus' privacy, which accords with Guelich's view, which is that Jesus' privacy diffuses the inevitable scandal that will result from His divine identity being made public. Such an announcement must be carefully timed, especially in light of Jesus' purpose in coming among men, which they will not understand at this point in His unique and contradictory pattern, since they expect a hero-god typical of the pattern of myth-culture.

Jesus then continues His fourth inversive and subversive "donor/council" motif by calling a very special "council" meeting. He climbed up a mountain and "summoned" to Himself certain individuals from among His followers (Mark 3:13). Jesus then "appointed twelve, so that they would be with Him, and that He could send them out to preach, and to have authority [to heal sicknesses, and] to cast out the demons" (3:14–15). So, at this special "council" Jesus also "donates" special powers and

28. Guelich, *Mark*, 149.

authority to enable the Twelve to fulfill their special mission, preaching the Gospel of the kingdom of God, and confirming the message with miraculous signs (attesting miracles) as Jesus does. Once again, this act of Jesus is inversive and subversive of myth-culture, in which the hero *receives* the "donated" tools and powers by the "council" of other gods to overcome the villain-god (see the descriptions of this motif in the Marduk and Zeus myths above). Instead, it is *Jesus* who calls the "council" of hand-picked disciples, made up of sinners who are thus among the source of the "lack/villainy," and *He* "donates" to *them* the tools and powers to overcome evil. Mark names the Twelve whom Jesus chooses as Simon (Peter), James (Jacob) and John the sons of Zebedee, Andrew, Philip, Bartholomew, Matthew, Thomas, James (Jacob) the son of Alphaeus, Thaddaeus, Simon the Zealot, and Judas Iscariot, "who [also] betrayed Him" (3:16–19).

From there, Jesus goes "home," perhaps again to Simon's in Capernaum,[29] and there He and His disciples are so inundated by a "crowd" in search of more "donations" that "they could not even eat a meal" (Mark 3:20). Jesus' "own people," meaning His family in this context,[30] are so scandalized at this when they hear of it that they attempt to "take custody of Him," saying, "He has lost His senses" (3:21). The scribes, "who came down from Jerusalem," say of Jesus to the crowd, "He is possessed by Beelzebul, He casts out the demons by the ruler of the demons" (3:22). It is the religio-political leaders of Israel who are "journeying"—in the position of the hero-god(s) of myth—all the way down from Jerusalem to engage their supposed "villain," Jesus, and they are doing so at the expected fourth motif point in the pattern of myth-culture, and with the expected purpose. With their irrational accusation that Jesus casts out demons by Satanic power, it appears that part of the plan that came out of the "council" of the scandalized religio-political leaders is to attempt to demonize Jesus, in order to turn the people away from Him.

Jesus' response to this scandal-driven attack is once again to diffuse the scandal with good "counsel," this time again with the diffusion tactic of logical reasoning. He calls the crowd to Himself and begins counselling them, asking the reasonable question, "How can Satan cast out Satan?" (Mark 3:23). Jesus goes on to answer His own question by explaining that if Satan is working against himself, "a kingdom . . . divided against itself," then it cannot stand but destroys itself. If Satan has indeed done this, Jesus says, "he is finished!" (3:24–26). Of Jesus' logical reasoning here, Guelich writes, "[Jesus'] argument that follows operates *reductio ad absurdum* with this premise to show that Satan has indeed 'met his end' (3:26)."[31] Jesus shows that the scribes have committed a logical fallacy, but He also seems to be hinting that although He Himself

---

29. Guelich, *Mark*, 172.

30. Guelich, *Mark*, 172.

31. Guelich, *Mark*, 175.

is not of Satan, Satan is indeed destroying himself, and being destroyed by Jesus' inauguration of His kingdom *via* His ministry.[32]

As such, Jesus continues His teaching, explaining that the "strong man" must first be bound before his kingdom can be plundered (Mark 3:27). He seems to be hinting that He intends to bind the "strong man," which is Satan, and then plunder his kingdom, speaking proleptically again of what is to come. This understanding agrees with Jesus' announcement of bringing "the kingdom of God" into the kingdom of Satan (Mark 1:15). As Guelich states:

> Few would question the applicability of this parable to Jesus' preaching of the kingdom. . . . Set against Jesus' ministry and Isa 49:24–25 (cf. 3:12), the details become transparent. Clearly the "strong man" . . . stands for Satan; his "possessions" . . . represent those possessed; the "binding" . . . of the "strong man" takes place in Jesus' ministry; and the "plundering" . . . bespeaks Jesus' own exorcisms of those "possessed."[33]

In this parable of Jesus, His out-of-sequence and out-of-character donations (in comparison with the expected order and meaning of myth-culture) of freedom from possession by Satan along with His out-of-sequence and out-of-character counsel to understand this deliverance, show that Jesus' pattern is indeed working at cross-purposes to the pattern of myth-culture represented by Satan and the religio-political leadership of Israel. Jesus is dismantling the pattern of myth-culture, the kingdom of Satan.

Jesus then makes a third point in His good "counsel" to the crowd, referring back to the scribes' irrational claim that He is "possessed by Beelzebul" and works for Satan. Jesus warns them that while "all sins shall be forgiven the sons of men," the sin of "blasphem(ing) against the Holy Spirit" of God results in "eternal [condemnation]" that "never has forgiveness" (Mark 3:28–29). Jesus is clearly working in the power of the Spirit of God and indeed is the Lord (Mark 1:1–11). Mark reiterates that Jesus is warning the leaders of Israel against rejecting the Holy Spirit (3:30).[34] Such a warning from Jesus constitutes very helpful good "counsel" for His enemies. In myth's pattern, the hero-god never offers good "counsel" to help his enemies.

At this point, and perhaps due to the failure of Jesus' wider family to "take custody of Him" (see Mark 3:21), Jesus' own mother and brothers arrive, having made a

---

32. See also Girard's treatment of this passage as recounted in chapter 3 above, the section entitled "Scandal" (see also Girard, *I See Satan*, 34–35).

33. Guelich, *Mark*, 176.

34. This warning will go unheeded. After Israel's leaders have rejected Jesus and His ministry of the Gospel of the kingdom of God, and He ascends back to Heaven, Jesus sends the Holy Spirit from Heaven, and the leaders of Israel also reject the Holy Spirit's ministry of the kingdom of God (see Acts 7:51–58). This rejection of the ministry of the Holy Spirit by Israel's leaders results in the Lord turning away from Israel for a season, to offer the Gospel of grace directly to all nations through a new creature, the Body of Christ (Rom 9–11; Eph 2–3).

scandal-driven "journey" to conduct a "family intervention," it seems, for their family-member who is embarrassing them (Mark 3:31–32). Like Israel's religio-political leaders who "journeyed" down from Mount Zion in Jerusalem in fulfillment of the myth-culture's pattern, Jesus' own immediate family make a mythological "journey," also in the expected fourth motif and with the expected meaning of the myth-culture's pattern. There is still a "crowd" surrounding Jesus, and they tell Him that, "Your mother and your brothers are outside looking for you" (3:32).

Jesus diffuses this gathering family scandal by offering more startling "counsel" to the "multitude," asking, "Who are my mother and my brothers?" (Mark 3:33). And again, He answers His own question by gesturing to those seated around Him and saying, "Behold, my mother and my brothers! For whoever does the will of God, he is my brother and sister and mother" (3:34–35). With this statement Jesus both alludes to His divine identity, and encourages His followers, and all Israel, to be part of the family/kingdom of God, to make that their primary identity. Jesus says to "do the will of God," and says that those who follow and listen to Him are doing God's will. Instead of being scandalized by Jesus like His family who have "journeyed" (likely from Nazareth) to apprehend Him, or like the scribes who have "journeyed" from Jerusalem to oppose and discredit Him, Jesus invites the multitude of Israel to receive His good "counsel" of divine diffusion. So, in His third inversive and subversive "donor/council" motif, Jesus "donates" to Israelites membership in the family of God, an incredible gift. As Guelich states:

> Jesus identifies his family on the basis of the response to him rather than natural kinship. The response of his natural family who sought to take him into their custody reflected their rejection of his ministry . . . [apparently out of] concern for his mental stability. The response of the crowd who sought his presence and gathered around him, doubtless to hear his teaching, reflected their acceptance of him.[35]

Jesus then begins an extensive period of "counselling," teaching the people if Israel "by the sea" of Galilee, with "such a very large crowd" that "He got into a boat in the sea" and from there "counseled" the multitude on the shore (Mark 4:1). Jesus was teaching them "many things in parables" (4:2). One word of "counsel" Jesus gives is a parable of the sower and the soils (4:3–9). Jesus tells of a sower who sows his seed, and it lands in four types of ground. The seed that lands by the road is eaten by birds of the air. That which falls in rocky soil has no depth and is scorched by the sun and dies. And that which falls amongst thorns is choked and produces no crop. But the seed that lands in good soil grows, increases, and yields great crops. Jesus finishes by saying to them, "He who has ears to hear, let him hear" (4:9). Jesus does not explain further to the crowd of Israel.

---

35. Guelich, *Mark*, 182.

Once Jesus' followers and twelve disciples are alone with Him in the house, they ask Him about the parables He has been teaching (Mark 4:10). Jesus answers by first explaining that only those who have decided to be His followers and disciples will "be given [to know] the mystery of the kingdom of God," while those "who are outside" (meaning, not following Jesus)[36] will only be given the parables (4:11). Jesus explains that He uses this method to fulfill Scripture: "While seeing, they may see and not perceive; and while hearing, they may hear and not understand lest they return again and [their sins] be forgiven" (4:12; Isa 6:9). Of the need to receive faith in Jesus in order to receive His "donations" and best "counsel," and the consequences of rejecting Jesus, Marcus writes:

> Our text in its Markan context shows the same sort of duality [as Pharaoh's hardening of heart: e.g., Exod 4:21; 7:3; 9:16]. "Those outside" are, in line with common usage and with the larger Markan context . . . Jesus' opponents, people who have deliberately excluded themselves from the circle of salvation by their attitude of hostility to Jesus. . . . The blind hatred and hard-heartedness that these opponents have been manifesting toward Jesus has been growing in the past two chapters of the Gospel (see particularly 3:5), so that in a way their condemnation to blindness and obduracy in 4:12 is just a ratification of a process already in motion.[37]

In other words, if a person who comes to hear Jesus does not choose to follow Jesus, as His followers and disciples have done, they will not be able to enter the family of God, the kingdom of God, or receive Jesus' "donations" and full "counsel." Marcus has also pointed out in the above quotation that Jesus' "hardening" of the hard-hearted is merely a response to a "process already in motion," a pattern of behavior in His opponents that has been developing through the account thus far. The "process" to which Marcus refers is evidently directly related to the pattern of myth-culture unfolding in those who refuse to receive Jesus. In this fourth motif of the second episode, they are "journeying" right on cue in the myth-culture's pattern, motivated by scandal right on cue, with intent to detain and/or destroy their opponent right on cue. They are mythological in identity, inured members of this world, the kingdom of Satan, who has possession of them.

After reprimanding His disciples for their lack of understanding (Mark 4:13), Jesus offers further "counsel" to His followers, explaining to them the parable of the sower and the soils (4:14–20). He explains that the seed is the Word, that is, the Word of God, and here it seems that He means the Gospel of the kingdom from Scripture (see Mark 1:15) that Jesus is ministering to the people of Israel (4:14). He says that the seed that falls by the road represents those from whom Satan immediately snatches the Word even as it is "sown [in their hearts]" (4:15). Jesus says that the seed that falls

36. Guelich, *Mark*, 181–84.
37. Marcus, *Mark 1–8*, 306.

on rocky soil represents those who do receive the Word "with joy," but have "no root," are "temporary," such that "when affliction or persecution arises because of the word, immediately they fall away" (4:16–17). In other words, some hearers of God's Word are uncommitted despite initially accepting it, not appreciating or accepting the cost of Jesus' discipleship. When scandal arises over Jesus' Word, they "fall away" (apostatize), they are literally "scandalized," being unable or unwilling to diffuse scandal as Jesus models and teaches.

He then says that the seed sown amongst thorns represents those hearing the Word, but for whom God's Word is choked out by "the worries of the world, the deceitfulness of riches, and the desires for other things" so that they become "unfruitful" (4:18–19). This third type of recipient of the Word is scandalized not by the opposition that naturally comes to him from the world over the Word itself, but rather he is scandalized by the fact that keeping and following God's word precludes worldly pursuits. Both cannot be pursued successfully; the person must choose. It is not that this one cannot or will not diffuse the scandal caused by receiving the Word. And he is not scandalized by the suffering the Word requires. Rather, this third type is scandalized by the requirement of the Word to set aside the cares, riches, and desires of the world (the 'p's, or "limited goods" the myth-culture strives after). So, Jesus is counselling His followers as to what sort of "soil" they must cultivate within themselves, in order to receive God's Word aright. As we can see from the examples He gives, it is often being scandalized by Jesus' Word that prevents people from entering the kingdom of God. Those who hear the Word and "accept it," diffuse their own scandal and "bear fruit" for God (4:20).

Jesus then offers further "counsel" in parables to His followers and twelve disciples as corollaries to His teaching on the need to properly and fully receive His Word. Marcus notes that proper understanding of the first parable Jesus taught of "the Sower" (or, the Diffuser?) unlocks "all the parables" (Mark 4:13b),[38] including these subsequent ones. The first corollary parable is that light is to be shed abroad, not hidden away (Mark 4:21). This parable seems to expand on what to do with the Word once a person has accepted it. To bear fruit for God from the Word, it must be set where it can be seen, and where it can diffuse light into the scandal-ridden darkness of the myth-culture of the world. Similarly, Jesus says that hidden and secret things are to be revealed, to be brought to light (4:22). Contextually, this seems to mean that a function of the Word, a way in which it bears fruit, is revealing hidden and secret things; the Word is revelation. That is, the Word diffuses (disseminates) the truth, diffusing (dispersing, scattering) scandal and lies,[39] bringing acceptance of the truth and

---

38. Marcus, *Mark 1–8*, 310.

39. The term "diffuse" can convey both of these meanings: disseminating or spreading, and dispersing or scattering. The term is apt here, as Jesus disseminates the Word and disperses scandalized opposition.

authority of God's Word, with understanding, clarity, and wisdom. Jesus then repeats His admonition, "If any man has ears to hear, let him hear" (4:23).

Jesus continues His corollaries on the parable of "the Sower," returning to types of "soil," saying, "Take care what you listen to," because in what "measure" you "measure," it will be measured to you (Mark 4:24a). That is, if you hear God's Word, so that it is your "measure," your authority for understanding, then "more shall be given you [who hear] besides" (4:24b). That is, you produce the sort of fruit that arises from the seed you receive into your "soil," and the amount of seed, and this modifies how, and how much, you grow. And you will steadily get more of what you sow in yourself, what you hear, and less of what you choke out or reject (4:25). That is to say, your soil's quality, and the quality of the growth, depends on how much seed of the Word you have in it already, so the more the "Word" is in your soil, the better the produce *and* the better the soil, and *vice-versa*. So, "Take care what you listen to," and thereby diffuse the ever-gathering, ever-threatening scandals of the types that the LORD Jesus lists here.

This corollary parable of Jesus suggests that a person chooses what sort of "soil" and growth he has based on what sort and amount of "seeds" he allows into his "soil." Marcus comments on how this personal reception of ("listening to") Jesus' "donation" of good "counsel," His Word, has a self-serving quality in terms of one's "soil" or one's self, saying, "Mark . . . reapplies the metaphor of the measure to epistemology: people will receive insight according to the measure of their attentiveness. . . . Apparently, one has an obligation not only to others but also to oneself, and that obligation is discharged by a turning of the self to God's word."[40]

Jesus continues to offer "counsel" to the people, always in parables, and only explaining them to those who choose to follow Him, His disciples (Mark 4:33–4). In one parable, Jesus likens the kingdom of God to a man casting seed on the ground. It sprouts, grows, and bears fruit, but how this happens the man does not know. Except that when the "crop permits," the man immediately "sends forth the sickle" because "the harvest has come" (4:26–29; see Joel 3:12–14; Rev 14:14–19).[41] Together with that parable, Jesus "compares" the kingdom of God to a mustard seed, which is very small as a seed, but grows to be larger than "all the garden plants" with large branches, so that the birds "can nest under its shade" (4:30–32; Ezek 17:23; 31:6; Dan 4:20–22). Marcus writes:

> The tiny size of the mustard seed . . . symbolizes the initial inconspicuousness
> of God's dominion (4:31). . . . The huge size of the full-grown mustard plant
> at the end of the parable (4:32) . . . [represents] a hope for the future. . . . The
> glory that the [Kingdom] can expect at the eschaton; if the final stage of the
> seed described in 4:26–29 is symbolic of the Second Coming, so must be the

40. Marcus, *Mark 1–8*, 320.

41. Jesus' references to the harvest and the sickle, in the context of related passages in Joel 3:12–14 and Revelation 14:14–19, show that this harvest is one of judgment, "the wrath of God," which immediately precedes the establishing of Jesus' kingdom on earth.

full development of the mustard plant. . . . This interpretation of the parable's end is supported by passages from Ezekiel and Daniel that form the background to the Markan picture of birds nesting in branches.[42]

These last two parables of the kingdom of God, then, continue Jesus' fourth inversive and subversive "donor/council" motif, speaking eschatologically of the divine diffusion of the Word that achieves the establishment of the Messianic (Christ's) kingdom on earth, in which "every kind of bird" (Ezek 17:23b), all tribes and nations dwell (Ezek 31:6b). This "counsel" of Jesus offers great hope for the future; Messianic hope with which His Israelite listeners would be familiar (e.g., Ezek 17:22–24), and which they eagerly await. Jesus intends to "donate" "the hope of Israel" to His followers, the believers of Israel; participation in the ingathering into His eternal kingdom of God.

Mark tells us that "on that day" in which Jesus was offering His "counsel" in parables, when evening had come, Jesus told His disciples that He wanted to cross to the other side of the Galilee (Mark 4:35). So, "leaving the crowd" they entered into boats and set off (4:36). And "there arose a fierce gale of wind" so that the waves crashed over the boats and began filling them up (4:37). Jesus was in the stern of one of the boats, "asleep on the cushion" (4:38a). They awoke Him and said, "Teacher, do You not care that we are perishing?" (4:38b). With this question the disciples express scandal over Jesus' seeming abandonment of them while in mortal peril. Jesus "rebuked the wind" and said to the sea, "Hush, be still," so that the wind dies and a great calm occurs (4:39).

Here, Jesus diffuses the scandal by again exercising His authority over His creation, "donating" deliverance to His disciples, even as He has already been doing for the people of Israel from demons and diseases:

> Jesus demonstrates his sovereign power over the elements. . . . Nor is this the only way that the Jesus of our passage is like the God of the Old Testament and Jewish traditions. For the latter, like the Markan Jesus, battles and triumphs over the power of the sea, which he "rebukes." Isa 51:9–10 . . . Job 26:11–12, several Psalms (18:15; 104:7; 106:9), and Isa 50:2 . . . our passage, then, reflects . . . a high Christology that goes a long way toward equating Jesus with the OT God.[43]

Jesus then reprimands His disciples for their fear and lack of faith in Him (Mark 4:40). Jesus' reprimand appears to fall on deaf ears, however, as the disciples continue to be "very much afraid" and continue in not believing in Jesus' identity, saying, "Who then is this, that even the wind and the sea obey Him?" (4:41). As Marcus notes, "The passage ends with a dialogue between Jesus and the disciples that reinforces the impression of his awesomely high identity, which the disciples are having difficulty in

42. Marcus, *Mark 1–8*, 330.

43. Marcus, *Mark 1–8*, 338–39.

grasping."[44] So, here we see the beginnings of scandal gathering in the disciples, which Jesus diffuses with "donations" of miracles (confirming signs), and "counsels" of reprimand and exhortation. Yet, scandal will continue to grow in the hearts of the disciples.

Jesus and the disciples safely arrive at the other side of the sea of Galilee, in the "country of the [Gadarenes]" (Mark 5:1). Just as Jesus disembarks, "a man from the tombs with an unclean spirit" meets Him (5:2). Mark tells us that this possessed man dwells "among the tombs," and that no one is able to bind him any more even with a chain (5:3). Evidently, the man used to be bound regularly with shackles and chains by his own people, but he would tear them apart and break them in pieces and none could subdue him (5:4). As such, "night and day," he wandered "among the tombs and in mountains," screaming "and gashing himself with stones" (5:5). Girard discusses the mimetic behavior of the demonized man in punishing himself:

> Mark's text suggests that the Gerasenes [*sic*] and their demoniac have been settled for some time in a sort of cyclical pathology. . . . The sick man [is] . . . *bruising himself with stones.* In Jean Starobinski's remarkable commentary on this text [*La Démoniaque de Gérasa*, 63–94] he gives a perfect definition for this strange conduct: *autolapidation.* But why would anyone want to stone himself? . . . He is fleeing from the stones that his pursuers may be throwing at him. . . . Perhaps because he never does become the object of stoning, the demoniac wounds himself with stones. In mythical fashion he maintains the peril with which he believes himself to be threatened.[45]

This man is imitating the desire of his persecutors, his scapegoaters. He knows that they believe he needs to be bound and punished. Instead of waiting for the community to punish him, he punishes himself to pre-emptively fulfill their desire. This demonized man helps his community maintain their cyclical pattern of myth-culture by scapegoating himself. When Jesus arrives, both the demons and the community are scandalized by Jesus' interference in their smoothly functioning cyclical pattern of myth-culture.

The demonized man notices Jesus coming from a distance and immediately recognizes Him for who He is. This recognition is in stark contrast to Jesus' own disciples, who just now demonstrated that they are as yet unable to identify who Jesus is despite all that He has said and done. And the demoniac runs up and bows down before Jesus (Mark 5:6). Of this, Yarbro Collins writes, "The act of bowing down before Jesus expresses the demon's recognition of Jesus' power and status."[46] The man, or demon within the man, cries out "with a loud voice" at Jesus, "What business do we have with each other, Jesus, Son of the Most High God? I implore you by God, do not torment me!" (5:7). Yarbro Collins notes that the demon's statement "serves to develop the

44. Marcus, *Mark 1–8*, 339.

45. Girard, *Scapegoat*, 168, 170.

46. Yarbro Collins, *Mark*, 267.

theme of Jesus' identity: the demon as a supernatural entity knows who Jesus is. The title 'God the Most High' was . . . an epithet of the God of Israel."[47] Here again we see Jesus' distinction reinforced. The evil spirits are not His rivals but His subjects, though rebellious in nature. His opponents are not His equals, as in myth.

As Satan and the demons before now, the demon in this man immediately recognizes the distinction of Jesus' identity, and is also scandalized by Jesus' presence there. Mark tells us that Jesus has already been exercising His full authority, commanding the demon, "Come out of the man, you unclean spirit!" (Mark 5:8). Jesus also asks the demon his name, and it replies, "My name is Legion; for we are many" (5:9). The demon pleads with Jesus "not to send them out of the country" (5:10), acknowledging Jesus' authority. Jesus insists on "donating" to the possessed man his freedom, but (seemingly) grants the "legion" of "[all the demons]" their request, giving them "permission" to enter into a great herd of swine, about two thousand in number, instead (Mark 5:11–12). Once they have entered into the pigs, they race down the hill into the sea and begin to drown (5:13). Of Jesus' apparent granting of the demons' request, Yarbro Collins writes, "Jesus has outwitted the demons. By allowing them to enter the swine, apparently foreseeing that the swine would go mad, Jesus has sent them into the sea. . . . The 'sea' is symbolically equivalent to the 'abyss,' and the 'abyss,' or 'Sheol,' is the home of the demons."[48] Seeing all of this, the swineherds run away and report these events to the city and surrounding country, so that the people come out to see what happened (5:14).

When the Gadarenes see the until-recently possessed man sitting down, "clothed and in his right mind," they are "frightened" (Mark 5:15). When it is explained to them by the swineherds that Jesus has done this to the man and the pigs (5:16), they are even further scandalized, pleading with Jesus "to leave their region" (5:17). The reason for Jesus' scandalization of the Gadarenes appears to differ from that of Israel's religio-political leadership and the people of Israel generally. Yarbro Collins notes:

> Dibelius concluded insightfully that here Jesus is presented "not as the benign Savior who helps, but as the strange miracle man who terrifies" [*From Tradition to Gospel*, 87]. As the local people tried to control the suprahuman power of the demoniac by binding him, here they try to control or ward off the suprahuman power of Jesus by asking him to leave their district . . . because they cannot bear the presence of his divine majesty [*Wunder und Glaube*, 33].[49]

Rather than being scandalized by Jesus' so-called blasphemous self-identification, as in the case of the religio-political leaders of Israel, the predominately Gentile (non-Israelite) population of the region of Gadara are scandalized by Jesus' terrible power.

---

47. Yarbro Collins, *Mark*, 268.

48. Yarbro Collins, *Mark*, 271.

49. Yarbro Collins, *Mark*, 273.

Jesus is happy to diffuse their scandal by again creating space, social distance, and boarding His boat to leave (Mark 5:18). The man whom Jesus set free asks "to be with Him," but Jesus gives him a mission instead, to "go home to your people and report to them what great things the Lord has done for you, and how He had mercy on you" (5:19).[50] The man does so throughout Decapolis, proclaiming "what great things Jesus had done for him," so that "everyone marveled" (5:20). Yarbro Collins notes the exchange of "Lord" with "Jesus" in these verses,[51] which reiterates Jesus' identity as the Lord incarnate. So, Jesus' "donation" of freedom to the man is shared in good "counsel" to all that region.

Jesus returns by boat to the other side, the Israelite side, of the Galilee again, and a "large crowd" gathers again around Him "by the seashore" (Mark 5:21). While there, a ruler of the synagogue named Jairus approaches Jesus, falls at His feet, and begs Him to come and lay His hands on his dying daughter "so that she will be saved and live" (5:22–23). Yarbro Collins notes, "Jairus's obeisance to Jesus and his words indicate complete confidence, or faith, that Jesus has the power to heal his daughter."[52] Jesus goes with Jairus to "donate" healing and life to the girl, and a large crowd follows and presses in on Him (5:24).

While on the way, a woman "who had had a hemorrhage for twelve years" (Mark 5:25), whom no physician could help (5:26), but had heard about Jesus, came to Him in the crowd and "touched His cloak" (5:27). She was saying to herself, "If I just touch His garments, I will be saved" (5:28). When she touches Jesus' cloak her blood-flow immediately stops and she is healed (5:29). Jesus immediately perceives that "power proceeding from Him had gone forth" when she touches His cloak, and so turns around saying, "Who touched My garments?" (5:30). His disciples are surprised that He asks this since many are pressing into Him (5:31). Jesus sees the woman, however, who trembles and falls before Him and tells Him the "whole truth" (5:32–33). And Jesus says to her, "Daughter, your faith has saved you; go in peace and be healed of your affliction" (Mark 5:34).

Jesus seemingly did not plan or intend to "donate" salvation and healing to this woman; but her faith, her trust in Jesus, won it for her.[53] In Mark four we learnt that if a person will not *receive* Jesus (become His follower), then he cannot receive His "counsels," His Word. Likewise, we learn here in Mark five that if a person will not *believe* in Jesus, then he cannot receive His "donations," His healing and resurrection. This message continues Jesus' fourth inversive and subversive "donor/council" motif of this second scandal-diffusion episode.

While Jesus is still speaking with the woman, people come from the house of Jairus the synagogue ruler and say, "Your daughter has died; why trouble the Teacher

---

50. Jesus' name is omitted twice in this chapter in the NU text. Here at 5:19 and earlier at 5:13.
51. Yarbro Collins, *Mark*, 273.
52. Yarbro Collins, *Mark*, 279.
53. Yarbro Collins, *Mark*, 284.

anymore?" (Mark 5:35). But Jesus says to Jairus, "Do not be afraid, only keep on believing" (5:36). As Yarbro Collins observes:

> The confidence, faith, or trust of the woman with the flow of blood was brought forward in order to illustrate for Jairus and the audience what kind of faith or trust Jesus is advocating. The exhortation "Do not fear" is both an expression of consolation and a call for courage. The encouragement "just trust" (μόνον πίστευε), as a present imperative, calls for continuing confidence in Jesus' ability to heal, in spite of the fact that death has intervened.[54]

Jesus would let only Peter, James (Jacob) and John go with Him to the house (Mark 5:37). People were weeping and wailing at the house of Jairus (5:38). Jesus goes in and says, "Why make a commotion and weep? The child has not died, but is asleep," and they laugh at Jesus (5:39). Jesus puts them all out of the house, takes the girl's mother and father with His three disciples, and enters the room where the child is (5:40).

This careful selection of companions seems to relate to the woman with the flow of blood, in that the crowd pressing Jesus were not saved and healed except the one who believed. Similarly, the crowd at the house laughs at Jesus, but the father believes. Jesus will only allow those with faith in Him to be present for this miracle, perhaps because it effects the outcome. This reading is confirmed by what happens next at Nazareth (Mark 6:5). Taking the child by the hand, Jesus says, "Talitha kum! (which translated means, 'Little girl, I say to you, get up!')" (Mark 5:41). Immediately the twelve-year-old girl gets up and walks, and the parents and disciples are "completely astounded" (5:42). Their faith evidently did not diminish their astonishment.

Once again, after "donating" healing and life in response to faith, Jesus orders the witnesses to keep it quiet, continuing to diffuse scandal over His identity and power with privacy, and says the girl should eat something (Mark 5:43). Jesus expresses practical concern for "donations" for the basic physical well-being of people, such as food, in addition to their spiritual well-being.[55] And this will not be the last time that Jesus commands others to feed the hungry, to "donate" toward the needs of others as He Himself "donates."

Jesus goes from there (likely Capernaum) to "His hometown" of Nazareth, followed by His disciples (Mark 6:1). On the Sabbath, Jesus begins "counselling" the people of Israel in the synagogue, and "astonished" the listeners. They were saying:

> Where did this Man get these things, and what is this wisdom given to Him, and such miracles as these performed by His hands? Is not this the Carpenter, the son of Mary, and brother of James [Jacob], and Joses, and Judas, and Simon? Are not His sisters here with us? And they took offense at Him [literally, "were scandalized by Him"]. (Mark 6:2–3)

---

54. Yarbro Collins, *Mark*, 285.

55. France, *Gospel of Mark*, 240.

This is the second time that scandal is the term literally used in the Greek to describe the response to Jesus and His Word in this fourth "donor/council" motif of the second scandal-diffusion episode (see Mark 4:16–17). Jesus responds saying that a prophet is not without honor except in his home town, among his own relatives and family (6:4).

And Mark tells us that Jesus could do "no miracle" there in Nazareth except laying His hands on "a few sick people" and healing them, as He "wondered at their unbelief" (Mark 6:5–6). France notes that, "Both evangelists [Matthew and Mark] attribute Jesus' 'minimal' miraculous activity to the ἀπιστία [unbelief or mistrust] of the people of Nazareth,"[56] which remember, relates to their scandal over Jesus' identity. So, in continuation of a key message of Mark's fifth chapter (and Jesus' fourth "donor/council" motif as a whole), without receiving Jesus, and having faith in Jesus, it is not possible to be saved, healed or taught by Jesus, to participate in His "donor/council" motif. Jesus diffuses the scandal of His relatives by creating space, social-distancing, moving on to other villages of Israel, "counselling" and "donating" where these gifts may be better received and believed (6:6).

Next, here in the midst of Jesus' inversive and subversive "donor/council" motif, He summons the twelve disciples for a second "council," at which He gives them a special expeditionary mission in pairs. To achieve it, Jesus "donates" to them further powers, "authority over the unclean spirits," and "counsels" them to take nothing for their journey except a single layer of garments on their backs, sandals on their feet, and a staff; no bread, bag, money, or second tunic (Mark 6:7–9). Jesus "counsels" them to stay in the same house they first enter when they reach a town, and whoever should not receive them or listen to them, they are to "shake the dust off the soles of their feet" when they leave as "a testimony against them" (6:10–11). And Jesus says to them, "[Truly I say to you, it shall be more tolerable for Sodom and Gomorrah in the day of judgment, than for that city.]" So, the disciples went out in pairs "preach(ing) that men should repent. And they were casting out many demons and were anointing with oil many sick people and healing them" (6:12–13). As we can see, while Jesus and His disciples continue the "journey" motif begun in the previous section (as mentioned, the motifs tend to be cumulative), Jesus is definitely focused on His atypical fourth "donor/council" motif in this portion of the Gospel account.

Mark then tells us what happened to John the Baptist after He had been imprisoned (see Mark 1:14). When King Herod Antipas hears of what Jesus is doing, because "[Jesus'] name had become well known," and "miraculous powers are at work in Him," Herod says, "John, whom I beheaded, has risen [from the dead]!" (Mark 6:14–16). Jesus' name and power have diffused throughout the land such that the people are saying that Jesus is either John raised from the dead, or Elijah returned as prophesied (Mal 4:5), or another prophesied prophet to come (Deut 18:18; Mark 6:14–15). France calls this the "popular estimate of Jesus."[57]

56. France, *Gospel of Mark*, 244.
57. France, *Gospel of Mark*, 252.

King Herod Antipas had personally sent and had John arrested and bound in prison (Mark 6:17). He had done this because John had given "counsel" to him saying, "It is not lawful for you to have your brother's wife" (6:18). John said this because Herod Antipas had married Herodias, his brother Philip's wife. Mark then tells us that Herodias "had a grudge against (John)," being scandalized and resentful of his public denunciation of their marriage (6:19). Herodias wanted to kill John the Baptist but could not, because King Herod "was afraid of John, knowing that he was a righteous and holy man" (6:20).[58] So, Herod had kept John safe from his unlawful wife Herodias. Mark tells us that though Herod was "very perplexed" at John's "counsels" and teachings, he "was hearing him gladly" nonetheless (6:21). This statement likely alludes to Mark's previous assertions that much of John's and Jesus' audience are seeing but not perceiving, and hearing but not understanding, because they do not receive the Word of God. Yet, most are happy to be entertained by it, like Herod Antipas.

On a "strategic" day, King Herod's birthday, he "gives a banquet" for "his lords, military commanders and the leading men of Galilee" (Mark 6:22). Herodias' daughter comes and dances for Herod and his guests. She pleases them so much that Herod offers her whatever she would ask of him, even "half of my kingdom" (6:22–23). The daughter goes and asks her mother, Herodias, who says, "The head of John the Baptist" (6:24). Immediately she comes back before Herod and his guests and asks, saying, "I want you to give me at once the head of John the Baptist on a platter" (6:25). Unwilling to refuse her because of his oaths and his guests, though very sorry, Herod Antipas sends an executioner to the prison in which he holds John, who beheads him (6:26–27). The executioner brings John's head on a platter to the girl, who gives it to her mother Herodias (6:28). When John's disciples hear, they come and take away John's body, at least, and lay it in a tomb (6:29).

This account of John's treatment at the hands of the people's leadership, for sowing the seed of the Word of God, further reveals the sameness and scandal of the pattern of myth-culture and their consequences—snare of striving, scapegoating, satiation, segregation—in a very powerful nutshell. France notes that Jesus "had come to regard Antipas as his enemy . . . [and] Mark records little public activity by Jesus within Antipas's territories after this point, and the narrative resumes with a 'retreat' to the other side of the lake."[59] This observation indicates that Jesus again diffuses His

---

58. France makes significant connections here, both between King Ahab and Jezebel's targeting of the prophet Elijah (John's prefigure), as well as Pontius Pilate and the priests targeting of Jesus later in the Gospel account. He writes, "These verses set up the contrast, strongly reminiscent of the story of Ahab and Jezebel (whose 'target' was, of course, John's model Elijah), which the rest of the story will work out between a resolutely hostile Herodias and a wavering Antipas, who will eventually be tricked into pronouncing sentence against his better judgment. The parallel with Pilate's ineffectual resistance to the determined hostility of the priests in 15:1–15 is remarkable . . . like Felix with another prisoner later in (Acts 24:24–26), [Herod Antipas] was at least open to persuasion; but he remained confused and undecided" (France, *Gospel of Mark*, 257).

59. France, *Gospel of Mark*, 254.

opponents' scandal over Him, this time that of Herod Antipas, by again creating social distance between them.

Mark then returns to Jesus and His disciples, telling us that the disciples who had gone out in pairs return to Jesus and "report to Him all that they had done and taught" (Mark 6:30). Jesus "counsels" them all to come away by themselves (in the boat) "to a secluded place and rest a while," because they were inundated by people such that they did not have time even to eat (6:31). So Jesus "donates" rest to His followers, and here practices again the diffusion of scandal method of creating distance, which will prevent both disciples and others from being scandalized by the exhaustion and frustration of their ministry; and as mentioned, it will diffuse the scandal of Herod Antipas and Herodias. So, they "went away in the boat to a secluded place by themselves" (6:32). However, the people see them going and will not leave them alone. They run around the lake of Galilee "on foot from all the cities, and got there ahead of them [and came together to Him]" (6:33). Disembarking, Jesus sees "a large crowd" and "felt compassion for them because they were like sheep without a shepherd"; so, Jesus begins to "counsel" them about "many things" (6:34).

When it grows "quite late" in the day, Jesus' disciples begin saying that the place they are in is "desolate" and the crowd must be sent off to buy "[themselves bread]" in the surrounding countryside and villages (Mark 6:35–36), "[for they have nothing to eat]." But Jesus says, "You give them something to eat!"; and they reply, "Shall we go spend two hundred denarii on bread?" (6:37). Jesus responds, "How many loaves do you have? Go look!" They check and say, "Five and two fish" (6:38). Jesus then commands everyone to "recline by groups" on the green grass, and they do so "in companies of hundreds and fifties" (6:39–40). Jesus takes the five loaves and two fish, looks up to heaven, "blessed and broke the loaves" and keeps giving the pieces to the disciples to set before the people, and He "divided up the two fish among them all" as well (6:41). All five thousand men "ate and were satisfied," and they even picked up twelve baskets full of left-over bread and fish (6:42–44). Jesus has performed an incredible miraculous "donation" of food to this great multitude of people. France writes of this miraculous "donation" by Jesus, as well as His next miracle hereafter: "These stories offer yet more evidence of the unique ἐξουσία [authority and supernatural power] of Jesus; the disciples may have been given ἐξουσία to heal and to exorcise, but here is power on a different level altogether."[60]

Jesus then makes His disciples get in the boat and sail "ahead of him" to the other side of Galilee, to Bethsaida (Mark 6:45), while He sends the multitude away. After bidding farewell to His five thousand (plus, if women and children were included) dinner guests, Jesus "left for the mountain to pray" (6:46). It seems that He personally needs to diffuse the potential of scandal as well, creating space and spending time in prayer in the Word of God, with the Father God and the Spirit God. For Jesus' disciples and the people were on the cusp of scandal prior to His miraculous feeding

60. France, *Gospel of Mark*, 259–60.

of these hungry "sheep without a shepherd." When Jesus needs a "donation" of help and "counsel," He goes to His Father in prayer.

Mark tells us that when it was evening, the boat-full of disciples was "in the midst of the sea" and Jesus was "alone on the land" (Mark 6:47). Jesus sees them "straining at the oars" with "the wind against them," and walks out to them at "about the fourth watch of the night" (between 3 and 6 a.m.), "walking on the sea," passing them by (6:48). When the disciples see Jesus walking on the sea, they think He is a ghost and cry out in fright (6:49); but Jesus immediately speaks to them saying, "Take courage; it is I, do not be afraid" (6:50). He then climbs into their boat and "the wind stopped" and the disciples were "greatly astonished" (6:51). France observes:

> [Jesus] comes to them as a figure of mystery and terror, not a familiar companion to be awakened in a crisis. While the earlier incident was sufficient to provoke a christological question (4:41), its more down-to-earth atmosphere contrasts with the numinous appearance and "impossible" behavior of Jesus in this pericope, after which the disciples are left not so much impressed as bewildered and (metaphorically) out of their depth. This response by the disciples leads to a surprisingly negative conclusion to the pericope in 6:52 . . . [with] the increasing inability of his disciples to cope with [Jesus' identity].[61]

Jesus miraculously "donates" smooth sailing to the disciples and demonstrates His identity to them perhaps more clearly than ever by walking on the sea. But Mark tells us that the disciples "had not gained any insight from the loaves" or Jesus' walking on and stilling the sea, because "their heart was hardened" (or "mind was closed, dull, or insensible" [Mark 6:52]).

Jesus diffuses the scandal of the disciples over hunger, and mortal peril on the water, with "donations" and "counsel" by His divine power, but they are evidently still not appreciating who it is that they are following. In fact, they appear to be scandalized by Jesus instead, not unlike His opponents. The language of hard-heartedness has been used previously only of the religio-political leaders of Israel who oppose Jesus (Mark 3:5; and implied in 4:11–12). It seems strange to see it used of Jesus' core twelve disciples; and yet we will see increasingly from here on just how alone Jesus is in His unique divine pattern, and also the incredible plan He is engaged in to change this solitude, so "whosoever will" can walk in Him, and in His pattern also, by means of the Cross and the promised baptism in the Holy Spirit (Mark 1:8).

They land and moor the boat at Gennesaret, disembark, and immediately the people recognize Jesus and run about the country bringing all their sick to Him on pallets, wherever they hear that Jesus is (Mark 6:53–55). At every village, city, and countryside that Jesus enters, the people lay the sick, and plead with Him to be free to "touch the fringe of His cloak," and "as many as touched it were being cured" (6:56). Again, Jesus continually busies Himself in His fourth inversive and subversive "donor/

---

61. France, *Gospel of Mark*, 270.

council" motif with "donating" healing, freedom and life to Israel, and offering them good "counsel" that liberates from the myth-culture's scandals, suffering and death.

The Pharisees and scribes again "journey" down from Mount Zion in Jerusalem in this fourth motif of the second episode—on cue in the expected order of the pattern of myth-culture that they follow, and with the expected meaning—and they "gathered together around Jesus" (Mark 7:1). These have not gathered around Him for His "donations" or "counsels," but to attack Him as a villain threatening their cosmos. The religio-political leaders of Israel are scandalized by Jesus' disciples' behavior, and have come to accuse Jesus and His followers of wrongdoing. They witness the disciples eating their bread with "impure hands, that is, unwashed" and "[they found fault]" (Mark 7:2). Mark explains that "the Pharisees and all the Jews do not eat unless they carefully wash their hands, thus observing the traditions of the elders" (7:3).[62] Additionally, Mark says that they sprinkle themselves with water when they come from the marketplace; they baptize their cups, pitchers and pots, "and there are many other things which they have received in order to observe" (7:4). So, Jesus and His disciples are "failing" to live by the received traditions of men, the prescribed myth-culture, and thus scandalize the leadership of Israel, who prize the words of men more than the Word of God. The Pharisees and scribes ask Jesus, "Why do your disciples not walk according to the tradition of the elders . . .?" (7:5). Stein observes, "The question addressed to Jesus concerning 'your disciples' . . . is an indirect attack on Jesus, for a teacher was responsible for the behavior of his disciples. . . . To 'walk' . . . means to live in accordance with the traditions of the elders."[63] Stein's observation of the Pharisees' and scribes' term "walk" demonstrates that they understand it as a pattern of life to be followed, yet Jesus shows that their traditional pattern is not His pattern, nor a pattern consistent with Scripture.

Jesus diffuses their scandal, as in the past, "donating" the good "counsel" of Scripture, saying, "Rightly did Isaiah prophesy of you hypocrites, as it is written:

'This people honors Me with their lips,

But their heart is far away from Me.

But in vain do they worship Me,

Teaching as doctrines the precepts of men.'"

(Mark 7:6–7; Isa 29:13)

---

62. Stein comments on these traditions to which the Pharisees and "all the Jews" adhere: "This expression (cf. Gal 1:14) refers to the traditions, supposedly given orally by God to Moses on Mount Sinai . . . that were codified into the Mishnah (ca. AD 200), which along with its Aramaic commentary, the Gemara, make up the Jerusalem Talmud (ca. AD 400) and the larger Babylonian Talmud (ca. AD 500). Jesus, in his defense against the specific teaching concerning defilement (7:2, 5), first directed his attack against the cause and origin of the teaching, that is, the tradition of the elders (7:6–13). The issue of whether eating with unwashed hands can defile a person would be addressed later, in 7:14–23. The practice of ceremonially washing hands, even though not prescribed by the Torah [Genesis through Deuteronomy], clearly existed in Jesus' day" (Stein, *Mark*, 339).

63. Stein, *Mark*, 340.

But Jesus is not finished. He continues His rebuke of these religio-political leaders of Israel, saying, "Neglecting the commandment of God, you hold to the tradition of men [like the washing of pots and cups; and you do many other such things]" (Mark 7:8). Jesus makes a sharp distinction between the rejected authority of God's written Word that saves and frees the people (as seen with the "seed" of the Word previously [Mark 4:1–34]), distinguishing it from the accepted ideas of the religio-political leadership of Israel that destroy and enslave the people.

Jesus then offers another example of the difference between the pattern that He teaches and exemplifies versus the pattern followed and taught by the religio-political leadership of the myth-culture, saying:

> You nicely[64] set aside the commandment of God in order to keep your tradition. For Moses said, "Honor you father and your mother" (Exod 20:12); and, "He who speaks evil of father or mother, let him die the death" (Exod 21:17); but you say, "If a man says to his father or his mother, anything of mine you might have been helped by is Corban (that is to say, given to God)," you no longer permit him to do anything for his father or his mother; thus invalidating the word of God by your tradition which you have handed down; and you do many things such as that. (Mark 7:9–13)

Stein notes how Mark translates the Hebrew-Aramaic term "Corban" into Greek as a "gift" (δῶρον),[65] or "donation," making Jesus' example literally on point in this, His fourth "donor/council" motif. Jesus' unique pattern, while consistent with the Word of God, is in subversive and inversive contradistinction to the myth-culture's pattern represented by His opponents. After quoting the LORD's rebuke of human hypocrisy from Isaiah—the practice of enforcing man-made ideas and laws while invalidating God-made ideas and laws—Jesus repeats the rebuke three times (Mark 7:8, 9, 13). Stein notes the three repetitions of Jesus, as well as Jesus' emphasis on the traditions' human origin in opposition to God's Word.[66] Jesus is again diffusing in both senses of scattering scandal and sowing the Word. This "counsel," if accepted, would enable the leaders of Israel to diffuse their scandal over Jesus and His disciples' behavior. They could be free from the oppressive man-made ideas and regulations that oppress themselves and the people, and free from the "snowballing" of scandals.

Jesus continues "donating" His good "counsel," "call(ing) the crowd" to hear a

---

64. Stein also notes Jesus' "ironical" use of "well" (καλῶς), translated "nicely" here in the NASB (*Mark*, 342), showing in part that Jesus is really "laying into" His homily on this matter with great passion. Together with His descriptor of the Pharisees and scribes as "hypocrites" here (7:6), it is clear that Jesus' "blood boils" at what may be termed the "virtue signalling" of the world's "righteous," making grandiose "donations" to God (purportedly) as they simultaneously neglect to actually help those in need, in this case their fathers and mothers, in contradiction of one of the ten commandments of God.

65. Stein, *Mark*, 342.

66. Stein, *Mark*, 341.

parable on this subject of defilement, as humans inured in the myth-culture see it, versus how God sees it (Mark 7:14). He explains to everyone that it is not what goes into a human that defiles him, but what proceeds out of a human that defiles him (7:15). Having dirty hands or dishes is not the problem, but having a dirty heart and mind. As Stein notes:

> Compare also the message of the OT prophets (Isa 1:11–17; Hos 6:6; Amos 5:21–27), where the spiritual meaning and the literal observance are seen not as contradictory but as supplementary. What Jesus's audience probably understood by these words was the importance of inner purity stemming from the heart. This was far more important than any outer ceremonial purity.[67]

And Jesus repeats the refrain of His fourth "donor/council" motif: "If any man has ears to hear, let him hear" (Mark 7:16). After leaving the multitude and entering "the house," Jesus' disciples ask Him "about the parable" (7:17). Jesus wonders aloud at their incomprehension. But He explains that what goes into a human does not enter the heart but the stomach, and thereafter goes out into the latrine. Mark tells us that in saying this Jesus also declares "all foods clean" (7:18–19). Jesus then says that it is what comes out of a human that defiles him (7:20):

> For from within, out of the heart of men, proceed the evil thoughts and fornications, thefts, murders, adulteries, deeds of coveting and wickedness, as well as deceit, sensuality, envy (an evil eye), slander, pride (arrogance) and foolishness. All these evil things proceed from within and defile the man. (Mark 7:21–23)

Jesus' "donation" of good "counsel" identifies the real source of evil and suffering for humanity, our filthiness, which is all humanity's sinfulness (listed by Jesus here) that defines the pattern of myth-culture, which He Himself has come to conquer (see Mark 1:5, 8, 15; 2:5–11). This enemy is a very different foe from those of heroes of myth-culture.

Jesus then travels to the "region of Tyre and Sidon" (Mark 7:24a), perhaps diffusing scandal again by creating more space after His stern rebuke of the Pharisees and scribes, or to avoid the "hostility of Herod Antipas" (one possibility proposed by Stein).[68] He enters a house there and tries keep His presence secret, but "He could not escape notice" (7:24b). As mentioned, this privacy is again likely a tactic for diffusion of scandal, related to His reason for being there. A woman of the Greek Syrophoenician tribe, whose daughter has an unclean spirit, hears of Jesus' presence, and immediately comes and falls at Jesus' feet (7:25). She is seeking a "donation" from Jesus of exorcism of her daughter's demon, asking Jesus repeatedly "to cast the demon out of her daughter" (7:26). Jesus responds that the children should be fed before the dogs

---

67. Stein, *Mark*, 344.
68. Stein, *Mark*, 350.

(7:27), evidently meaning that His ministry—access into the kingdom of God—is to the Israelites first and the other tribes of humanity (the Gentiles) second.[69]

The mother is persistent, however, and argues that crumbs nevertheless fall from the children's table that the dogs eat up (Mark 7:28). Jesus accepts her argument, saying that "because of this word" of hers she should go her way, saying, "the demon has gone out of your daughter" (7:29). When she gets home the woman finds her daughter thrown on her bed and the demon gone out of her (7:30). So, Jesus "donates" freedom from demons to a non-Israelite, despite His determined adherence to the prophetic order of the gift of salvation—to the Jews first and then to the Gentiles through Israel (e.g., Isa 42:1; 49:6)—as described in the Scriptures that He came to perform "as it is written" (e.g., Mark 1:2; 9:12; 14:21).[70] It is therefore a very gracious "donation" by Jesus here; and it diffuses considerable potential scandal.

Then, apparently careful to keep diffusive distance from the gathering scandal in Israelite Galilee for the time being, Jesus travels through Sidon to the Decapolis side of the lake of Galilee (Mark 7:31). The people there bring to Him a deaf man with a speech impediment, and they ask Jesus "to lay His hand upon him" (7:32). Jesus happily "donates" healing to this man. Taking him away from the multitude, Jesus puts His fingers into the man's ears, then apparently spits on His fingers and touches the saliva to the man's tongue (7:33). Looking toward heaven, Jesus heaves a deep sigh and says to the man, "'Ephphatha!' that is, 'Be opened!'" (7:34). The man's ears are opened, the bond of his tongue is loosed, and he begins speaking plainly (7:35).

After this "donation," Jesus seeks to diffuse scandal, continuing His practice of telling the people to keep the healing private. But, "the more He ordered them, the more widely they continued to proclaim it" (Mark 7:36). The people are astonished, saying, "[Jesus] has done all things well; He makes even the deaf to hear, and the dumb to speak" (7:37). The Word of Jesus—who He is and what He is offering the world—is being diffused abroad despite Jesus' efforts at containment or "controlled release" to avoid scandal's hindrance of His ministry. As Stein remarks, "Mark portrays Jesus as not seeking notoriety or fame but despite this receiving great fame and notoriety. Jesus, the Son of God, is too great to be kept hidden."[71]

Jesus continues His fourth "donor/council" motif and ministry to the people of Israel, now with another mass feeding. There was again a great multitude, with nothing to eat, following Jesus (Mark 8:1). Jesus summons His disciples and says, as He did the last time (see Mark 6:34–38), "I feel compassion for the crowd because they have remained with Me now three days, and have nothing to eat" (8:2). He worries aloud that if He sends them away, they will faint on the way (8:3). Edwards remarks on both of Jesus' mass feedings, which notably occur within His fourth "donor/council" motif:

69. Stein, *Mark*, 352–53. Jesus alludes perhaps to Isaiah 42:1; 49:6.

70. Stein, *Mark*, 352–54.

71. Stein, *Mark*, 362.

"Both emphasize Jesus' compassion on the crowds."[72] The people have spent time with Jesus listening to His good "counsel," and now Jesus again seeks to "donate" towards their physical well-being as well.

Jesus' donations are not for allies on the side of the "hero," as seen in myth-culture, but for sinners whom He has come nevertheless to save, and for people that the "righteous" of the myth-culture would never help. As Edwards observes, "In Mark this word [*splangnizomai*, compassion] is not used of people for whom one would naturally feel compassion (such as friends or compatriots), but for those far removed and even offensive [scandalous]: lepers (1:41), revolutionaries (6:34), Gentiles (8:2), and demon-possessed (9:22)."[73] Based on location as well as other indicators, it seems that the first mass feeding was of Israelites or Jews, while this second mass feeding is of Gentiles;[74] with this, Edwards notes an interesting difference in the response of the Gentiles:

> In describing the crowd Mark uses a rare and intensified form of the word for "remain," *prosmenein*, connoting a special adherence and commitment to Jesus. . . . This is an unusually positive description of a crowd in Mark. Jesus again finds a reception among Gentiles that he has not found among Jews.[75]

And once again, Jesus' disciples express scandal and disbelief at the possibility of feeding so many people "here in the wilderness" (Mark 8:4). Jesus asks His disciples how many loaves of bread they have, and they say "seven" (8:5). Jesus decides to perform another miraculous "donation." He directs the multitude to sit down, and just as before, He takes the loaves, gives thanks to the Father, breaks them, and hands them to His disciples to serve the multitude, who do so (Mark 8:6). Jesus then does the same thing with "a few small fish" that they had (8:7). Mark tells us that all ate and were satisfied, and they picked up seven baskets full of left overs. "About four thousand" men, presumably not including women and children, were fed by Jesus, and then He sent them away (8:8–9).

Jesus immediately enters the boat with His disciples and they sail to "the district of Dalmanutha" (Mark 8:10). The Pharisees come out and begin arguing with Jesus, demanding a "sign (attesting miracle) from Heaven, to test Him" (8:11). They are clearly continuously scandalized by Jesus' actions and words. Their demand is strange, because He has been performing many miracles that attest to the legitimacy of His identity and "counsels," yet they ask for another. Edwards notes, "Jesus is accosted

---

72. Edwards, *Mark*, 227.

73. Edwards, *Mark*, 230.

74. Edwards, *Mark*, 230. Evidently, the appeal made by the Syrophoenician woman has had a farther-reaching impact on Jesus' ministry than she herself intended. With the scandal over Jesus so great amongst the Israelites, resulting in Him spending more and more time among the Gentiles, Jesus is blessing the Gentiles instead. Israel's hardness of heart results in blessings for the nations. This situation occurred in the past (with Elijah and Elisha) and is one that will be repeated, but even more profoundly, in the future (see Rom 9–11).

75. Edwards, *Mark*, 229.

by the Pharisees. . . . Mark reads 'came out' . . . as if in military rank. They not only 'question' him, but they 'dispute' or 'oppose' him. . . . Likewise, the word for 'test' . . . does not mean an objective test to discover the merit of something, but an obstacle or stumbling block [scandal] to discredit."[76] Jesus diffuses this by refusing to perform on demand for these leaders of Israel, who clearly have other motives for their demand than a desire to repent and believe in Him. He was "sighing deeply in His spirit" (the Greek term expresses utter dismay),[77] and says to them, "Truly I say to you, no sign [attesting miracle] will be given to this generation" (8:12).[78] Jesus then gets back in the boat with His disciples and sails to "the other side" (8:13), probably again creating social distance as a diffusive tactic. Edwards views this encounter between Jesus and the religio-political leaders of Israel as a low-point for Jesus' ministry; and it does indeed occur near the end of the second scandal-diffusion episode, at the height of scandal thus far. He writes, "The Pharisees' intractable opposition and Jesus' utter dismay in the previous story (8:11–12) marked a nadir in the Galilean ministry."[79]

Mark tells us that the disciples had forgotten to bring bread with them, and had but one loaf with them in the boat (Mark 8:14). Meanwhile, Jesus is "counselling" them, "giving orders" that they, "Watch out! Beware of the leaven of the Pharisees and the leaven of Herod" (8:15). Leaven symbolizes harbouring unbelief while claiming to be a believer (e.g., Luke 12:1; 1 Cor 5:6–8; Gal 5:8–10). The disciples then begin to complain aloud about their lack of bread (8:16), and Jesus rebukes them, evidently for having in them the same "leaven" as the Pharisees and Herodians, the religio-political leaders of Israel, in that they do not believe in Him. And it seems their unbelief is at risk of leading to their scandal over Jesus as well, like the Pharisees:

> Jesus has not left the opposition behind with the Pharisees on the lakeshore.
> It is with him in the boat. . . . Jesus is moved to outright exasperation. Like the
> prophet Ezekiel, he is an exile among his own people. "Son of man, you are
> living among a rebellious people. They have eyes to see but do not see and ears
> to hear but do not hear" (Ezek 12:2).[80]

Evidently, despite seeing what He has just been doing, Jesus' own core disciples still do not accept who He is and so what He can do. Jesus says, "Do you not yet see or understand? Do you [yet] have a hardened heart?" (Mark 8:17). And paraphrasing the

---

76. Edwards, *Mark*, 235.

77. Edwards, *Mark*, 236.

78. Jesus makes a solemn oath here similar to one He also made to the religio-political leaders earlier. As Edwards states, "The solemn declaration, 'I tell you the truth,' has been used only once before in Mark [actually, twice in the Received Text] with reference to the scribes' accusing Jesus of complicity with the devil. The repeat of the declaration here suggests that the Pharisees' antagonism is in league with the opposition of 3:22" (*Mark*, 236).

79. Edwards, *Mark*, 237.

80. Edwards, *Mark*, 237.

prophet Ezekiel, Jesus says, "Having eyes, do you not see? And having hears, do you not hear?" (8:18; Ezek 12:2).

Jesus then asks the disciples whether they can remember what He has just done in His two mass feedings for the five thousand Israelites and the four thousand Gentiles, and how many left-overs there were (Mark 8:19–20). Then Jesus says, "Do you not yet understand?" (8:21). Edwards calls Jesus' "counsel" here a "fusillade of seven questions combining pleading with censure."[81] Jesus' own disciples, like the religio-political opposition, still do not realize who He is, despite His many astonishing miraculous "donations" and "counsels" confirming His identity and His offer of the kingdom of God to Israel.

Jesus arrives at Bethsaida with His disciples, and the people there bring Him a blind man and plead for Him "to touch him" (Mark 8:22). Jesus decides to make another miraculous "donation," taking the blind man by the hand, bringing him out of the village, and similarly to His miraculous healing of the deaf and mute man (Mark 7:33), Jesus touches His own saliva to the blind man's eyes (8:23). Jesus asks, "Do you see anything?" The man says essentially that he sees rather blurrily (8:24). Jesus repeats the treatment, touching his eyes a second time, "[and made him look up]," and then the blind man "began to see everything clearly" (8:25).[82] Edwards remarks:

> We are immediately struck by Mark's emphasis on sight in the present miracle as opposed to the emphasis on blindness and lack of comprehension in the previous story (8:14–21). The juxtaposition of the two stories is a clue that the lingering blindness of the disciples may also be relieved . . . by the continued touch of Jesus. . . . The two-stage cure in the present miracle thus suggests a *process* of revelation—as much for the disciples, we suspect, as for the blind man at Bethsaida. . . . The ability to see, both physically and spiritually, is a gift of God, not of human ability. . . . His healing from failed sight to partial sight to complete sight comes solely from the repeated touch of Jesus. His healing exemplifies the situation of the disciples, who move through the same three stages in Mark, from non-understanding (8:17–19) to misunderstanding (8:29–33) to complete understanding (15:39). . . . Only at the cross and resurrection will they, like the man at Bethsaida, see "everything clearly."[83]

It appears that these three stages of understanding align with the three broad stages of the pattern we are tracing; the three passages Edwards cites here fall within the first-second episodes, third-fourth episodes, and fifth-sixth episodes. After this "donation"

---

81. Edwards, *Mark*, 239.

82. Edwards also observes: "In English translations several of the words used for sight are the same, but in the original Greek there are eight different words used for nine instances of seeing in 8:23–25! The redundancy of [eight to nine] references to sight and seeing provides a counterbalance to the redundancy of [seven] accusations of blindness and misunderstanding in the previous story" (*Mark*, 243).

83. Edwards, *Mark*, 241, 244.

of miraculous healing, Jesus sends the man to his home with "counsel," saying, "[Neither] enter the village, [nor tell it to anyone in the village]" (8:26). Jesus is still practicing the diffusion of scandal here, using privacy.

This fourth "donor/council" motif of Mark's Gospel account is by far the longest motif of Jesus' unique divine pattern, comprising about five chapters of the sixteen total. This means that the longest of the twelve motifs of Jesus' pattern consists of Jesus' miraculous "donations" of healing of diseases, salvation from death, freedom from demons, and feeding of multitudes of the hungry, as well as astonishing "counsel" toward freedom from sin and death, and from the scandal of the myth-culture's pattern. In the pattern of myth-culture laid out in combat myths, the "donor/council" motif is quite brief, and consists of the hero-god receiving tools and counsel from other gods to defeat the villainous monster-god(s). Here in the Gospel account, the "donor/council" motif has Jesus, in place of the hero (or villain?), "donating" to and "counselling" sinners (everyone but Himself), all the while they passively resist Him, and at times actively oppose Him!

The sin of the people of Israel (and certain Gentiles) and its effects are the monsters of the world, the myth-culture, in which Jesus operates, and the source of "lack/villainy." This sin nature frequently places the people at enmity with Jesus, yet He "donates" to and "counsels" them toward freedom from sin and death. Jesus graciously does this for the benefit of the "monstrous," "villainous," and weak of the world, for all humanity, both Jews and Gentiles, and all the while He is opposed by the "righteous" and powerful of the world (see Mark 2:17).

Stein remarks on the two clear and opposing patterns of the Gospel account, in terms of the eventual cause of Jesus' death: "The human cause of his death was due to the hostility of those who honored God with their lips but whose heart was far from him. The divine cause for Jesus' death still awaits explanation, but this will come shortly (8:31)."[84] Stein clearly points to the pattern of myth-culture in the sense of the opposition to Jesus, as well as the unique pattern of Jesus in terms of the divine plan. Eventually, Jesus will be opposed by everyone of the mythological world, as will be predicted in the third snare of striving-deference episode, and will be seen in the fourth scapegoat-deliverance episode.

Social-Science

Social-scientifically, this fourth "donor/council" motif section continues to be comprised of diffusion exhibited by the LORD Jesus, continuing His unique evangelical pattern, intermingled with scandal exhibited by both demons and the people, especially at the leadership level, continuing the myth-culture's pattern. Beginning in this fourth motif, however, the common people of Israel, including Jesus' own disciples,

---

84. Stein, *Mark*, 348.

begin to be caught up in the gathering ("snowballing") scandal more and more as the second episode reaches its conclusion. The social-science lenses of Girard and Malina aid us in perceiving this chiastic bi-pattern.

At this point in the pattern of myth-culture we typically continue to see scandal preeminent. However, not so in the Gospel account due to the evangelical pattern here in Jesus Christ. Instead, Jesus exhibits diffusion of scandal, in opposition to those who embody the pattern of myth-culture around Jesus. Divine diffusion in Jesus continues to subvert the scandalous meaning expected of this episode, and continues to invert the myth-sequence so that this episode also contains a strong anti-satiation element as well.

While in Jesus' third "journey" motif of this second scandal-diffusion episode there occurred seven escalating scandals over Jesus, in Jesus' fourth and longer "donor/council" motif of the second episode, there are nineteen such events described by Mark, involving more and more divisions of the people. Not only the demons and religio-political leadership, but now also the common people of Israel and neighboring Gentiles, Jesus' own family, and Jesus' own disciples are being scandalized by Him. Clearly, despite Jesus' diffusive actions and words, the unbelief, scandal and resentment (harbored scandal) are accumulating against Him. It his hard to find someone that Jesus has not offended, despite good and miraculous "donations" and "counselling" to everyone, as well as other genuine attempts to diffuse scandal using His five methods listed previously.

However, Jesus expands His methods of diffusion in this motif. As He focuses on "donations" and "counselling," Jesus not only heals many more diseases and exorcises many more demons but also "donates" (1) miraculous amounts of food to thousands of hungry people on two separate occasions; (2) life-saving miracles from storms on the water to His disciples on two different occasions; (3) greater powers to perform miracles to His disciples, and sends them out in pairs to make "donations' to many more Israelites. Jesus also engages in lengthy "counselling" sessions for the people, the religio-political leadership, and His disciples. He freely offers them extensive good "counsel" against scandal and all forms of sin.

In doing all of this, Jesus is working very hard to diffuse the regular scandal over His astonishing identity, His miraculous deeds, and His incredibly wise teaching. Nevertheless, the scandal spreads to everyone around Him, and grows in intensity day by day. Jesus "counsels" everyone that the scandal comes from within each of them, not from outside of them (Mark 7:14–23), not from Jesus, but they do not seem to understand or accept the "counsel." As we will see in the next fifth motif that begins the third episode, Jesus knows they are incapable of properly understanding and receiving His "counsel," and so has planned two extraordinary "donations" to give them in the near future that are far more remarkable than anything He has done thus far, and which will achieve deliverance from the very source of scandal within, which is sin, the real "chaos-monster" of Jesus' unique evangelical pattern (see Mark 1:4–5, 15).[85]

Jesus' divine diffusion is subversive of the mythological scandal of everyone around Him, but His actions and words are also inversive of mythological satiation, pre-emptively undercutting the pattern of myth-culture which "requires" scapegoating to achieve the satiation of the people. As demonstrated in this motif by Mark's account of the beheading of John the Baptist (Mark 6:14–32), first the scandalizing scapegoat is slain, and *then* his head is taken on the platter to the collective feast, temporarily sating the hunger of sinners for evil, bringing them temporary return to segregation and peace. The peace is very temporary, always requiring a repetition of the pattern of myth-culture, another scapegoat, as seen in King Herod's complaint about Jesus, "John, whom I beheaded, He has risen [from the dead]!" (6:16). As France states: "In contrast to the unedifying banquet in Antipas's palace, the story goes on with a very different meal; the food is basic, but the circumstances and the reminiscences of OT events in the narrative mark out this simple meal as of more ultimate significance than the tetrarch's lavish birthday party. For those with eyes to see it, this will be a foretaste of the messianic banquet."[86]

Instead of myth's sequence of events and their meaning, in Jesus' unique divine pattern He satiates the even more fundamental needs and desires of the people's souls, the unmeetable desires that drive them continually and repeatedly through the pattern of myth-culture. Jesus physically satiates with food thousands miraculously on two separate occasions, but He also "donates" freedom to great numbers from demons, diseases, and death, and gives them extensive reliable "counsel" on how to be free and satisfied in life, and for eternity in the kingdom of God. Jesus' pattern achieves a better result than the myth-culture's pattern achieves, and He does it without the human-sacrifice (scapegoating) employed by the mythological culture, which ever achieves only temporary satisfaction at the expense of someone else. Somehow, unknown to everyone around Him, Jesus has power to meet the deepest needs and desires of the people of Israel, and her Gentile neighbors, without the sadistic and masochistic methods of sinful humanity. In this fourth "donor/council" motif that concludes the second scandal-diffusion episode, Jesus successfully subverts scandal and inverts satiation.

---

85. These two greatest donations are (1) Jesus' Cross and Resurrection (see Mark 8:31–38); and (2) His Spirit, which John the Baptist also prophesies that Jesus will donate (Mark 1:8).

86. France, *Gospel of Mark*, 260.

7

Episode 3

Mark 8:27–11:33: Snare of Striving and Deference

Snare of Striving	Deference
"What is the source of quarrels and conflicts among you? . . . You lust and do not have; so you commit murder. You are envious and cannot obtain; so you fight and quarrel." (Jas 4:1–2a)	"[Jesus] . . . said to them, 'If anyone wishes to come after Me, he must deny himself, and take up his cross and follow Me . . . whoever loses his life for My sake and the gospel's will save it.'" (Mark 8:34–35)

OVERVIEW

The LORD Jesus' two miraculous feedings of the multitudes make up the last major events of the second episode of the Gospel account. They are followed by Simon Peter's confession of belief that Jesus is the Messiah (see table c for the first and last verses of the episode). This account of Peter's confession of belief in Jesus begins the third social-scientific episode of the chiastic bi-pattern. The third episode consists of the mythological snare of striving in the people of Israel (involving striving to ensnare the rival), especially within Israel's leadership, as well as Jesus' unique evangelical pattern's inversive and subversive divine deference in Jesus (figure 1; table c).

Just as for the two previous episodes, the first and last verses of this third episode are identified based upon their positions at the beginning and end of the snare-deference content, as seen through the social-science lens, as well as the beginning and end of the "battle" and "defeat" motifs, as seen through the narratological lens. According to the pattern of myth-culture, we expect at this point in the account to encounter "battle" and then "defeat" for the hero-god, in that order, just as seen in

159

the Zeus-Typhon and Marduk-Tiamat examples. But as we have been seeing in the first two episodes, and their first four motifs, the two motifs of the third episode are again found to be in reverse order (inversive) for Jesus in the Gospel account, as well as possessing antithetical meanings in Jesus (subversive) by comparison with their meanings in myth-culture. In Jesus' identity, actions and words in the third episode, the evangelical pattern of the Gospel account continues to be not in accordance with the logic of the combat myth, the pattern of the myth-culture.[1]

Unlike in myth-culture, the "defeat" motif occurs in first position for Jesus. The episode begins with Simon Peter's confession that Jesus is the Christ, the Messiah (Mark 8:29). With this confession of Jesus' identity, Jesus then teaches them that according to the Scriptures, apparent "defeat" is necessary for the Christ at the Cross before Him (8:31), as well as for the Christ's followers who must take up their own crosses (8:34–38). But Peter rebukes Jesus, saying that He will not be "defeated," and Jesus tells Satan—whose viewpoint is evidently expressed through Peter—to get behind Him (8:32–33). So, Jesus defers to the Cross, to the Father's will that He should be "defeated," and so subverts the snare of worldly striving. His deference inverts and displaces the "defeat" motif in sequence as well. Jesus spends much of the remaining third episode teaching His disciples and all people Israel to defer to the way of the Cross that He Himself is taking, rather than remaining in the snare of striving.

As before, we see that the previous motifs and episodes continue in a cumulative manner. While new emphases take over in this third episode, Jesus continues to give good "counsel," make good "donations," etc. Likewise, the opposition to Jesus continues to grow, and continues to exercise the expected pattern of myth-culture.

After Jesus' unexpected fifth "defeat" motif, the out-of-order and out-of-character sixth "battle" motif is found in Jesus, which concludes the third snare-deference episode. Jesus arrives in Jerusalem, received (initially) by the people like a conquering hero, and "battles" with the religio-political leadership, the sixth motif again being inversive and subversive in Jesus. Jesus "battles" with the leadership of Israel at the Temple, casting out the market-place set up in the Temple precinct (Mark 11:15–17), and refuting the chief priests, scribes and elders who are still seeking to destroy Him (11:18). Jesus debates them into silence (11:33). So, the third social-science episode, and the sixth narratological motif, end in the Gospel account with Jesus' arrival in Jerusalem prior to His death and resurrection, and His "battle" with Israel's leaders there.

Just as the first two episodes, this third episode continues the chiastic bi-pattern. The people continue to follow the pattern of myth-culture in which they are helplessly inured. At the same time, continuing His evangelical pattern, Jesus is unexpectedly embodying God's gracious deference to all recalcitrant sinners, which is inversive and subversive of the myth-culture's behavior. Jesus does not respond to His opponents in kind, according to the

---

1. The "defeat" motif (the two motifs are separated by a bold black line in table 1C), here in the form of Jesus taking the Way of the Cross and teaching others to do likewise, occurs first, and is found in Mark 8:27–10:45. Jesus' "battle" motif is then found, also out of mythological sequence, in Mark 10:46–11:33.

myth-culture's pattern, which in every episode is a critical, surprising and incomprehensible development. This unique behavior of Jesus in the world is what forms the chiastic bi-pattern between the expected mythological pattern and the Gospel pattern in Jesus.

GOSPEL According to MARK			
WORLD'S SNARE		JESUS' DEFERENCE	
	8:27–28		
		8:29–9:4	
	9:5–6		
		9:7–9	
	9:10–11		
		9:12–13	
	9:14–18		
		9:19–31	
	9:32–34		
		9:35–37	
Battle	9:38		Defeat
		9:39—10:1	
	10:2		
		10:3–12	
	10:13		
		10:14–21	
	10:22–26		
		10:27–32a	
	10:32b		
		10:32c–34	
	10:35–37		
		10:38–40	
	10:41		
		10:42–45	
		10:46–47	
	10:48a		
		10:48b—11:4	
	11:5		
		11:6–17	
Defeat	11:18		Battle
		11:19–26	
	11:27–28		
		11:29–30	
	11:31–33a		
		11:33b	
TABLE 1C: Snare and Deference, Battle and Defeat			

MARK 8:27–10:45: JESUS' "DEFEAT"[2]

Narratology

Narratologically, this section of the Gospel account is comprised of the "defeat" motif for Jesus, but inversive in sequence and subversive in significance when compared with the pattern of myth-culture. The expected mythological motif of "battle" does predominate here in Israel's leadership, and all opposition to Jesus, but not in Jesus Himself. At this point in the combat myth, the "battle" motif is foremost. But at this point in the Gospel account, which contains the unique divine pattern in Jesus Christ, we instead see the "defeat" motif preeminent. Not only is the sequence of the motifs reversed, however, but their significance as well. Jesus' "defeat" is not like the typical "defeat" of myth-culture experienced by the hero-god there.

The "defeat" motif begins for Jesus as He heads out to the "villages of Caesarea Philippi," followed by His disciples. As they make their way, Jesus questions His disciples, saying, "Who do people say that I am?" (Mark 8:27). They respond that some say He is John the Baptist, others that He is Elijah the Prophet, and others say He is one of the prophets (8:28). Then Jesus asks His disciples, "But who do you say that I am?" It is Peter who answers, and says, "You are the Christ" (8:29). In response to Peter's confession of Jesus' identity as Israel's prophesied Messiah, Jesus warns His disciples "to tell no one about Him" (8:30), continuing His diffusive practice as before (the motifs and episodes tend to be cumulative, as mentioned previously). But additionally, evidently because His identity as Messiah has now been recognized, Jesus begins to describe the prophesied suffering of the Messiah. That is, Jesus responds to Peter's confession of belief in who He is by announcing His "defeat." With this announcement, Jesus initiates the third episode, which emphasizes deference to the will of God, including that the Christ should suffer.

As such, Jesus begins His inversive and subversive "defeat" motif here with this teaching (counsel) to His disciples: "the Son of Man must suffer many things and be rejected by the elders and the chief priests and the scribes, and be killed, and after three days rise again" (Mark 8:31). Mark tells us that Jesus is very matter-of-fact about this unexpected announcement (unexpected, that is, from the perspective of the pattern of myth-culture). Peter, who has just made the crucial confession of belief in Jesus' identity, nevertheless responds to Jesus Christ's pre-emptive declaration of "defeat" by initiating the expected "battle" motif of myth-culture's pattern, by "battling" Jesus and falling into the snare of striving with Jesus. Peter "took Him aside and began to rebuke Him" (8:32), which is a surprisingly bold and rivalrous thing to do, especially after the acknowledgment he just made. Peter seems to be arguing that Jesus should be starting His "battle" motif now, leading the myth-culture's expectation of striving against the corrupt and oppressive leadership of Israel, rather than declaring apparent "defeat."

---

2. Please refer to appendix 1 for the complete text of Mark's account for this motif.

So, once again it is not Jesus but the mythologically inured people around Jesus, even His own disciple here, that continue the pattern of myth-culture.

Craig A. Evans, in his commentary on the second half of the Gospel according to Mark (in continuation of Guelich's commentary),[3] makes the following observations on this first pericope of Jesus' fifth "defeat" motif: "Mark 8:27–33 attempts to bring together these two seemingly contradictory elements. On the one hand, Jesus is the Messiah; yet, on the other, his destiny is to die. What resolves the tension is the prediction that Jesus will be resurrected. Thus his death on the cross is not defeat (as Jews and Romans alike would assume) but a prerequisite for accomplishment of mission and attainment to office."[4] Evans deftly observes the culturally unexpected order and meaning of Jesus' words, actions and deeds. Jesus announces "defeat" when He should be entering into His first "battle" motif according to the myth-culture's pattern. He is flouting the prescribed pattern of the hero-god in both sequence and significance. Evans continues, "That Jesus' disciples find all of this baffling is understandable. They too shared much of the popular expectation."[5]

Jesus sees the other disciples watching this rivalrous behavior by Peter and rebukes Peter, saying, "Get behind me, Satan; for you are not setting your mind on God's interests, but man's" (Mark 8:33). Peter is trying, with good intent no doubt, to drag Jesus into conformity with the expected pattern of myth-culture, to get Him back on track. Jesus, however, re-asserts His unique divine evangelical pattern that does not conform to the myth-culture's pattern. Jesus even declares Peter's desire and perspective to be of Satan, and of sinful humanity, which two entities (Satan and humanity) Jesus closely links in His statement. Jesus will not conform to the world's myth-culture, but defer instead to "God's interests."

Girard views Peter's statement here, and Jesus' response, as a critical moment for both master and disciple: "And there Jesus says, move away from me, *vade retro*, Satan," states Girard, paraphrasing in his mimetic-scapegoat reading, "Peter says to Christ, imitate my desire. I have a desire for success. I'm part of your enterprise. And

---

3. Evans describes his approach to the Gospel according to Mark in the following way: "'Mark's meaning,' Gundry avers, 'lies on the surface. He writes a straightforward apology for the Cross' [1]. . . . This commentary is in essential agreement with Gundry. . . . Perhaps it would be wise to see if Mark makes sense, as it stands, in the context of the first-century Roman Empire. Herein lies what I think is the essential point behind Mark's Gospel. His work does indeed constitute an apology for the cross, as Gundry has argued. But it is an apologetic that boldly challenges the emperor's claim to divinity and his demand for the absolute loyalty of his subjects. . . . For Mark it is all or nothing. If Jesus really is the fulfillment of OT prophecies . . . then he must be recognized and proclaimed as the *true* son of God. Jesus can have no rivals" (*Mark*, xi–xii). With this view, Evans affirms that the Gospel account contains the internal opposition that this book proposes between the pattern of myth-culture, of which the Roman imperial cult of Caesar based on the people's combat myths is a great and concurrent example, and the pattern of the LORD Jesus. Evans elaborates on his approach further when discussing the purpose of Mark, noting that the Caesars are explicitly equated with the hero-gods of myth (including Zeus) and their achievements are expressed in combat-myth terms (*Mark*, lxxxi–xciii).

4. Evans, *Mark*, 20.

5. Evans, *Mark*, 20.

I tell you your enterprise is not going to fail. . . . And Jesus says, that's what Satan is."[6] Peter's mythological desire and expectation for Jesus is being threatened by Jesus' statement about His death. Meanwhile, Jesus' divine desire and expectation for God's will for humanity is being threatened by Peter's suggestion that Jesus will not die.

Peter's suggestion, which Jesus attributes to Satan, is strangely reminiscent of the Serpent's suggestion to Eve and Adam in Genesis 3:4: "You surely will not die!" This event, beginning in Mark 8:27, constitutes the moment of the development of the myth-culture's pattern from scandal to snare-of-striving, with Peter and Satan striving to ensnare Jesus. For Jesus' part, this moment is His transition from diffusion to deference in His unique divine evangelical pattern. Jesus is changing the emphasis from diffusing scandals to deferring to His Father's will and plan, in contrast with Adam's response in a similar moment of temptation. Jesus alone will succeed where the First Adam and all his other descendants failed, thus becoming the Last Adam (1 Cor 15:45), and saving humanity from the curse of sin, its consequences of myth-culture and death.

Jesus continues on in this new emphasis of the third deference-snare of striving episode, and the subversive sense of His out-of-sequence "defeat" motif, summoning the multitude and His disciples and counselling them, saying, "If anyone wishes to come after Me, let him deny himself, and take up his cross, and follow Me. For whoever wishes to save his life[7] shall lose it; and whoever loses his life for my sake and the Gospel's shall save it" (Mark 8:34–35). Not only is Jesus demonstrating the unique divine evangelical pattern instead of the pattern of myth-culture, but He expects His followers to do the same! With this statement, Jesus also explicitly indicates the coming method of His murder, which is by crucifixion. Jesus suggests that the "battle" mythological people usually engage in at this point in the pattern, ensnared in striving to "save their lives," actually results in them "losing their lives," which is why such striving is a snare.

Paradoxically, Jesus promises life to those who willfully lose their lives for the LORD Jesus' sake and the Gospel's sake, even as His "defeat," His death, will actually be His victory when "after three days He rises again." So, Jesus' fifth "defeat" motif is not only inversive of myth-culture's sequence, coming before the "battle" motif, but also subversive of myth-culture's significance, in that Jesus' "defeat" is actually eternal victory. This saying of Jesus in Mark 8:35 is a "nutshell" expression of the entire chiastic bi-pattern of the Gospel account, describing the completely antithetical relationship between the pattern of myth-culture and Jesus' unique, divine, evangelical pattern.

Jesus continues His good counsel on deference instead of snare-of-striving, asking His disciples and the multitude, "For what does it profit a man to gain the whole

---

6. Girard, "Scapegoat," 22.

7. The NASB translation uses the hyphenated term "soul-life" to capture the Greek sense of the term ψυχή (psyche). It is important to note that Jesus is referring to the salvation of not merely the physical and temporal life but saving one's spiritual and eternal life as well.

world, and forfeit his soul?[8] For what shall a man give in exchange for his soul?" (Mark 8:36–37). Jesus is making a clear distinction here between the victory gained by the myth-culture's pattern, which is only death even if the whole world is won, and the victory won by His own divine pattern, the evangelical pattern. Jesus encourages will-ful acceptance of what seems like "defeat" in the world's eyes, according to the world's flawed wisdom and logic, in order to gain eternal life. Jesus' pattern, including this apparent "defeat" must be chosen, instead of the myth-culture's truly self-defeating "battle" to gain what is really a living death in this life, followed by eternal condemna-tion hereafter. As Evans remarks, "In other words, the true disciples of Jesus must be prepared to share Jesus' fate. . . . Is it worth denying oneself, taking up a cross, and following Jesus? Yes, it is asserted."[9]

Jesus then states a powerful conclusion to His assertion of the need for defer-ence to God's will instead of the snare of striving, and/or striving to ensnare the rival-double: "For whoever is ashamed of Me and My words in this adulterous and sinful generation, the Son of Man will also be ashamed of him when He comes in the glory of His Father and the holy angels" (Mark 8:38). Jesus reinforces the eternal conse-quence of the choice His hearers must make between the two patterns laid out here. If a person is ashamed of the voluntary "defeat" Jesus requires of him, the cross with which he must follow Jesus, then Jesus will be ashamed of that person when He comes again, evidently to judge the choice of humans between the two patterns.[10]

If a person chooses the "battle" of myth-culture for the world, instead of Jesus' inversive and subversive "defeat" that is the way of the Cross for the eternal life of his soul, that person will lose everything. Evans notes, "Gundry remarks that here 'discipleship plays second fiddle to Christology' [*Mark*, 434]. He is right, for the focus is upon whether one is 'ashamed' of Jesus and his words (8:38). . . . The true disciple will embrace and follow the crucified Jesus because he is the heavenly 'son of man' who will come in glory."[11]

Jesus then says that some of those listening to His counsel "shall not taste death until they see the kingdom of God after it has come with power" (Mark 9:1). Marcus notes, "It was expected among Jews that when the latter event occurred, when the dominion of God came in power (cf. 9:1), not only the Messiah but the whole of redeemed humanity represented by Adam would regain the splendor that had been lost through the fall."[12] Six days later, Mark tells us, Jesus takes three of His disciples—Peter, James (Jacob) and John—and brings them up a high mountain by themselves.

8. The term translated "soul" here is the same ψυχή translated "life" just previously. This abrupt change in translation value is unhelpful, and yet for most readers, neither "life" nor "soul" fully cap-tures what Jesus is talking about here, which is the entire eternal existence of a human being, both physical and spiritual.

9. Evans, *Mark*, 30.

10. And notably, with this statement, Jesus also reinforces His distinctive identity as the LORD.

11. Evans, *Mark*, 30.

12. Marcus, *Mark 8–16*, 637.

These appear to be the "some of you" whom Jesus allows to see the kingdom of God in power, because Jesus is then "transfigured before them" (9:2). Jesus' clothes "become radiant and exceedingly white, as no launderer on earth can whiten them" (9:3).

Then, Elijah and Moses appear and begin talking with Jesus before the three disciples' very eyes (Mark 9:4). This encounter provides a glimpse of the future kingdom of God, involving believers in Jesus of all ages alive on earth once more, in glorified form. Mark tells us that they are terrified by what they are seeing, and because he "did not know what to answer" Peter makes another myth-cultural statement, saying to Jesus, "Rabbi, it is good for us to be here; and let us make three tabernacles, one for you, and one for Moses, and one for Elijah" (9:5–6). Once again, Peter attempts to disrupt Jesus' divine pattern with the pattern of myth-culture, no doubt with as good intent as a member of "this adulterous and sinful generation" can muster. Peter equates Jesus with the other two significant yet nevertheless human-only persons, potentiating the sameness that leads to scandal and snare-of-striving.

Peter is quickly rebuked, not by Jesus this time, but by the Father God. Mark says that a cloud appears, overshadowing them, and a voice comes out of the cloud, saying, "This is my beloved Son, listen to Him!" (Mark 9:7). This is the second time the Father's voice has been audible from heaven, declaring Jesus' divine identity (see Mark 1:11). Immediately, the three disciples see "no one with them any more, except Jesus only" (Mark 9:8). The disciples were unable to glimpse God's kingdom come with power without bringing their myth-culture with them into it, treating other humans as though they were the same as the LORD God. The Father had to re-assert Jesus' sovereignty in God's kingdom for them, so that they would defer to Jesus and "listen to Him," and so defer to the Father's will for them as well. So, in this is the subversive nature of Jesus' fifth "defeat" motif in comparison with the myth-culture's pattern:

> In the transfiguration, then, the Markan audience has been shown a vision of Jesus in his Adamic, messianic glory, a vision that counterbalances the strong emphasis in the preceding pericopes on the necessity of joining in Jesus' march to extinction (8:31–37) and thus "remov[ing] the offence of the cross from the disciples' heart" (Leo the Great, *Sermon 51*) . . . transfiguration and crucifixion are two sides of the complex, divine-but-human identity of the Son . . . "in whom the eschatological pattern of suffering-vindication, tribulation-salvation must play itself out. Therefore in fulfilling the prophets and their ancient oracles of doom and consolation, Jesus is humiliated and exalted, surrounded by saints and ringed by sinners, clothed with light and yet wrapped in a garment of darkness" [Davies and Allison, *Matthew*, 2:706].[13]

As they make their way down the mountain, Jesus orders Peter, James (Jacob) and John "not to relate to anyone what they had seen, until the Son of Man should rise

---

13. Marcus, *Mark 8–16*, 640–41.

from the dead" (Mark 9:9).[14] The three disciples do not seem to understand that Jesus means that He will literally rise from the dead, despite Jesus saying that after that event they may openly discuss their glimpse of the kingdom of God. Instead of accepting the plain sense of Jesus' statement, they ask each other "what rising from the dead might mean" (9:10). Yet, while there is a clear meaning in terms of Jesus' personal bodily resurrection, the disciples' question may not be so obtuse or unbelieving. As Marcus observes, "It is evident from 1 Cor 15:20–28 that this was an issue that exercised early Christians, for here Paul is concerned to establish the correct order of resurrections: first Christ's, as a kind of 'first-fruits'; then, at his 'coming,' that of the people who belong to him (i.e., Christians); finally, perhaps, everyone's (cf. 1 Thess 4:13–17)."[15]

Then the three disciples ask Jesus about the prophet Elijah, why "the scribes say that Elijah must come first?" (Mark 9:11).[16] Jesus explains to them, "Elijah does first come and restore all things" (9:12a). But Jesus interjects a question of His own to these three disciples, "And yet how is it written of the Son of Man that He should suffer many things and be treated with contempt?" (9:12b). Then Jesus says that Elijah already came, "and they did to him whatever they wished, just as it is written of him" (9:13). So, Jesus appears to be saying at least three things in Mark 9:12–13: (1) By redirecting them to the Son of Man and His prophesied suffering and contemptuous treatment, Jesus seems to be chiding their continued focus on Elijah while He the LORD is with them, even as the Father God just audibly rebuked them for the same thing on the mount of transfiguration. With this, Jesus appears to be saying that it may seem strange that Elijah should fare better than the Son of Man. (2) Jesus appears to be saying that the return of Elijah already happened (though see note 17), and he had deferred to the purpose of God as written (see Mark 1:4–9), achieving what he was to do in preceding the Messiah, the LORD (see Mark 1:2–3). (3) Then, Elijah was ill-treated (see Mark 1:14a, 6:14–29), all happening "as it is written."[17]

Jesus' descriptions of the treatment of both "Elijah" and the Messiah, the Son of Man, are in keeping with His fifth inversive and subversive evangelical "defeat" motif. As Marcus notes,

14. Jesus' diffusive tactic of privacy receives additional explanation here. As Marcus notes regarding Jesus' statement, "Its climactic position suggests that it has programmatic significance and that the earlier injunctions may fall under the same limit. Secrecy [privacy is a more accurate term] until the resurrection makes sense because the transfiguration is an anticipation of the resurrection, and the healings about which Jesus has previously forbidden publicity foreshadow the power that will become operative in the world through that event" (*Mark 8–16*, 648).

15. Marcus, *Mark 8–16*, 648.

16. The scribes of whom Peter, James (Jacob), and John speak were evidently basing their view that Elijah precedes the LORD's coming on Malachi 3:1; 4:5.

17. Mark's account may seem to indicate that John the Baptist is "Elijah" himself. However, reading contextually with the parallel accounts in the other three Gospels, we find that John came "in the spirit and power of Elijah" (Luke 1:17; Matt 11:14) but was not Elijah himself. When asked directly if he is Elijah, John the Baptist explicitly answered, "I am not" (John 1:21). Jesus Himself says here (Mark 9:12; Matt 17:11) that Elijah will yet return, that is, before Jesus' second coming.

The scriptural expectation that Elijah will play the forerunner role by restoring all things is played off against the biblical expectation that the Son of Man will suffer, and the resolution is to affirm that Elijah *will* go before the Messiah, but in the way of death rather than in a mode of conventional triumph, "as it has been written concerning him." . . . Elijah himself must be a suffering figure: the servant is not above his master, but shares his fate.[18]

Both the "Elijah" John and Jesus the Son of Man defer to the will of God to suffer "defeat" for the Gospel of the kingdom of God, "as it is written," instead of following the pattern of myth-culture by conforming to the "battle" of the snare of striving (and/or striving to ensnare).

When Jesus and the three disciples have returned to where they had left the other nine, they see that a large crowd has surrounded them, including some scribes who are arguing with the disciples who were left behind (Mark 9:14). The scribes are "battling" with Jesus' followers, evidently striving to ensnare Jesus' disciples in reproaches for their failure to exorcise a demon (Mark 9:18b).[19] When the "entire crowd" sees Jesus (it appears that Jesus' nine disciples did not notice Jesus return, being caught up in their argument with the scribes), they are "amazed" (perhaps Jesus still radiating glory) and run up to greet Him (9:15). Jesus asks the crowd, "What are you discussing with them?" (9:16).

It is interesting that Jesus asks the crowd rather than the disciples this question, perhaps because the crowd noticed Jesus while His own disciples did not. Someone in the crowd answers, telling Jesus that he had brought his son, who is possessed with a spirit that makes him mute and causes seizure-like symptoms, but Jesus' disciples were unable to cast the spirit out (Mark 9:17–18). Jesus answers the man and His disciples saying, "O unbelieving generation, how long shall I be with you? How long shall I put up with you? Bring him to Me!" (9:19). Jesus seems to express His readiness to complete His time with humanity and depart already. His nine other disciples have experienced their first "defeat," out-of-order of myth-culture's pattern and out-of-character of myth. Jesus attributes this defeat to *everyone's* unbelief, including the father's, which in previous healing miracles appears to have been a decisive factor (e.g., Mark 5:40). Unbelief is synonymous with the control of the "chaos-monster" sin in a person, as expressed at the outset of the Gospel account (Mark 1:4–5, 15).

When they bring the boy to Jesus, the spirit in the boy sees Jesus and throws the boy "into a convulsion" so that he falls to the ground, rolling and foaming at the mouth (Mark 9:20). Jesus asks his father how long this has been happening to his son, and the man says, "from childhood" (9:21), adding that the spirit has often thrown the boy into fire and water in order to destroy him. The father pleads with Jesus, saying, "But if You can do anything, take pity on us and help us!" (9:22). Jesus responds,

18. Marcus, *Mark 8–16*, 649–50.

19. Marcus, *Mark 8–16*, 660.

"If You can!," showing His frustration with the father's continued unbelief, his doubt of Jesus' power. And Jesus says, "All things are possible to him who believes" (9:23). At once the boy's father "cried out" saying, "I do believe, [Lord]; help my unbelief" (9:24). Clearly, Jesus has told the father that he must defer to Him, believing that Jesus is Lord for help in trouble, and the man then explicitly confesses this truth. But the father also acknowledges that he has difficulty deferring to Jesus, to the Lord, and asks for help to defer better. Human incapacity is emphasized here with the need to defer to, to rely upon, the Lord and His power, His will.

Jesus' perspective and will contrast starkly with the human striving "battle" of the scribes, and perhaps also with Jesus' nine disciples who seem to have been "battling" back with the scribes. Similarly, the father of the possessed boy, as well as the crowd, appear to have been in "battle" with unbelief. The conflict with the sin of unbelief is a "battle" that Jesus does not struggle with. Rather, and in keeping with His unique "defeat" motif here, Jesus affirms "defeat" before God that enables victory over the sin of unbelief. Jesus asserts complete faith in God's omnipotence (Mark 9:23). "The father of the epileptic boy is therefore, in this double-mindedness, a perfect symbol for the Christian disciple. Whereas logically faith and unbelief are opposites, in Christian experience they are simultaneous realities; the one who believes is always concurrently involved in a battle against disbelief."[20] The two patterns, of Jesus and of myth-culture, are in conflict within the one who has chosen to follow Jesus, as exemplified by this believing yet unbelieving father.

Jesus, seeing that a crowd is rapidly gathering, "rebukes the unclean spirit" saying, "You deaf and dumb spirit, I Myself command you, come out of him and do not enter him again" (Mark 9:25). After "crying out" the spirit throws the boy into "terrible convulsions" before coming out of him, leaving the boy "so much like a corpse that most of them said, 'He is dead!'" (9:26). But Jesus takes the boy by the hand and "raises him" so that he gets up (9:27). When Jesus comes into the house, His disciples privately ask Him, "Why is it that we could not cast it out?" (9:28). Jesus replies to these men to whom He has given the authority to cast out demons, "This kind cannot come out by anything but prayer [and fasting]" (9:29). This type requires deference to the Father God, taking it to Him in prayer along with fasting. Jesus' deference to the Father during His forty-day fast as He began His ministry comes to mind. It requires not a "battle," but a "defeat" of human strength and initiative, with deference to God rather than striving. In this we see the inversive and subversive fifth narratological motif continue, as well as the inversive and subversive third social-science episode continue.

Mark tells us that Jesus and His disciples went out from there "to go through Galilee," and Jesus "did not want anyone to know about it" (Mark 9:30), continuing His diffusive practice of privacy. But Mark tells us another key reason that Jesus is keeping a "low profile" at this point, "For He was teaching His disciples and telling

20. Marcus, *Mark 8–16*, 663.

them, 'The Son of Man is to be delivered up into the hands of men, and they will kill Him; and when He has been killed, He will rise again three days later'" (9:31). For the second time (see Mark 8:31) in Jesus' inversive and subversive fifth "defeat" motif of the third snare of striving-deference episode, Jesus is explaining that He is deferring to "defeat" according to the will of God, "as it is written," that He must soon suffer, die and rise the third day. Instead of striving, "battling" for the world as the myth-culture expects, and as practiced by Jesus' opponents here, Jesus is accepting "defeat," and deliberately walks toward it. With this statement, among other things, Jesus affirms that He is to be "betrayed into the hands of men," again implying His divine distinction, and also explaining His policy of privacy as He travels. He seems to be attempting to time His death and resurrection just right; not wanting to attract too much attention ahead of schedule, as it were. But Jesus' disciples "did not understand this statement, and they were afraid to ask Him" (9:32).

They arrive at Capernaum and enter "the house" (presumably Simon Peter's), where Jesus asks His disciples, "What were you discussing on the way?" (Mark 9:33). The disciples are silent in the face of Jesus' question because, "they had discussed with one another which of them was the greatest" (9:34). Jesus knows what they discussed "on the way," that they are caught in the snare of striving with each other, in "battle" with each other for pride of place according to the pattern of myth-culture as expected of this fifth motif.

Marcus points out that Mark is probably emphasizing the term "way" here to bring the audience's mind to the two ways, or patterns, being contrasted in the Gospel account:

> This phrase ["on the way"] is immediately repeated for effect in 9:34. . . . This repetition of "on the way" is another instance of Markan irony; God's way, "the way of the Lord," which has been the Gospel's subject from its opening verses (1:1–3) . . . is, as we shall immediately learn (9:35; cf. 10:41–45), a way of selfless service, of putting oneself last, in order that others may be benefited and God's triumph may be announced.[21]

Jesus sits down, calls the twelve, and counsels them to defer to the "defeat" that the LORD God requires of them, saying, "If any one wants to be first, let him be last of all, and servant of all" (Mark 9:35). Jesus then illustrates this lesson on divine deference instead of human striving by taking a child and standing him in their midst. Jesus then receives the child into His arms, saying, "Whoever receives one child like this in my name is receiving Me; and whoever receives Me is not receiving Me, but Him who sent Me" (9:36–37). Embracing the child represents "serving all," making oneself "last of all."

Putting a child first in your life represents willful acceptance of "defeat," deferring to the will of God rather than the desire of humanity inured in the pattern of

---

21. Marcus, *Mark 8–16*, 680.

myth-culture. This deference is "defeat" instead of the striving of the world's "battle" for gain. And when a child is not rejected, but received "in Jesus' name," the recipient is not merely receiving Jesus, but receiving the Father God. Deferring to the child is deferring to Jesus, which is deferring to the Father God, rather than striving to make oneself god to the neglect of children, the neglect of Jesus, the neglect of the Father God. It is a powerful illustration for the evidently ambitious men around Jesus, and for men and women of all times and places.

Then the disciple John says to Jesus, "Teacher, we saw someone casting out demons in Your name, and we tried to hinder him because he was not following us" (Mark 9:38). John's statement again shows that Jesus' disciples are having trouble staying out of the snare of striving, of "battling" with others for pre-eminence in the fifth motif of the mythological pattern. The disciples were actually scandalized by this other man, who was "not following them" yet following Jesus, and they actually "laid a snare" for him, attempting to "hinder" him. That Jesus chose these twelve is going to their heads in the manner of myth-culture. Jesus replies, "Do not hinder him, for there is no one who shall perform a miracle in My name, and be able soon afterward to speak evil of Me" (Mark 9:36).

The disciples are not to attempt to hold a monopoly over the discipleship of Jesus, as if they are now doorkeepers of who can follow Jesus and work in His name. That behavior belongs to the pattern of myth-culture, not the unique, divine, evangelical pattern of Jesus. It is the snare of striving, the prideful "battle" rather than the humble "defeat" that drives such falsely authoritative behavior. The kingdom of God does not operate according to the pattern of myth-culture. Jesus reiterates, "For he who is not against us is for us" (Mark 9:40), suggesting that it is not the permission of humans that gives access to Jesus' kingdom, but rather the call of Jesus and a personal decision ("follow Me" [Mark 1:17–20]).

Jesus continues to counsel His disciples on this theme of divine deference, being great in God's kingdom by serving all rather than striving with and ruling all. He says that a person will be rewarded even just for giving you a cup of water "because of your name as followers of Christ" (Mark 9:41). That is, if a person gives a known follower of Jesus even the smallest gift (if he gives it because he knows the recipient follows Jesus), the giver will be rewarded. Jesus' kingdom is incredibly open and welcoming to all, being entered by the humble ("defeated") rather than the proud ("battling").

Jesus continues to illustrate the deferential, rather than striving, pattern of behavior expected of His followers and accepted by Jesus, saying, "And whoever causes one of these little ones who believe [in Me] to stumble [be scandalized], it would be better for him if, with a heavy millstone hung around his neck, he had been cast into the sea" (Mark 9:42). The LORD Jesus declares that whoever views one of His followers with sameness (as a rival double), scandalizing and being scandalized, striving with and ensnaring in striving, would be better off if he had suffered a terrible demise before he had done that. The follower of Jesus is to make himself "servant of all," "last of all," accepting "defeat." Marcus explicitly identifies Jesus' teaching here as the "ancient motif of the Two Ways, which is found in the OT (Deut 30:19; Ps 1:1–6), early Judaism . . . and nascent Christianity. . . . The 'way of life' is set forth first, with its eschatological reward . . . followed by a description of the 'way of death' and its eschatological punishment."[22]

Jesus then reinforces this counsel toward divine "defeat," deference to the LORD's will, with a triad of warnings for believers in Jesus against scandalizing others, as is typical of the "battle" motif of the pattern of myth-culture. The disciples must also walk in Jesus' "defeat" of the Cross according to His unique, divine, evangelical pattern. Jesus says if your hand, your foot, or your eye causes you to scandalize or be scandalized, it is better to cut them off and enter eternal life, the kingdom of God, crippled, lame or half-blind, than to enter the unquenchable fire of Gehenna (γέεννα, which is the Lake of Fire)[23] "where their worm does not die and the fire is not quenched" (Mark 9:43–48; Isa 66:24). The LORD Jesus describes the final abode of unbelievers, who are resurrected bodily to eternal condemnation in the Lake of Fire (Rev 21:8). Jesus really hammers this warning home, repeating it three different ways, and quoting the prophet Isaiah on the physical, fiery torment of Gehenna. Marcus explains Jesus' tripartite warning as increasingly intentional opposition to the "chaos-monster" sin, to avoid that terrible and eternal judgment:

> "If your *hand* offends you . . . ": Don't *commit* sins! (9:43)
>
> "If your *foot* offends you . . . ": Don't *go anywhere* where you may commit sins! (9:45)
>
> "If your *eye* offends you . . . ": Don't even *think* about committing sins! (9:47)[24]

Finally, Jesus offers one more illustration of the consequential need to walk in His way of the Cross, the way of divine deference instead of the mythological snare of striving; to choose "defeat" instead of "battle." He offers three sayings involving salt: "For everyone will be salted with fire [and every sacrifice will be salted with salt]. Salt is good; but if the salt becomes unsalty, with what will you make it salty again? Have salt in yourselves, and be at peace with one another" (Mark 9:49–50). Jesus is building here on all His previous counsel toward divine deference for those who go in Jesus' name. He contrasts the fire suffered by those in the coming eternal life, those who refuse to have "fire/salt" in them in this mortal life, with those who "have salt/fire in themselves" in this mortal life, and thereby escape the fire of Gehenna. "In the OT and Christian texts," writes Marcus, "fire can have both [destructive and purgative] aspects. . . . The same ambiguity might apply to the fire symbol in our saying; the eschatological

---

22. Marcus, *Mark 8–16*, 694.

23. Gehenna is translated "Hell" here in the NASB, but this is a mistake. Reading the Scriptures contextually, we can see that Gehenna is synonymous with the Lake of Fire, while Hell is synonymous with that compartment of Hades/Sheol holding the souls of unbelievers. Synonyms for Hell in Scripture are Abaddon and the Pit. See Fruchtenbaum's discussion of these terms and locations (*Footsteps*, 737–61).

24. Marcus, *Mark 8–16*, 697.

fire will punish the wicked but refine the righteous."[25] At that time, if a believer in the Gospel of the kingdom loses his saltiness in this life by striving and "battling" for gain, scandalizing and being scandalized—abandoning the deferential way of the Cross in which the believer makes himself last of all and endures the "defeat" of fiery trial in this life—then he is doomed in the next life to fire. Whereas, if a person "has salt/fire in himself," being "at peace with one another" because of deferential behavior when facing the snare of striving, he will live forever in the kingdom of God.[26]

Jesus then gets up and goes out from Capernaum and the Galilee "to the region of Judea, and beyond the Jordan" (Mark 10:1a). Crowds gather around Jesus again, and "according to His custom" He teaches them, continuing to offer good counsel (10:1b). As Jesus was teaching, the Pharisees approach Him to continue the fifth "battle" motif of myth-culture, striving to ensnare Him. Mark says the Pharisees begin "testing Him," questioning Jesus as to "whether it is lawful for a man to divorce a wife" (Mark 10:2). Jesus' response is to ask, "What did Moses command you?" (10:3). The Pharisees respond that Moses permitted a man to write "a certificate of divorce" and send her away (10:4). Jesus replies that Moses only allowed this practice "because of your hardness of heart" (10:5). This statement "implies," says Yarbro Collins, "that divorce is not the will of God but was allowed by Moses only because of the people's stubbornness."[27] In other words, because the people then, and now in Jesus' day, were not committed to divine deference but inured in the snare of striving, being committed to the myth-culture's "battle" rather than the LORD's way of "defeat" (being "servant of all," putting the spouse ahead of oneself [Mark 9:35]), Moses allowed them to practice divorce.

So, Jesus says that a concession was made in the law of Moses that is not God's original intention for marriage. Jesus takes His audience back to His creation of marriage to explain:

> But from the beginning of creation, God "made them male and female" (Gen 1:27; 5:2). "For this cause a man shall leave his father and mother (and shall cleave to his wife), and the two shall become one flesh" (Gen 2:24); consequently they are no longer two, but one flesh. What therefore God has joined together, let no man separate. (Mark 10:6–9)

Jesus demands deference to God's design and purpose for marriage as instituted from the beginning of His creation of humanity, as recorded in the law of Moses in Genesis

25. Marcus, *Mark 8–16*, 698.

26. Given the severity of this passage, it behooves me to comment further on this warning by Jesus. Contextually, observe that it is made to believers of Israel in Him at that time, believing in the Gospel of the kingdom of God, and awaiting that kingdom according to prophecy. This warning does not apply to those who believe today in Jesus, in the Gospel of His grace according to the mystery, first delivered by Jesus to His Apostle Paul directly to all nations, and not through Israel (e.g., Rom 16:25; Eph 2:8–9).

27. Yarbro Collins, *Mark*, 467.

1–2, which Jesus explicitly quotes. As Yarbro Collins remarks, "In the speech of Jesus, 'for this reason' refers to the act of God in creating humanity. It is because God made man and woman as a unit that a man shall cling to his wife."[28] Jesus perfectly defers to the law of Moses, and He expects Israel to also. In deferring to the authority of Scripture during His "test" by the Pharisees, and reasoning logically (presupposition-ally) from the letter of the text, Jesus out-manoeuvres their "snare" in which they were striving to catch Him. It is fascinating to find the topic of marriage and divorce in this fifth motif, in which the mythological world emphasizes "battle" (of the sexes?) and Jesus emphasizes "defeat." And so appropriately, we find "defeat" in marriage in this third episode, in which the myth-culture emphasizes the snare of striving against the LORD's will and one another, while Jesus emphasizes deference to the divine will and to one another.

When Jesus is back "in the house" with His disciples, they privately ask Him again about what He said regarding divorce (Mark 10:10). Jesus responds by describing the practical application of the Scriptures that He quoted, and their logical corollary that He expressed to the Pharisees. He says to His disciples, "Whoever divorces his wife and marries another woman commits adultery against her; and if she herself divorces her husband and marries another man, she is committing adultery" (10:11–12). In other words, according to Jesus, marriage requires the ultimate act of divine deference to the spouse, instead of resorting to the snare of striving. The LORD demands of the husband and wife willful "defeat" by each other instead of "battle" (and Apostle Paul will affirm this for the Church [Eph 5:22–33]).

Mark then tells us that the crowds began bringing their children to Jesus, "so that He might touch them," but His disciples where "rebuking" the children and their parents (Mark 10:13). When Jesus sees His disciples' behavior He is "indignant" and says to them, "Permit the children to come to Me; do not hinder them; for the kingdom of God belongs to such as these" (10:14). The disciples' behavior is particularly shameful, not merely because of their scandalizing (being model-obstacles to) the children and their parents, but because Jesus has just given them extensive instruction to defer to children and not strive against them, within this very same fifth motif and third episode (see Mark 9:33–50). Consistent with Jesus just telling His disciples that "God's kingdom belongs to the children," He told them at that time that if they desire to be great in God's kingdom, they must receive the children in Jesus' name (9:37). Not only that, but Jesus had sternly warned them three times that "whoever scandalizes one of these little ones" would be better off having been drowned in the sea (9:42). "The connection between these two passages," writes Yarbro Collins, "suggests that receiving the kingdom of God as a child means receiving it without the ambition to be a figure of authority, but being content to be 'last of all and servant of all' (Mark 9:33–37)."[29]

---

28. Yarbro Collins, *Mark*, 467.
29. Yarbro Collins, *Mark*, 473.

In light of this context, the disciples' behavior here is astonishingly perverse. So, Jesus repeats His warning to the disciples that, "Whoever does not receive the kingdom of God like a child shall not enter it at all" (Mark 10:15). Jesus again demonstrates to them, as before (9:36), how to treat children deferentially, and so how to enter and be great in the kingdom of God: "And He took [the children] in His arms and began blessing them, laying His hands upon them" (Mark 10:16). Rather than striving against children, "battling" and rejecting them, as the myth-cultural world does according to its pattern, Jesus is willfully "defeated" by children, deferring to them, according to His unique divine pattern.

Jesus has been traveling steadily southward from Galilee toward Jerusalem to fulfill His twice-made prediction of His "defeat" in this fifth motif and third episode (Mark 8:31; 9:31). As He is about to continue that journey a man runs up to Him and kneels before Him, asking, "Good teacher, what shall I do to inherit eternal life?" (Mark 10:17). Jesus responds, "Why do you call me good? No one is good except God alone" (10:18). Jesus seems to be speaking somewhat ironically here, both criticizing the man's sloppy and possibly sycophantic use of the term "good," and yet hinting that the Lord is nevertheless before him. Jesus quickly moves along from this seemingly off-hand jibe, however, and says, "You know the commandments, 'Do not commit adultery, Do not steal, Do not bear false witness,' Do not defraud, 'Honor your father and mother'" (Mark 10:19; Exod 20:12–16; Deut 5:16–20). The man responds to Jesus, "Teacher, I have kept all these things from my youth up" (10:20; notice the term "good" has not been repeated). Jesus looks at the man and "feels love for him," and says, "One thing you lack: go and sell all you possess, and give it to the poor, and you shall have treasure in heaven; and come, [take up the cross, and] follow Me" (10:21). Jesus demands that the man cease his inurement in the snare of striving in the world for gain, that He leave it all behind, and instead defer completely to the Lord, embracing the "defeat" of the way of the cross like Jesus, instead of "battle," and so storing up his treasure in the eternal kingdom of God, by following the unique, divine pattern of Jesus.

At Jesus' words the man's "face fell, and he went away grieving, for he was one who owned much property" (Mark 10:22). Yarbro Collins observes, "The man does not respond in the way that Simon (Peter), Andrew, James, John, and Levi did. . . . On the contrary, he is appalled at Jesus' suggestion and goes away distressed."[30] And now the initial "jibe" that Jesus made to the man that "only God is good" takes on meaning. This Israelite, who does desire the kingdom of God, is nevertheless not following Jesus, following the pattern of the only "good God," and that is his problem. He is walking in the pattern of the myth-culture. The man's own goodness and success in the world, his "gaining the whole world," will not save his life, just as Jesus said at the outset of His fifth "defeat" motif, at the beginning of this third snare-deference episode (Mark 8:36–38). If the Law-abiding rich man will not accept "defeat" with Jesus,

30. Yarbro Collins, *Mark*, 480.

ceasing his "battle" for gain, and taking up his cross and following Jesus, he will lose his soul (8:34–35). Although this man has kept the law of Moses well, and succeeded in the world, he nevertheless remains a doomed sinner (Mark 1:4–8, 15) if he will not receive and follow Jesus. According to the Gospel of the kingdom, faith in Jesus and walking in His pattern faithfully are both required to enter the kingdom.[31]

As the man goes away grieving, Jesus looks around and says to His disciples, "How hard it will be for those who are wealthy to enter the kingdom of God!" (Mark 10:23). The disciples are "amazed" at Jesus' exclamatory statement, but He repeats it saying, "Children, how hard it is to enter the kingdom of God [for those who trust in wealth]!" (10:24). Then, in other words, Jesus says a third time, "It is easier for a camel to go through the eye of a needle than for a rich man to enter the kingdom of God" (10:25). Obviously, that is an impossible feat, and the disciples agree, being "even more astonished" and asking Jesus, "Then who can be saved?" (10:26). Looking at them Jesus says, "With men it is impossible, but not with God; for all things are possible with God" (10:27). In other words, all the human striving and "battling" people do, according to the pattern of myth-culture, will avail them not at all. They must defer to the will of God, the pattern of Jesus Christ, embracing what appears to be "defeat" in this world's view, to win eternal life: "For Jesus, it is God, not human beings, who is in control, even in matters that seem to center on human choices and decisions."[32]

Peter says to Jesus, "Behold, we have left everything and followed You" (Mark 10:28). He seems anxious to distinguish himself from the rich man and show that he and the other disciples have indeed ceased their striving and deferred to God, leaving myth-culture's pattern with its "battle" and accepting supposed "defeat" in the world's view, the "defeat" of the Cross. Leaving all else behind and taking up their crosses, they are following Jesus' divine pattern. Jesus affirms their actions, saying:

> Truly I say to you, there is no one who has left house or brothers or sisters or mother or father [or wife] or children or farms, for My sake and for the Gospel's sake, but that he shall receive a hundred times as much now in the present age, houses and brothers and sisters and mothers and children and farms, along with persecutions; and in the world to come, eternal life. (Mark 10:29–30)

So, Jesus confirms for His followers that there is indeed far superior reward from God, in both this life and the next, for following His pattern instead of the culture's myth-pattern; though the LORD's rewards come only ever "with persecutions" by the myth-culture, the world.

---

31. Thank God that today, because of the revelation of the mystery of His grace, we are saved and secure in Christ apart from works (Rom 3:24, 28; 4:16; 5:1–2; 6:14; 11:6). Certainly, we are to walk in Jesus' unique divine pattern also, however (e.g., Rom 6:15; 13:14). But praise the LORD, this has no bearing on our salvation into the Kingdom of God, into which we have already been transferred by grace through faith (Col 1:13–14), and in which we are secure in Jesus (Rom 8:35–9; Eph 1:13–14; 4:30).

32. Yarbro Collins, *Mark*, 481.

But Jesus, perhaps seeing satisfied looks on His disciples' faces, concludes by saying, "But many who are first, will be last; and the last, first" (Mark 10:31). With this statement Jesus seems to warn once more against comparing rewards with other disciples and other people, falling into the snare of striving once more, as if the pattern of myth-culture could yet be followed while also following Jesus' unique, divine, evangelical pattern (see Mark 9:33–34). Yarbro Collins notes the contrasting rewards of the two patterns in this way: "Many of the rich, who appear to be those to whom the kingdom of God belongs, will *not* enter into it, whereas many of the poor, who seem to be abandoned by God, *will* enter into it."[33] Jesus is repeating in other words, therefore, that to be first in God's kingdom is to defer, embrace "defeat," and make yourself last of all (see Mark 9:35).

Mark tells us that they are "on the road, going up to Jerusalem, and Jesus was walking on ahead of them" (Mark 10:32a). The followers are "amazed" and "fearful" at what Jesus is doing, and so are trailing behind, with Jesus leading them along the way of the Cross; and Jesus takes "the twelve" aside again and tells them for the third time in this fifth "defeat" motif of the third episode "what is going to happen to Him" (10:32b). Jesus says:

> Behold, we are going up to Jerusalem, and the Son of Man will be delivered up to the chief priests and the scribes; and they will condemn Him to death, and will deliver Him up to the Gentiles. And they will mock Him and spit upon Him, and scourge Him, and kill Him, and three days later He will rise again. (Mark 10:33–34; see also 8:31; 9:31)

Jesus has now told His disciples three times, in His inversive and subversive "defeat" motif, that He is deliberately going to His own "defeat" (followed by resurrection victory), instead of "seeking to save His life," as do the heroes of myth-culture in their fifth "battle" motif.

As if James (Jacob) and John, the sons of Zebedee, have not heard Jesus' repeated warnings against the snare of striving, but instead deferring to the Cross—the "defeat" instead of "battle" that results in eternal victory—these two approach Jesus privately with an embarrassingly grasping request, saying, "Teacher, we want You to do for us whatever we ask of You" (Mark 10:35). Jesus says, "What do you want Me to do for you?" (10:36). And they say, "Grant that we may sit in Your glory, one on Your right, and one on Your left" (10:37). This request shows that they have completely missed all that Jesus has been saying and doing. Their minds are still in the pattern of myth-culture, thinking that they can pursue God's kingdom in the same way that gain in the world is achieved. "Their request creates a jarring contrast," writes Yarbro Collins, "with the prediction of Jesus' suffering and death in vv. 33–34 and constitutes the

---

33. Yarbro Collins, *Mark*, 483.

climactic example of the disciples' misunderstanding of (or refusal to accept) Jesus' revelation, in the middle section of the Gospel, that the messiah must suffer."[34]

Jesus responds that, "You do not know what you are asking for" (Mark 10:38a). They are literally ignorant of the inversive and subversive structure of God's kingdom compared with this mythological world's structure. So, Jesus asks them, "Are you able to drink the cup that I drink, or to be baptized with the baptism with which I am baptized?" (10:38b). It is a wonder whether they have appreciated that He is referring to the terrible death He is about to suffer, but they answer, "We are able" (10:39a). And then Jesus says, "The cup that I drink you shall drink; and you shall be baptized with the baptism with which I am baptized" (Mark 10:39b). But the apparent goal of pride of position, that they seek in this bargain, Jesus will not vouchsafe to them, saying, "But to sit on My right or on My left, this is not Mine to give; but it is for those for whom it has been prepared" (Mark 10:40). Perhaps James (Jacob) and John regret their request now, though it is not really a change for them. Jesus has already promised them persecutions and "defeat" if they follow Him.

However, the other ten disciples get wind of the Zebedee brothers' "battling," striving request, and "they began to feel indignant toward James [Jacob] and John" (Mark 10:41), so the "battle" escalates. Jesus then calls them all together and, perhaps more plainly than ever, repeats His continuous teaching and example in His fifth motif and third episode to embrace "defeat" instead of "battle," deference instead of striving, saying:

> You know that those who are recognized as rulers of the Gentiles lord it over them; and their great men exercise authority over them. But it is not so among you, but whoever wishes to become great among you shall be your servant; and whoever wishes to be first among you shall be slave of all. For even the Son of Man did not come to be served, but to serve, and to give His life a ransom for many. (Mark 10:42–45)

Jesus very plainly compares those who are great in this temporary mythological culture, the world, with those who are great in the eternal kingdom of God. Worldly rulers gain the whole world by following the pattern of myth-culture, "battling" and striving with each other and against the LORD, and at each other's expense. Yarbro Collins observes that this saying of Jesus definitively distinguishes the believer's identity from the human's identity in the myth-culture: "As a unit, vv. 42–45 is intended to shape [a believer's] identity both in terms of internal relations and in contrast to the practices of other social groups."[35] Once more, and as the final event of Jesus' fifth "defeat" motif in His unique divine pattern, Jesus emphasizes that even as He Himself came to be willingly "defeated" to serve and save many, any follower of Jesus' pattern must do the same.

---

34. Yarbro Collins, *Mark*, 495.

35. Yarbro Collins, *Mark*, 500.

Social-Science

Social-scientifically, this fifth motif in the third episode is comprised of deference exhibited by Jesus, continuing His unique, divine, evangelical pattern. Jesus' pattern is intermingled with the snare of striving exhibited by Israel's leadership, and especially His own disciples in this motif, continuing the myth-culture's pattern. The social-science lenses of Girard and Malina aid us in perceiving this chiastic bi-pattern.

At this point in the pattern of myth-culture we typically see snare of striving preeminent. However, not so in the Gospel account due to the evangelical pattern here in Jesus Christ. Instead, Jesus exhibits divine deference instead of the snare of striving. Deference in Jesus subverts the snare-of-striving meaning expected of this episode, and inverts the myth-sequence so that this episode also contains a strong anti-scapegoating element.[36]

In Jesus' fifth inversive and subversive "defeat" motif of Mark's account, there are twelve instances of snare of striving (or "battling") behavior, none of which are exhibited by Jesus. These strivings or "battles" take the form of (1) the people, and the disciples themselves, pitting Jesus against others, as if there is or could be rivalry between them (e.g., Jesus vs Elijah); (2) the disciples striving with each other for pre-eminence; (3) the Pharisees striving with Jesus; (4) the disciples striving with little children; (5) a "good" rich man striving with Jesus' criteria for entering the kingdom of God; (6) and the disciples striving against this "defeat" motif of Jesus' pattern, the way of the Cross, and the need to willfully embrace "defeat" as the world (the myth-culture) sees it.

The behavior of the people of Israel in response to Jesus' command and example to reject the "battle" and choose "defeat" to gain eternal life in the kingdom of God can be summarized by the adage, "The problem with living sacrifices is they are always crawling off the altar."[37] Jesus requires deference to the will of God, His pattern instead of myth's, and deference to one another, even and especially to little children. This last form of deference is emblematic according to Jesus. It is both literally necessary to enter God's kingdom, and symbolic of how to enter. Jesus' disciples especially are struggling to understand and walk in the way of the Cross, along which He is physically and spiritually leading them.

This pre-emptive deferential self-sacrifice in which Jesus is engaging, and is modelling to others, not only subverts the snare of striving but unexpectedly inverts the scapegoating that (according to the pattern of myth-culture) should not take place until the next

---

36. As shown in the methodology, while the narratological chiasm is within each episode, involving the switching (inverting) of the two motifs and their meanings, the social-scientific chiasm involves the switching of the entire account's sequence of episodes and their meanings, inverting one and six, two and five, three and four. These two narratological and social-scientific aspects of the inversive and subversive chiastic relation of Jesus' pattern and myth-culture's pattern is demonstrated as we go along.

37. My father is the source of a great many words of wisdom, including this one, and a scholar always happily credits his source.

(fourth) episode. Three times throughout Jesus' fifth "defeat" motif in the third episode, He explicitly describes His coming murder at Jerusalem, and His resurrection three days later. Jesus deliberately journeys south from the Galilee to Jerusalem as He makes these three successive declarations of "defeat," of deference to God's will for the Messiah, the Christ, "as it is written" of Him. But Jesus' actions are not peculiar to Himself. He makes it abundantly clear that anyone who would follow Him in the divine, evangelical pattern, and thereby enter into eternal life in the kingdom of God, must take up His own cross and live according to Jesus' pattern instead of the myth-culture's pattern (e.g., Mark 8:34–38).

GOSPEL According to Mark			
WORLD'S SNARE		JESUS' DEFERENCE	
	8:27–28		
		8:29—9:4	
	9:5–6		
		9:7–9	
	9:10–11		
		9:12–13	
	9:14–18		
		9:19–31	
	9:32–34		
		9:35–37	
Battle	9:38		Defeat
		9:39—10:1	
	10:2		
		10:3–12	
	10:13		
		10:14–21	
	10:22–26		
		10:27–32a	
	10:32b		
		10:32c–34	
	10:35–37		
		10:38–40	
	10:41		
		10:42–45	

		10:46–47	
	10:48a		
		10:48b—11:4	
	11:5		
		11:6–17	
Defeat	11:18		Battle
		11:19–26	
	11:27–28		
		11:29–30	
	11:31–33a		
		11:33b	

TABLE 1C: Snare and Deference, Battle and Defeat

MARK 10:46–11:33: JESUS' "BATTLE"[38]

Narratology

Narratologically, this section of the Gospel account makes up Jesus' sixth "battle" motif, but as is now perhaps expected, it is atypically inversive in sequence and subversive in significance when compared with the pattern of myth-culture. The expected sixth mythological motif of the hero's "defeat" occurs here in the myth-culture's leadership, the opposition to Jesus, so that they continue in the pattern of myth-culture in opposition to Jesus' unique, divine, evangelical pattern. Israel's leadership treat Jesus as though He were a chaos-monster. As He nears Jerusalem, Jesus begins to "battle." In addition to being inversive in sequence, Jesus' "battle" is subversive in significance, having a very different meaning to that of myth-culture.

As mentioned previously, due to Jesus' divine distinction, He is not actually imperiled by opposition in the manner of humans and/or mythological gods. In His "battle" motif, Jesus moves into Jerusalem, the capital city, as a conquering hero, fearlessly full of confidence and authority, despite His stated and intended purpose in being there as laid out in His previous "defeat" motif. While the leadership do intend to defeat Jesus, it is they who will experience the mythologically expected "defeat," right on cue in the myth-pattern.

At this point in the combat pattern of myth-culture, the "defeat" motif is foremost. But at this point in the Gospel account, which contains the unique, divine pattern in Jesus Christ, we instead see the "battle" motif preeminent in Jesus. The expected mythological "defeat" motif predominates only in the religio-political leaders who oppose Jesus. The sequence of the motifs is inverted by Jesus, and He subverts their

---

38. Please refer to appendix 1 for the complete text of Mark for this motif.

significance as well, so that Jesus' "battle" is not like the typical "battle" of myth-culture experienced by the hero-god there.

Mark tells us that Jesus' and His disciples' southward journey along the way of the Cross brings them to Jericho (Mark 10:46a). Jesus' arrival at Jericho at the outset of His sixth "battle" motif may well be intended to evoke Joshua's (itself a Hebrew form of Jesus' name) arrival at Jericho that began the battles and conquest of the Promised Land to establish the LORD's kingdom of Israel (Josh 5–6). (This also occurred at the time of Passover; 5:10.) As Jesus leaves Jericho to continue on to Jerusalem, He is accompanied by His disciples and "a great multitude" (10:46b).

Outside Jericho, "a blind beggar named Bartimaeus" is sitting by the road (Mark 10:46c). This beggar contrasts sharply with the rich man in the previous "defeat" motif, who would not join Jesus' in His "defeat" and deference to the Father's will.[39] When blind Bartimaeus hears that it is "Jesus the Nazarene" who passes by, he begins crying out, saying, "Jesus, Son of David, have mercy on me!" (Mark 10:47). "Many" people in the multitude "sternly tell him to be quiet," but the blind man will not be "defeated." He "battles" on, "crying out all the more, 'Son of David, have mercy on me!'" (10:48). France notes how unusual and new Bartimaeus' statement is, calling Jesus the "Son of David":

> This is the only time in Mark when Jesus is addressed as υἱέ Δαυίδ. . . . The voicing of David's name increases the loading of royal and nationalistic ideology. . . . No other onlooker has interpreted Jesus in messianic (as opposed to merely prophetic) terms in this gospel. . . . His words open up a new phase in the gradual disclosure of Jesus in Mark. For it is now time.[40]

France has observed that this moment represents a shift. With these terms, timing, and location, Jesus marches to "battle" with a "great host" to establish the kingdom of God at Jerusalem. France therefore notes this shift as Jesus' move to a "battle" footing, a "change in the nature of Jesus' activity. Private teaching gives way to public confrontation . . . both Jesus and the religious authorities issue challenges and manoeuvre for position," and Jesus is about to "throw down the gauntlet to the Jerusalem authorities and challenge them to respond."[41]

The blind man himself has had to "battle" with the multitude accompanying Jesus, and his unwavering "battle" meets with success, as Jesus stops and says, "Call him here" (Mark 10:49a). The multitude immediately changes its tune, saying to the blind man, "Take courage, arise! He is calling for you" (10:49b). The blind man casts aside his cloak, which is perhaps his only possession as a beggar, contrasting sharply with the wealthy man previous (Mark 10:22). France also notes this contrast.[42] Blind

39. France, *Gospel of Mark*, 422.
40. France, *Gospel of Mark*, 423.
41. France, *Gospel of Mark*, 426–28.
42. France, *Gospel of Mark*, 422.

beggar Bartimaeus jumps up, and comes to Jesus (10:50), and Jesus asks him, "What do you want Me to do for you?" And he says, "Rabboni (My Master), I want to regain my sight!" (Mark 10:51). Jesus replies, "Go your way, your faith has saved you." Immediately the blind man receives his sight and begins following Jesus on the road (10:52).

So, it is a blind beggar's saving faith in Jesus, the "son of David," that introduces us to the nature of Jesus' "battle" motif, a very different sort of battle than that of myth-culture's pattern. In the face of certain and voluntary "defeat" by God's will, the "battle" of the believer, walking in Jesus' unique, divine, evangelical pattern is to have unwavering faith in God to save him. Like Jesus, the believer must practice divine deference instead of falling into the human snare of striving, "crying out all the more" to Jesus when opposed (see Mark 11:22).

Jesus and His disciples approach Jerusalem from the east, and "at Bethphage and Bethany, near the Mount of Olives," Jesus sends two of His disciples on ahead (Mark 11:1). Jesus instructs His two messengers, saying:

> Go into the village opposite you, and immediately as you enter it, you will find a colt tied there, on which no one yet has ever sat; untie it and bring it here. And if anyone says to you, "Why are you doing this?" you say, "The LORD has need of it"; and immediately he will send it back here. (Mark 11:2–3)

Jesus' two disciples go ahead and find the colt tied at a door outside in the street, just as Jesus said, and they untie it (Mark 11:4). France notes here an allusion to a messianic prophecy in Genesis 49:10–11.[43] Again, as Jesus suggested, however, before they can make their way back some bystanders say to them, "What are you doing, untying the colt?" (11:5). Remembering Jesus' instructions, the two disciples answer as Jesus had commanded, saying, "the LORD has need of it," and the bystanders give them permission to take the colt (Mark 11:6).

As observed from the first verses of Mark, Jesus' identification, and here His self-identification, as the unique, eternal LORD Himself, is critical. "The κύριος [LORD] has been variously interpreted as God ('it is needed on divine service')," writes France, "to reflect the regular Jewish use of the phrase as a divine title. In that case the password asserts that the donkey is needed for God's service, a bold claim by Jesus for the significance of his own arrival in Jerusalem."[44] And in this event, Jesus continues, unexpectedly according to the sixth motif of myth-culture's pattern, to meet with success instead of defeat. He "battles" onward toward Jerusalem, now with a colt to ride upon and surrounded by a great throng of Israelites.

The two disciples bring the colt to Jesus, putting their own garments upon it, and Jesus rides the colt (Mark 11:7). Then many people in the multitude spread their garments in the road before Jesus, while others spread "leafy branches which they had cut from the fields" (11:8). While this event is often referred to as Jesus' "triumphal

---

43. France, *Gospel of Mark*, 431.
44. France, *Gospel of Mark*, 432.

entry" into Jerusalem, Jesus' entry is not a scene of great triumph, so that while it is no "defeat" as expected in myth-culture, it is not a "victorious entry" either. Jesus is there to do "battle," and approaches on the foal of a donkey rather than a war horse. All of this is out-of-character from the myth-cultural expectations.

As He approaches, Jesus' multitude goes before Him and follows after "crying out," saying, "Hosanna ('Save us now')![45] Blessed is He who comes in the Name of the LORD (Ps 118:25–26); Blessed is the coming kingdom of our father David [that comes in the Name of the LORD]; Hosanna in the highest!" (Mark 11:9–10). In such (unusual, unmythological) pomp Jesus enters Jerusalem and comes into the Temple in Zion, in Jerusalem (11:11a). And after "looking all around" Jesus departs "for Bethany with the twelve, since it is already late" (11:11b). France describes Jesus' behavior here as "reconnaissance for the next day"[46] in preparation for His "battle" with the religio-political leaders of Israel.

The next day, Jesus departs from Bethany with His disciples to return to Jerusalem, and becomes hungry (Mark 11:12). He sees a fig tree from a distance that is "in leaf," so He goes to see if there is any fruit on it. Finding nothing but leaves, "for it was not the season for figs" (11:13), Jesus says to the tree, "May no one ever eat fruit from you again!" and His disciples were listening (11:14). As becomes clear as we read through the remainder of Jesus' fifth "battle" motif (Mark 11), and on into chapter 12 in the seventh motif and fourth episode, Jesus' prophetic judgment of the fig tree is also and actually a prophetic judgment on Jerusalem (the city and mountain of the LORD) and the house of Judah that govern it, which are all symbolized by the fig tree, with its lack of fruit and its withered leaves.[47]

As France observes, "The withering of the fig tree . . . conveys in pictorial form an equally vehement repudiation of the status quo. . . . It points forward to the radical teaching of chapter 13 on the terminal decline and replacement of the Jerusalem régime, focused in the failure and the coming dissolution of the temple worship."[48] Once again, the "defeat" does not belong to Jesus in His sixth motif but is (or soon will be) His opponents' "defeat" in this motif, as expected of those who follow the myth-culture's pattern, those who are rejecting their Christ, the Messiah. Once again it is

---

45. France, *Gospel of Mark*, 433.

46. France, *Gospel of Mark*, 442.

47. See Jeremiah 8:1–22, to which Jesus evidently alludes here in Mark 11:13–14, directly referencing Jeremiah 8:13: "I will surely consume them, saith the LORD: there shall be no grapes on the vine, *nor figs on the fig tree*, and the leaf shall fade; and the things that I have given them shall pass away from them." Luke also cites Jeremiah 8:12 in this moment, as "the time of their visitation" (Luke 19:44) in which "they will be cast down." Also see the result of Jesus' curse in Mark 11:20, which is also stated in Jeremiah 8:13. Jesus actually quotes Jeremiah 7:11 in Mark 11:17, concerning how Judah has turned Jerusalem's Temple into a "robbers' den," suggesting that Jesus has Jeremiah 7–8 in mind as He engages in His 'battle' motif in Jerusalem. The LORD Jesus' arrival in Jerusalem signals Israel's destruction, because "they have rejected the Word of the LORD" (Jer 8:9b).

48. France, *Gospel of Mark*, 428.

Jesus' opponents who continue in the pattern of myth-culture, while Jesus "battles" on toward victory in His own unique pattern.

Jesus and His disciples enter Jerusalem again, and go into the Temple. Jesus begins "casting out those who are buying and selling in the Temple, and overturning the tables of the money-changers and the seats of those who are selling the doves" (Mark 11:15). Jesus also prohibits everyone from carrying vessels of any kind through the Temple (Mark 11:16). The LORD Jesus engages in physical "battle" against the turning of the LORD's house into a business, and succeeds, rather than meeting "defeat" as in the myth-culture's pattern. Jesus explains His actions by again quoting Scripture, counselling the people of Israel, saying, "Is it not written, 'My house shall be called a house of prayer for all the nations?' But you have made it a 'robbers' den'" (Mark 11:17; Isa 56:7; Jer 7:11).

France observes, "Those who heard might have reflected that Jeremiah's sermon went on to predict the destruction of the temple (7:12–15), and that that prediction was fulfilled soon after; Jesus will soon be making the same prediction (13:2)."[49] Jesus clearly has Jeremiah chapters 7–8 in mind (see note 534) as He takes His actions against the symbolic fig tree and the Temple corruption by Jerusalem's leadership. With Jeremiah, Jesus declares their looming "defeat" and ruin. With Jesus' curse on the symbolic fig tree and prophetic actions and words in the Temple, His opponents fulfill the sixth "defeat" motif of the pattern of myth-culture, in the expected sequence and meaning, while Jesus continues to fulfill His inversive and subversive divine, evangelical pattern instead. France concludes:

> Both actions claim a unique status and authority for Jesus, and neither is cal-
> culated to win the goodwill of the religious authorities; a direct challenge to
> Jesus' credentials will quickly follow (11:27–33). . . . In presenting himself as
> Jerusalem's messianic "king," Jesus has in effect already placed himself above
> the Sanhedrin as the ultimate authority in the holy city. . . . None of these texts
> [Ezek 37:26–28, 40–48; Zech 6:12–13; 14:21; Mal 3:1–4] is directly alluded
> to in Mark's wording, but they would be likely to occur to an observer with
> a reasonable knowledge of the OT and of current messianic expectation. . . .
> Seen in that light, this was not an attempt at short-term reform of the system
> but a symbolic declaration of eschatological judgment.[50]

The "chief priests and the scribes" hear what Jesus is saying and doing in the Temple, and they (yet again) "began seeking how to destroy Him" (Mark 11:18a). Mark tells us their reason—though it is quite clear from the context as well—is because, "They were afraid of Jesus, for all the multitude was astonished at His teaching" (11:18b). The myth-cultural leadership of Israel is losing the support of the people, who are going over to Jesus instead. Judea's leadership is being "defeated" by Jesus, continuing their pattern of myth-culture, while Jesus "battles" on victoriously, continuing His unique pattern.

---

49. France, *Gospel of Mark*, 446.
50. France, *Gospel of Mark*, 428, 438.

Mark tells us that whenever evening came, Jesus and His disciples would go out of the city of Jerusalem and then come back again in the morning (Mark 11:19). So, Jesus evidently "battled" daily in the Temple for several days. When they pass by the cursed fig tree the following morning, "they see the fig tree withered from the roots up" (11:20; see Jer 8:13 and note 534). Peter is reminded of what Jesus had said to it before, and says, "Rabbi, behold, the fig tree which You cursed has withered" (11:21). Jesus answers, saying to them all, "Have faith in God" (11:22). And Jesus continues, saying, "Truly I say to you, whoever says to this mountain, 'Be taken up and cast into the sea,' and does not doubt in his heart, but believes that what he says is going to happen, it shall be granted him" (11:23). France notes that Jesus is teaching verbal deference to the LORD as the victorious "weapon" of the Christ-follower's "battle": "It is Jesus' powerful word, not coincidence, which has destroyed the tree, and the following verses will take up the theme of God's power operating dramatically through a human word."[51]

Though the LORD Jesus seems to be expressing a general principle to live by as part of His unique evangelical pattern, His example of "this mountain" which they are looking at from the Mount of Olives, which is Zion, Jerusalem, and the house and temple of the LORD, is clearly not chosen arbitrarily. Jesus is still operating in the context of fulfilling Jeremiah 7–8. Jesus is connecting His curse on the fig tree with a curse on "this mountain," Zion, which is to be "taken up and cast into the sea." It will be "cast out of the LORD's sight" (Jer 7:15), and "snatched away" (Jer 8:13) into exile (Jer 8:19).

The AD 70 destruction of Jerusalem and the Temple, and the exile of the Jews, is clearly depicted on the Arch of Titus (ca. AD 82; on the *via Sacra*, Rome). Judah and Jerusalem are to be utterly "defeated" and destroyed, as was done to Ephraim and Shiloh where the Tabernacle rested beforehand (Jer 7:11–15). As the chief priests and scribes plot Jesus' defeat, it is they that are "defeated" here by Jesus, inverting and subverting myth-culture's pattern. Jesus "battles" by declaring the fulfillment of the prophecies of the LORD through Jeremiah, rather than the means of "battle" employed by myth-culture's heroes.

Jesus also continues His good counsel, in this sixth motif, that His unique, evangelical pattern's "battle" is won by faith in God (see Mark 10:52). It is unwavering, undoubting faith that saves (Mark 11:23). Jesus says, "Therefore I say to you, all things for which you pray and ask, believe that you [received] them, and they shall be granted you" (11:24). This divine deference is the means for "battle" for the believer in Jesus: "What Jesus has just done is a model for how true believers may also draw on the power of God. For those who have faith the impossible is achievable."[52] Continuing His counsel on how to pray, according to the Gospel of the kingdom for Israel, and through Israel for the nations, Jesus says, "Whenever you stand praying, forgive, if you have anything against anyone; so that your Father also who is in heaven may forgive you your transgressions. [But if you do not forgive, neither will your Father who is in

51. France, *Gospel of Mark*, 447.
52. France, *Gospel of Mark*, 448.

heaven forgive your transgressions]" (Mark 11:25–26). So, Jesus' unique evangelical "battle" is won (*inter alia*) not merely by faith in Jesus, but forgiving your enemies, which is very unmythological behavior. God gives victory in "battle" to the believing and forgiving person. Jesus' sixth "battle" motif is indeed subversive in meaning in relation to myth-culture's "battle" motif.

Jesus and His disciples enter Jerusalem again, and as Jesus walks in the Temple, "the chief priests, and scribes, and elders" come to Him (Mark 11:27). France states, "[Jesus] has thrown down the gauntlet, and now it will be taken up, first by the full 'panel' of Sanhedrin authorities."[53] As they have been plotting how to destroy Jesus (see Mark 11:18) since He began His "battle" in the Temple, the question they now ask Jesus seems designed to catch Jesus in what they will define as blasphemy, so that they can have a supposed justification to destroy Him. Israel's leaders say to Jesus, "By what authority are You doing these things, or who gave You this authority to do these things?" (Mark 11:28).

Jesus' "battle" is not over yet, and neither is their "defeat." Jesus responds by saying, "I will ask you one question, and you answer me, and then I will tell you by what authority I do these things" (Mark 11:29). So, Jesus asks His question, "Was the baptism of John from heaven, or from men? Answer Me" (11:30). Jesus knows that He has defeated them with this question, and He has also very cleverly answered their question implicitly with His own question, without "incriminating" Himself in their eyes by explicitly telling them the truth about His identity and resultant authority. Jesus implies that His authority is from heaven, just as was John's.

The chief priests, scribes and elders reason amongst themselves, very aware of their "defeat," saying, "If we say, 'From heaven,' He will say, 'Then why did you not believe him?' But shall we say, 'From men'?" (Mark 11:31–32a). In short, Jesus' question has silenced them and their attempt to defeat Jesus. Instead, they are "defeated" as expected in the sixth motif, in accordance with the pattern of myth-culture's sequence. Meanwhile, Jesus "battles" them successfully, not in keeping with myth, but in keeping with His own unique, divine, evangelical pattern. Mark tells us of the religio-political leaders of Israel here, that "they were afraid of the multitude, for all considered John to have been a prophet indeed" (11:32b).

Finally, the leaders, knowingly lying and willfully unbelieving, say, "We do not know." So, Jesus says, "Neither will I tell you by what authority I do these things" (Mark 11:33). Of course, Mark has suggested that the people know, and that even those religio-political leaders know, that Jesus performs His miraculous deeds and counsels by means of authority from Heaven. But the leaders suppress the truth in their unrighteousness (see Jer 7:28; 8:8–9), following the pattern of myth-culture rather than the pattern of God lived by Jesus. France concludes, "The cumulative effect of this sequence of controversy is to leave the reader with the impression of Jesus

---

53. France, *Gospel of Mark*, 451.

locked in combat with a wide coalition of the most influential people in Jerusalem, but holding his own and ultimately having the last word."[54]

Social-Science

Social-scientifically, this inversive sixth "battle" motif of Jesus (and "defeat" motif for the religio-political leaders of Israel) continues to be comprised of divine deference exhibited by Jesus, continuing His unique evangelical pattern, intermingled with the snare of striving exhibited by the other humans around Him, and especially the leadership of Israel in this sixth motif, that concludes the third deference-striving episode, continuing the myth-culture's pattern. The social-science lenses of Girard and Malina aid us in perceiving this chiastic bi-pattern.

At this point in the pattern of myth-culture, we typically continue to see snare of striving preeminent. However, not so in the Gospel account due to the evangelical pattern here in Jesus Christ. Instead, Jesus exhibits divine deference in place of snare of striving, in opposition to those who embody the pattern of myth-culture around Jesus. Divine deference in Jesus continues to subvert the snare-of-striving meaning expected of this third episode, and continues to invert the myth-culture's sequence, so that this episode also contains a strong anti-scapegoating element as well.

There are five instances of the snare of striving in this sixth motif of the third episode. All five instances are not found in Jesus, but people around Jesus. Jesus continues to be all divine deference here, just as in the fifth motif. And it is amazing that although this is Jesus' "battle" motif, it is so subversive of the typical myth-meaning that there is no snare of striving on Jesus' part in His "battle." He is easily victorious in all His "battles"; opposition simply melts away every time.

The first exhibit of being caught in the snare of striving is many people in the multitude following Jesus striving against the blind beggar, Bartimaeus, sitting by the road from Jericho to Jerusalem (Mark 10:46–52). Bartimaeus cries out for Jesus to have mercy on him, and many people "sternly tell him to be quiet." The man is dauntless and "cries out all the more" to Jesus. Only when Jesus stops and tells the people to call the blindman to Him do they *volte-face* and encourage the blindman in his plea. Jesus defers to the will of God to save this man, halting His march toward Jerusalem to heal him, and defers to the man's request for sight because of his great faith. Bartimaeus is the first onlooking Israelite to openly declare Jesus as the Messiah (of course, Peter first acknowledges Jesus to be the Christ), and the first Israelite altogether, to identify Jesus as the "son of David." And Jesus replies, "Your faith has saved you."

The second instance of snare of striving is in the owners (or perhaps the neighbors of the owners) of the unridden colt near Bethphage and Bethany, near the Mount of Olives overlooking Jerusalem (Mark 11:1–7). Jesus anticipates that His two disciples

---

54. France, *Gospel of Mark*, 451.

will encounter opposition when they go to borrow this colt for His "victorious" procession into Jerusalem, so He gives them a "password" that He knows will appease the owners (and/or their neighbors), which is "The LORD has need of it." While these "bystanders" initially strive with the disciples over taking the colt, when the disciples say, "The LORD has need of it," they defer to the LORD's need. Jesus is not striving against the people with the colt. He is deferring to the will of God, and so do those with the colt, fulfilling Israelite prophecy that Mark quotes in 11:9–10.

The third occurrence of snare of striving in this sixth motif in the third episode is found in the chief priests and scribes, who are livid at Jesus for casting their roaring business out of the Temple (Mark 11:15–18). As before, they are "seeking how to destroy Him" for what He is saying and doing with respect to their profiteering from the Temple worship. But they proceed carefully against Jesus, because "they are afraid of Him, for all the multitude is astonished at His teaching." Jesus pays them no mind, however, but carries on deferring to His Father's will, "battling" victoriously against their abuses of His house.

The fourth occurrence of snare of striving is again in the chief priests, scribes and elders who approach Jesus in the Temple to enact an attempt to catch Jesus in His words, to justify destroying Him as planned (Mark 11:27–28). They demand to know "by what authority" Jesus says and does what He says and does, and "who gave Him such authority." As we soon find out, though, and as we know from previous encounters between Jesus and these leaders of Israel, they already know the answer that both Jesus and the people of Israel give to those questions. So, the Jewish leadership do not genuinely seek the answer, but rather the opportunity to accuse Jesus of blasphemy when He answers it.

Rather than engaging in the snare of striving with these men over His identity and authority, however, Jesus "battles" them in another unexpected way. He proposes that they answer His question, and then, if they answer, He will answer theirs. Jesus then asks them whether John's baptism was from heaven or from men, from God or from humans. Jesus shows here, implicitly though very clearly, what His answer is to their question, while also exposing their evil motives in asking Him their question. In answering this way, with a revelatory question of His own, Jesus defers to God's will and purpose without giving them opportunity to condemn Him. Simply by asking that question of the leaders, Jesus wins the "battle" decisively, and is undefeated by them.

The fifth and final instance of striving, a continuation of the last, is these religio-political leaders of Judea willfully avoiding acknowledgement of the truth (Mark 11:31–33a). They know they are beaten by Jesus' question, being unable to answer either way without endangering themselves. Jesus defers to the Father God by answering them without answering them, clearly indicating that His own authority is from heaven, from His Father, as was John the Baptist's. The leaders already knew this, but refuse to accept it, and yet will not now admit their unbelief openly because "they are afraid of the multitude," who believed in John and believe in Jesus. So, they finally say, "We do not know," and Jesus replies that He will not answer their question then either, even though He already has, very cleverly.

Those "heroes" of the myth-culture are "defeated" as expected in this sixth motif of the pattern of myth, while Jesus is not, but "battles" victoriously and unexpectedly, according to His unique, evangelical pattern. The religio-political leaders of Israel engage in the snare of striving, as expected by myth-culture's pattern, while Jesus does not. Jesus remains all divine deference, fulfilling the purpose of God and the needs of His people Israel. Throughout, Jesus makes explicit reference to Jeremiah 7–8 and Isaiah 56 in His words and actions in this sixth motif, and somehow "battles" without being ensnared in striving against the opposition. He meets with immediate victory in all His forays, contrary to myth-culture, and certainly meets no "defeat," also contrary to myth's pattern.

Jesus' divine deference according to His unique, evangelical pattern is not only subversive of the third snare-of-striving episode of myth-culture's pattern, however, but inversive of the fourth scapegoating episode as well. As in the previous fifth motif, Jesus' sixth motif that concludes the third snare-deference episode does not see Him being scapegoated by the people or the leadership of Israel (yet), and Jesus certainly does not scapegoat others. Jesus walks deliberately to His death and resurrection in the fifth and sixth motifs. Far from being hated by the mob or defeated and captured by the "heroes" or "villains" of the myth-culture of Israel (the leadership), Jesus boldly enters Jerusalem and the Temple, being welcomed like a victorious conqueror by the people, and is untouchable by Israel's leaders. Jesus is hailed by the people as the LORD and the king, in lineage from David (Mark 11:8–11). In all this, Jesus inverts the next intended and expected scapegoating episode and its myth-cultural meaning.

By the time Jesus enters the following fourth episode, in which He is expected (according to the myth-culture) to be scapegoated by the heroes (if He is the villain), or engage in scapegoating of others *as* the hero (if He is the hero-god), Jesus has preemptively redefined that fourth scapegoating episode of myth-culture, by means of His anticipatory inversion of it in this third snare of striving episode. And this snare of striving episode has been successfully subverted by Jesus' divine deference, as we have now seen. He will complete His conquest of the scapegoating episode in the upcoming fourth episode, by subverting scapegoating there with His divine deliverance. Thus, the chiastic bi-pattern of the Gospel account will reach its apex, as the LORD Jesus overcomes this world, with its pattern of myth-culture, at the Cross.

8

Episode 4

Mark 12:1–14:52: Scapegoat and Deliverance

Scapegoat	Deliverance
"It is expedient for you that one man die for the people, and that the whole nation not perish" (John 11:50)	"The Son of Man did not come to be served, but to serve, and to give His life a ransom for many" (Mark 10:45)

OVERVIEW

After Jesus' final arrival in Jerusalem prior to His death, His preparation "half" of His unique pattern is complete, and His fulfillment "half" begins. Jesus' unique, divine, evangelical structure parallels the problem and solution "halves" of the myth-culture's pattern. In the Gospel account, this second "half" continues the chiastic bi-pattern, beginning with the fourth episode of mythological scapegoating of Jesus, by everyone around Jesus, concurrent with the inversive and subversive divine deliverance from the sins of the whole world (1 John 2:2), performed by Jesus.

The fourth episode begins with Jesus' parable of the Lord of the Vineyard and His scapegoated Son (table c; figure 1). Jesus is still speaking with the chief priests, scribes and elders (the vine-growers of the parable; the tenant-farmers, or stewards of Israel) who questioned Jesus' authority while He was in the Temple. Social-scientifically, the episode focuses on the matter of scapegoating, or the salvific human sacrifice of another to save one's cosmos from chaos, and Jesus' opposition to it *via* divine deliverance, laying down His own life, the Father God's only Son's life, to save His sinful children (Mark 2:17; 10:45). The fourth episode ends with Jesus' address to the lynch mob—sent from the chief priests, scribes and elders of Israel—that has come to arrest Jesus as their scapegoat.

As said of the three preceding episodes, the first and last verses of the fourth episode are selected based upon their positions at the beginning and end of both the content of the next two combat myth motifs, the seventh and eighth, as well as the scapegoating and divine deliverance content of the fourth episode; myth-culture's pattern intermingled with Jesus' unique, divine pattern. The expected combat myth motifs of episode four are the seventh "enemy ascendant" and eighth "hero recovers," in that order. In keeping with Jesus' unique evangelical pattern thus far, in this fourth scapegoat-deliverance episode these two myth-motifs are found out of typical order (or inversive) in Jesus, but in the correct mythological order in Jesus' opponents. Not only are the motifs inversive in Jesus, but just as in the three episodes previous, Jesus subverts the mythological significance of the "hero's recovery" and the "enemy's ascendance."[1]

Antithetical to the two mythological motifs of this episode, Jesus' seventh "hero's recovery" motif occurs in first position, and in the form of Jesus' prediction of the coming victory of "the rejected stone" (Mark 12:10–11), which contextually is clearly Jesus Himself. In His unique evangelical pattern, Jesus' inversive and subversive form of the motif is like those before it. In the third episode, we saw that instead of myth-culture's "defeat" motif, Jesus taught divine deference to "defeat" in the Way of the Cross. Here in the fourth episode, instead of myth-culture's "hero's recovery," Jesus employs biblical prophecy to predict the result of His resurrection, which is a "recovery" that involves the establishment of His kingdom, the kingdom of God.[2]

Then, Jesus' eighth "enemy's ascendance" motif occurs out of the sequence expected of myth-culture, concluding the fourth episode. When Jesus no longer describes His own post-crucifixion recovery, and the establishment of His kingdom on earth from Jerusalem (the seventh motif), He begins the eighth inversive and subversive motif by telling of the ascendance of the Enemy, starting with the approaching total destruction of Jerusalem and her Temple, as well as the great Tribulation that His people Israel will undergo. Finally, regarding their present time, Jesus tells His disciples that His own time has come to suffer death, and so the Enemy's hour of ascendance has come. The fourth episode ends with Jesus finally being arrested by a lynch-mob sent from the religio-political authorities, the leaders of Israel.

---

1. Jesus' "hero's recovery" comes out of sequence in first position (the two motifs are separated by a bold black line in table 1D), and not in keeping with the expected mythological form, and is found in Mark 12:1–44. Jesus' "enemy's ascendance" comes second, concluding the scapegoat-deliverance episode, and is found in Mark 13:1—14:52.

2. E.g., Stein, *Mark*, 537.

GOSPEL According to MARK			
WORLD'S SCAPEGOATING		**JESUS' DELIVERANCE**	
Enemy Ascendant		12:1–2	Hero Recovers
	12:3–5		
		12:6	
	12:7–8		
		12:9–11	
	12:12–15a		
		12:15b–17	
	12:18–23		
		12:24–7	
	12:28		
		12:29–44	
Hero Recovers		13:1–37	Enemy Ascendant
	14:1–2		
		14:3	
	14:4–5		
		14:6–9	
	14:10–11		
		14:12–42	
	14:43–47		
		14:48–49	
	14:50–52		
TABLE 1D: Scapegoating and Deliverance, Enemy Ascendant and Hero Recovers			

MARK 12:1–44: JESUS' "HERO'S RECOVERY"[3]

Narratology

Narratologically, this section of the Gospel account is comprised of Jesus' seventh "hero recovers" motif, but inversive in sequence and subversive in significance when compared with the pattern of myth-culture. The expected mythological motif of "enemy ascendant" does predominate here in Israel's leadership, the opposition to Jesus, but not in Jesus Himself. At this point in the combat myth, the "enemy ascendant" motif is foremost. But at this point in the Gospel account, which contains the evangelical pattern in Jesus Christ, we instead see the "hero recovers" motif preeminent in Jesus. Not only is the sequence of the motifs reversed, however, but their significance as well. Jesus' "heroic recovery" is not like the typical "hero's recovery" of myth-culture experienced by the hero-god there. This seventh inversive and subversive "hero recovers" motif begins with Jesus still speaking with the chief priests, scribes

---

3. Please refer to appendix 1 for Mark's complete text of this motif.

and elders in the Temple precinct in Jerusalem, who had approached Him to publicly question Him, and hopefully undermine His authority (see Mark 11:27–33), but they are unsuccessful. Jesus now begins to speak to the religio-political leaders of Judea "in parables" (Mark 12:1a). Stein notes that this parable that Jesus offers is clearly meant as an answer to the question of the source of Jesus' authority.[4] He starts by quoting Isaiah 5:2 about a man who built a vineyard, rented it out to tenant farmers, and left "on a journey" (12:1b). Jesus says that at harvest time, the owner of the vineyard sent a slave to the tenant farmers (vine-growers) to receive some of the produce of the vineyard (12:2). But the tenant vine-growers took the owner's slave, "beat him, and sent him away empty-handed" (12:3). The lord of the vineyard sent another slave whom the tenant vine-growers treated similarly to the first, [and cast stones at him] (12:4). The third servant the lord sent was killed by the tenant farmers, and they continued thereafter to beat and/or kill many more messengers sent from the lord of the vineyard (12:5). Jesus then says to the religio-political leaders that the lord of the vineyard had one more person, a beloved son, to send. The owner sent his son last of all, saying, "They will respect my son" (12:6). But when the tenant farmers saw the lord's son approaching, they said to each other, "This is the heir; come, let us kill him, and the inheritance will be ours!" (12:7). And they took the lord's son, says Jesus, and those tenant vine-growers killed the lord's son, and threw his body out of the vineyard (12:8).

The man who owns and built the vineyard is explicitly the LORD Himself, and the vineyard is Israel, as understood from the context of Isaiah 5:1–7, to which Jesus explicitly alludes with His quotation of Isaiah 5:2. Stein affirms these "allegorical analogies . . . a man = God; the vineyard = Israel; and the tenants = the leaders of Israel: the chief priests, scribes, and elders . . . servants = the prophets (12:2–5); beloved son = Jesus, the Son of God (12:6–11); and killing the son = the crucifixion of Jesus, the Son of God (12:7–8)."[5] Jesus has told Israel's leaders a paraphrastic story about themselves. But more broadly, it is about the history of Israel's leaders' reception of the LORD's servants, the prophets, and then their reception of the LORD's own Son, Jesus Himself, whom they are about to crucify.

In Jesus' parable to the religio-political leaders of Israel, we see not Jesus' "enemy ascendant," though they certainly attempt to make themselves ascend through terrible acts of evil against their LORD and His servants, and finally His Son also. Rather, it is the LORD Himself who is ascendant, despite the evil actions of His unfaithful tenants. That is, the Lord of the Vineyard of Israel has a "hero's recovery" in the face of seeming defeat by His enemies. This is evident since Jesus next describes His "hero's recovery" despite His enemies' supposed victory, so that it is Jesus' enemies whose enemy is ascendant. In this way, the chief priests, scribes and elders of Israel continue to fulfill the pattern of myth-culture, while Jesus continues His chiastic, unique, divine, evangelical pattern.

4. Stein, *Mark*, 530.

5. Stein, *Mark*, 534–35.

After finishing the parable, Jesus rhetorically asks the religio-political leaders before Him, "What will the owner (lord) of the vineyard do? He will come and destroy the vine-growers, and will give the vineyard to others" (Mark 12:9). Stein writes concerning this prophecy of Jesus, "The destruction of the temple, alluded to in Jesus' cleansing of the temple (Mark 11:15–19) and the clear prophecy of its destruction in 13:1–37, was fulfilled in AD 70 and came upon not only the leaders of the nation but the people of Israel as well."[6] Jesus bases His "heroic recovery" conclusion on a prophecy of the Hebrew Bible (Old Testament), saying to Israel's leaders:

> Have you not even read this Scripture: "The stone which the builders rejected,
> This became the chief corner *stone*; This came about from the LORD, And it is
> marvelous in our eyes"? (Mark 12:10–11; Ps 118:22–23)

With this quotation Jesus expresses confidence that it is the religio-political leaders' enemy that is ascendant, not Jesus' enemy. Jesus claims a "hero's recovery," though not of the sort expected by myth-culture's pattern. And the religio-political leader's enemy who is ascending here is the Lord of the Vineyard, the LORD of Israel, whom Mark makes clear is Jesus and His Father.

Stein remarks on how Jesus' quotation points out the irony of the situation, in that while the religio-political leaders of Israel willfully reject the Stone, it is also the LORD's doing, which is "marvellous in our eyes": "The rejection of the stone was, ironically enough, ultimately the Lord's doing."[7] This duality affirms the presence of the two opposing yet unfolding patterns in the Gospel account. None of this meaning appears to be lost on the chief priests, scribes and elders listening to Jesus in the Temple at Jerusalem, because they are immediately "seeking to seize Him; and yet they feared the multitude" (Mark 12:12a). Mark tells us, "they understood that Jesus had spoken the parable against them." But because they feared the people, "they left Him, and went away" (12:12b).

But Israel's seditious "tenant vine-growers" are not done attempting to scapegoat the LORD's Heir of the vineyard of Israel. They evidently intend to fulfill (and are bound to fulfill) the parable, and the prophecy from Isaiah, that Jesus has just spoken against them. They send some of "the Pharisees and Herodians to Jesus, in order to trap Him in a statement" (Mark 12:13). They come to Jesus with flattery, nevertheless "the content of their flattery is true."[8] They say, "Teacher, we know that You are truthful, and defer to no one; for you are not partial to any, but teach the way of God in truth" (12:14a). Then they pose their question that they hope will trap Jesus, saying, "Is it lawful (permissible) to pay a poll-tax to Caesar, or not? Shall we pay, or shall we not pay?" (12:14b–15a).

6. Stein, *Mark*, 537.

7. Stein, *Mark*, 538.

8. Stein, *Mark*, 543.

Mark says that Jesus "knows their hypocrisy" in coming and asking Him this question, and He says to the Pharisees and Herodians, "Why are you testing Me? Bring Me a denarius to look at" (Mark 12:15b). They bring one to Jesus, and Jesus asks them, "Whose likeness and inscription is this? And they reply, Caesar's" (12:16). Jesus says to them, "Render to Caesar the things that are Caesar's, and to God the things that are God's"; and Mark tells us that the Pharisees and Herodians "were amazed (greatly marveling) at Jesus" (12:17). Stein observes, "Once again the greatness of Jesus is seen in that even his bitter opponents marvel at him and in so doing acknowledge his great wisdom and authority (cf. 2:12)."[9] And so, the religio-political leaders of Israel continue to see their "enemy ascendant," fulfilling in themselves the seventh motif of the pattern of myth-culture, while Jesus' continues His seventh "hero recovers" motif, inversive and subversive of myth-culture's pattern, so fulfilling instead His own divine, evangelical pattern.

Because Jesus' "recovery" is pre-emptory, and does not follow a defeat as in myth's pattern, His unbroken ascent with back-to-back successes, all deliberately moving toward His willful crucifixion, completely shatters any possible mythological meaning expected according to the pattern of myth-culture. Jesus is heading to the Cross undefeated, more successful as each moment passes. As such He is no mere scapegoat, despite being so treated in this fourth episode; rather, Jesus is the Deliverer. Meanwhile, those opposing Jesus continue to "tick all the boxes" of each motif of the pattern of myth-culture, in the right order, and with the right meaning expected of myth-culture.

Having now debated into silence the chief priests, scribes, elders, Pharisees and Herodians—most of Israel's unbelieving leadership—Jesus continues His "hero's recovery," which is simultaneously the mythological leaders' "enemy's ascent," by next engaging the Sadducees, who also come to try and trap Him. Mark tells us that the Sadducees do not believe in the resurrection, and they come to Jesus with a question based upon their unbelief (Mark 12:18). They initially seem to base their question on a sound reading of Scripture, saying:

> Teacher, Moses wrote for us *a law* that "if a man's brother dies," and leaves
> behind a wife, "and leaves no child, his brother should take the wife, and raise
> up offspring to his brother." (Mark 12:19; Deut 25:5)

The Sadducees then tell Jesus a story, saying that there were seven brothers, the first of whom took a wife and then died childless (Mark 12:20). The second brother, keeping the commandment through Moses, married the widow of his deceased brother, but he also died childless. Likewise, said the Sadducees, the third brother married the widow, and finally all seven brothers had married the widow yet none had produced a single child before dying. Then the widow of the seven brothers died also (12:21–22). Now

---

9. Stein, *Mark*, 547.

the Sadducees pose their clever question to Jesus, saying, "In the resurrection, when they rise again, which one's wife will she be? For all seven had her as wife" (12:23).

As the Sadducees do not believe in the resurrection, they are happy to poke fun at something they obviously have taken no trouble to understand. And Jesus says so, asking them a question in turn (as He often does), saying, "Is this not the reason you are mistaken, that you do not understand the Scriptures, or the power of God?" (Mark 12:24). Jesus then proves both of these charges against the unbelieving Sadducee leaders, and their supposedly clever trap, continuing His inversive and subversive preemptory "heroic recovery" (though having never been defeated in the myth-culture's sense). Meanwhile, the seditious regicidal "vine-growers" continue to see their "enemy ascendant" before their eyes, despite their best traps.

First, Jesus shows the Sadducees' mistake in "not understanding the power of God" (Mark 12:24), with respect to the resurrection of the dead, in which they do not believe. Jesus affirms not only His own coming resurrection on the third day, which He has repeatedly declared to His disciples (e.g., Mark 10:34), but the resurrection of all who follow Him (e.g., Mark 8:34–35; 9:43–48; 10:21, 30, 37), saying, "For when they rise from the dead, they neither marry, nor are given in marriage, but are like angels in heaven" (12:25). This statement by Jesus on the resurrection is an expression of His inversive and subversive "hero recovers" motif. Not only Himself, but many others will be raised and live forever like the angels of God, experiencing divine deliverance and "heroic recovery," instead of the scapegoating and "enemy's ascendance" experienced in this world of myth-culture.

Second, Jesus shows the Sadducees' mistake in "not understanding the Scriptures . . . regarding the fact that the dead rise again" (Mark 12:24–26a). Jesus asks them, "Have you not read in the book of Moses, in the passage about the burning bush, how God spoke to him, saying, 'I am the God of Abraham, and the God of Isaac, and the God of Jacob'?" (12:26b; Exod 3:6). The LORD God tells Moses that He is presently the God of the patriarchs, even though their bodies died hundreds of years before Moses' day. From this verse Jesus logically deduces, "He is not the God of the dead (of corpses), but of the living; you are greatly mistaken" (12:27). Stein writes:

> Moses, who recorded God's command in Deut 25:5–6 [cited by the Sadducees], also records God referring to himself as the God of Abraham, Isaac, and Jacob. . . . Moses indicates that Abraham, Isaac, and Jacob, who had died, are alive. . . . The "everlasting" covenant God made with them (Gen 17:7, 19) involved an "everlasting" relationship that cannot be terminated by death. . . . Having proven that the patriarchs are alive, the consequence is that there will be a resurrection in the future.[10]

And Stein quotes Wright, who observes, "Prove the first [that the patriarchs are still alive], and (within the worldview assumed by both parties in the debate, including

---

10. Stein, *Mark*, 550.

any listening Pharisees) you have proved the second."[11] With these two points refuting the Sadducees' argument, Jesus affirms the "hero's recovery" of His divine, evangelical pattern, which is very different from the hero's recovery of the pattern of myth-culture. Also, Jesus adds the Sadducees to His list of defeated opponents, so that His enemies are not ascendant but declining rapidly.

One of the scribes overhears Jesus and the Sadducees arguing in Jerusalem's Temple, and he "recogniz(ed) that Jesus has answered them well" (Mark 12:28a). The scribe decides to pose Jesus a question, saying, "What commandment is the foremost of all?" (12:28b). Jesus answers, "The foremost is, 'Hear, O Israel; The LORD our God is one Lord; And you shall love the LORD your God will all your heart, and with all your soul, and with all your mind, and with all your strength [; this is the first commandment]'" (12:29–30; Deut 6:4–5). Jesus continues, "The second is this, 'You shall love your neighbor as yourself' (Lev 19:18), There is no commandment greater than these" (12:31). Among other things, Jesus has just stated the guiding principles of His unique, divine, evangelical pattern that criss-crosses the pattern of myth-culture. Could a human being consistently live by these two commandments, he would entirely invert and subvert the myth-culture's pattern, the way of the world. The Gospel account documents one man uniquely doing just that.

The scribe who posed the question to Jesus answers, "Right, Teacher, You have truly stated that 'He is One; and there is no one else besides Him' (Deut 4:35); 'and to love Him with all the heart and with all the understanding [and with all the soul] and with all the strength' (Deut 6:5), 'and to love one's neighbor as himself' (Lev 19:18), is much more than all burnt offerings and sacrifices'" (1 Sam 15:22; Hos 6:6; Mic 6:6–8; Mark 12:32–3). Jesus sees that the scribe has "answered intelligently," and says to him, "You are not far from the kingdom of God" (Mark 12:34a).

Stein notes that Jesus seems to call the scribe's response wise, due to his additional comment that these two commands are greater than burnt offerings and sacrifices.[12] He continues, "Love is more important than ritual. . . . In the context of Jesus's prediction of the temple's destruction . . . and his teaching in 12:29–31, the scribe's wise statement (12:32–33) would take on great importance. . . . The once-for-all sacrifice of Jesus (14:22–25; cf. Heb 7:27; 9:12; 10:10) and the twofold love command provided [believers] with what was necessary for holy living."[13] Jesus' ascendance and "hero's recovery" seems complete here, with this scribe forming allegiance to Jesus, and Jesus declaring that divine deliverance is attainable for this man. Mark says that, "After that, no one would venture to ask him any more questions" (12:34b). Jesus has silenced his last challenge. No one in the Temple dares challenge Him anymore. His enemies are not ascendant, and His own "hero's recovery" has been confidently assured, in complete antithesis to the pattern of myth-culture.

11. Wright, *Christian Origins*, 425.

12. Stein, *Mark*, 563.

13. Stein, *Mark*, 563.

Jesus remains teaching a "great crowd" in the Temple at Jerusalem unassailed, continuing to attack the unbiblical teaching of the scribes and other religio-political leaders, all of whom He has silenced. He says, "How is it that the scribes say that the Christ is the son of David?" (Mark 12:35). Answering His own question (since no one else dares to any longer), Jesus responds, "David himself says by the Holy Spirit, 'The LORD said to my Lord, 'Sit at my right hand, until I put Your enemies beneath Your feet'" (12:36; Ps 110:1). Jesus once again logically deduces from the text of Scripture, saying, "David calls Him 'Lord'; and so in what sense is He his son?"; and Mark says that the "great crowd enjoyed listening to Jesus" (12:37).

Stein remarks, "Mark wants to indicate that he is much more. Jesus is the Messiah—Son of David, but more important, he is the Messiah—Son of God ([Mark] 1:1; 14:61–62)! . . . [Psalm 110:1] should be understood, 'The Lord [God] said to my [David's] Lord [The Messiah].'"[14] Jesus' statement regarding the Christ, the Messiah, is very provocative, and yet Mark, and Jesus in Mark's account, has been declaring this to be the identity of Jesus from the outset. Once again in Mark's Gospel account, Jesus is referred to, and is referring to Himself, as the Lord sitting at God's right hand. In quoting this Scripture, Jesus is also indicating that it is about to be fulfilled, with Jesus' ascension and return to His throne, until the Father puts His enemies beneath His feet. And in turn, "This would bring to mind Jesus's triumph over sin and death by his death and resurrection, and his coming to judge the world (8:38; 13:26–27)."[15] Stein rightly notes that, while the Cross and resurrection are great victories by the LORD Jesus over sin and death, He will thereafter ascend to the right hand of the Father, until the Father puts all His enemies under His feet, as prophesied. Jesus is increasing, the "ascendant enemy" of the world's leaders, and He enjoys an atypical "hero's recovery," while His opponents are decreasing, which is not in accordance with the myth-culture's pattern. Jesus is bringing divine deliverance, about to lay down His own life, at the stage in which we expect to see the hero scapegoating the chaos-monster(s) to save the cosmos. The religio-political leaders are still attempting to scapegoat Jesus, but Jesus intends to save them, His scapegoaters, with His own death and resurrection.

Jesus teaches the great crowd at the Temple, saying, "Beware of the scribes who like to walk around in long robes, and like respectful greetings in the market places, and chief seats in the synagogues, and places of honor at banquets. They are the ones who devour widows' houses, and for appearance's sake offer long prayers; these will receive greater condemnation" (Mark 12:38–40). In this warning, Jesus loosely summarizes the six 'S' behaviors of the pattern of myth-culture, which if performed successfully result in fine living in the world, but ultimately result in "greater condemnation." Stein concludes, "The scribes serve as examples of those who do not love God with all their heart, soul, mind, and strength (12:29–30). . . . They also serve as

14. Stein, *Mark*, 570–71.
15. Stein, *Mark*, 571.

examples of those who do not love their neighbors as themselves (12:31)."[16] Jesus is determined that the people receive the deliverance that He is offering, rather than practicing the scapegoating of the pattern of myth-culture, which may gain you the world but will cost you your soul.

The final event of Jesus' seventh chiastic "hero recovers" motif, and of the first part of the fourth scapegoat-deliverance episode, is Jesus going and "sitting down opposite the treasury" at the Temple in Jerusalem, "and observing how the multitude are putting money into the treasury" (Mark 12:41a). Jesus sees many rich people "putting in large sums" (12:41b). Then a poor widow—perhaps one "devoured" by the scribes—approaches and "puts in two small copper coins (lepta), which amount to a cent (quadrans)" (12:42). Jesus calls His disciples and says to them, "Truly I say to you, this poor widow put in more than all the contributors to the treasury; for they all put in out of their surplus (abundance), but she, out of her poverty, put in all she owned, all she had to live on" (12:43–44).

To give all that one has, especially when it is so little, is a great act of trust in the LORD's deliverance of one's life. This poor widow's faith in God to deliver her from all her troubles, evidenced by giving the LORD everything, contrasts sharply with the rich young ruler who possesses "the whole world" and yet is on track to "lose his soul." And this widow contrasts sharply with the scribes, who pretend to serve the LORD while actually serving worldly gain, in part by scapegoating widows. Stein remarks, "The woman's action involves her doing exactly what Jesus told the young ruler to do (10:21). . . . Her action follows exactly what Jesus taught the disciples."[17] Once more then, Jesus affirms divine deliverance over mythological scapegoating as the way to eternal life. The poor widow gave everything, losing her life for the LORD, trusting in His deliverance to take it up again (see Mark 8:35).

Jesus has experienced and articulated an inversive and subversive "hero's recovery" in this seventh motif, while the leaders of the cosmos have continued in the pattern of myth-culture, experiencing and articulating the expected "enemy's ascendance" of myth-culture, seeing Jesus ascend despite their best efforts to scapegoat Him. Yet Jesus intends to allow Himself to be murdered by them, and very soon. In the next eighth motif that concludes this fourth episode, Jesus will perform the divine deliverance, all the while the religio-political leaders of Israel perform the mythological scapegoating.

Social-Science

Social-scientifically, this seventh motif in the fourth episode is comprised of deliverance exhibited by Jesus, continuing His unique, evangelical pattern, intermingled with the scapegoating exhibited by every branch of Israel's leadership, continuing the myth-culture's pattern. The up-coming eighth motif continues and concludes this

16. Stein, *Mark*, 575–76.

17. Stein, *Mark*, 578.

fourth episode. The social-science lenses of Girard and Malina aid us in perceiving the chiastic bi-pattern.

At this point in the pattern of myth-culture we typically see scapegoating pre-eminent. However, not so in the Gospel account due to the evangelical pattern here in Jesus Christ. Instead, Jesus exhibits deliverance instead of scapegoating. Deliverance in Jesus subverts the scapegoat-meaning expected of this episode, and inverts the myth-sequence so that this episode also contains a strong anti-snare of striving element.[18] As such, because it is the first motif in the first episode of the second half of the pattern, in this seventh motif in the fourth episode, Jesus begins the inversion of what is expected (if it were myth) to come before.

There are six expressions of scapegoating in this seventh motif in the fourth episode, all performed by the various branches of Israel's leadership, but never by Jesus. Jesus' response and posture are ever according to His purpose of divine deliverance instead of scapegoating, His unique, divine, evangelical pattern instead of the pattern of myth-culture. Jesus subverts the mythologically expected scapegoating with His divine deliverance, His self-giving to save the whole world at enmity with Him.

The first instance of scapegoating is a reference to a past pattern of events, as Jesus describes in a parable the behavior of the tenant farmers/vine-growers (Israel's leaders throughout history) toward the servants of the Lord of the Vineyard (the LORD's prophets). These servants were sent to receive from the tenants some of the produce of the land (Mark 12:3–5). The tenants beat and/or killed the lord's servants. Mark's text makes it clear that Jesus means that the vineyard is Israel, its owner and lord is the LORD, the tenant-farmers are the religio-political leadership of Israel, and the servants are the LORD's prophets. The leaders of Israel, says Jesus to their faces, have a documented proclivity to systematically scapegoat the LORD's representatives.

The second description of scapegoating is, in the same parable told by Jesus, when the lord of the vineyard (the Father God) has only his own son left to send to the tenant-farmers (the Son of God), but thinks that they will respect his son (Mark 12:6). However, the tenants see in the son the opportunity to steal the vineyard from their lord its owner, by murdering the son of their lord (12:7). So, the tenants take the son of the lord, kill him, and throw him out of the vineyard (12:8). In this statement by Jesus, He describes the very scapegoating behavior in which the religio-political leaders of Israel are engaging at the very moment of their discussion with Jesus in the Temple at Jerusalem. Jesus predicts to their faces the manner in which they are collectively attempting to treat Him.

---

18. As shown in the methodology, while the narratological chiasm is within each episode, involving the switching (inverting) of the two motifs and their meanings, the social-scientific chiasm involves the switching of the entire account's sequence of episodes and their meanings, inverting one and six, two and five, three and four. These two narratological and social-scientific aspects of the inversive and subversive chiastic relation of Jesus' evangelical pattern and the myth-culture's pattern is being demonstrated as we go along.

The third instance of scapegoating in this Gospel account's seventh motif and fourth episode is that—in their anger at Jesus' explicit prediction of their scapegoating of Him, and His prediction of how the LORD will deal with them as a result (Mark 12:9–11)—the chief priests, scribes and elders "were seeking to seize Jesus" (12:12). However, they feared the multitude who had just welcomed Jesus like a king, so they left Him alone for the time being.

The chief priests, scribes and elders may have retreated for the moment, but they have not given up seeking to scapegoat Jesus, so they send two other arms of their establishment, the Pharisees and Herodians, "in order to trap Jesus in a statement" from another angle (Mark 12:13). And this constitutes the fourth instance of scapegoating in this seventh motif that begins the fourth episode. These leaders of Israel begin with some flattering words, perhaps hoping to soften Jesus up, and then they lay the trap, asking whether it is lawful (permissible) for an Israelite to pay the poll-tax to Caesar (12:14–15a). Mark says that Jesus "knows their hypocrisy," and He asks them, "Why are you testing Me?" (12:15b). The denarius used to pay the tax has the "likeness and inscription" of Caesar upon it, which may be a reason why it could be considered unlawful for an Israelite to handle the coinage, as it is a "graven image" (e.g., Deut 4:16).[19] Also, to pay the tax with it may be to tacitly acknowledge Caesar's mythological claims about his "divine" identity, constituting idolatry.

As such, the Pharisees and Herodians are hoping to catch Jesus in idolatry (in conforming to the myth-culture with them), or get Him in trouble with the Romans, or both. They are seeking to destroy Him. Stein summarizes the trap: "Regardless of whether Jesus would answer yes or no, the Pharisees and Herodians would succeed in bringing an end to his popularity and ministry."[20] Jesus delivers Himself, and all of them, from both pitfalls, by saying, "Render to Caesar the things that are Caesar's, and to God the things that are God's" (12:17).

Now that the chief priests, scribes, elders, Pharisees and Herodians have made their attempts to scapegoat Jesus, it is the Sadducees' turn. Their attempt is the fifth occurrence of scapegoating in this seventh motif and fourth episode. They do not believe in the biblical doctrine of the resurrection, as Mark tells us, and this is the angle from which they come at Jesus (Mark 12:18–23). The Sadducees attempt to trap Jesus in mishandling the Scriptures, and seek to persuade Him to join them in doubting the power of God. It is easy for them to scapegoat Him, as all He must do is disagree with their peculiar unbelief. But Jesus challenges them on their unbelief in the resurrection, saying that their problem is not knowing the Scriptures, as well as their denial of the power of God (12:24–27).

The sixth and final attempt at scapegoating comes from a scribe who overhears the Sadducees' question of Jesus, and Jesus' authoritative answer. The scribe was impressed by Jesus' response, and it is not clear whether he means his own question as

19. Evans, *Mark*, 247.

20. Stein, *Mark*, 544.

a test for Jesus (so that he may not be looking for an excuse to scapegoat Jesus as the others evidently were), but he goes ahead and questions Jesus also (Mark 12:28). The scribe asks Jesus what commandment is the foremost of all. Jesus answers that it is that the LORD God is one, and to love the LORD with all that you are, and the second is to love your neighbor as yourself (12:29–31). The scribe affirms what Jesus says as true, so that Jesus declares the scribe to be "not far from the kingdom of God" (Mark 12:34). Mark tells us that after this battery of questions from all the leadership of Israel, "no one would venture to ask Him any more questions" (12:34). Jesus had demonstrated His superior knowledge and authority over all the leadership of Israel, and had stated and affirmed the way for them to be delivered, all the while they attempted by diverse means to scapegoat and destroy Him.

Jesus is never found to be engaging in scapegoating in any of these six instances. But He is the victim of scapegoating in all of them, and He subverts scapegoating in every case. Jesus' stated and active purpose is divine deliverance for everyone, including those attempting to scapegoat Him. After Jesus offers divine deliverance in response to these six attempts to discredit Him by the leaders of Israel, toward their goal of scapegoating Jesus, Jesus continues to teach in the Temple, unchallenged now, on how divine deliverance is received.

Jesus states that the Messiah cannot be David's son as the scribes say, or rather not merely so, because David calls the Messiah "Lord" (Mark 12:35-7). With this statement, Jesus is restating for the crowds, who love to hear Him, that they should understand who the Christ is and the salvation He brings through the Scriptures, rather than the teaching of the scribes. Then Jesus warns them explicitly against listening to the scribes, because they have selfish, proud and hypocritical motivations (12:38–40). Finally, Jesus watches a poor widow making a selfless contribution to the Temple treasury, and watches the rich make their contributions. From this, Jesus reaffirms for His disciples the cost of discipleship and salvation; of deliverance. The widow represents losing one's life in this world to gain eternal life (deliverance), while the rich represent saving their lives in this world, and forfeiting eternal life. While the scribes win themselves this world and its wealth through scapegoating widows and the like (12:40), the widow wins herself deliverance into eternal life by giving all her livelihood, her life, to the LORD (Mark 8:35).

Jesus' divine deliverance according to His unique, evangelical pattern is not only subversive of the scapegoating episode of myth-culture's pattern, however, but inversive of the snare-of-striving episode as well, continuing the formation of the chiastic structure of the two patterns. Jesus certainly contends with all those who come against Him, striving with Him in order to scapegoat Him if possible. But Jesus' "striving" is not of the sort of myth-culture. He cites Scripture in all His six engagements with the leadership of Israel who are seeking to scapegoat Him, and He sends each of them away in silence. He is not striving with them in order to destroy them, to scapegoat them, or overcome them in a mythological sense. Rather, Jesus is correcting them with His authority, the authority of the Word of God. To the final scribe that comes to Him with a question, Jesus says, "You are not far from the kingdom of God." Jesus offers deliverance even to His scapegoaters.

GOSPEL According to MARK			
WORLD'S SCAPEGOATING		JESUS' DELIVERANCE	
Enemy Ascendant		12:1–2	Hero Recovers
	12:3–5		
		12:6	
	12:7–8		
		12:9–11	
	12:12–15a		
		12:15b–17	
	12:18–23		
		12:24–27	
	12:28		
		12:29–44	
Hero Recovers		13:1–37	Enemy Ascendant
	14:1–2		
		14:3	
	14:4–5		
		14:6–9	
	14:10–11		
		14:12–42	
	14:43–47		
		14:48–49	
	14:50–52		

TABLE 1D: Scapegoating and Deliverance, Enemy Ascendant and Hero Recovers

MARK 13:1–14:52: JESUS' "ENEMY ASCENDANT"[21]

Narratology

Narratologically, this section of the Gospel account makes up the eighth "enemy ascendant" motif for Jesus, out of place from the vantage of the myth-culture's pattern. As is now perhaps expected, Jesus' eighth motif is atypically inversive in sequence and subversive in significance when compared with the pattern of myth-culture. The expected mythological motif of the "hero's recovery" occurs here only in the myth-culture's leadership, the opposition to Jesus, so that they continue in the pattern of myth-culture, while Jesus continues His anti-mythological, unique and evangelical pattern. In addition

21. Please refer to appendix 1 for the complete text of Mark for this motif.

to being inversive in sequence, Jesus' "enemy ascendant" motif is subversive in significance, having a very different meaning to that of myth-culture. A part of this subversive meaning is that Jesus' betrayal and capture by His "enemies" is all according to His predetermined and pre-declared plan, in fulfillment of the Scriptures (Mark 14:49).

As mentioned previously, due to Jesus' divine distinction, He is not actually imperiled by opposition in the manner of humans and/or mythological gods. Satan and the world's leadership are not Jesus' rivals in the mythological sense. Unlike myth, the biblical view of the LORD's relation to Satan is not the dualistic relationship of the hero and the villain. Jesus and His Father are ultimately in control of all the events unfolding (Mark 14:36, 49), unlike events in myth. In His "enemy ascendant" motif, Jesus deliberately walks into the hands of the traitorous "tenant-farmers" of Israel, full of confidence and authority. The leaders of Israel finally have their scapegoat, so they achieve their "hero's recovery" in this eighth motif, in keeping with and continuing myth-culture's pattern. And yet, their "hero's recovery" assures their destruction, as predicted by Jesus (Mark 12:9). The mythological victory they think they achieve is no victory at all, and is very short-lived (e.g., Mark 13:2).

At this point in the combat myth, the "hero's recovery" motif is foremost. But at this point in the Gospel account, which contains the evangelical pattern in Jesus Christ, we instead see the "enemy ascendant" motif preeminent for Jesus. The expected mythological "hero's recovery" motif predominates only in the religio-political leaders who oppose Jesus. The sequence of the motifs is inverted by Jesus, and He subverts their significance as well, so that Jesus' "enemy ascendant" is not like the typical "enemy ascendant" of myth-culture experienced by the hero-god there.

Jesus' eighth motif, concluding the fourth episode, begins with Him leaving the Temple precinct in Jerusalem (Mark 13:1a). One of Jesus' disciples remarks on how great are the stones and buildings of the Temple (13:1b), and Jesus responds by spending all of the thirteenth chapter of Mark's account describing His "enemy's ascendance," which is His opponents' "hero's recovery." His enemies include the "tenant-farmers" who control the Temple, Jerusalem, and the whole "vineyard" of Israel. But Jesus will also describe His disciples' "enemies' ascendance," the nations' leaders who will persecute them (Mark 13:7–13). For, as was the case with Jesus' "hero's recovery," Jesus describes His "enemy's ascendance" as occurring both in the present or near future, and also far into the distant future.

Edwards states, "Chapter 13 . . . is cast in the form of a final discourse of Jesus. . . . The subject is eschatology, in which future events, including some as distant as the coming of the Son of Man in final judgment, are prefigured by the destruction of the temple and the fall of Jerusalem."[22] Jesus makes it clear that the consequences of His "enemy's ascendance" against Him, their Lord, will be severe. So, the meaning of the "enemy's ascendance" is not only inverted in order of occurrence, but subverted in meaning in Jesus' unique, divine, evangelical pattern.

22. Edwards, *Mark*, 383.

In the near future, says Jesus, because of Israel's tenant-farmers' "ascendance" against their Lord (Mark 12:9) to scapegoat Him, the Temple will soon be completely razed to the bedrock with "not one stone left upon another" (Mark 13:2). So, although Israel's leaders will have their "hero's recovery" over Jesus their "enemy" in this motif (see Mark 14:1–2, 10–11, 18–21, 43–52), in keeping with myth-culture's pattern, scapegoating Jesus will not save their Temple and nation from destruction, as scapegoating is intended to do. Because they will have rejected their King, and crucified the Son of their Lord, they and their City, their Temple and their nation, will be destroyed.

Having left the Temple, and crossed the Kidron valley again, over onto the Mount of Olives, Jesus sits down "opposite the temple," and (Simon) Peter, James (Jacob), John and Andrew "question Jesus privately" about the total destruction of which Jesus spoke (Mark 13:3). They ask Jesus, "When will these things be?," and "What will be the sign when all these things are going to be fulfilled?" (13:4). It is important to note that these four disciples do not ask only about the destruction of the Temple. In fact, based upon their phrase "all these things," they evidently refer to all that Jesus has been saying since this episode began in Mark 12, when He declared that the vineyard of Israel would be taken from its current leadership, and would be given to another generation of Israel in the future. In short, the disciples want to know when Jesus will give to Israel the kingdom of God. This larger context must be borne in mind as we read Jesus' answer.

Jesus answers their two questions, first answering the second question concerning signs of "all these things" fulfilled (Mark 13:5–13).[23] Jesus begins with what are *not* to be taken as signs, but what must take place before "all these things" are fulfilled. In His answers in this eighth motif, Jesus speaks of His "enemy's ascendance" against His disciples—in the right place and with the right meaning from the view of myth-culture's pattern—into a more distant future than they may have imagined. From His answer, it is evident that in the disciples' phrase "all these things," Jesus understands the period of the destruction of the present generation of evil "tenant-farmers" of Israel, and the giving of Jerusalem, the Temple, and the kingdom of Israel to others, a later generation of Jews who will believe (as predicted: Mark 12:9).

Jesus uses the phrase "those days" (e.g., Mark 13:19–20) regarding the events (signs) just prior to the time when the Father God will put Jesus' enemies beneath His feet (as predicted: Mark 12:36; Ps 110:1), and Jesus will return and rule over His "vineyard," a believing Israel that accepts Jesus' kingship, at last (as predicted: Mark 12:10–11, Ps 118:22–23), along with other events of "those days." As Edwards writes:

> "Those days" is a stereotype for the eschaton in the prophets (Jer 3:16, 18;
> 31:29; 33:15; Joel 3:1), and it appears likewise in Mark 13. Chap. 13 is thus
> constructed according to a twofold scheme of tension and paradox, alternating

23. This passage, called the "Olivet Discourse," glaringly shows how important it is to read the Bible contextually. In order to understand Mark 13, it must be read alongside its parallel accounts in Matthew and Luke. Our study of Mark 13 will therefore keep these synoptic accounts in view.

between the immediate future (related to "these things") and the end of time (related to "those days"), in which the destruction of the temple and the fall of Jerusalem function as a prefigurement for the Parousia.[24]

Concerning events that precede "those days," Jesus begins His answer to the four disciples' second question with a warning, saying, "See to it that no one misleads you" (Mark 13:5), because, "Many will come in My name, saying, 'I am He!' and will mislead many" (13:6). Edwards notes, "The Greek of v. 6 reads simply, 'I am,' which is the name for God in the OT (Exod 3:14). "I am" is the same claim Jesus has made of Himself (6:50; 14:62)."[25] Jesus' "enemy's ascendance," His opponents' "heroic recovery" into the future, will involve a great deal of deception and attempted deception of believers in Jesus by people who claim to be who Jesus is, the Messiah of Israel.

Jesus prophesies that many people will be deceived by these pretenders in the time before "those days." Edwards cites Josephus' record of such pretenders: "In the years preceding the Jewish Revolt in AD 66 several messianic pretenders arose. In the mid-forties Theudas (Acts 5:36) boasted of various signs . . . that, according to Josephus, 'led many astray' (*Ant.* 20.97–98)," as well as an Egyptian pretender (Josephus, *War* 2.261–63).[26] These false-messiahs were followed by Simon Bar-Cochba, "the leader of the second Jewish revolt against Rome, in AD 132–135."[27] And they would continue throughout this Church age: "More recent false messiahs were Jacob Frank of Poland (1726–1791) and Menachem Schneerson (1902–1994)."[28] So, the first sign Jesus gives His disciples is His "enemies ascending" through lies and pretence in Jesus' name, pretending to be the Christ of Israel who would give the kingdom to Israel.

The second sign that will precede Jesus' return to give the kingdom of God to Israel is the occurrence of "wars and rumors of wars" (Mark 13:7a). Jesus tells the disciples not to be frightened by this, because "those things must take place, but that is not yet the end" (13:7b). The eventuality of various local wars, and rumors of them, will come to pass, but should not be considered signs of "all these things" fulfilled, and the imminent coming of the kingdom of God, says Jesus. They "must take place," but are not signs of "the end" of this age, and the beginning of the age of the kingdom of God. And since constant local wars and rumors of them is a sign of sin at work on earth, and war will be done away with in the Christ's kingdom (e.g., Isa 2:4), these local wars are also times of Jesus' "enemy ascending."

But Jesus next describes a different type of war that will take place, and this type of war *will* be a sign of "the end," and so of the soon fulfillment of the kingdom of God being given to Israel, since Jesus calls it "the beginning of birth pangs" (Mark 13:8c). This war will be an extraordinary conflagration, indicated by Jesus' use of a phrase

24. Edwards, *Mark*, 385–86.

25. Edwards, *Mark*, 391.

26. Edwards, *Mark*, 391.

27. Fruchtenbaum, *Yeshua*, 467.

28. Fruchtenbaum, *Yeshua*, 467.

from the Old Testament: "For nation will rise against nation, and kingdom against kingdom" (13:8a). This idiom (e.g., Isa 19:1–4; 2 Chr 15:1–7)[29] describes "total war" in the region specified in the context. So, Jesus describes His "enemy's ascendance" as involving the occurrence of "total war" fought on a global scale (see note 29), as the context of Mark 13 clearly indicates. The first global war was fought from 1914 to 1918, and was continued from 1939 to 1945. Therefore, the first sign of the beginning of "the end" began in AD 1914.[30]

Jesus adds that this sign of "total war" on a global scale will be accompanied by "earthquakes and famines [and troubles] in various places" (Mark 13:8b). Unlike the two preceding events prior to "those days," which are not signs of "the end," Jesus says that this global war, accompanied by earthquakes, famines and troubles, is indeed "the beginning of birth pangs" (13:8c). By this sign, believers will know that "the end" of the age has now begun. The LORD Jesus uses the prophetic imagery of a woman laboring to give birth (e.g., Isa 66:5–11) to describe this global war accompanied by earthquakes, famines and troubles in various places. Labor contractions, once begun, increase in frequency, intensity and duration until the baby is born. That is, "the end" begins with these signs, but the signs intensify until the LORD Jesus returns to set up His kingdom for Israel. Jesus' enemies will enjoy more and more "ascendance" until His return to set up His kingdom, and the Father puts them all under Jesus' feet.

Jesus then changes topics in Mark 13:9 to His disciples' personal experiences that precede "the end" that begins with the global war.[31] Jesus warns His disciples that they personally will be rejected by the leadership of Israel, just as Jesus Himself, being "delivered up to the courts," being "flogged in synagogues," as well as the leadership of the nations, "standing before governors and kings for Jesus' sake, as a testimony to them" (Mark 13:9). Jesus' disciples are going to be scapegoated by the myth-culture's authorities on a broad scale, again showing the "enemy's ascendance." But these persecutions of Jesus' followers will be opportunities for them to bear witness to Jesus, the Christ and coming King.

---

29. In both of these passages, the phrase is used to describe total war in the region described in the passage. That means that in our context, in Mark 13, the region described indicates the scale of this total war. In Mark 13, the region that the LORD Jesus explicitly and repeatedly refers to is the entire world: "nation against nation" and "various places" (13:8); "all nations" (13:10); "beginning of creation which God created until this time" (13:19); "no flesh" (13:20); "from the four winds" and "uttermost part of the earth" (13:27). Contextually, then, the total war that Jesus describes as the first birth-pang of "the end" is a global war. The first global war occurred in 1914–1918, followed by a sequel global war in 1939–1945. 1914 was therefore the beginning of birth pangs that lead up to the LORD Jesus giving the kingdom of God to Israel.

30. Fruchtenbaum, *Yeshua*, 468–69.

31. Many readers and commentators fall into the temptation of decontextualizing this passage so as to refer to all believers of all times and places. However, it is clear in the context that Jesus is describing experiences particular to His disciples to whom He is speaking. Of course, some experiences would be similar for Christians of later times and places. But it is critical not to confuse such application with the basic interpretation of the text.

After this prophecy of the disciples' persecution and testimony, Jesus says that "the gospel must first be preached to all the nations" (Mark 13:10). Jesus has entrusted to His disciples the Gospel of the kingdom, which He Himself has been ministering to them and to Israel. The twelve disciples are hereby entrusted with delivering the Gospel of the kingdom through Israel to all nations (this would occur first at Pentecost; Acts 2:5–11). We see here also that Jesus' "enemy's ascendance" against His disciples is in response to them preaching the Gospel of the kingdom to the nations, so that the nations haul believing Jews before their leaders for scapegoating and punishment.

Jesus offers His twelve disciples some good counsel on how to persevere and be delivered in these moments of persecution for His sake, saying:

> When they arrest you and deliver you up, do not be anxious beforehand about what you are to say, but say whatever is given you in that hour; for it is not you who speak, but it is the Holy Spirit. (Mark 13:11)

The Holy Spirit will miraculously speak through the disciples in these moments of state persecution. This is one of the many Pentecostal powers the disciples will have for the ministry of the Gospel of the kingdom. They need not worry about what to say, it will be given them from the LORD what to say, so that the Holy Spirit speaks through them. We see examples of this supernatural speech by the Spirit of God, through Apostles Peter and John during trial by the Sanhedrin, in the first chapters of the book of Acts (e.g., Acts 4:1–13).

Jesus also warns His disciples that, just as was His experience, their families would reject and betray them for their faith in Jesus as Messiah. He says that brother will betray his brother to death, and father will betray his child to death, and children will rise up against their parents and put them to death (Mark 13:12). So, Jesus' "enemy's ascendance" will involve family members scapegoating each other, putting their own family to death, over their testimony for Jesus.

And Jesus says that His disciples will be "hated by all on account of Jesus' name" (Mark 13:13a). Jesus' "enemy's ascendance" involves the disciples being hated and scapegoated by everyone. And in the face of this rampant hatred of them, Jesus calls for "endurance" from His disciples in order to be delivered, saying that the disciple "who has endured to the end will be saved" (Mark 13:13b). The twelve disciples, soon to be apostles (ones sent by Jesus), must endure the "enemy's ascendance" until "the end," persevering in Jesus' unique, divine, evangelical pattern in the face of the myth-culture's pattern of persecution.

Then Jesus transitions from discussing His disciples' personal experiences prior to "the end" to once again answering their questions about the signs of "the end." He says that, "when you see the Abomination of Desolation [spoken of by Daniel the prophet] standing where it should not be (let the reader understand)" (Mark 13:14a; Dan 9:27; 11:31; 12:11),[32] and so the believers' "enemy's ascendance" has reached the

---

32. Fruchtenbaum writes, "In 167 BC, the Greek king Antiochus Epiphanes profaned the Temple

very heart of Jerusalem, then must the believers of Israel, "who are in Judea flee to the mountains" (Mark 13:14b). This flight is also prophesied in Revelation 12:13–17.

Then Jesus offers more good counsel on what those believers of Israel, living in Judea, must do when this event takes place in order to be delivered. When it comes time to flee from Jerusalem and Judea, because of the Abomination of Desolation set up in the temple in the middle of the Tribulation (see note 32), believers should not go back into their houses to collect anything, even if they are on the roof or right outside their door (Mark 13:15). Likewise, Jesus says that if they are in the field when it is time to flee, they should not even go back to collect their cloak from wherever they left it while working (Mark 13:16). Jesus is impressing on the believers of Israel the immediacy with which they must flee when their "enemy ascends" fully, when the Abomination of Desolation is "where it should not be." Jesus adds, "But woe to those who are with child and to those who nurse babes in those days!" (Mark 13:17). Finally, Jesus says that the believers should, "pray that [their flight] may not happen in the winter" (13:18). Obviously, children and young mothers would have the most difficulty fleeing from Judea, but everyone would be impeded by wintry weather.[33]

From that mid-point of the Great Tribulation, spoken of by Daniel the prophet, as marked by the Abomination of Desolation and the believers fleeing from Jerusalem and Judea, the LORD Jesus declares the beginning of a persecution such as has never occurred before it, nor shall ever be thereafter:

> For those days will be a time of tribulation such as has not occurred since the beginning of the creation which God created, until now, and never shall. And unless the Lord had shortened those days, no life (flesh) would have been saved; but for the sake of the elect (chosen ones) whom He chose, He shortened the days. (Mark 13:19–20)

Jesus' "enemy's ascendance," the "hero's recovery" of the opponents of Jesus Christ and His followers, will have become so acute that not only the believers, and not only all humans, but all flesh, all life on earth, would not survive if the LORD did not cut those days short by personally and physically stepping in (see Mark 13:26). Jesus says there has not been a time since the LORD created all things (not even the global flood!), and there will not ever be another time, when the earth's troubles will be so great as during this "Great Tribulation." Thankfully, we know through prophecy that the LORD Jesus will step in

---

in Jerusalem by setting up an altar to Zeus. . . . While Daniel's prophecy in chapter 8 speaks of events fulfilled in 167 BC . . . chapters 9 and 10 [of Daniel] clearly predict an incident that will occur during the tribulation. The prophecy states that the abomination of desolation will occur exactly in the middle of the tribulation [Dan 9:27b]" (*Yeshua*, 475–76).

33. As Fruchtenbaum observes, during winter in Judea, "weather conditions can also limit a speedy escape especially through *wadis* such as the one leading to Petra" (*Footsteps*, 633). According to prophecy, Petra (Bozrah) is the location to which the believers of Israel will flee at that time (Mic 2:12–13; Isa 34:1–10; 63:1–6; Hab 3:3).

personally, to bring to an end His "enemy's ascendance," three and a half years after the Abomination of Desolation occurs (see Dan 7:25, 12:7; Rev 11:2, 12:6, 12:14, 13:5).

And during this final half of the Great Tribulation, the second three-and-a-half-year period, Jesus prophesies that there will come false followers of Christ declaring false Christs, and false prophets, and false gods who would pretend to hold Christ's place:

> And then if anyone says to you, "Behold, here is the Christ (Messiah)"; or, "Behold, he is there"; do not believe him; for false Christs (Messiahs) and false prophets will arise, and will show signs and wonders, in order, if possible, to lead the elect (chosen ones) astray. (Mark 13:21–2)

In the latter half of the Great Tribulation, believers of Israel will be told to believe this or that person is Jesus (see 2 Thess 2:3–4), or prophets of Jesus (see 2 Thess 2:8–10; Rev 13:11–15), of God, and they are not to believe them. "Ironically," writes Edwards, "the message and signs of the false Christs will be believed . . . on the other hand, the message of the true Christ has not been believed (8:14–21)."[34] Jesus concludes this warning of His "enemies' ascendance" as deceptive pretenders just prior to "the end," saying, "But take heed; behold, I have told you everything in advance" (13:23).

Then Jesus describes the way in which this greatest Tribulation, that accompanies His "enemy's" greatest "ascendance" thus far, will be "shortened" by His own return to earth:

> But in those days, after that tribulation, "The sun will be darkened, and the moon will not give its light, and the stars will be falling" [Isa 13:10; 34:4] from heaven, and the powers that are in the heavens will be shaken. And then they shall see the Son of Man coming in the clouds with great power and glory [Dan 7:13–14]. (Mark 13:24–26)

In verses 24–25, Jesus says that this three-and-a-half-year period concludes with what may be termed a universal "black-out," in which all the lights of the heavens either cease to give their light, or their light is severely diminished. And then, Jesus the Son of Man will return, seen by those on the earth, as in that darkness He will return in the brightness of His glory. We know that this "Son of Man" is Jesus Himself, because Jesus said as much to His disciples previously regarding the death and resurrection of the Son of Man, Himself, and speaks of Himself as the Son of Man who will come in His Father's glory with the angels (see Mark 8:31, 38; 9:31; 10:33–4).

"'The Son of Man coming in the clouds' (v. 26) is taken from the vision of Dan 7:13. What remarkable irony this is, coming from a man who has predicted his humiliation and death (8:31; 9:31; 10:33–34) and who even now is preparing for his shameful treatment at the hands of Jews and Romans alike."[35] Jesus says here, then, that His future "enemy's ascendance," involving the greatest "Tribulation" the earth has ever

---

34. Edwards, *Mark*, 401.

35. Edwards, *Mark*, 403.

seen or will see, ends with His own coming again. For Jesus' enemies, however, this time of tribulation will evidently be their grand "hero's recovery," in accordance with the pattern of myth-culture. And it will be ended by Jesus Himself.

And then, when Jesus the Son of Man comes on the clouds, "He will send forth the angels, and will gather His elect [chosen ones] from the four winds, from the farthest end of the earth to the farthest end of heaven" (Mark 13:27). Here, Jesus describes the final regathering of His elect believers of Israel from both earth and heaven. Many of Israel's prophets also describe this event (Isa 11:11—12:6; 43:5–7; Jer 23:5–8; 31:7–14; Ezek 11:16–21; 20:40–42; 36:22–31). As Fruchtenbaum observes, "The prophets spoke of two regatherings: one in unbelief in preparation for the judgment of the tribulation and one in faith in preparation for the blessings of the kingdom. This passage clarifies that the latter will only occur after the second coming."[36]

This regathering of believing Israel that Jesus describes is also spoken of by Moses: "If any of your outcasts be in the uttermost parts of heaven, from there will the LORD your God gather you, and from there He will fetch you" (Deut 30:4). It is fascinating to read of this final regathering of Israel, which is from both all the earth and all of heaven. Both the survivors of believing Israel on the earth, as well as believing Israel awaiting their resurrection in Heaven (including Abraham, Isaac, Jacob, and all the believers of the Old Testament, and pre-Church period; Isa 26:19–21; Dan 12:2), will be resurrected and gathered together into Jesus' kingdom on earth, centered at Jerusalem, on that day.

Jesus then transitions in His discourse again, telling these four disciples to learn a parable: "Now learn the parable from the fig tree: when its branch has already become tender and puts forth its leaves, you know that summer is near. Even so, you too, when you see these things happening, recognize that it is near, right at the door(s)" (Mark 13:28–9). Jesus has already engaged with a fig tree in a metaphorical way in Mark's account. In Mark 11:12–23, as we saw during Jesus' "battle" motif and Israel's leaders' "defeat," Jesus associates the unbelieving leaders of Israel, of Judea, with the fig tree that bears no fruit. Jesus therefore curses the fig tree. There is a parallel passage in Luke's account:

> And He began telling this parable: "A man had a fig tree which had been planted in his vineyard; and he came looking for fruit on it and did not find any. And he said to the vineyard-keeper, 'Behold, for three years I have come looking for fruit on this fig tree without finding any. Cut it down! Why does it even use up the ground?'" (Luke 13:6–7)

Both of these passages from Mark and Luke build on the prophetic parable of Isaiah concerning the vineyard of Israel, which Jesus also alluded to in Mark 12: "For the vineyard of the Lord of hosts is the house of Israel / *And the men of Judah His delightful*

---

36. Fruchtenbaum, *Yeshua*, 482.

plant. / Thus, He looked for justice, but behold, bloodshed; / For righteousness, but behold, a cry of distress" (Isa 5:7).

What we are seeing here is a constellation of references to the leaders of Judah as a fig tree in the vineyard of Israel, from which the LORD expects fruit, but which bears none. Therefore, the LORD curses the fig tree, the leaders of Judah, to destruction (which occurred beginning in AD 70, but also in AD 135). However, Jesus here says this fig tree will one day come back to life (also see Ezek 37).[37] When it does, it will be a sign of the end of the age, the Great Tribulation, and the return of Jesus Christ to set up His kingdom because "it is near, right at the doors." As Morris writes:

> These and other Scriptures tell us that, in the latter days, the people of Israel will come back to their own land. When they first return, however, they will still be in unbelief. The bones have flesh and skin, but there is no breath. The fig tree will bud, but with no fruit as yet. . . . When we see this, however, Jesus said we could know that His coming is "near, even at the doors!"[38]

So, although Jesus is describing the "enemy's ascendance" into the future, even during the first return of Israel to her Land in unbelief, Jesus also assures His disciples and the believers of Israel that their hope of the kingdom of Israel is surely yet coming. Amazingly, we today, in combination with the first sign of "the end," which is the global war and accompanying famines and plagues, can see the leadership of Israel once again in the Land of Israel, in Judea, in Jerusalem, "putting forth its leaves," but no fruit (the nation of Israel remains largely unbelieving, and the leadership is thoroughly unbelieving). We are witnessing the sign of the fig tree.

And of this event, Jesus says, "Truly I say to you, this generation will not pass away until all these things take place. Heaven and earth will pass away, but my words will not pass away" (Mark 13:30-1). That is, the generation that witnesses "all these things," the signs of "the end" that Jesus has just laid out, "will not pass away" before Jesus returns in power to set up His kingdom.[39] Jesus then assures His disciples, and all the believers of Israel, that His words are entirely trustworthy, and will certainly be literally fulfilled just as He has said. He guarantees this by declaring His words to be more permanent than this universe itself.

Jesus then transitions again, saying, "But of that day or hour no one knows, not even the angels in heaven, nor the Son, but the Father alone" (Mark 13:32). Edwards notes an "amazing paradox" in this verse:

---

37. As the passage in Ezekiel 37 states, in agreement with Jesus' parables of the fig tree (along with many other prophecies), Israel returns to the land and flourishes *without* bearing fruit. That is, Israel returns and is re-established in *unbelief*. This is a fact that is commonly missed. Many Christians will not support Israel today because it is largely unbelieving in Jesus, and therefore they mistakenly think that it is not the fulfillment of prophecy. But even in this first return of Israel, the "enemy" is still "ascendant."

38. Morris, *Creation*, 63.

39. Morris, *Creation*, 183.

> In this the only passage of the Gospel of Mark where Jesus explicitly calls him-
> self "the Son," he admits to what he does *not* know and *cannot* do. . . . Jesus
> does not claim the prerogatives of divine sonship apart from complete obedi-
> ence to the Father's will but rather forsakes claims and calculations in favor of
> humble confidence in the Father's will.[40]

Jesus Himself relies upon divine deliverance from scapegoating during the "enemy's
ascendance," even as He exhorts His disciples and the believers of Israel to wait on
and watch for His return and deliverance from scapegoating, while Jesus' enemies
enjoy their "hero's recovery." Even after providing all these signs of His return and the
kingdom of God coming to Israel, Jesus emphasizes that "the end" cannot be known
by anyone, any being, except the Father God.

For this reason, after His promise of deliverance from the "enemy's ascendance"
in Jesus' eighth inversive and subversive motif, from tribulation full of scapegoating,
through cutting the time short and His returning on the clouds, Jesus once again
exhorts His disciples to be ever watchful, ready, and prayerful, saying, "Take heed,
keep on the alert [and pray]; for you do not know when the appointed time is" (Mark
13:33). He then offers a final parable as a reminder to these four disciples who asked
Him about how to discern "the end" of "all these things." Jesus says the time of the end
and His return is like a man going away on a journey, who leaves his house with his
slaves in charge, and commands his doorkeeper to stay on the alert (Mark 13:34). It
is evident that Jesus is the man, and His disciples and believers of Israel are the slaves
and doorkeeper.

Then Jesus rephrases His warning, saying, "Therefore, be on the alert—for you
do not know when the Master of the house is coming, whether in the evening, at
midnight, at cockcrowing, or in the morning—lest He come suddenly and find you
asleep" (Mark 13:35–36). Edwards concludes, "Temptations come in many forms.
False prophets raise false hopes; mistaken signs raise fears and anxiety; the delay of
the Parousia induces complacency and neglect; lack of knowledge induces resignation
and defeat. . . . Living faithfully in the present, being attentive to the signs, and being
ready at any hour for the return of the master is not one job among others; it is the
doorkeeper's *only* job."[41]

Finally, Jesus expands this command not only to His disciples and the believers
of Israel, but "to all," saying "watch out!" For the sixth time (in one way or another)
in this thirteenth chapter, Jesus says "watch out!": "And what I say to you I say to all,
'Be on the alert!'" (Mark 13:37). Jesus is so insistent with His message of warning,
seeming desperate that no one be so foolish as to be unprepared for the greatest
"ascendance" of Jesus' "enemy," and for His own second coming, and so be found
"asleep." The enemies of Jesus are going to have an extraordinary mythological "hero's

40. Edwards, *Mark*, 407.
41. Edwards, *Mark*, 408.

recovery" in the future as "the end" approaches, and Jesus is eager that everyone be delivered, giving this repetitive warning "to all."

Thus concludes Jesus' discussion of the future on the Mount of Olives, overlooking Jerusalem and the Temple, in response to these four disciples' questions about what are the signs of "the end" and the giving of the kingdom of God to Israel. We now return to the present, AD 33,[42] with Mark telling us that the feast of Passover and Unleavened Bread was only "two days off" (Mark 14:1a). And "the chief priests and the scribes were seeking how to seize (Jesus) by stealth, and kill Him" (Mark 14:1b). Jesus has deliberately come to Jerusalem and the Temple to meet His death at the hands of the religio-political leaders of Israel, the fruitless fig tree, and rise again on the third day.

In this eighth motif Jesus' present "enemies" are "ascendant," which is not in keeping with the pattern of myth-culture in order or significance of events, but rather according to His own unique, evangelical pattern. As we are about to see, the current religio-political leaders are enjoying their eighth "hero's recovery" motif, themselves keeping the pattern of myth-culture. Mark tells us that these "tenant farmers" hoped to kill their Lord "by stealth," saying, "Not during the festival, lest there be a riot of the people" (Mark 14:2). Evans observes the initiation in the present of Jesus' "enemy's ascendance" here, which is His opponents' "hero's recovery":

> In the immediate context (13:33–37) Jesus has just warned his disciples of impending persecution and the need to be alert and watchful for the coming danger. Notice of the priests' and scribes' plotting follows naturally, almost expectedly. The report of the ruling priests and scribes' murderous intentions sets the tone for the Passion Narrative that will now unfold.[43]

We are then told that Jesus was having dinner at the home of "Simon the leper" in Bethany, on the eastern slope of the Mount of Olives (Mark 14:3a). While reclining there, a woman comes to Him "with an alabaster vial of costly perfume of pure nard," and she breaks the vial and pours its perfume over Jesus' head (Mark 14:3b). Some of those with Jesus remark indignantly to each other, "For what purpose has this perfume been wasted?" (Mark 14:4). They think it could have served a better purpose than anointing Jesus' head, saying, "this perfume might have been sold for over three hundred denarii (a year's income), and the money given to the poor" (Mark 14:5a). These Israelites were collectively scolding the woman (Mark 14:5b).

But Jesus answers their question as to the purpose of the woman's actions. He first tells these people off, delivering the woman from persecution, from scapegoating, saying, "Leave her alone; why do you bother her? She has done a good deed to Me" (Mark 14:6). Jesus then explains that they always have the poor with them, and they can do good to the poor any time they like, but they do not always have Him with

---

42. Humphreys and Waddington, "Date of Crucifixion," 2–10.

43. Evans, *Mark*, 355.

them (Mark 14:7). Evans remarks, "The emphasis falls on her extravagance, on her gift. . . . She has recognized Jesus as the Messiah and has expressed her faith in him and love for him in an extravagant manner."[44]

Jesus explains her actions, saying, "She has done what she could; she has anointed My body beforehand for the burial" (Mark 14:8). This statement reminds everyone that Jesus fully intends and expects to be killed, dead and buried in the very near future. And it expresses Jesus' "enemy's ascendance," in that because Jesus is certainly going to His death, what the woman has done is one of the only good things left to be done for Jesus. He says that the thing the woman has done for Him is so good, in fact, that, "wherever the gospel is preached in the whole world, that also which this woman has done shall be spoken of in memory of her" (Mark 14:9), as it is this day.

The woman's grandly self-sacrificial act while being persecuted by Jesus' disciples—in keeping with the poor widow, "devoured" by the scribes, sacrificing her all—anticipates Jesus' self-sacrificial divine deliverance, *while* suffering personal persecution and scapegoating, and her trust in and dependence upon Jesus' sacrifice. These two women's acts "book-end" Jesus' teaching in the fourth scapegoat-deliverance episode on how the believer is to live amid scapegoating/persecution, and both help the reader to see what Jesus is doing as He approaches the Cross:

> In one of the most poignant stories in the Gospels we witness an act of remarkable generosity, devotion, and faith on the part of the woman who anointed the head of Jesus with an ointment that was worth a small fortune. The woman's selfless act stands in stark contrast to Judas's act of treachery and greed . . . [and] the disciples at the very moment of her deed. She was concerned with no one but Jesus. . . . This episode in many ways encapsulates the essence of the passion story itself.[45]

Jesus Himself, *while* being scapegoated, willfully and selflessly goes to the Cross to deliver many from sin and death. Jesus repeatedly draws our attention to the person who, while already suffering for the LORD, yet continues to give all he/she has for Jesus.

Then the religio-political leaders of Israel enjoy a genuine mythological "hero's recovery" moment, on cue in this eighth motif, and Jesus experiences a serious "enemy ascendant" moment, when one of His twelve disciples, Judas Iscariot, "goes off to the chief priests, in order to betray Him to them" (Mark 14:10). Evans suggests Judas' motivations from the context, which remind one of Jesus' parable of the seed-sower and the soils, and the type of heart "soil" Judas seems to have (Mark 4:16–19: "affliction or persecution arises because of the word" and/or "the deceitfulness of riches, and the desires for other things"):

> Mark's readers might infer that Judas has given up on Jesus, who continues to speak of his death. The insertion of the anointing story (14:3–9) . . . seems

44. Evans, *Mark*, 361.

45. Evans, *Mark*, 362–63.

to support this inference. When the woman anoints Jesus and so recognizes his messianic identity, how does Jesus respond? He interprets her extravagant deed as preparation for burial. With this, Judas "went away to the ruling priests, so that he might hand him over to them" (14:10). Perhaps from Judas' perspective, it is Jesus who has betrayed the cause. Having given up on the hope of inaugurating the kingdom of God now and establishing a new government in Jerusalem (in which Judas may play a part), Jesus seems determined to pursue a reckless and pointless course of martyrdom. Judas will have none of it; he wants out. . . . Judas Iscariot exemplifies human weakness, and all [believers] should know that the discouragement and temptation that overtook him could overtake them as well.[46]

So, perhaps Judas refused to accept the delay of the kingdom of God. Or perhaps he interpreted Jesus' goals according to the myth-culture's pattern from the beginning, and Jesus' refusal to abide by his myth-cultural expectations has resulted in a profound sense of betrayal. This "betrayal" justified Judas' actions, in his mind, in seeking reward and fulfillment of his own goals elsewhere, and at Jesus' expense, by scapegoating Him. As for the chief priests, the "tenant-farmers" of the Lord's Vineyard Israel, "they are glad when they hear this, and promise to give (Judas Iscariot) money, and he begins seeking how to betray Jesus at an opportune time" (Mark 14:11). Of course, the religio-political leaders have been anxious to scapegoat Jesus for some time, and Judas has finally given them the means to do it "by stealth" as they desire.

Then Mark tells us that on the first day of the feast of Unleavened Bread, "when the Passover lamb was being sacrificed" (Mark 14:12a; Deut 16:5–6), Jesus' disciples said to Him, "Where do You want us to go and prepare for You to eat the Passover?" (14:12b). The apposition of Judas' betrayal of Jesus to the chief priests, and the day when the Passover lamb is being sacrificed, is no coincidence. It highlights that Jesus' death will be the result of scapegoating, as a collective sacrifice by the people of Israel's priestly leadership, adhering to the myth-culture's pattern. Simultaneously, however, it highlights that Jesus' death is for the deliverance of the people of Israel, and all tribes of Adam's race, in His unique, divine, evangelical pattern. Deliverance from sin and death is the original and historical purpose of the Passover lamb's death (Exod 12:1–14, 21–33). The atoning death of the lamb is prefigured further back in biblical history, however, even to the historical entrance of sin and death into God's universe, when the LORD Himself slew the first animal to cover the shame of Adam and Eve's sin in the Garden of Eden (Gen 3:21). That is, the LORD Jesus goes to the Cross to deliver all humanity from sin and death.

Jesus sends two of His disciples into the city of Jerusalem, and tells them that "a man will meet you carrying a pitcher of water" and they are to follow him (Mark 14:13). Wherever the man enters, Jesus tells His two disciples that they are to enter and tell the master of that house, "The Teacher says, 'Where is My guest room in which

46. Evans, *Mark*, 366.

I may eat the Passover with My disciples?'" (Mark 14:14). Jesus says that the master will show them "a large upper room furnished and ready," and the two are to prepare for Him there (Mark 14:15). The two disciples go and do as Jesus says, and it literally unfolds just as Jesus prophesied, and "they prepare the Passover" (Mark 14:16). Jesus' "enemies" are "ascendant," enjoying their "hero's recovery," and He is about to be scapegoated. Jesus knows this, which is also signalled by the apparent clandestine manner with which He organizes this Last Supper.[47] Yet, Jesus is determined and deliberate about effecting His divine deliverance, and achieving His purpose. As Evans remarks, "Again Jesus is portrayed as master of the Situation."[48]

Mark then tells us that, "when it was evening (Jesus) came with the twelve" (Mark 14:17) to the undisclosed Upper Room that Jesus secured for the Passover meal. Mark's remark that it is evening is important because, as alluded to previously by Mark (Mark 14:12; Deut 16:5–6), the Passover is to be sacrificed at evening, which is at the time the Israelites came out of Egypt. Jesus has evidently gone into the Temple precinct to have a lamb slaughtered with His disciples that afternoon (Mark 14:12; which is when they ask Him where He wants to eat it), and stays in Jerusalem to have His Passover meal with the disciples, all to keep and fulfill this command of the LORD through Moses.[49]

As they recline at the Passover table in the upper room in Jerusalem, Jesus says, "Truly I say to you that one of you will betray Me—one who is eating with Me" (Mark 14:18). The twelve disciples are "grieved," Mark tells us, and they say to Him "one by one, 'Surely not I?'" (Mark 14:19). Jesus replies:

> It is one of the twelve, one who dips with Me in the bowl. For the Son of Man is to go, just as it is written of Him; but woe to that man by whom the Son of Man is betrayed! It would have been good for that man if he had not been born. (Mark 14:20–1)

Evans notes Jesus' allusion to Psalm 41:9 here: "Even my close friend in whom I trusted, / Who ate my bread with me, / Has lifted up his heel against me,"[50] which likely forms a part of what Jesus means by His death happening "just as it is written." Jesus makes it clear that He knows His enemies are about to make Him their sacrifice, their scapegoat to save themselves according to myth-culture's pattern.

The one who betrays Jesus to His enemies will be one of His own, of the twelve. He makes clear what a terrible evil this act is for His betrayer, yet He willingly allows His "enemy's ascendance." Jesus the Son of Man will go "just as it is written of Him." He is fulfilling the divine plan for deliverance laid out in the Hebrew Bible (Old Testament). And yet, the one who betrays Jesus is committing a terrible crime. Evans notes:

---

47. Evans, *Mark*, 373–74.
48. Evans, *Mark*, 375.
49. Evans, *Mark*, 373.
50. Evans, *Mark*, 375.

> Jesus' mastery of the situation is seen in the fact that he is able to foretell his fate. He has announced his forthcoming suffering and death, even the manner of it (10:32–34); now he foretells the betrayal. Later he will foretell the disciples' desertion and Peter's three denials. At every point Jesus is in command of the unfolding events; nothing takes him by surprise, nothing causes him to stumble and shrink back from fulfilling his mission.[51]

Evans' observations show that Jesus' unique, divine, evangelical pattern is entirely in His hands. It is in Jesus' control from beginning to end, despite the pattern of myth-culture simultaneously unfolding against Jesus all the while.

Jesus explicitly makes His own sacrifice of Himself, one that is for deliverance from a very different villain, a very different monster, than that of myth-culture. Mark tells us that while they were eating:

> (Jesus) took some bread, and after a blessing He broke it, and gave it to them, and said, "Take [eat]; this is My body." And when He had taken a cup, and given thanks, He gave it to them, and they all drank from it. And He said to them, "This is My blood of the [new] covenant, which is poured out for many. Truly I say to you, I shall never again drink of the fruit of the vine until that day when I drink it new in the kingdom of God." (Mark 14:22–25)

Jesus is giving His body to His friends and enemies to eat, and His "blood of the new covenant" to His friends and enemies to drink, in order to save (deliver) His friends and enemies; His body broken and His blood shed "on behalf of many." In so doing, Jesus encourages His "enemies" even in their "ascendance," because it achieves what is "written." The "heroes" of the pattern of myth-culture are certainly having their "recovery," but only because the LORD has also purposed it. After Jesus has handed out His body and blood, He says that He will not drink wine, which He has made to symbolize His death for the sin (the non-mythological monster) of Adam's race, until He has returned to set up His kingdom on earth from Jerusalem.

Evans notes that Jesus' words in Mark 14:24, "This is my blood of the new covenant, which is shed (poured out) on behalf of many," make allusion to Exodus 24:8; Jeremiah 31:31; Zechariah 9:11: "As for you also, because of the blood of My covenant with you, / I have set your prisoners free from the waterless pit"; as well as Isaiah 53:12b: "Because He poured out Himself (His soul) to death."[52] Finally, in Jesus' statement regarding the bread and the wine, He clearly anticipates future victory and feasting with His disciples (Mark 14:25), despite laying down His life right now, in keeping with His vow to rise from the dead on the third day.

Then Jesus sang a hymn to the LORD with His disciples, and they went out of the upper room, out of Jerusalem, across the Kidron Valley, and made their way back up onto the Mount of Olives (Mark 14:26). Along the way, Jesus says to His disciples,

51. Evans, *Mark*, 379.
52. Evans, *Mark*, 392–93.

"You will all fall away (be scandalized) [because of Me this night], because it is written, 'I will strike down the shepherd, and the sheep will be scattered'" (Mark 14:27; Zech 13:7). The disciples will be scandalized by Jesus Christ and His willful capture that night, and they will all flee instead of standing with Him, "because it is written." The disciples will take the side of Jesus' "enemies" in the moment of their "ascendance," implicitly joining in scapegoating Jesus, even as He walks the lonely road of the Deliverer, even for such disciples as these, and many others such as these. In saying this, Jesus also indicates that the "heroes" of the mythological world are about to enjoy their full "recovery," right on schedule in their myth-cultural pattern.

Jesus does not condemn His disciples for this, however, and even assures them that He will return to them very soon, saying, "But after I have been raised, I will go before you to Galilee" (Mark 14:28). Jesus again comments on His resurrection from the dead three days after His imminent murder, and assures the disciples, who He knows are about to betray Him, that He will rejoin them after His resurrection. Jesus' "enemy's ascendance"—the religio-political leaders' "heroic recovery"—is not an obstacle to His own divine pattern, but actually fulfills His unique pattern, even though it is the opposite in every way of the pattern of myth-culture. Though His disciples join in scapegoating Jesus, His deliverance of them will result in their soon reunion. Jesus' own disciples' betrayal of the pattern He is modelling for them is not an obstacle to His love for them either, or the achievement of His desired plan. Jesus promises to return to them and lead them onward very soon. Evans observes Jesus' combative terminology here, indicating a renewed "military" campaign that is to continue: "The military usage of προάγειν, 'to go before.' . . . As their commander, Jesus will continue to lead his disciples in Galilee."[53]

Simon Peter objects to Jesus' (and Zechariah's) prophecy, saying, "Even though all may fall away (be scandalized), yet I will not" (Mark 14:29). Peter attempts to assure Jesus that he himself will not betray Jesus even if all the others do, despite Jesus saying that all will, "because it is written." Once again (as when Jesus first told His disciples that He was going to die and rise again), and apparently due to continued myth-cultural expectations for Jesus' behavior, Peter neglects and even opposes Jesus' word. Jesus assures Peter that he will indeed betray Him along with everyone else, saying, "Truly I say to you, that you yourself today, on this very night, before a cock crows twice, shall three times deny Me" (Mark 14:30). Even with Jesus' additional, more specific prophecy concerning the imminent event of Peter's personal betrayal of Jesus, he still insists that he will not, repeatedly saying, "Even if I have to die with you, I will not deny you!" And Mark says that all the others were saying to Jesus the same thing as Peter (Mark 14:31). Evans observes:

> The point is that Jesus is vastly superior in power, insight, and faith in comparison with his own disciples. . . . What ordinary people fail to comprehend and

53. Evans, *Mark*, 402.

fear, Jesus comprehends and faces with dignity and composure. He is prepared
to face death, even if his closest friends betray and abandon him. . . . In a group
and unthreatened, [the disciples] are brave. As it turns out, however, it is the
predictions of Jesus that come true, not the assurances of his disciples. Mark's
reader will discover that at every point Jesus gets it right.[54]

Peter has evidently led something of a mutiny against Jesus, albeit with intent to be
faithful to Jesus; Peter's expectations are myth-cultural, being upside-down and back-
ward compared with Jesus' unique, divine pattern. The disciples deny Jesus' word,
instruction, and the Scripture that Jesus is fulfilling, by refusing to accept Jesus'
prophecy. Yet even now, with *everyone* arrayed against Jesus' purpose and evangelical
pattern, His divine pattern continues unhindered, even as the myth-culture's pattern
continues in His opponents.

Mark tells us that Jesus and the disciples arrive at a place on the Mount of Olives
called Gethsemane, where Jesus tells His disciples, "Sit here until I have prayed" (Mark
14:32). Jesus takes just Peter, James (Jacob) and John with Him, as on the Mount of
Transfiguration, and goes and prays, becoming "very distressed and troubled" (Mark
14:33). Jesus says to the three disciples with Him, "My soul is deeply grieved to the
point of death; remain here and keep watch" (Mark 14:34). Evans notes in Jesus' statement an allusion to Psalms 42 and 43, and Jonah 4:9.[55] The actual events of Jesus'
betrayal, scapegoating, and death are imminent. Jesus' soul is severely grieved by the
situation, by what He is about to willingly suffer "on behalf of many," on behalf of His
"ascendant enemies."

Jesus then goes a little farther from the three disciples by Himself, and begins
falling to the ground and praying that "if it were possible, the hour might pass from
Him" (Mark 14:35). He prays aloud, "Abba! Father! All things are possible for You;
remove this cup from Me; yet not what I will, but what You wilt" (Mark 14:36). Jesus is
overwrought with grief, and clearly desires that He not have to undergo the scapegoating, suffering and death before Him. Yet, He is willing to do the Father's will, "because
it is written." Jesus' statement to Peter two verses later ("the spirit is willing, but the
flesh is weak" [Mark 14:38b]) explains the tension between Jesus' request and Jesus'
submission. Ultimately, the victory of the Father's will in Jesus demonstrates that His
pattern is certainly not the myth-culture's pattern. In this eighth motif of the fourth
episode, Jesus' "enemies are ascendant" having their "heroes' recovery," and He allows
it, to do the Father's anti-mythological will.

Jesus returns to the three disciples and finds them sleeping. He says to Peter,
"Simon, are you asleep? Could you not keep watch for one hour? Keep watching and
praying that you may not come into temptation; the spirit is willing, but the flesh
is weak" (Mark 14:37–38). With this instruction to Simon Peter, Jesus seems to be

---

54. Evans, *Mark*, 402–3.
55. Evans, *Mark*, 410.

explaining His own predicament as well. Jesus' flesh is unwilling to do what the Father has commanded, yet His spirit is full-willing. Jesus is giving His disciples a model of how to endure the most extreme trials that befall the believer, as he takes up his cross and follows Jesus in His unique, divine, evangelical pattern. When the "enemy is ascendant" it is extremely difficult not to be tempted to embrace the pattern of myth-culture, save oneself, and join the scapegoaters.

Jesus then again goes beyond the three disciples and prays, saying the same words to the Father as before (Mark 14:39), watching and praying. And again, He returns to the three disciples and finds them sleeping a second time, "for their eyes were very heavy; and they did not know what to answer Him" (Mark 14:40). Then Jesus goes again a third time to watch and pray, and comes back to His disciples to find them asleep, and He says,

> Are you still sleeping and resting? It is enough; the hour has come; behold, the
> Son of Man is being betrayed into the hands of sinners. Get up, let us be going;
> behold, the one who betrays Me is at hand! (Mark 14:41–42)

Jesus says a number of things here to His disciples. The disciples have failed to watch and pray, the hour of Jesus' "enemy's ascendance" is upon Him. His enemies, whom He calls "sinners," are about to experience a full "hero's recovery" in keeping with the mythological pattern. Jesus distinguishes Himself from sinners in saying this. He has consistently followed the unique, divine pattern while all those around Him, including His own disciples much of the time, have been following the pattern of myth-culture that is typical of sinners. And finally, Jesus tells His sleepy disciples to get up and get going with Jesus to meet His pre-determined and willful murder, because "the one who betrays Me is at hand." Evans remarks, "Jesus' prescience is here demonstrated. Before the actual arrival of the party sent out by the ruling priests, scribes, and elders (14:43), Jesus already knows who they are. Even more impressive, he knows that Judas Iscariot himself is with them."[56]

Mark says that while Jesus is still speaking this way to His disciples, "Judas, one of the twelve, comes up accompanied by a crowd with swords and clubs, who are from the chief priests and the scribes and the elders" (Mark 14:43). The religio-political leaders of Israel are having their full "hero's recovery" in this moment, and Jesus' "enemies" are certainly "ascendant," though Jesus has deliberately and willingly approached this moment, speaking of it often since before He departed from Galilee.

Judas had given his lynch-mob a signal, saying, "Whomever I kiss, he is the one; seize him and lead him away safely" (Mark 14:44). Then Judas went "immediately" to Jesus, "saying, 'Rabbi!' and kissed Him" (Mark 14:45). And the mob from the chief priests, scribes and elders, "laid hands on (Jesus) and seized Him" (Mark 14:46). Evans notes, "Now that Jesus has been identified, the priests' deputies seize him, no doubt wishing to make him secure as Judas had urged. Seizure at night was intended

---

56. Evans, *Mark*, 418.

to render Jesus' following leaderless and so discourage a coordinated counterattack (which those doing the priests' bidding may have feared)."[57] So now, in this eighth motif of the fourth episode, the religio-political leaders' mob have their scapegoat in hand. Unlike myth-culture's pattern, Jesus' "enemies are ascendant" and He Himself is fulfilling His divine mission of deliverance, while the "heroes" of myth-culture are enjoying their "recovery," in keeping with and fulfilling myth's expected pattern.

Then a scuffle occurs, as "one of those who stood by drew his sword, and struck the slave of the high priest and cut off his ear" (Mark 14:47). Notice that the violence toward the myth-culture's leaders does not come from Jesus, but the disciple Peter (John 18:10), who is once again tempted into the pattern of myth-culture, seeking his own "heroic recovery" in this eighth motif. Evans observes,

> The disciple who struck the servant of the high priest is identified in John 18:10 as Simon Peter. . . . We should perhaps see the disciple's action as a brave attempt to protect Jesus by intercepting a man who was advancing on Jesus to deliver a blow. . . . It may have been that Peter, still smarting from Jesus' prediction that he would not only fall away with the others but would deny Jesus . . . was eager to prove his loyalty.[58]

If this was indeed Simon Peter's intent, he was certainly living by the expectation of the myth-culture's pattern in that moment, rather than the pattern of Jesus Christ. But Jesus says to the lynch-mob:

> Have you come out with swords and clubs to arrest Me, as you would against a robber? Every day I was with you in the temple teaching, and you did not seize Me; but this has taken place to fulfill the Scriptures. (Mark 14:48–49)

Here, Jesus reiterates to the leaders of Israel's mob that what is happening is according to the Lord's timing, and according to the Lord's prophetic word in the Hebrew Bible (Old Testament). Jesus also indicates that their method for capturing Him, with swords and clubs, is ridiculous since He is no sinner (Jesus gives the example of a robber) who needs to be seized by the authorities as though He has done anything wrong. Evans observes, "Jesus is unfazed; his time in prayer has prepared him for this moment. . . . Not only is Scripture fulfilled, but Jesus' own predictions begin to be fulfilled."[59]

And then, all Jesus' disciples "left (Jesus) and fled" (Mark 14:50), just as Jesus foretold that they would (Mark 14:27), and despite the disciples' repeated assurances that they would sooner die than abandon Him. A young man who was wearing nothing but "a linen sheet over his naked body" was yet following Jesus, and the mob

---

57. Evans, *Mark*, 424.

58. Evans, *Mark*, 424–25.

59. Evans, *Mark*, 426–27.

seized him as well (Mark 14:51). But the young man "pulled free of the linen sheet and escaped naked" (Mark 14:52). Evans concludes,

> Whereas *Jesus* is prepared for the temptations and dangers that lie ahead, his *disciples* are not. When the arresting party approaches, the disciples fall into panic and disorder. One strikes at the high priest's servant, all flee, and then a young man, perhaps a would-be follower, narrowly escapes, fleeing in utter disgrace. All of this underscores the stunning accuracy of Jesus' prediction that they all would fall away. In stark contrast to his disciples' failure of nerve, Jesus stands his ground, ready to drink the cup that his Father has given him.[60]

So here at the end of the eighth motif, Jesus is completely alone in His unique, divine, evangelical pattern, fulfilling the Scriptures, doing His Father's will, with His "enemies" fully "ascendant." Of course, only the fully God, fully human, Lord Jesus Christ could keep His unique pattern, and so, only He does. Therefore, Jesus stands alone. Israel's leaders are enjoying their "heroes' recovery," as expected of the myth-culture's pattern, which they follow. Jesus is now their scapegoat, but also the "Passover lamb" (Mark 14:1, 12, 22–4) of the Scriptures, the Deliverer of Adam's race.

Social-Science

Social-scientifically, this inversive eighth "enemy ascendant" motif of Jesus, and "hero recovers" motif of the religio-political leaders, continues to be comprised of deliverance exhibited by Jesus continuing His unique, divine pattern, intermingled with scapegoating exhibited by the leadership of Israel, and ultimately everyone, apart from Jesus (Mark 14:50), continuing the myth-culture's pattern. The social-science lenses of Girard and Malina aid us in perceiving this chiastic bi-pattern.

At this point in the pattern of myth-culture we typically continue to see scapegoating preeminent. However, not so in the Gospel account due to the unique evangelical pattern in Jesus Christ. Instead, Jesus exhibits deliverance in place of scapegoating, in opposition to those who embody the pattern of myth-culture around Jesus. Divine deliverance in Jesus continues to subvert the scapegoat meaning expected of this fourth episode, and continues to invert the myth-culture's sequence, so that this episode also contains a strong anti-snare of striving element as well.

There are five expressions of scapegoating experienced by Jesus in this eighth motif that concludes the fourth episode, performed by both Israel's leadership and Jesus' own disciples, but never by Jesus. Jesus' response and posture are ever according to His purpose of divine deliverance instead of scapegoating, His unique pattern instead of the pattern of myth-culture. Jesus subverts the mythologically expected scapegoating with His divine deliverance, His self-giving to save the world at enmity with Him.

60. Evans, *Mark*, 429.

Also, however, in Mark 13, Jesus prophesies coming times of scapegoating of His disciples and believers of Israel during His "enemies' ascendance" into the unspecified future. Therefore, prior to the five instances of Jesus' deliverance in the face of scapegoating, in Mark 13 Jesus prophesies His believers' deliverance from scapegoating into the distant future, all the way to the "the end" (Mark 13:7), when Jesus the Son of Man comes again on the clouds with great power and glory (Mark 13:26). Jesus says that while the believers of Israel will be hated by all because of Jesus' name (Mark 13:13a), those who endure to the end will be saved (Mark 13:13b), and Jesus will gather to Himself His elect (chosen ones) from the four winds (Mark 13:27), from all earth and all heaven, to enter His kingdom with Him. Those who take up their crosses and follow Jesus in His unique, evangelical pattern, instead of the pattern of myth-culture, are promised scapegoating by this mythological world. But believers in Jesus are also promised deliverance in this life, and most importantly in the next, life everlasting (e.g., Mark 13:13, 26–27).

The first instance of the scapegoating of Jesus in this eighth motif and fourth episode is in Mark 14:1–2, when Mark tells us that the feasts of Passover and Unleavened Bread were two days away, and the chief priests and scribes were seeking how to seize Jesus by stealth and kill Him. But these religio-political leaders of Israel were afraid of the people of Israel, and so were reluctant to do it during the festival in case the people rioted. Yet, the leaders have designated Jesus a scapegoat, and are eager to seize Him and kill Him as soon as possible.

The second instance of scapegoating in this eighth motif in the fourth episode is of a woman in Bethany, by some of those with Jesus (perhaps disciples). Jesus is reclining at supper in the house of Simon the leper, and a woman comes with a vial of costly perfume and pours it over Jesus' head. Some of those with Jesus are indignant, calling it a waste, saying that the vial (worth a year's wages) should have been sold for money and given to the poor. They are scolding the woman therefore (Mark 14:4–5). This example of scapegoating is subtle and interesting, because the woman is being attacked by a number of people for recognizing Jesus as the promised Deliverer (rather than a scapegoat), and she is being scapegoated herself for buying into and participating in the unique, divine, evangelical pattern that Jesus is modelling. She puts the LORD Jesus first, before the poor and everything else, and Jesus praises her, defends her, and delivers her from their scorn and scolding.

The third instance of scapegoating in this eighth motif in the fourth episode is when Judas Iscariot, one of the twelve disciples, goes to the chief priests in order to betray his master Jesus to them (Mark 14:10–11). Judas knows that the religio-political leaders want to get rid of Jesus, and he offers to make that possible. He actively joins in the scapegoating of Jesus. The chief priests offer to give Judas money in exchange for Jesus, and "Judas began seeking how to betray Jesus at an opportune time."

The fourth instance of scapegoating is the actual physical event of Judas leading a mob of soldiers from the chief priests to capture Jesus and "bring Him in" (Mark

14:43–7). It is the night of the first day of Passover, and Jesus has just finished praying the third time in Gethsemane on the Mount of Olives, and Judas arrives right on
schedule, "accompanied by a multitude with swords and clubs, from the chief priests
and the scribes and the elders." Judas approaches Jesus, says, "Rabbi," and kisses Him.
That is the signal to the mob, who then take hold of Him. The religio-political leaders
now have their scapegoat in hand. The "heroes" have "recovered," Jesus' "enemy" is fully
"ascendant." Yet Jesus is simultaneously right on schedule to affect His divine deliverance. One of those who follows Jesus, the disciple Peter, is again unable to follow the
unique, evangelical pattern Jesus is modelling, and so again reverts to the pattern of
myth-culture. Simon Peter, "drew his sword, and struck the slave of the high priest, and
cut off his ear."

The fifth and final instance of scapegoating in the eighth motif, and in this fourth
scapegoating-deliverance episode, is when all Jesus' disciples leave Him and flee (Mark
14:50–52). They have all vowed to stay with Him and even die with Him, but when the
time comes, the moment of scapegoating by the cosmic authorities, one betrays Jesus
and the other eleven abandon Him. So, all Jesus' disciples participate in scapegoating
Him either explicitly or implicitly. Jesus knew that they would and told them so in
advance. He told them that all of their actions were in fulfillment of prophecies of
Scripture. Mark tells us that after Jesus' disciples had fled, there was yet a "certain
young man" following Jesus and wearing only a linen sheet (Mark 14:51). The mob
grabs this young man too, but then he also flees naked, leaving his sheet behind (Mark
14:52). Jesus the scapegoat is utterly alone, and Jesus alone is delivering Israel, and all
humanity, by willingly going to shed His blood for many, and rise again the third day.

Jesus' behavior, including His five responses to these five acts of scapegoating, is
ever according to His unique, divine purpose of deliverance. Jesus offers deliverance
in place of scapegoating: (1) While the chief priests and scribes in Jerusalem plot to
seize Jesus by stealth for their scapegoat, and kill Him (Mark 14:1–2), Jesus is waiting
nearby at the house of Simon the leper in Bethany (very near Jerusalem [Mark 14:3a]),
willingly preparing Himself to die to deliver the people. (2) While people with Jesus
at Simon's house scold a woman for helping Jesus to prepare for His imminent salvific
death (Mark 14:4–5), Jesus stops them and praises her for aiding Him in His mission
of deliverance through His death and resurrection (Mark 14:8).

(3) While Judas Iscariot goes to betray his master Jesus to the chief priests in
order to help them acquire Him as their scapegoat, in exchange for filthy lucre, Jesus
is preparing Himself—even as the Passover lamb is being sacrificed (Mark 14:12)—to
sacrifice His own life at Passover to save the people (Mark 14:14). Jesus knows He is
being betrayed by Judas (Mark 14:17–21), and does not try to stop Judas or flee from
scapegoating and death, but willingly and deliberately goes to His death to deliver
"many" (Mark 14:24). Jesus describes Himself as a sacrificial victim, His body as bread
to be eaten for the deliverance of all who believe in Him (Mark 14:22), His blood as
wine to be drunk for the deliverance of all who believe in Him (Mark 14:23). But

Jesus says He will drink wine again in the kingdom of God (Mark 14:25), signaling His resurrection and glorious future. Jesus' divine, evangelical pattern is diametrically opposed in order and meaning to the pattern of myth-culture. The religio-political leaders and even Jesus' own disciples, meanwhile, simultaneously continue in the pattern of myth-culture, out of which they are evidently unable to rise.

(4) While Judas leads an armed mob from the chief priests and scribes and elders to capture Jesus their scapegoat (Mark 14:43–47), Jesus has been praying to the Father to prepare Himself for His self-sacrificial deliverance of the people (Mark 14:32–42). Then Jesus asks the mob why they come for Him armed with swords and clubs as though He were a robber, when He has been speaking openly for days in the Temple in Jerusalem and they did not seize Him (Mark 14:48–49a). With this question Jesus indicates that He is being scapegoated, since He is innocent of wrongdoing, and His death sentence by the world's leaders is immoral and unlawful, and so is done by stealth under cover of darkness. Jesus concludes that their actions are dictated by "the Scriptures," which all parties are "fulfilling" in that moment (Mark 14:49b). They think to scapegoat Him, but Jesus' actions are for their deliverance according to "the Scriptures."

(5) Finally, while all Jesus' disciples join implicitly in scapegoating Him, fleeing for their lives and forsaking their master (Mark 14:50–52) just as He predicted and they denied, Jesus willingly goes alone to His death for them to deliver them and many more. Jesus alone walks the strange, unique, evangelical pattern of the Cross, that no one else walks. All others, even Jesus' closest disciples, instead continue in the pattern of myth-culture, joining in scapegoating.

Jesus' divine deliverance according to His evangelical pattern is not only subversive of the scapegoating episode of myth-culture's pattern, however, but inversive of the snare-of-striving episode as well, continuing the formation of the chiastic structure of the two patterns. Jesus certainly contends with all those who come (and will come in the future [Mark 13]) against Him and His mission of deliverance, those who strive against Jesus in order to scapegoat Him and those who follow Him. But Jesus' contention in this fourth episode for maintenance of His unique, evangelical pattern is *not* the striving to ensnare others, the snare of striving that makes up the third episode of the pattern of myth-culture.

As Jesus focuses on His mission of deliverance in this fourth episode, He contends against attempts to dissuade Him and against those who oppose His divine purpose. As He does this, Jesus cites the Scriptures in His predictions of His disciples' future scapegoatings (when they will begin to walk in His unique, divine, evangelical pattern [Mark 13]), and during His five personal sorrows of scapegoating (Mark 14). Part of Jesus' contending for His faith is praying earnestly to the Father for the strength to do the Father God's will, instead of the will of "the flesh" (Mark 14:35–39). Just as previously, when His mythological opponents were unable to counter the power of His statements and deeds, no one who speaks or acts against Jesus in this eighth motif in the fourth episode is successful. Even though their mythological plans and deeds go forward, continuing unabated in the pattern of myth-culture, their words and actions have no effect toward hindering Jesus in His own pattern. In fact, Jesus says that what they do "fulfills the Scriptures" (Mark 14:49).

So, Jesus' inverted striving, His contending, in this fourth scapegoat-deliverance episode does not occur at the point that striving occurs in the myth-culture's pattern, and it does not mean what striving means in the myth-culture's pattern. Jesus "strives" to deliver His scapegoaters, to save treacherous "sinners" as He calls them (Mark 14:41). Jesus self-sacrificially "strives" to offer deliverance even to His scapegoaters, while they have striven to scapegoat an innocent man for personal gain.

9

Episode 5

Mark 14:53–15:41: Satiation and Dispersive Display

Satiation	Dispersive Display
"Come with us. . . . Let us swallow them alive like Sheol . . . fill our houses with spoil; Many bulls have surrounded me. . . . They open wide their mouth at me, as a . . . roaring lion" (Prov 1:11–13; Ps 22:12–13)	"If [a grain of wheat] dies, it bears much fruit; so must the Son of Man be lifted up, so that whoever believes in Him will have eternal life" (John 12:24; 3:14–15)

OVERVIEW

The transition to the fifth episode of the Gospel account begins with the Judas-led lynch-mob, which came from the chief priests, scribes and elders, taking Jesus back to these leaders (tenant-farmers) of Israel (Mark 14:53). Jesus the scapegoat being "brought in" initiates the satiation episode of the pattern of myth-culture, inverted and subverted by the divine dispersive display of the evangelical pattern in Jesus (table c; figure 1). The fifth satiation episode is so named as it is characterized by the myth-culture's sating of itself on the body and blood of its victim(s), while at the same time the Gospel account's fifth episode is also called the divine dispersive display because God in Christ is dispersing and displaying His glorious gift of deliverance "for many," continuing the chiastic bi-pattern.

Jesus clearly stated previously three times, but especially in Mark 10:33–34, that His death would graphically display His love for them, even as the leaders of Israel and of the gentiles (or nations, led by Rome) are sated upon the suffering of their scape-goat. In the Gospel account, the fifth episode ends with darkness, the death of the

LORD Jesus, the tearing of the Temple's veil, and the women disciples and converted centurion looking on as eye-witnesses of all of these events (Mark 15:37–41).

The first and last verses of this episode are selected based upon their positions at the beginning and end of the content of this episode that parallels combat myths. The two combat myth motifs that help us see the beginning and end of this fifth episode, in addition to the change of focus from the scapegoat-deliverance emphasis and content to the satiation-dispersion emphasis and content, are the ninth motif of "battle rejoined" and the tenth motif of "victory," in that order. But again, unlike the combat myth pattern, as seen for example in the Zeus-Typhon combat and Marduk-Tiamat combat, the motifs' order is inversive and their significance is subversive in the Gospel account, in Jesus, when compared to myth.[1]

Unlike the myth-culture's pattern, in Jesus' unique, evangelical pattern "victory" comes first, and is not a mythological victory but an anti-mythological victory. Jesus' victory consists of Him proving unimpeachable and perfect before the high priest, Sanhedrin council, and the Roman governor Pilate. At the same time, Jesus declares Himself to be the Messiah (Christ), the LORD (as Son of God), and the King of Israel (assaulted by envious "tenant-farmers," as noted by Pilate [Mark 15:10]). And yet, Jesus is condemned to death by Israel's leaders and the leader of the nations (in Pilate). Jesus' "victory" is therefore not a mythological "victory" motif.

Then Jesus' "battle rejoined" comes second, out of order in comparison with myth-culture's pattern. Jesus' "battle rejoined" is not the type of mythological "battle rejoined" seen in myth. He willingly suffers terribly, not fighting at all with His scape-goaters, and is brutally murdered by them. Jesus' "battle rejoined" is to faithfully suffer as His Father wills, and He succeeds gloriously. But this behavior is certainly not the "battle rejoined" of the myth-culture's pattern. As Jesus dies, He quotes Psalm 22:1 (Mark 15:34), which is also quoted by Mark in the descriptions of the behavior of Jesus' crucifiers throughout the account of the crucifixion (e.g., Mark 15:24 quotes Ps 22:18; Mark 15:29 quotes Ps 22:7). Psalm 22 clearly speaks not of defeat but of victory, of eternal life despite terrible suffering and death. It implies a resurrected victim, and Jesus has promised three times to rise again on the third day.

The "tenant-farmers" of the LORD's Vineyard of Israel have done exactly what the Hebrew prophets and Jesus said to their faces that they would do, and the LORD Jesus is doing exactly what He said He would do. The myth-culture's pattern continues unhindered in the religio-political leaders of Israel, even as the divine, evangelical pattern continues unhindered in Jesus. The leaders of Israel experience their ninth mythological "battle rejoined" motif against Jesus right on cue in the myth-culture's pattern, taking Him to "court" to attempt to prove Him a blasphemer worthy of death (Mark 14:64). This motif is followed by their tenth mythological "victory" motif over

---

1. The out of order "victory" motif of Jesus occurs in first position and is found in Mark 14:53—15:14 (the two motifs are separated by a bold black line in table 1E). The seconded (in comparison) motif of Jesus' "battle rejoined" concludes the episode and is found in Mark 15:15–15:41.

Jesus, again in keeping with the pattern of myth-culture, as they convince the Roman governor Pilate to crucify Jesus, and take pleasure in mocking Jesus as He suffers and dies. At the same time, Jesus offers no defence of Himself to the myth-culture's authorities. He has already won His victory during the "kangaroo court," even as His scapegoaters think they have finally beaten Him. The LORD Jesus then goes to the Cross, as silent as a Passover lamb to the slaughter, and dies.

GOSPEL According to MARK			
WORLD'S SATIATION		**JESUS' DISPERSIVE DISPLAY**	
	14:53–55a		
		14:55b–59	
	14:60		
		14:61a	
	14:61b		
		14:62	
Battle Rejoined	14:63—15:1		Victory
		15:2	
	15:3		
		15:4–10	
	15:11–13		
		15:14a	
	15:14b		
	15:15–27		
		15:28	
	15:29–33		
Victory			Battle Rejoined
		15:34	
	15:35–36		
		15:37–41	

TABLE 1E: Satiation and Dispersive Display, Battle Rejoined and Victory

MARK 14:53—15:14: JESUS' "VICTORY"[2]

Narratology

Narratologically, this section of the Gospel account is comprised of Jesus' ninth "victory" motif, strangely preceding His tenth "battle rejoined" motif. Unlike myth, it is inversive in sequence and subversive in significance compared with the pattern of myth-culture. The expected ninth mythological motif of "battle rejoined" does predominate here in the Israel's leadership, the opposition to Jesus, but not in Jesus Himself. At this point in the combat myth, the "battle rejoined" motif is foremost. But

---

2. Please refer to appendix 1 for the text of Mark for this motif.

at this point in the Gospel account, which contains the unique, evangelical pattern in Jesus Christ, we instead see the "victory" motif preeminent in Jesus, and "battle rejoined" only in the leadership ("tenant farmers") of Israel. Not only is the sequence of the motifs reversed, however, but their significance as well. Jesus' "victory" is not like the typical "victory" of myth-culture experienced by the hero-god there.

Jesus' ninth inversive and subversive "victory" motif begins with the lynch-mob led by Judas Iscariot bringing in Jesus, into the presence of the high priest at his palace in Jerusalem, where "all the chief priests and the scribes and the elders gathered together" (Mark 14:53). These leaders have gathered for the commencement of their mythologically typical ninth "battle rejoined" motif. Mark tells us that the disciple Peter "had followed Jesus at a distance, right into the courtyard of the high priest" (Mark 14:54a). Marcus notes the phrase "at a distance" as an allusion to Psalm 38:11:

> The same expression will be used later for the women who watch him die (15:40). This expression implies a criticism . . . and the critical nuance is strengthened by the echo of Ps 38:11 . . . where the speaker complains that his closest friends stand at a distance (*apo makrothen*) from his travail. The psalmist goes on to say that he does not open his mouth in complaint (38:14) . . . a feature that appears later in the Markan narrative (14:61a).[3]

Peter was even sitting with the officers (servants) of the high priest, warming himself at their light (fire) (Mark 14:54b). Marcus continues, "Seen in this biblical context, Peter is a shadowy figure, flirting with defection though still trying to follow 'the light'—a theme suggested by the unusual choice of *phōs* to describe the fire beside which he attempts to warm himself. . . . But he is gradually being pulled into the dark orb of his master's enemies."[4] Peter may not know it in this moment, but he is again participating in the pattern of myth-culture, engaging in "battle rejoined" to save his own skin at Jesus' expense, while Jesus continues in His unique, divine pattern of "victory" through self-sacrifice for Peter and the whole world.

The chief priests and "the whole council (Sanhedrin) kept trying to obtain testimony against Jesus to put Him to death" (Mark 14:55a). These "tenant farmers" have "rejoined" in their mythological "battle" to destroy their scapegoat, their "chaos-monster" who threatens their control over the Vineyard that they have stolen from its rightful Lord. Marcus observes, "Here Jesus is arraigned in a trial with a predetermined verdict. . . . This seems to echo another Righteous Sufferer psalm . . . 'The sinner watches the righteous, and seeks to kill him' [37:32]."[5] Mark tells us that despite their efforts, the "tenant-farmer" leadership of Israel "were not finding any" testimony against Jesus (Mark 14:55b). Many people were giving false testimony against Jesus, but their testimony was not consistent (Mark 14:56). Jesus' unimpeachability is a

---

3. Marcus, *Mark 8–16*, 1013.

4. Marcus, *Mark 8–16*, 1013.

5. Marcus, *Mark 8–16*, 1013.

dispersive display of His divinity, and is a victory for Him, even as His enemies falsely try to impugn Him as a fraud and an evildoer. When Jesus is attacked, His glorious light only shines brighter and broader for all to see.

Then some people stand to give false testimony and say, "We heard Jesus say, 'I will destroy this temple [sanctuary] made with hands, and in three days I will build another made without hands'" (Mark 14:57–58). While this statement does sound similar to Jesus' remarks about His death and resurrection on the third day, as well as His prophecy that the Temple would soon be razed to the bedrock, Mark tells us that "not even in this respect was their testimony consistent" (Mark 14:59).

Then the high priest "joins" in the "battle" personally, standing and coming forward to question Jesus (Mark 14:60a). The high priest says to Jesus, "Do You not answer? What is it that these men are testifying against You?" (Mark 14:60b). The high priest appears to be attempting to catch Jesus in a "process crime," impugning Himself merely by responding to the charges. Jesus does not take the bait, "But He kept silent and did not answer" (Mark 14:61a), silent as a Passover lamb. Of this encounter between Jesus and the high priest, Marcus notes,

> Confronted with the high priest's question about the Temple charge, however, Jesus remains silent—partly in fulfillment of his role as the Suffering Just One of the Psalms and Isaiah 53, but partly perhaps because the Temple charge is in a way true: God will, within a generation, destroy the present Temple. This destruction will be related to the fate of Jesus. God will . . . build a new Temple.[6]

The high priest then questions Jesus directly about His identity, saying, "Are you the Christ (Messiah), the Son of the Blessed One?" (Mark 14:61b). The high priest has asked Jesus if He is both Messiah and LORD, since the Son of God was understood to mean God Himself in the messianic prophecies of the Hebrew Bible.

Marcus notes that, ironically, the high priest has himself declared Jesus' victory for Him:

> This, then, is one of several ironic instances in the Markan passion narrative in which the enemies of Jesus inadvertently proclaim the very Christological truths they abhor (cf. 14:2, 65; 15:2, 18, 26, 29–32). . . . Jesus does not proclaim his messianic divine sonship but lets his enemies announce it for him. And that they do so, even against their will, is one of the subtle signs in the Markan passion narrative that, despite Jesus' apparent subjection to their power, God is still in control and his victory march ongoing . . . the phrasing of the high priest's question . . . is almost identical with that of the demons in 3:11. . . . The high priest is therefore unmasked by his own question; it is not Jesus who is on the side of Satan, but the high priest and his collaborators.[7]

---

6. Marcus, *Mark 8–16*, 1015.

7. Marcus, *Mark 8–16*, 1016.

Jesus responds in the affirmative, saying, "I am; and you shall see 'the Son of Man sitting at the right hand of Power' (Ps 110:1), and 'Coming with the clouds of heaven' (Dan 7:13)" (Mark 14:62). Jesus declares His victory here, affirming His identity as Christ the LORD, and His coming victory as prophesied in the Hebrew Bible (Old Testament). Evidently, Jesus' apparent defeat and imminent death are not going to be obstacles to His victory.

In response to Jesus' declaration of His identity and victory, the high priest tears His clothes and says, "What further need do we have of witnesses? You have heard the blasphemy; how does it seem to you?" (Mark 14:63–4a). The high priest has referred to Jesus' declaration of His identity as the LORD God of the Bible as "blasphemy," meaning that Jesus' claim to be "the Son of the Blessed One" is a claim to be the LORD God. Jesus has demonstrated His divine identity with His attesting miracles (signs), and the people of Israel have been waiting for their leadership, the tenant-farmers (fig tree) of the LORD's Vineyard, to affirm Jesus' identity, but they reject Him here (the fig tree bears no fruit). Despite Jesus' explicit claim, the entire leadership of Israel declare His claim to be "blasphemy." Mark tells us, "And they all condemned Jesus to be deserving of death" (Mark 14:64b). Marcus writes,

> The high priest's action is itself blasphemous because Jesus *is* the Son of God, and that title implies participation in the divine glory. . . . The real blasphemy is *not* to recognize Jesus' words and deeds as the saving activity of God. . . . The narrative thus deconstructs the high priest's protestation of concern for God's honor, and exposes his injustice further by having him declare Jesus' guilt *before* polling his fellow justices. . . . The farcical logic of the Markan Sanhedrin trial, then, approaches that enunciated by the Red Queen: "Sentence first—verdict afterwards."[8]

Then the real satiation on their scapegoat begins, as the leadership ("tenant-farmers") of Israel begin to verbally and physically abuse their LORD, Jesus. Marks says that, "Some began to spit at Jesus, and to blindfold Jesus (cover his face), and to beat Jesus with their fists, and to say to Him, 'Prophesy!' And the officers received (treated) Jesus with slaps (blows with rods) in the face" (Mark 14:65). Marcus notes an allusion to Isaiah 50:6 here, and states, "For the evangelist and biblically literate readers . . . the echoes of the Suffering Servant passages in Isaiah 50–53 (silence before judges, spitting, slapping) may suggest that this absorption of abuse is actually effecting the defeat of the rulers of this world."[9] Their behavior is a grotesque "battle rejoined" for those in the pattern of myth-culture, and yet an antithetical "victory" for Jesus in His unique, divine, evangelical pattern.

Mark tells us that as this beating of Jesus ensues at the palace of the high priest, the disciple Peter is still "below in the courtyard" (Mark 14:66a). A servant-girl of the

---

8. Marcus, *Mark 8–16*, 1017.

9. Marcus, *Mark 8–16*, 1017.

high priest then sees Peter "warming himself" at their light, and she says to him, "You also were with Jesus the Nazarene" (Mark 14:66b–7). She is continuing her master's "battle rejoined" against Jesus' followers now also. As prophesied by Jesus, though not yet recognized by Peter, he denies the slave-girl's assertion, saying, "I neither know nor understand what you are talking about" (Mark 14:68a). Peter himself is continuing in the pattern of myth-culture; having implicitly joined in the scapegoating of Jesus, he is now joining in the mythological mob's satiation on Jesus.

Peter is clearly afraid that he will become a scapegoat too, because he then leaves the warm light and goes "out onto the porch (forecourt/gateway) [and the rooster crowed]" (Mark 14:68b). The servant-girl of the high priest sees Peter there, and again says to the bystanders around him, "This is one of them!" (Mark 14:69). Peter denies any association with Jesus a second time (Mark 14:70a). After a little while, the other bystanders themselves say to Peter a third time, "Surely you are one of them, for you are a Galilean too, [and your speech is alike]" (Mark 14:70b). Peter's different accent from theirs, which is the same as Jesus' and reminds them of Him, shows He is Galilean and not Judean, and gives Him away, associating him with Jesus the scapegoat. Cursing and swearing, Peter denies Jesus a third time saying, "I do not know this Man you are talking about!" (Mark 14:71). Immediately a rooster crowed a second time (Mark 14:72a).

Peter has sated himself on Jesus, just like the leadership of Israel. He has betrayed Jesus, "joining" in the "battle" against Jesus to save himself. When the rooster crows the second time, Mark says that Peter "remembered how Jesus had made the remark to him, 'Before a rooster crows twice, you will deny Me three times.' And (Peter) began to weep" (Mark 14:72b). Even here in this dark moment, there is a combination of the opponents' "battle rejoined" and Jesus' inversive and subversive "victory," an intermingling of mythological satiation and divine dispersive display. Marcus observes,

> At the very moment, then, that Jesus is being mocked as a prophet (14:65), his prophecy of Peter's denial (14:30) is coming to pass, as Peter confirms by recalling it word for word (14:72). . . . Importantly, for the question of Peter's fate, this prophecy was embedded in a graceful context: Jesus foretold that Peter and the other disciples would abandon him, but he added the coda that he would later lead them back into battle at his side (14:28).[10]

The LORD Jesus' prophecies are all coming true, as well as the prophecies of the Hebrew prophets from which Jesus has quoted, and to which He has alluded.

Jesus' enemies are now sating themselves upon Him, "having their way" with Him (as prophesied). And Jesus is already beginning to achieve His divine dispersive display through His body broken and shared out to the world, and His blood poured out "for many." Marcus adds, "The hopeful implication does not change the fact

---

10. Marcus, *Mark 8–16*, 1024–25.

that the last remnant of Jesus' inner circle has now abandoned him and he has been condemned to death by the highest religious authority."[11] The opponents' ninth "battle rejoined" motif seems to be going very successfully at present. Yet, as the LORD's foretold will is being fulfilled and accomplished through Jesus, it is nevertheless a great ninth "victory" motif for Him; though certainly atypical of the myth-culture's "victory."

Mark tells us that early that morning, "the chief priests with the elders and scribes and the whole council (Sanhedrin), immediately held a consultation; and binding Jesus, they led Him away and delivered Him to Pilate" (Mark 15:1). Yarbro Collins comments that this "delivering" of Jesus, or "handing over," "evokes Isa 53:12 . . . according to which the servant of the Lord is handed over to death. Further, the handing of Jesus over to Pilate by the chief priests here fulfills the next part of the most detailed prediction of the passion, [Mark] 10:33: 'and they will hand him over to the nations.'"[12] The leaders of Israel's ninth "battle rejoined" motif continues against Jesus. They need to arrange for His death, and they intend that Pilate the Roman governor should do it. Yarbro Collins notes, "The council had no jurisdiction over capital cases; only the Roman governor had authority to impose the death sentence."[13] Pilate questions Jesus, saying, "Are you the King of the Jews?" (Mark 15:2a) Jesus replies, "It is as you say" (Mark 15:2b). With this affirmation, Jesus declares His LORDship over Israel a second time, now to the Roman governor, the representative of the nations. Immediately, the chief priests "begin to accuse Jesus harshly of many things [but He answered nothing]" (Mark 15:3). In response, Pilate questions Jesus again, saying, "Do You not answer? See how many charges they bring against You!" (Mark 15:4). But Jesus makes no further answer, so that "Pilate is amazed" (Mark 15:5).

Apart from successful fulfillment of prophecy and so the Father's will, there is another critical "victory" in this for Jesus (as becomes clearer in the following verses), which is inversive and subversive of myth-culture's expectation, in that Pilate openly recognizes the legitimacy of Jesus' claim (or pretends to for political ends), while also recognizing the illegitimacy of Israel's religio-political leaders' motives for condemning Jesus. The upshot is a public declaration of Jesus' Kingship, a dispersive display for all to see and hear.

Mark says that at the feast of Passover, the first daylight period of the first day of which is just now beginning, Pilate has a habit of releasing one prisoner to the people of Israel, whomever they request (Mark 15:6). He then tells us that at that time, Pilate is holding a man named Barabbas, "who had been imprisoned with the insurrectionists who had committed murder in the insurrection" (Mark 15:7). Expecting Pilate to keep his custom of releasing a prisoner, the people of Israel who are there for the feast

---

11. Marcus, *Mark 8–16*, 1025.

12. Yarbro Collins, *Mark*, 712.

13. Yarbro Collins, *Mark*, 712.

of Passover and Unleavened Bread, started "[crying aloud,] and began asking Pilate to do as he had been accustomed to do for them" (Mark 15:8).

Pilate expects the people to ask for, and evidently desires himself to perform, the release of Jesus. So, he answers the people by saying, "'Do you want me to release for you the King of the Jews?' For Pilate was aware that the chief priests had handed Jesus over because of envy" (Mark 15:9–10). Yarbro Collins observes, "This explanation implies that Pilate expected the people to ask for Jesus. The envy of the chief priests . . . is due to Jesus' popularity with the crowd."[14] This is a "victory" for Jesus, that Pilate acknowledges Jesus as King of Israel, and acknowledges the false accusations of the "tenant-farmers" of Israel out of envy for the LORD's possession of Israel. But Mark tells us that the chief priests "stir up the crowd" against the LORD Jesus (Mark 15:11a), continuing their "battle rejoined" against the LORD Jesus. Yarbro Collins suspects, "It may even be implied that the chief priests organized the crowd so that they would ask for Barabbas."[15] The chief priests encourage the crowd to ask Pilate "to release Barabbas for them instead" (Mark 15:11b).

Pilate responds by again asking them about Jesus, saying, "Then what shall I do with Him whom you call the King of the Jews?" (Mark 15:12). The people shout back, "Crucify Him!" (15:13). Pilate asks a third time, and more pointedly, "Why, what evil has He done?" (15:14a). But the people "shout all the more, 'Crucify Him!'" (Mark 15:14b). The leadership of Israel has convinced the people to join them in condemning Jesus to death. Roman governor Pilate will do their bidding, as is his custom. Yarbro Collins concludes, "It is striking that the sentence of Jesus (crucifixion) is determined here by the crowd and not by Pilate, who, as governor, was the only person with the authority to pass such a sentence at the time. Pilate's question in v. 14, 'What evil has he done?' . . . is a clear indication that . . . Pilate believed Jesus to be innocent and that he ought to have been released."[16]

Yet, Jesus' opponents have now had a successful ninth "battle rejoined" motif, in keeping with both the sequence and significance of myth-culture. Jesus Himself has not, but rather has enjoyed an inversive and subversive ninth "victory" motif, fulfilling the Father's will and being declared the King of Israel. It is certainly not a mythological "victory," however. Leading the nation along with them, the religio-political leaders of Israel have begun enjoying the fifth satiation episode on Jesus their scapegoat; beating, mocking, accusing and condemning Him to death. At the same time, Jesus has been engaging in His fifth divine dispersive display episode, dispersing Himself and displaying Himself for the whole Sanhedrin (the fig tree), the crowd (the vineyard), and all nations (the Romans) to see: Jesus the LORD, the King of Israel, the King of the universe.

14. Yarbro Collins, *Mark*, 720.

15. Yarbro Collins, *Mark*, 720.

16. Yarbro Collins, *Mark*, 720–21.

Social-Science

Social-scientifically, this ninth motif in the fifth satiation-dispersive display episode is comprised of dispersive display exhibited by Jesus, continuing His divine, evangelical pattern, intermingled with the satiation exhibited by every branch of Israel's leadership, as well as Jesus' disciples represented by Peter and ultimately all the people, continuing the myth-culture's pattern. The up-coming tenth motif continues and concludes this fifth episode. The social-science lenses of Girard and Malina aid us in perceiving the continued chiastic bi-pattern in the Gospel account.

At this point in the pattern of myth-culture we typically see satiation preeminent. However, not so in the Gospel account due to the evangelical pattern here in Jesus Christ. Instead, Jesus exhibits divine dispersive display instead of myth-culture's satiation. Dispersive display in Jesus subverts the satiation-meaning expected of this fifth episode, and inverts the myth-sequence so that this episode also contains a strong anti-scandal element.[17]

It is difficult to separate out the instances of the world's satiation on the LORD Jesus the scapegoat in this ninth motif in the fifth episode. But I count eleven expressions of satiation here. All satisfying of self on the victim is performed by various members of Israel's leadership, and their servants, and Jesus' disciples represented by Peter, and the crowd of people in Jerusalem for the feast of Passover, and Pontius Pilate the Roman governor. Everyone participates in the satiation on the scapegoat.

The expressions of satiation include: (1) the gathering of all Israel's leadership together at the palace of the high priest to take part in condemning Jesus (Mark 14:53), on the very day of the feast of Passover when the pure lamb is sacrificed to save the people of Israel; (2) the chief-disciple Peter gathering with the servants of the high priest to warm himself at their light (Mark 14:54); (3) the chief priests and whole council (Sanhedrin) attempting to find testimony against Jesus to put Him to death (Mark 14:55); (4) the high priest himself coming forward to condemn Jesus to death for blasphemy for claiming to be Christ (Messiah) and LORD (Son of the Blessed One) (Mark 14:61, 63); (5) the entire council (Sanhedrin) joining the high priest in condemning Jesus to death (Mark 14:64); (6) members of the council and the high priest's officers (servants) collectively spitting on, blindfolding, mocking, beating, and slapping Jesus (Mark 14:65); (7) the attempts by servants of the high priest to also condemn those associated with Jesus, namely the disciple Peter (Mark 14:66–72); (8) Peter's three denials of association with Jesus to save himself (Mark 14:68, 70–71); (9) the chief priests, elders, scribes and whole council (Sanhedrin) holding a consultation

17. As shown in the methodology, while the narratological chiasm is within each episode, involving the switching (inverting) of the two motifs and their meanings, the social-scientific chiasm involves the switching of the entire account's sequence of episodes and their meanings, inverting one and six, two and five, three and four. These two narratological and social-scientific aspects of the inversive and subversive chiastic relation of Jesus' unique pattern and myth-culture's pattern are demonstrated as we read through Mark's account.

early in the morning, binding Jesus and sending Him to the Roman governor Pontius Pilate (Mark 15:1); (10) the chief priests accusing Jesus of many things before Pilate (Mark 15:3); (11) the chief priests stirring up the crowd to release a known criminal and condemn innocent Jesus to death by crucifixion out of envy (Mark 15:10–14).

Jesus is never found to be engaging in satiation in any of these eleven instances. He is the victim of satiation in all of them, and He subverts satiation in every case. Jesus' stated and active purpose is divine dispersive display for everyone (e.g., Mark 14:62), including those sating themselves on Him. Jesus says to the high priest, "I am (the Christ, the Son of the Blessed One), and you shall see 'the Son of Man sitting at the right hand of Power' (Ps 110:1), and 'Coming with the clouds of heaven' (Dan 7:13)." What a dispersive display of His divine glory is this statement, quoting Hebrew Messianic prophecy as concerning Himself, to the high priest and the entire leadership of Israel! Jesus displays and disperses His divine glory throughout these eleven satiations by the leaders and people of Israel, His own disciple Peter, and the Roman governor Pilate.

In total, I note seven instances of Jesus' divine dispersive display in this ninth motif in the fifth episode, including: (1) no reliable testimony being found against Jesus, confirming His innocence and purity (Mark 14:55b–59); (2) Jesus' silence in the face of false accusations (Mark 14:61a); (3) Jesus' clear declaration of His messiahship and divinity (as noted; Mark 14:61b–62); (4) Jesus' declaration of Himself as King of Israel (Mark 15:2); (5) Jesus' silence before the chief priests' false accusations a second time (Mark 15:5); (6) Pilate's awareness of Israel's leaders' envious motivation, and his attempt to have Jesus released (Mark 15:9–10); (7) Pilate's vocal acknowledgement of Jesus' innocence (Mark 15:14). All of these seven elements contribute to Jesus' dispersive display of His divine glory, subverting the mythological satiation of everyone around Jesus.

Jesus' divine dispersive display according to His divine, evangelical pattern is not only subversive of the fifth satiation episode of myth-culture's pattern, however, but inversive of myth-culture's second scandal episode as well, continuing the formation of the chiastic structure of the two patterns. Jesus is certainly a scandal to everyone who interacts with Him in this fifth episode, but the scandal is not caused by Him, but by the envy, hate and self-interest in the hearts of those around Him. Mark states that governor Pilate knows that the leaders ("tenant-farmers") of Israel condemn Jesus to death "out of envy" (Mark 15:10). In the social-science chapters previous, we noted that Girard and Malina describe envy as a key characteristic of the scandal episode, and a driving factor in the escalation of the myth-culture's pattern from sameness toward striving, scapegoating, and satiation.

Jesus inverts scandal here by not being scandalized in turn by the high priest's and ruling council's refusal to acknowledge His rightful claim to being Christ, Son of God and King of Israel. They call Jesus' claim "blasphemy," denying the return of their King, just as Jesus' parables prophesied. Jesus shows no sign of being scandalized by their denial. He simply quotes Scriptural prophecies (e.g., Daniel) affirming His claim, and otherwise remains silent. Jesus' accusers have been envious and scandalized by Him since the second episode, and envy still drives them here in the fifth episode, but Jesus is not scandalized by them in turn. Therefore, Jesus' dispersive display of divinity also inverts scandal here.

GOSPEL According to MARK			
WORLD'S SATIATION		JESUS' DISPERSIVE DISPLAY	
Battle Rejoined	14:53–55a		Victory
		14:55b–9	
	14:60		
		14:61a	
	14:61b		
		14:62	
	14:63—15:1		
		15:2	
	15:3		
		15:4–10	
	15:11–13		
		15:14a	
	15:14b		
Victory	15:15–27		Battle Rejoined
		15:28	
	15:29–33		
		15:34	
	15:35–36		
		15:37–41	

TABLE 1E: Satiation and Dispersive Display, Battle Rejoined and Victory

MARK 15:15–41: JESUS' "BATTLE REJOINED"[18]

Narratology

Narratologically, this section of the Gospel account makes up the tenth "battle rejoined" motif for Jesus, out of place and out of character from the vantage of the myth-culture's pattern. Jesus' tenth motif is atypically inversive in sequence and subversive in significance when compared with the pattern of myth-culture, and it concludes the fifth satiation-dispersive display episode. The expected tenth mythological motif of "victory" clearly occurs here only in the myth-culture's leadership, the opposition to Jesus, so that they continue in the pattern of myth-culture, while Jesus continues His

18. Please refer to appendix 1 for the complete text of this motif in Mark's account.

anti-mythological evangelical pattern. In addition to being inversive in sequence, Jesus' "battle rejoined" motif is subversive in significance, having a very different meaning to that of myth-culture. A part of this subversive meaning is that Jesus' crucifixion and death at the hands of His enemies is all according to His pre-determined and pre-declared plan, in fulfillment of the Scriptures and the Father's will, according to Jesus (Mark 8:31; 9:31; 10:33–34; 14:21).

As mentioned previously, due to Jesus' divine distinction, He is not actually imperiled by opposition in the manner of mere humans and/or mythological gods. In the Gospel account, Satan and the world's leadership are not Jesus' rivals in the mythological sense. Unlike myth-culture, the biblical view of the LORD's relation to Satan is not the dualistic relationship of the hero and the villain. Jesus, His Father and His Spirit (e.g., Mark 1:10–12) are ultimately in control of all the events unfolding (see Mark 14:36, 49), unlike events in myth-culture. In His tenth "battle rejoined" motif, Jesus willingly and quietly undergoes the grotesque satiation of the "tenant-farmers" of Israel, and giving a mighty shout, a great dispersive display of His divinity, as He dies. The leaders of Israel finally have sated themselves on their scapegoat, enjoyed their mythological "victory" in this tenth motif, in keeping with and continuing myth-culture's pattern. And yet, their "victory" assures their destruction, as prophesied by the LORD Jesus (Mark 12:9). The mythological "victory" they think they achieve is no "victory" at all, and it is very short-lived (e.g., Mark 13:2).

At this point in the combat myth, the "victory" motif is foremost. But at this point in the Gospel account, which contains the evangelical pattern in Jesus Christ, we instead see the "battle rejoined" motif preeminent in Jesus. The expected mythological "victory" motif predominates only in the religio-political leaders who oppose Jesus. The sequence of the motifs is inverted by Jesus, and He subverts their significance as well, so that Jesus' "battle rejoined" is not like the typical "battle rejoined" of myth-culture experienced by the hero-god there.

Jesus' tenth motif in this fifth episode begins with Mark telling the reader that the Roman governor Pilate "wishes to satisfy the crowd" (Mark 15:15a). France remarks, "The idiom τὸ ἱκανὸν ποιῆσαι τινι probably means 'to satisfy.' . . . Pilate is not willing or able to oppose either part of the crowd's demand."[19] In order to satiate the crowd, then, Pilate releases the insurrectionist murderer Barabbas to them as requested, and then "hands Jesus over to be crucified" (Mark 15:15b). This event begins the tenth mythological "victory" motif for the leaders of Israel, and Jesus' tenth evangelical "battle rejoined" motif. Jesus has been sentenced to a brutal and shameful death on full display to the world, which has gathered at Jerusalem for the Passover feast.

The Roman soldiers take Jesus away into the palace of the praetorium, or Roman fortress, and call the whole cohort (battalion) together (Mark 15:16).[20] The soldiers

19. France, *Gospel of Mark*, 634.

20. This event occurred on the so-called "Temple Mount," upon which sits the Muslim Dome of the Rock today (Martin, *Temples*, 3, 59), contrary to the claims of many scholars. Herod's Temple was

dress Jesus in purple, twist a crown of thorns together and put it on His head (Mark 15:17). They then begin to acclaim Jesus, saying, "Hail, King of the Jews!" (Mark 15:18). Then they begin to beat Jesus' head repeatedly with a reed-staff, spitting on Him, and kneeling and bowing before Him (Mark 15:19). France observes, "The mixture of mockery and cruelty in dressing Jesus up is continued in the soldiers' actions, as the homage of royal acclamation and of kneeling before the 'king' is combined with beating and spitting."[21] When they are done mocking Jesus, they take the purple robe off of Him, put His own clothes back on Him, and lead Him out to crucify Him (Mark 15:20). All of these acts of satiation upon and "victory" over their scapegoat Jesus are typical of this point in the combat myth pattern, and of the heroes' treatment of their "chaos-monster," as noted by Girard and Malina as well as combat myth scholars discussed previously.

The Roman soldiers "press into service" a passer-by coming in from the country named Simon of Cyrene, whom Mark notes is the father of Alexander and Rufus; they force this Simon to bear Jesus' cross (Mark 15:21). And they bring Jesus to a place called Golgotha, meaning "Place of a Skull" (Mark 15:22).[22] They try to give Jesus "wine mixed with myrrh, but He does not take it" (Mark 15:23). Then the Roman soldiers crucify Jesus; and they divide up His garments amongst themselves by casting lots for them to decide who gets what (Mark 15:24). France observes, "A further level of reflection is introduced by the clear echo of Ps 22 in v. 24. Ps 22 is one of those which depict the suffering of God's faithful servant exposed to the malice of the ungodly . . . a prefiguring of the passion of Jesus. The psalm will not be quoted verbatim until v. 34, but echoes of it run through the Golgotha narrative."[23] Jesus' "battle rejoined" is clearly one of continued willingness to suffer in the Father's will, toward the glorious purpose that Jesus and the prophets (including the Psalmist [Ps 22:22–31]) have expressed. Jesus' "battle rejoined" is a very different "battle rejoined" than that of myth-culture,

---

razed to bedrock in AD 70, as prophesied by the LORD Jesus (Mark 13:2) and the prophets of Israel (e.g., Mic 3:12). Only the Roman fortress Antonia remains to this day (Josephus, *Jewish War* 7.1.1; 7.8.7), and the Praetorium in which Jesus was flogged by the Romans stood where the Dome of the Rock stands today. That is, the "Temple Mount" is no such thing; it is the Roman fortress in which Jesus was flogged.

21. France, *Gospel of Mark*, 638.

22. Golgotha was upon the Mount of Olives (Martin, *Secrets of Golgotha*, 96–103), east of the Temple, facing its doors. This is critical to understand for the events of Jesus' crucifixion to make sense as recorded in the Gospel accounts. Once again, however, as with the actual location of the Temple, most scholars do not know or recognize that Golgotha was upon the Mount of Olives.

23. France, *Gospel of Mark*, 640. France has more to say regarding the allusions to Psalm 22 in Jesus' tenth "battle rejoined" motif as He marches toward and endures the Cross: "The story has been moulded to some extent by the wording of the psalm which will provide Jesus with the only words he speaks from the cross in this gospel. The following echoes are clear: Mark 15:24 Psalm 22:18 | Mark 15:29 Psalm 22:7 | Mark 15:34 Psalm 22:1 and further echoes are likely both in the general theme of scorn (cf. Ps 22:6) and in the words of mockery in vv. 30–31 concerning being 'saved' (cf. Ps 22:8) . . . the cumulative effect of this language is to assure the reader who is familiar with Ps 22 . . . that what is happening is, even in detail, 'according to scripture,' as Jesus had predicted" (*Gospel of Mark*, 640).

while the religio-political leaders' "victory" is very typical of that of myth-culture, as satiation usually involves the dividing up of the spoil of their victim as he dies.

Mark tells us that it is "the third hour" (9 a.m.) when the Roman soldiers crucify Jesus (Mark 15:25), and that the charge that the Romans inscribe for Jesus, for all to see, is, "The King of the Jews" (Mark 15:26). France notes, "The phrase ὁ βασιλεὺς τῶν Ἰουδαίων is the same as that used at the trial (v. 2) and represents the charge on which Jesus has been convicted . . . a claim to be a king under the Roman empire . . . was treasonable. Placed over a man dying in agony and disgrace it was both a cruel joke and a powerful deterrent."[24] This charge ironically glorifies Jesus in His "battle rejoined" suffering, as it confirms His claim in His "victory" declaration in the last motif. The soldiers also crucify two robbers with Jesus, "one on His right and one on His left" (Mark 15:27). With this act, Mark says that the Scripture is fulfilled which reads, "And He was numbered with the transgressors" (Mark 15:28; Isa 53:12).

Once Jesus is hanging on the cross, the people increasingly enjoy their mythological "victory" and sate themselves on Jesus. As they pass by over the Mount of Olives, in and out of Jerusalem and the Temple, they take pleasure in "blaspheming" Jesus, "hurling abuse at Him," and "wagging their heads" (Ps 22:7), saying, "Ha! You who are going to destroy the temple and rebuild it in three days, save Yourself, and come down from the cross!" (Mark 15:29–30). France observes just what a dispersive display of Jesus' atypical, anti-mythological, divine glory this is: "There is scope for ironical reflection on the sort of δόξα Jesus now enjoys. . . . In recording such general mockery Mark is of course reflecting the effect that public humiliation and punishment have always been able to evoke in any culture. . . . The popular support which Jesus' teaching had at least begun to gain during the preceding week has now evaporated."[25]

The chief priests and scribes also enjoy their "victory," taking pleasure in satisfying themselves at Jesus' expense. Marks says that "in the same way the chief priests also, along with the scribes, are mocking Jesus among themselves and saying, 'He saved others; can He not save Himself? Let this Christ, the King of Israel, now come down from the cross, so that we may see and believe!'" (Mark 15:31–32a). The chief priests and scribes' mythological view of the nature and behavior of the messiah as a typical hero-god of myth-culture is displayed in these mocking jibes: "A 'deliverer' who cannot even secure his own survival is a poor sort of Χριστός for others."[26] Finally, we are told that the two robbers being crucified beside the LORD Jesus are also insulting Him (Mark 15:32b). Even while being crucified, these two men join the leadership and people of Israel, and the Romans, in mythological satiation upon their scapegoat. "Mark's readers are aware that at a deeper level all these [mock titles and claims of Jesus] are true, and that ironically it is by being where he is that Jesus is fulfilling this mission."[27]

24. France, *Gospel of Mark*, 646.
25. France, *Gospel of Mark*, 646–47.
26. France, *Gospel of Mark*, 648.
27. France, *Gospel of Mark*, 648–49.

When it becomes noon, darkness falls "over the whole land" until three in the afternoon (Mark 15:33). At three o'clock, "Jesus cried out with a loud voice, 'Eloi, Eloi, Lama Sabachthani?' meaning, 'My God, my God, why have You forsaken Me?'" (Mark 15:34; Ps 22:1a). As noted by France above, Jesus quotes from a Psalm here that describes the nature of the Messiah's "battle rejoined" and ultimate eternal triumph (Ps 22:25–31), a Psalm that later states that the LORD has *not* "hidden His face from Him" (Ps 22:24). France observes here that, "The unnatural darkness tells us that this is a crucifixion unlike any other, and prepares us to hear Jesus' dreadful last shout from the cross, and then to witness the striking manner in which he died."[28]

But bystanders think that Jesus is "calling for Elijah" (Mark 15:35). France notes that this confusion is evidently due to the possible similarity of the words "my God" and "Elijah" as pronounced in Hebrew and Aramaic (אלי).[29] One of them runs and fills a sponge with sour wine, puts it on a reed, and gives Jesus a drink, saying, "Let us see whether Elijah will come and take Him down" (Mark 15:36). Perhaps this response and behavior of the onlookers indicates something of the "victory" of the pattern of myth-culture, in their total incomprehension of what they are witnessing and participating in, and ignorance of Jesus' quotation, with a "loud voice," from the Psalms and its significance. In Jesus' "battle rejoined" He has shouted to His audience the meaning of His death from Psalm 22, and they have missed it.

Jesus then again "utters a loud cry," a great shout (in part of exasperation at the dullness of His audience?), and "He breathes His last" (Mark 15:37). In that moment of Jesus' death, "the veil of the Temple is torn in two from top to bottom" (Mark 15:38),[30] which is visible to the witnesses from Golgotha, on the Mount of Olives, where Jesus is crucified.[31] France notes:

> In Herod's temple Josephus again describes two καταπετάσματα [curtains] . . . (Josephus, *War* 5.212, 219; cf. *Ant.* 8.75); he says that the huge outer curtain hung in front of and was the same height as the doors, which were fifty-five cubits high. . . . The outer curtain, which Josephus describes rapturously as a magnificent work of Babylonian tapestry in rich colours symbolizing earth, sea, and sky (*War* 5.212–14), was the only one visible to anyone except the priests who served in the Holy Place.[32]

28. France, *Gospel of Mark*, 649–50.

29. France, *Gospel of Mark*, 654.

30. France quotes Juel, who states, "The event is for Mark the fulfillment of the 'prophecy' made in 14:58 and 15:29. With Jesus' death, the old religious order comes to an end; those who have rejected Jesus, the religious leaders, have now been rejected by God" (Juel, *Messiah and Temple*, 206, in France, *Gospel of Mark*, 657).

31. France also notes scholars (including Ernest Martin) who argue that Golgotha, where Jesus was crucified, was on the Mount of Olives, so that the veil of the Temple was indeed visible to everyone at the crucifixion site (Jackson, "Death of Jesus," 24–25; Martin, *Secrets of Golgotha*; France, *Gospel of Mark*, 658).

32. France, *Gospel of Mark*, 656.

Taken together, the entire event of Jesus' death is an incredible dispersive display of Jesus' identity, glory, and battle against sin and death, as well as divine judgment of the leadership of Israel, the figless fig tree. We are told that when the centurion standing in front of Jesus sees the way that He dies, "[having thus cried out,] and breathed His last" (Mark 15:39a)—amid a queer darkness, with a mighty shout, and the tearing of the Temple's veil—he exclaims, "Truly this Man was the Son of God!" (Mark 15:39b). France observes that this Roman centurion is:

> The first human witness to describe Jesus as υἱὸς θεοῦ and mean it, and that witness not a disciple or even a Jew at all, but a Gentile army officer with no previous connections with Jesus. What the Jewish leaders have denied and declared to be blasphemy and even the disciples have not yet grasped, this ordinary soldier perceives in the unlikely context of Jesus' final defeat and death.[33]

Thus, Jesus finishes His tenth "battle rejoined" motif, having willfully endured terrible evil and suffering right to His death, in order to "give His life a ransom for many" (Mark 10:45). At the same time, the mythological world (everyone has participated in some fashion, except Jesus) completes its tenth "victory" motif, murdering the LORD Jesus Christ. The world is satiated on its scapegoat, and Jesus has dispersed and displayed His divine glory and love as "Passover lamb" "for many" (Mark 14:24).

Mark tells us that there are "some women looking on from a distance," witnessing all of these events in Jesus' dispersive display of divinity, in His out of order and out of character "rejoined battle," including "Mary Magdalene, Mary the mother of James (Jacob) the Less and Joses, and Salome" (Mark 15:40). When Jesus was in Galilee, these women "followed Him and ministered to Him"; and "there were many other women" besides these there, who came up with Jesus from Galilee to Jerusalem, and who witness His divine dispersive display (Mark 15:41). France comments, "Mark lets us know that all the time there has been a female element to Jesus' entourage, who are now ready to pick up where the men have left off."[34]

Social-Science

Social-scientifically, this inversive tenth "battle rejoined" motif of Jesus, and tenth "victory" motif of the religio-political leaders of Israel, continues to be comprised of dispersive display exhibited by Jesus continuing His divine, evangelical pattern, intermingled with mythological satiation exhibited by the leadership of Israel, and the people themselves, continuing the myth-culture's pattern. The social-science lenses of Girard and Malina aid us in perceiving this chiastic bi-pattern.

At this point in the pattern of myth-culture we typically continue to see satiation

33. France, *Gospel of Mark*, 659.
34. France, *Gospel of Mark*, 662.

preeminent. However, not so in the Gospel account due to the evangelical pattern here in Jesus Christ. Instead, Jesus exhibits dispersive display in place of satiation, in opposition to those who embody the pattern of myth-culture around Jesus. Divine dispersive display in Jesus continues to subvert the satiation meaning expected of this fifth episode, and continues to invert the myth-sequence, so that this episode also contains a strong anti-scandal element as well.

There are perhaps nine expressions of satiation in this tenth motif in the fifth episode, performed by Israel's leadership as well as the people of Israel and the Romans, but never by Jesus. Jesus' response and posture are ever according to His purpose of dispersive display of His unique divinity instead of satiation, His evangelical pattern instead of the pattern of myth-culture. Jesus subverts the mythologically expected satiation with His display, His self-giving to save the world at enmity with Him.

The expressions of satiation on Jesus in this tenth motif and fifth episode are: (1) Because Pilate wishes to "satisfy" the crowd, he releases the murdering insurrectionist Barabbas to the people, and has the innocent Jesus scourged, and then hands Him over to be crucified (Mark 15:15). (2) The Roman soldiers take Jesus away to the court of the Praetorium, call together the entire battalion, dress Jesus in purple, twist a crown of thorns onto His head, and mock Him exclaiming, "Hail, King of the Jews!" (Mark 15:16–18). (3) The soldiers then beat Jesus repeatedly in the head with a reed-staff, spit on Him and kneel and bow before Him (Mark 15:19). (4) They then put Jesus' own clothes back on Him and lead Him out of the Roman fortress, out of the Temple precinct and out of Jerusalem, to crucify Him (Mark 15:20). (5) The satiation continues as the soldiers bring Jesus to a place called Golgotha, eastward across the Kidron valley on the Mount of Olives, in view of most of the City, and in view of the veiled entrance of the Temple (Mark 15:38). They try to give Jesus wine mixed with myrrh, and they crucify Him (Mark 15:22–24a). (6) The soldiers divide up the "spoils" of Jesus garments between themselves by casting lots for them (Mark 15:24b). (7) The many people passing by (it is presumably a busy road, especially on the high holiday of Passover, and as it is the main route across the valley and into the Temple) collectively sate themselves on Jesus, by hurling blasphemy and insults at Jesus, as He hangs on the cross under the charge "The King of the Jews" (Mark 15:29, 26). They "wag their heads" at Jesus and mockingly command Him to save Himself (Mark 15:30). (8) The chief priests and scribes also join in the collective satiation with the people, mocking Jesus as He hangs, saying, "He saved others; can He not save Himself?" (Mark 15:31). They exclaim that if Jesus will save Himself and come down from the cross, then they will believe in Him (Mark 15:32a). (9) The mythological satiation on the scapegoat is so unanimous that even the robbers being crucified on each side of Jesus insult Him, joining in the collective feast on the innocent victim (Mark 15:32b).

Jesus' behavior, including His responses to these acts of satiation, is ever according to His divine purpose of dispersive display of divine love for the mythological mob. Jesus undergoes some nine instances of satiation, but He Himself engages in His divine dispersive display instead every time. Jesus is not recorded as saying anything during the scourging, beatings, spitting, mocking, and most of the crucifixion throughout His passion; His suffering to save the world. When Jesus does speak, it is only Scripture and gracious words to His persecutors, His scapegoaters. Mark records only two utterances of Jesus throughout His "battle rejoined": Jesus crying out, with a loud voice from the cross, the first line of Psalm 22, which describes the suffering and glory of the Messiah (Mark 15:34); and Jesus giving a "loud cry" as He breathes His last (Mark 15:37).

Included in the great dispersive display of Jesus' glory as He suffers and dies are: the exclamation of the centurion who, when he sees the way in which Jesus dies, says, "Truly this man was the Son of God" (Mark 15:39b); the darkness over the land at mid-day, from twelve noon until three in the afternoon (Mark 15:33); and the tearing of the great curtain or veil of the Temple from top to bottom as Jesus gives His last shout and dies (Mark 15:37). It is an incredible display that clearly impacted the onlookers deeply. Mark says that many women who had followed and ministered to Jesus from Galilee to Jerusalem were watching and bearing witness to all this divine display (Mark 15:40-1), and they will soon disperse the news of what they have seen and heard. The satiation of myth-culture is powerfully subverted by the dispersive display of the LORD Jesus' suffering and death.

Jesus' dispersive display of His divine glory and love according to His unique, evangelical pattern is not only subversive of the satiation episode of myth-culture's pattern, however, but inversive of the scandal episode as well, continuing the formation of the chiastic structure of the two patterns. The envy of Israel's leadership, and the scandal of the people and the Romans over Jesus, has fed the unfolding of myth-culture's pattern to this point of satiation, and still inspires their mocking scorn and abuses of Jesus throughout their "feasting" upon Him. Jesus shows no sign of scandal or offense at the way He is being treated by everyone around Him, even His onlooking disciples and the robbers beside Him. He is mostly silent and always gracious, focusing on His Father's will, which He is performing as planned and expressed. Jesus' dispersive display of love and glory inverts the scandal of the mythological world, which seeks its own glory in its selfish pride over against its rival. Jesus, the self-affirmed Messiah, declared King of the Jews and of Israel, Son of the Blessed One and Son of God, is not proud or selfish, suffering and dying the most humiliating and painful death imaginable—on display for all to see—to save not His friends but His enemies, all humanity except Himself. Envy and scandal could not be more powerfully inverted.

10

Episode 6

Mark 15:42—16:20: Segregation and Deification

Segregation	Deification
"But woe to you, scribes and Pharisees, hypocrites! For you shut up the kingdom of heaven against men; for you neither go in, nor do you allow those who are entering to go in" (Matt 23:13 NKJV)	"Through [Jesus] you may be partakers of the divine nature, having escaped the corruption in the world caused by evil desires; . . . I am in My Father, and you in Me, and I in you" (2 Pet 1:4b;[1] John 14:20)

OVERVIEW

The sixth and final episode of the Gospel account begins with Joseph of Arimathea's burial of Jesus in his own tomb, and ends with Jesus' resurrection, His appearing to and spending time teaching His disciples, as well as Jesus' ascension to the right hand of the Father in Heaven, and the disciples going out to preach the Gospel of the kingdom everywhere. This myth-cultural segregation episode is inverted and subverted by divine deification through Jesus (figure 1; table c), which completes the chiastic bi-pattern, the two inversive and subversive patterns of the Gospel account.

As with the previous five episodes, the first and last verses of this episode are selected based on their positions at the beginning and end of the content of this episode in combat myth. Here again in the final episode, while we can distinguish the change of content and emphasis from satiation-dispersion to segregation-deification (*not* Jesus' deification, but those who believe in Him [Mark 16:14, 16–18]), we can see

---

1. Author's translation.

perhaps more clearly the transition points when we consider the two mythological motifs. Though once again, the motifs are evidently inverted in order of appearance, when compared to the combat myth pattern, and subverted in significance. In other words, the criss-crossing or mirror-relation between Jesus and myth-culture is expressed in this regard as well.

The final two, eleventh and twelfth, combat myth motifs are "enemy punished" and "triumph," in that order (table A).[2] Looking for the content of these two motifs that make up the sixth episode, we can pinpoint the transitions just as before. The mythological pattern continues in the expected order in the religio-political leaders, who have their "enemy punished" with Jesus' burial in the tomb under the earth. But Jesus' "triumph" occurs out of order in first position in His unique, evangelical pattern, with His resurrection from the dead, His "triumph" over death. In terms of meaning, unlike Zeus's "triumph" or Bel-Marduk's "triumph," and the other mythological gods of the myth-culture's pattern, who win the cosmos by overcoming evil gods (chaos monsters) for themselves and their friends, Jesus wins heaven and earth back from His stated enemy of sin (in the first motif of the first episode), and His "triumph" is *for* His enemies. Jesus' "triumph" is not for Himself or His friends, but for His betrayers like Peter, and for His persecutors like Sanhedrin council member Joseph of Arimathea. And Jesus' "triumph" is over His enemies sin and death, as He said and demonstrated throughout the Gospel account (e.g., Mark 1:4–5, 15; 2:5–10; 8:38; 10:29–30; 14:41; 16:6, 16).

Jesus having His "enemy punished" occurs out of order in last position, and also does not conform to the mythological meaning. Jesus' enemy is sin, which is clear in the first episode of Mark's Gospel account. Sin enjoys a final "triumph" on cue as the twelfth and final motif. This mythological "triumph" occurs with the repeated sin of unbelief by the disciples, refusing to believe in the reports of Jesus' resurrection. Jesus began, in His first inversive and subversive episode, by commanding the people to "repent (of sin) and believe in the Gospel (of the kingdom)" (Mark 1:15). Jesus' "punishment of the enemy" does not occur in the myth-culture's meaning, but subverts the pattern of myth-culture. When Jesus appears bodily before His disciples, He sternly rebukes their sin of unbelief in Him, their unbelief in His promise of resurrection on the third day, and the reports of His resurrection. It is sin that is punished by Jesus. So that when Jesus commands His disciples to "go into all the world and preach the gospel (of the kingdom) to all creation," He also declares that those who believe and are baptized will be saved, but those who persist in the sin of unbelief will be condemned (Mark 16:16). The sin of unbelief in the Gospel of the kingdom is the enemy that Jesus punishes in His twelfth and final "enemy punished" motif of His unique, divine, evangelical pattern.

2. Jesus' out of order "triumph" motif is found in Mark 15:42—16:8 (the two motifs are separated by a bold black line in table 1F). Jesus' second "enemy punished" motif comes last, Mark 16:9–20.

In this final sixth episode, we see the myth-culture's segregation re-establishing itself on the corpse of the "consumed" scapegoat, in the disciples' mourning and weeping over Jesus, and in their fleeing to the countryside from Jerusalem, where kingdom of God is to be set up by Jesus (Mark 16:10, 12). These disciples are abandoning the Gospel of the kingdom, and allowing themselves to be re-segregated back into their allotted positions in the world, because of their sin of unbelief in Jesus and His promises. Nevertheless, Jesus graciously grants His disciples deification, meaning union with God through His Spirit, and the eternal life it brings (e.g., Mark 1:8; 3:28–29; 10:29–30; 13:11). Instead of being divided up and running in fear and grief, Jesus unites them with Himself, in His Spirit (Mark 1:8; 13:11; 16:20). And Jesus gives His twelve (currently eleven) apostles the great commission to carry out, preaching the Gospel of the kingdom to all creation in all the world (Mark 16:15). Jesus says that His twelve apostles will go in His own name and perform wonders (Mark 16:17–18), and that He Himself will go with them, even while He Himself is bodily in heaven (Mark 16:19–20).

GOSPEL According to MARK			
WORLD'S SEGREGATION		**JESUS' DEIFICATION**	
Enemy Punished	15:42–6		Triumph
		15:47—16:8a	
	16:8b		
Triumph		16:9–10a	Enemy Punished
	16:10b–11		
		16:12–13a	
	16:13b		
		16:14–20	
TABLE 1F: Segregation and Deification, Enemy Punished and Triumph			

MARK 15:42–16:8: JESUS' "TRIUMPH"[3]

Narratology

Narratologically, this section of the Gospel account is comprised of Jesus' eleventh "triumph" motif, unexpectedly preceding His twelfth "enemy punished" motif, inversive in sequence and subversive in significance compared with the pattern of myth-culture. The expected eleventh mythological motif of "enemy punished" is clear here in the burial of Jesus in the tomb. The enemies of Jesus, the mythological "heroes" including the religio-political leaders of Israel presumably enjoy the death, burial and entombment of Jesus. But more-so perhaps, Jesus' declared enemies of sin, death, the Devil and his demons, enjoy the Author of Life's death and segregation in the tomb.

---

3. Please refer to appendix 1 for Mark's complete text of this motif.

At this point in the combat myth, the "enemy punished" motif is foremost. But at this point in the Gospel account, which contains the unique, evangelical pattern in Jesus Christ, we instead see the "triumph" motif preeminent in Jesus. Not only is the sequence of the motifs reversed, however, but their significance as well. Jesus' "triumph" is not like the typical "triumph" of myth experienced by the hero-god there. As Stein observes:

> By his account of Jesus' burial, Mark prepares his readers for a real resurrection three days after Jesus's death (8:31; 9:31; 10:34). This will involve not merely a resuscitation from death, such as experienced by Jairus's daughter (5:35–43) . . . for [she] would . . . experience death again. Jesus's resurrection will be of a different order. It will be "the" eschatological event of history, for with his resurrection, death is not merely escaped for a period of time but is conquered forever.[4]

Jesus' eleventh inversive and subversive "triumph" motif, which coincides with His opponents' mythologically typical eleventh "enemy punished" motif, begins the evening of Jesus' death on the cross at Golgotha, on the Mount of Olives. It is the day of preparation for the Sabbath (Mark 15:42). Because of this, Mark tells us, Joseph of Arimathea hastens to request Jesus' body to bury Him before time runs out, as he cannot work on the Sabbath: "There was little time to obtain permission from Pilate for the body of Jesus, purchase the necessary supplies for burial, and prepare the body for burial."[5]

This Joseph is described as a prominent member of the ruling council of Israel (Mark 15:43a), or Sanhedrin, which just that morning had unanimously voted for Jesus to be put to death for blasphemy (Mark 14:55, 64). Despite presumably voting for Jesus' death, Mark tells us that this Joseph was also "a man who was himself waiting for the kingdom of God" (Mark 15:43b), suggesting that the Arimathean had a foot in each camp, making his motives here unclear. Stein avers that, based on Mark's description of him, this Joseph "should be listed among those who had responded to Jesus's pronouncement in 1:15."[6] In either case, it may be that the leadership of Israel wanted one of their own to bury Jesus, so that His own disciples could not have opportunity to take the body, and to ensure Jesus was safely entombed beneath the earth for good. It may be that Joseph of Arimathea was ideal for both sides, Jesus' disciples also knowing that he was sympathetic to Jesus, and believed in the Gospel of the kingdom. In any case, having one of their own council members bury Jesus and seal Him in a tomb in the earth is the final "punishment of the enemy" by the leaders of Israel. Joseph of Arimathea "gathers up courage and goes before Roman governor Pilate, and asks for the body of Jesus" (Mark 15:43c).

4. Stein, *Mark*, 726.

5. Stein, *Mark*, 723.

6. Stein, *Mark*, 724.

Evidently, Pilate wonders to hear that Jesus is already dead by this time (Mark 15:44a). He summons the centurion and questions him as to whether Jesus is already dead (15:44b). "Crucified victims normally lived for at least a day or two."[7] This is the same centurion who was standing right in front of Jesus as He died at three that afternoon, and said, "Truly this Man was the Son of God!" (Mark 14:39b). The centurion, who witnessed Jesus' death, confirms for Pilate that Jesus is dead (Mark 15:45a), and then Pilate grants Jesus' body to Joseph (Mark 15:45b).

Joseph buys a linen sheet, takes Jesus' body down from the cross, wraps Him in the sheet, and lays Him "in a tomb that had been hewn out in the rock; and he rolls a stone against the entrance of the tomb" (Mark 15:46). The leaders of Israel have their "enemy punished." While Joseph has done the LORD Jesus a service in treating His body as properly as time allowed, he has also done the high priest and his own fellow council-members a service in ensuring Jesus' body is safely entombed in the earth. Yet Mark tells us that Mary Magdalene and Mary the mother of Joses, "are looking on to see where Jesus is laid" (Mark 15:47). Israel's leaders' representative in Joseph of Arimathea may have carefully kept Jesus' body from His disciples, but they have managed to observe its location.

The Sabbath passes, and when it is over, Mary Magdalene, Mary the mother of James (and Joses?; see Mark 15:40, 47), and Salome buy spices, "that they might come and anoint Jesus" (Mark 16:1). "Very early on the first day of the week," these three women go to the tomb in which two of them had seen Joseph of Arimathea bury Jesus, arriving "when the sun had risen" (Mark 16:2). Edwards notes how remarkable it is that women are the prime witnesses of this key event, given that "Jewish opinion of women . . . was not always positive."[8] But this view of women appears to be another pagan influence on Israel, since it was generally held in the ancient myth-cultural world, so that, "Some two centuries after the Gospels were written [when the early Church fathers were defending the Gospel accounts from the charge of being mythological], the pagan Celsus could still needle Origen on 'the gossip of women about the empty tomb.'"[9] Edwards also points out the subversive nature of Jesus' pattern in having women witnesses: "The testimony of women is, however, entirely 'in character' with the divine economy: those whose testimony is discounted in human society [myth-culture] are the first to be included in the divine society [kingdom of God]."[10] In opposition to the myth-culture and the expectation of this sixth episode, women

---

7. Stein, *Mark*, 724.

8. Edwards, *Mark*, 491–92. Edwards cites Rabbinic sources that have terrible things to say of women regarding the quality of the evidence they bring as witnesses (*m. Rosh HaSh.* 1:8), their worthiness to be taught (*b. Sot.* 19a), their value as human beings (*b. Qid.* 82b), and the standard morning prayer of Rabbinic Jewish men (Edwards, *Mark*, 492).

9. Edwards, *Mark*, 492.

10. Edwards, *Mark*, 492.

are not segregated in Jesus' kingdom of God, and they are given the honor of being the first witnesses of Jesus' inversive and subversive "triumph."

The three women were saying to each other, "Who will roll away the stone for us from the entrance of the tomb?" (Mark 16:3). "The anxiety of the women about this significant detail is due," says Edwards, "in part, to the fact that all the men were hiding (John 20:19)."[11] The men are segregated by their fear of the religio-political leaders, and are evidently not looking for Jesus' promised resurrection. But looking up, "(the women) see that the stone had been rolled away, although it was extremely large" (Mark 16:4). "The removal of the stone suggests that in all respects the resurrection of Jesus is entirely God's work. The human role in the event is that of witness, not worker."[12]

Upon entering the tomb, they "see a young man sitting at the right, wearing a white robe; and they are amazed" (Mark 16:5). Edwards observes, "The 'white robe' . . . the 'young man' . . . and the women's response indicate an angelic encounter."[13] The "young man" says to them, "Do not be amazed; you are looking for Jesus the Nazarene, who has been crucified. He has risen; He is not here; behold, here is the place where they laid Him" (Mark 16:6). "The response of the angel," writes Edwards, "can be taken as a mild rebuke. The women, intent on their funereal errand, are preoccupied with death. They endeavor with their spices and anxieties to bring some kind of closure. . . . But all their preparations leave them unprepared for the reality they encounter."[14]

Here is Jesus' unexpected inversive and subversive eleventh "triumph" motif. Jesus has risen from the dead! He has been victorious over sin, as an innocent and even perfect Man (e.g., Mark 15:14), and due to His identity, and sinlessness, the LORD Jesus has now "triumphed" over the tomb, over death. Edwards concludes, "The visit to the tomb is vintage Markan irony: the living are consumed with death, but the Crucified One is consumed with life."[15] Jesus' opponents' "punishment" of their "enemy" in the tomb has been fruitless, as has all their previous opposition to the LORD Jesus. Edwards observes how non-ethereal, how unmythological, Jesus' resurrection is, "The women are not directed to a mystical or spiritual experience or to a numinous encounter. They are directed specifically to Jesus, who died by a crucifixion they witnessed, was buried in a place they witnessed, and now has been resurrected."[16]

The "young man" gives instructions to the three women, saying, "But go, tell Jesus' disciples and Peter, 'He is going before you into Galilee; there you will see Him, just as He said to you'" (Mark 16:7). Not only has Jesus risen, but He is going to visit His disciples again soon; even Peter who betrayed Jesus, worse perhaps than the others. This

---

11. Edwards, *Mark*, 492.

12. Edwards, *Mark*, 493.

13. Edwards, *Mark*, 493.

14. Edwards, *Mark*, 494.

15. Edwards, *Mark*, 494.

16. Edwards, *Mark*, 494.

reminder points to the deification of Jesus' followers, in that they will now be reunited with the LORD forever. Death is no obstacle to union with God: "The first act of Jesus' ministry was the calling of four fisherman into community with himself (1:16–20); and the first word of the resurrected Jesus is the reconvening of the same community of disciples (14:27–28)."[17] The "young man" says that Jesus will visit them again "just as He said to you." Jesus promised that He would go before them after His resurrection into Galilee (Mark 14:28), and the "young man" reminds the three women of this promise now. The world's leaders may have "punished their enemy," but Jesus has had His "triumph" anyway, out of sequence and not with the myth-culture's meaning.

Importantly, Jesus' resurrection is not for Himself here, but "the kingdom of God is at hand" for those who "repent and believe in the Gospel (of the kingdom)" (Mark 1:15). Jesus says that He sheds His blood "on behalf of many" (Mark 14:24), and that eternal life—resurrection from the dead and eternal life in the kingdom of God—is for those who believe in Jesus until the end (see Mark 10:29–30; 13:13, 27; 16:16). Unlike myth-culture, then, Jesus' "triumph" is for those who betray Him, those who persecute Him; it is for sinners (Mark 14:41). There is no segregation as in myth-culture; the "triumph" is not for Himself and for other gods, as with Zeus and Marduk.

Having received the message from the "young man" in the empty tomb, Mary Magdalene, Mary the mother of James, and Salome, "went out [quickly] and fled from the tomb, for trembling and astonishment had gripped them" (Mark 16:8a). The "triumphant" resurrection of Jesus, and the appearance of the "young man" with his "triumphant" message, have astonished and overwhelmed these three women, such that they run pell-mell back the way they came. Initially, after this encounter, Mark tells us that the three women, "say nothing to anyone; for they were afraid" (Mark 16:8b). Perhaps their fear is due, at least in part, to the possibility that they would be accused of having moved Jesus' body if they told anyone that it is missing. Edwards notes, "It is clear that Mark does not intend v. 8 to imply reverence and faith on the part of the women, but fear and flight."[18] And so, in this eleventh motif, we have seen the leaders of the people of Israel have their "enemy punished," in keeping with myth-culture's pattern and meaning. But at the same time, Jesus has had His "triumph," not in keeping with the myth-culture's pattern or meaning.

Social-Science

Social-scientifically, this eleventh motif in the sixth segregation-deification episode is comprised of deification (union with God) provided to sinners through Jesus' resurrection, continuing His unique, divine, evangelical pattern, intermingled with the segregation enforced by sin, death, and by the Israel's leadership, continuing the myth-culture's pattern. The up-coming twelfth motif continues and concludes this sixth episode, as well

17. Edwards, *Mark*, 495.

18. Edwards, *Mark*, 496.

as concluding the two chiastic patterns that make up the Gospel account. The social-science lenses of Girard and Malina aid us in perceiving the continued chiastic bi-pattern.

At this point in the pattern of myth-culture we typically see segregation preeminent. However, not so in the Gospel account due to the unique, evangelical pattern here in Jesus Christ. Jesus achieves divine deification of sinners, instead of myth-culture's oppressive segregation of Adam's race. Deification through Jesus subverts the segregation-meaning expected of this sixth episode, and inverts the myth-culture's sequence, so that this episode also contains a strong anti-sameness element.[19]

There appear to be at least two expressions of segregation in this eleventh motif of the sixth episode. Segregation is performed or imposed by Israel's leadership, as well as the sin of unbelief and fear of death. The expressions of segregation are: (1) A "prominent member" of the Sanhedrin council that unanimously condemned Jesus to death for blasphemy, Joseph of Arimathea, hurrying to get Jesus' dead body from Pilate before the Sabbath begins. Presumably, he acts as a representative of the high priest and council in doing this, ensuring that the body of Jesus is not acquired by His disciples, but securely entombed in the earth immediately. Quickly entombing Jesus' body re-establishes the control of the priests and council over the people of Israel, keeping them from the kingdom of God, and so controlling the "chaos" purportedly caused by the LORD Jesus. (2) After Jesus' resurrection, the three women disciples who discover His absence are so afraid of telling anyone that Jesus is not in the tomb, that they keep silent about it. In part at least, the women are evidently terrified of Israel's leadership and the authorities, which is evidence that they have been cowed into submission, despite the good news that they saw and received at the empty tomb. Also, it seems that they have not truly believed what they saw and heard there. They were told to tell the disciples and Peter the message that Jesus has risen, and is going ahead of them into Galilee as He promised. But it is only after Jesus begins to appear bodily to them, first to Mary Magdalene, that they begin to boldly declare what has happened to the other disciples.

Of course, Jesus is not found to be engaging in mythological segregation in this eleventh motif of the sixth episode. He and His disciples are the victims of segregation, by His body's removal from His disciples and entombment, and Jesus subverts segregation with His resurrection from the dead and escape from the tomb. Jesus' stated and active purpose is divine deification, meaning eternal union for everyone with God in His kingdom (e.g., Mark 8:34–38; 10:29–30, 35–45; 13:26–27). Jesus offers deification in this eleventh motif, in the sixth episode, in two ways: (1) Through Jesus' messenger in the tomb, the "young man" in the white robe, the three women disciples are told that Jesus has risen. This good news confirms the promise Jesus repeatedly

19. As shown in the methodology, while the narratological chiasm is within each episode, involving the switching (inverting) of the two motifs and their meanings, the social-scientific chiasm involves the switching of the entire account's sequence of episodes and their meanings, inverting one and six, two and five, three and four. These two narratological and social-scientific aspects of the inversive and subversive chiastic relation of Jesus' pattern and myth-culture's pattern are demonstrated as we read through Mark's account.

made to them all that He would rise the third day. In so doing, Jesus confirms His promise that they who believe in Him, and take up their crosses and follow Him, will inherit the kingdom of God. Because Jesus has risen, they can be confident that their eternal place with Jesus in God's kingdom, their "deification," is assured. As Jesus said, they will be "like angels in heaven" (Mark 12:25–27). (2) Also, through the "young man" Jesus repeats the promise He made to His disciples, that after His resurrection from the dead, He would go ahead of them into Galilee and be with them there. They are all to be reunited very soon, and are never to be truly apart ever again, as we will see in the final twelfth motif of this final sixth episode.

Jesus' provision of divine deification according to His evangelical pattern is not only subversive of the sixth segregation episode of myth-culture's pattern, however, but inversive of myth-culture's first sameness episode as well, bringing to conclusion the formation of the chiastic structure of the two patterns in the Gospel account. Jesus is certainly viewed in terms of myth-cultural sameness by the religio-political leaders of Israel. They view Him as merely a typical myth-cultural rival for the affections and loyalty of the people, a rival-double for control of their world, a mimetic rival of the same nature and intention as themselves. However, with His resurrection, Jesus has demonstrated what the Gospel account claims from the beginning, which is that this Man is the LORD, who has come to inaugurate His kingdom come (Mark 1:1–9). It is a kingdom open to all in Israel, and through Israel all among the nations, through repentance from sin and belief in the Gospel of the kingdom (Mark 1:15).

As such, Jesus is not the same as those who have made themselves His enemy. He is not a rival double of the Devil and his demons, or of sin and death, or of the religio-political leaders of Israel, or anyone else. Jesus is distinct, and offers liberation from sameness and all that follows from it. Jesus offers deification, baptism in the Holy Spirit (Mark 1:8), so that Jesus' Spirit speaks in them, to them and through them in need (Mark 13:11), and so that they may endure to the end and be saved (Mark 13:13), entering into the eternal kingdom of God (Mark 10:29–30).

GOSPEL According to MARK			
WORLD'S SEGREGATION		**JESUS' DEIFICATION**	
Enemy Punished	15:42–46		Triumph
		15:47—16:8a	
	16:8b		
Triumph		16:9–10a	Enemy Punished
	16:10b–11		
		16:12–13a	
	16:13b		
		16:14–20	
TABLE 1F: Segregation and Deification, Enemy Punished and Triumph			

MARK 16:9–20: JESUS' "ENEMY PUNISHED"[20]

Narratology

Narratologically, this final section of the Gospel account makes up the twelfth "enemy punished" motif for Jesus, out of place from the vantage of the myth-culture's pattern. Jesus' twelfth motif, like the eleven that precede it, is also atypically subversive in significance when compared with the pattern of myth-culture. The expected twelfth mythological motif of "triumph" clearly occurs here in the sin of unbelief in the disciples, and in the effect that the actions of Israel's leadership have had on the LORD Jesus' disciples, continuing and concluding the pattern of myth-culture. Simultaneously, Jesus' twelfth "enemy punished" motif continues and concludes His anti-mythological, unique, evangelical pattern.

At this point in the combat myth, the final "triumph" motif is foremost. But at this point in the Gospel account, which contains the divine, evangelical pattern in Jesus Christ, we instead see the twelfth "enemy punished" motif preeminent in Jesus. The expected twelfth mythological "triumph" motif predominates only in the effects of the religio-political leaders' actions on Jesus' disciples, and in the sin that continues to rule in Jesus' disciples. Just as in the five preceding episodes, in this sixth and final episode, the sequence of the motifs is inverted by Jesus, and He subverts their significance as well. Jesus' "enemy punished" is not like the typical "enemy punished" motif of myth-culture experienced by the hero-god there.

Before discussing the content of this twelfth and final motif, it needs to be noted that there will be precious little additional scholarly commentary on these last twelve verses of Mark's Gospel account. This dearth is due to most scholars today discussing how, while these twelve verses are supposedly not original (overlooking the abundant evidence that shows they certainly are original),[21] there was likely a longer ending that has supposedly been lost. There is a widespread but unfounded belief that Mark 16:9–20, the so-called "long ending," is a late, non-Markan addition to the text.[22] However, and interestingly for our purpose, we cannot complete the two concurrent patterns of the Gospel account, that of myth-culture and that of Jesus, without these last twelve verses. Without them, both patterns would possess only eleven motifs in Mark's account, and the account and the patterns would then be incomplete.

Evans notes that ancient readers confronted with copies lacking the longer ending of Mark (16:9–20) viewed the account as incomplete:

> The two endings of Mark . . . testify to the widespread belief that Mark's narrative did not abruptly conclude with frightened, silent women at the tomb,

---

20. Please refer to appendix 1 for Mark's complete text of this final motif.

21. See John Burgon's timeless defense of the last twelves verses of Mark (*Last Twelve Verses*), cited previously, as well as William Cooper's recent defense of their authenticity (*Gospels*).

22. Evans, *Mark*, 545.

ostensibly unwilling or unable to obey the mysterious young man who commanded them to tell the disciples and Peter that the risen Jesus would go before them in Galilee.[23]

Stein lays out various compelling reasons to agree with these readers, ancient and modern, who notice the absence of the ending.[24] This writer certainly agrees that Mark's account was never intended to end at verse 8.[25] But furthermore, we can be absolutely certain that the so-called "long ending," 16:9–20, is the original ending written by Mark. The reasons for this certainty are perhaps best laid out by John Burgon, some of which I briefly summarize in appendix 2. In short, the reason is that hundreds of years before manuscripts appear that lack Mark 16:9–20, early Church fathers are quoting from and alluding to them. It is fascinating, given what we are about to discover concerning the final enemy that Jesus punishes in this last motif of the Gospel account, which is the sin of unbelief, that the final twelve verses of Mark's Gospel have been one of the most contended portions of the Bible's text.

Jesus' final twelfth motif in this final sixth episode of Mark's Gospel account begins by recounting Jesus' bodily appearances after His resurrection. After Jesus has risen early on the first day of the week, the first person to whom He appears is Mary Magdalene, "from whom He had cast out seven demons" (Mark 16:9). This woman whom Jesus has saved from the terrible spiritual affliction of a truly monstrous demon-possession is honored with the first visit by the resurrected LORD Jesus. Mary goes at once and reports this appearance of the resurrected Jesus to "those who had been with Him," His disciples, "while they were mourning and weeping" (Mark 16:10).

In the weeping and the mourning of Jesus' disciples we see the myth-cultural pattern's "triumph" of the religio-political leaders of Israel. To the minds and hearts of Jesus' disciples, the "tenant farmers" of Israel have succeeded in defeating Jesus, their "chaos-monster," who threatened their control over "their" cosmos, the vineyard of Israel. Mark tells us that when the disciples hear from Mary Magdalene the report that Jesus "is alive and has been seen by her, they refuse to believe it" (Mark 16:11). In this refusal to believe in Jesus' resurrection is also a refusal to believe the promise Jesus made many times that He would indeed rise on this third day, and a refusal to believe in Jesus and in the Gospel message of the kingdom, that He preached. So, in the disciples' refusal to believe is the myth-cultural pattern's "triumph" of Jesus' enemy sin. The sin of unbelief has its "triumph" here, right on cue to conclude the pattern of myth-culture.

23. Evans, *Mark*, 550–51. There is a less-prevalent so-called "short ending" that is also included in the NASB translation (see appendix 1), which seems to be recognized by all as certainly not original (Evans, *Mark*, 550).

24. Stein, *Mark*, 734–37.

25. As also believed by Gundry, *Mark*; Evans, *Mark*; Witherington, *Gospel of Mark*; Edwards, *Mark*; France, *Gospel of Mark*; Wright, *Resurrection of the Son God*; Stein, *Mark*.

After Jesus' appearance to Mary Magdalene, He appears "in a different form" to two of Jesus' followers "while they are walking along on their way to the country" (Mark 16:12). These two go and report this appearance of Jesus "to the others" (meaning the eleven disciples, it seems), but Mark records, "but they did not believe them either" (Mark 16:13). The disciples have refused to believe a second report of Jesus' resurrection and bodily appearance. The sin of unbelief in the LORD Jesus' word and in the Gospel of the kingdom—contrary to Jesus' command (Mark 1:15; 8:31)—continues its "triumph" over Jesus' followers here, the last motif of the pattern of myth-culture.

The third appearance of the resurrected Jesus in Mark's Gospel account is to the disciples themselves. He appears "to the eleven themselves as they are reclining at the table" (Mark 16:14a). When He appears this third time to His eleven disciples, Jesus "reproaches them for their unbelief and hardness of heart, because they have not believed those who have seen Him after He has risen" (Mark 16:14b). Here, Jesus has His "enemy punished," in that He punishes sin, the sin of unbelief. Jesus reproaches the unbelief and hardness of heart of His disciples. Jesus' "enemy punished" motif is not in the expected place in the order of motifs as found in myth-culture, coming last, nor does it possess the expected mythological meaning. Jesus' twelfth motif is therefore inversive and subversive of myth-culture's twelfth motif. In myth-culture, the "enemy's punishment" is a subjugation, humiliation, and death or imprisonment of a person. Here, the LORD Jesus "punishes" the sinful behavior of His disciples with a severe reprimand.

Then, Jesus immediately commands His disciples to get back to work for Him and for the Gospel of the kingdom, saying, "Go into all the world and preach the gospel to all creation" (Mark 16:15). The disciples are now apostles, having been sent. Jesus commands His apostles to continue the mission that He began, and trained them to perform, calling everyone everywhere to "repent and believe in the gospel" (Mark 1:15). Then Jesus declares, "He who has believed and has been baptized shall be saved; but He who has disbelieved shall be condemned" (Mark 16:16). Jesus declares that His eternal salvation is for everyone, all Israel, and all nations through Israel, who believe in Him and is water baptized (Of this eternal life in Jesus, see Mark 8:35; 10:29–30; 13:27). Jesus also declares that there is eternal condemnation for unbelief. Concerning Jesus' warnings on the nature of this condemnation, see Mark 9:43–48.

So, Jesus says that His "enemy's punishment," His punishment of sin, will continue into eternal condemnation, if the sin of unbelief continues in a person. Jesus similarly spoke of this condemnation when He asked, "For what does it profit a man to gain the whole world, and forfeit his soul?" (Mark 8:36–38). As in other motifs in which Jesus speaks of present and future iterations of the motif, Jesus speaks in this twelfth motif of both a present punishment of His enemy sin (the reprimand), and a future eternal punishment of sin (in Gehenna, the Lake of Fire).

Jesus then promises His eleven apostles that certain confirming miraculous sign gifts (or "attesting miracles") will "accompany those who have believed" (Mark 16:17a). Jesus promises them that in His name, those who believe in Him: "will cast out demons," "will speak in new tongues," "will pick up serpents," will not be hurt by drinking deadly poison, and "will lay hands on the sick, and they will recover" (Mark 16:17b–18). Such miraculous signs will accompany those who believe in Jesus in response to the apostles' preaching of the Gospel of the kingdom. In these miraculous signs, we also see that Jesus is empowering those who believe in Him, through His apostles' witness, to "punish" some of His "enemies." Certainly demons, sickness and death are enemies of the LORD Jesus, enemies that He has battled victoriously throughout Mark's account as He Himself preached the Gospel of His kingdom.

Mark tells us that after Jesus has thus spoken to His disciples, "He was received up into heaven and sat down at the right hand of God" (Mark 16:19; Ps 110:1). Evidently the disciples watch Jesus rise into the sky, and perhaps remembering His words about where He is going (e.g., Mark 14:62), or being allowed to glimpse it, know that Jesus again takes up His throne in heaven. Finally, Mark writes, "And they went out and preached everywhere, while the LORD worked with them, and confirmed the word by the signs (attesting miracles) that followed" (Mark 16:20). The eleven apostles obey Jesus' command, and set about the work He prepared and empowered them to do, preaching the Gospel of the kingdom to all creation. Mark says that the LORD works with the apostles, and confirms the word of the Gospel with the signs or attesting miracles that He had given them.

These miraculous sign gifts are one of the ways that Jesus gave to His apostles participation in the divine nature, or deification. He has also promised to baptize them in the Holy Spirit, which will soon occur at Pentecost, also resulting in participation in the divine nature, or deification. And, in addition to these things, just as Jesus lived His unique, divine, evangelical pattern in the face of the pattern of myth-culture, lived-out by everyone else around Him, the LORD Jesus also sent His apostles to live His unique, divine pattern, instead of the pattern of myth-culture, by the Holy Spirit's power. The expectation and the ability given to walk in Jesus' pattern, the way of the cross, is also participation in the divine nature, or deification.

Social-Science

Social-scientifically, this inversive twelfth "enemy punished" motif of Jesus, and the expected twelfth mythological "triumph" motif of the religio-political leaders and of Jesus' enemy sin, continue and conclude this sixth episode. The divine deification of the disciples performed by the LORD Jesus, and the mythological segregation of His opponents, bring to a close the two patterns, Jesus' and myth-culture's. As before, Jesus' pattern is intermingled with the myth-culture's pattern. Here, segregation is imposed by the "tenant-farmer" leadership of Israel, and the sin of fear and unbelief within the disciples themselves. The social-science lenses of Girard and Malina aid us in perceiving this chiastic bi-pattern.

At this point in the pattern of myth-culture we typically continue to see segregation preeminent. However, not so in the Gospel account due to Jesus' unique, evangelical pattern. Instead, Jesus performs deification of those who believe in Him and His Gospel of the kingdom (e.g., Mark 16:16a) instead of segregation, and in opposition to those around Jesus who embody and impose the segregation of myth-culture. Divine deification through Jesus continues to subvert the segregation meaning expected of this sixth and final episode, and continues to invert the myth-sequence, so that this episode also contains a strong anti-sameness element as well.[26]

There are three expressions of myth-culture's segregation in this final twelfth motif in the final sixth episode, imposed by Israel's leadership, and self-imposed by Jesus' own disciples, but never by Jesus. Jesus' response and posture are ever according to His purpose of deification for others, giving them entry into God's eternal kingdom, involving eternal communion with Himself already in this life, instead of the oppressive segregation characteristic of this myth-cultural world. The LORD Jesus' presence with and empowerment of His disciples is directed toward saving the world at enmity with Him, through belief in His Gospel of the kingdom.

The expressions of segregation of Jesus' followers in this twelfth motif and sixth episode are: (1) when Mary Magdalene comes to tell the disciples that Jesus has appeared to her, they are mourning and weeping. This behavior shows that the disciples have not believed Jesus' repeated promise that He will rise the third day. They have not believed in Him and in the Gospel message of the kingdom that Jesus preached to them and confirmed for them with miraculous signs. They are mourning and weeping over Jesus' death, evidently believing that it is all over, the kingdom is not coming to Israel, and perhaps now fearing for their own lives and the lives of their families. In other words, they have allowed themselves to be segregated back into their place in the myth-culture's world, intimidated by the religio-political leaders of Israel, who do not enter the kingdom, and do not allow others to either. They likely believe that the leadership of Israel has won, has defeated Jesus, and that they are now mere outlaws, most likely with prices on their heads like Jesus. So, they mourn and weep.

(2) Then, when the disciples hear Mary Magdalene's message, that Jesus is alive and has been seen by her, they refuse to believe it. Jesus' closest disciples, the eleven, do not merely express doubt or uncertainty. They refuse to believe that Jesus has risen and appeared to Mary. The disciples are engaged in the sin of unbelief. Jesus' enemy sin, named in the first episode in place of the "chaos-monster" that Jesus' "emerged" to

---

26. As stated in the methodology and demonstrated in this textual analysis, while the narratological chiasm is within each episode, involving the switching (inverting) of the two motifs and their meanings, the social-scientific chiasm involves the switching of the entire account's sequence of episodes and their meanings, inverting one and six, two and five, three and four. These two narratological and social-scientific aspects of the inversive and subversive chiastic relation of Jesus' pattern and myth-culture's pattern are demonstrated as we read through Mark's account.

conquer, has evidently "triumphed" over Jesus' disciples here, segregating them from Jesus and His kingdom that He promised them. Believing in Jesus and His Gospel is described as requisite for salvation and entry into God's kingdom, but Jesus' disciples here do not believe.

(3) Finally, after Jesus appears to two other disciples leaving (fleeing from?) Jerusalem for the countryside, and they return and report to the eleven that they have seen Jesus, the disciples do not believe their report either! Jesus' eleven core disciples are sunk in the sin of unbelief. They are inured and hardened in the sin of unbelief, Jesus' enemy. And it separates, segregates them from Him and His kingdom.

Jesus' behavior, including His responses to these acts of myth-cultural segregation, is ever according to His divine purpose of deification for those who believe in Him. Jesus has appeared to Mary Magdalene, despite her silence (along with the other two women) concerning Jesus' resurrection and His messenger at the empty tomb. Jesus is returning to and reuniting with His disciples, yet in a way that seems to be testing their belief in Him and His promises. For His disciples to be "deified" in this sense of being united with Him and entering into His eternal kingdom, they must be believing. After His disciples refuse to believe Mary's report, Jesus appears to two disciples on their way to the countryside. These two believe as did Mary, but the eleven still refuse. Jesus then appears a third time, in Mark's account, to the eleven themselves. Jesus must personally appear to each one for them to believe, despite all that He formerly said and did.

He reproaches them for their unbelief in Him and His word, and for their hardness of heart. Yet, Jesus again gives them the opportunity to believe, with the expectation to confirm belief with water baptism. And Jesus directly gives miraculous powers to those who believe and are water baptized, to be able to do attesting miracles, as they are sent on His mission to preach the Gospel of the kingdom everywhere. And just so, Jesus works with them, despite having ascended into heaven. In these ways, Jesus "deifies" His disciples, reuniting them with Himself, with God. Jesus does not segregate as the heroes of myth-culture, but makes it possible for humans to enter into communion with Him, and into His eternal kingdom, to be "deified," through belief in Him and His Gospel of the kingdom.

The LORD Jesus' deification of those who believe in Him, His gracious welcoming of them into His eternal kingdom, His work, and His presence, according to His unique, evangelical pattern, is not only subversive of the segregation episode of myth-culture's pattern, however, but inversive of the sameness episode as well, continuing and concluding the formation of the chiastic structure of the two patterns in the Gospel account. In the myth-culture's pattern, the two opponents both view themselves as gods, and as having a right to control of the cosmos. It is not clear in myth-culture who will overcome, in part due to the merely relative power and authority of the contending rival-double gods.

In the Gospel account, Jesus is immediately declared to be the LORD God of the Hebrew Bible, or Old Testament, and He states and demonstrates as much Himself in the course of the account, resulting in the charge of blasphemy being leveled against Him by the envious, unbelieving high priest and Sanhedrin council of Israel. But as the LORD, Jesus' power and authority are without equal, and without legitimate contender. Just as sameness is inverted in the first episode, it is inverted in this final sixth episode as well, though in a different way. Jesus has welcomed His disciples, even disciples inured in sin, into participation in His mission, and into His eternal kingdom, through belief in Him. Jesus has not made them His equals by "deifying" them, but He has made them as close to gods as possible under His own absolute deity and sovereignty. Jesus has made them similar, though not the same, as Himself, asserting that His twelve apostles will sit upon twelve thrones with Him in His kingdom, judging the twelve tribes of Israel (Mark 10:35–40; Matt 19:28). Clearly, Jesus' deification of those who believe in Him is inversive of the sameness of myth-culture. Jesus shows that becoming like gods is not achieved through the pattern of myth-culture; not by exalting oneself, but by denying oneself, and taking up one's cross, and following Jesus in His unique, divine, evangelical pattern. And this achievement is never one's own, but is achieved by Jesus Christ's work and His Spirit's work in you.

11

Conclusion

The LORD Jesus' Conquest of Myth-Culture

"For God,

who commanded the light to shine out of darkness,

hath shined in our hearts,

to give the light of the knowledge of the glory of God

in the face of Jesus Christ."

(2 COR 4:6)

I have argued that the Gospels are not mythological, and that Jesus Himself is not mythological. This fact has now been confirmed in various ways. As stated in the introduction, the Gospel accounts are broadly historically verified, which has already been demonstrated many times over by other scholars and researchers. This study was given to testing the claim that the Gospels and Jesus are mythological by comparing and contrasting the Gospel accounts, and Jesus in particular, to the pattern of myth as found in global combat myths (narratology), as well as comparing and contrasting the Gospel accounts, and Jesus in particular, to the pattern of myth-culture (social-science), which is directly related to those combat myths at the heart of cultures. For if Jesus were mythological, He would conform to the pattern of myth. However, we have now found that Jesus "fails" to conform to the pattern of myth, and "fails" to conform to the pattern of myth-culture. The LORD Jesus actually combats and defeats those entire patterns. That is, not only is Jesus *alone* not mythological, but it is everyone else who *is* mythological in the account. And similarly, we are all inured in the pattern of myth-culure, unlike Jesus Christ. And what we encounter in the Gospel account is the LORD Jesus alone setting humanity free from the pattern of myth-culture.

As we saw in the Gospel account, everyone around Jesus does conform to the pattern of myth, and the pattern of myth-culture. Does this mean that the Gospels are mythological, or that they contain myth? Certainly not, because it is evident from this study that all human beings, in all times and places, except Jesus Christ Himself, are mythological in the same way that everyone around Jesus in the Gospel accounts are mythological. By *this* use of the term "myth," we do not mean "unreal" or "unhistorical," but rather, we mean that all human beings except Jesus are characterized in our identity, thoughts, words and deeds by the six episodes of myth-culture's pattern, and the twelve motifs of the combat myth's pattern. It is a pattern inherently characterized by self-delusion producing self-interested violence or carelessness toward others. In other words, "let God be true, but every man a liar" (Rom 3:4b NKJV), and,

> [Human beings] are of [their] father the devil, and the desires of [their] father [they] want to do. He was a murderer from the beginning, and does not stand in the truth, because there is no truth in him. When he speaks a lie, he speaks from his own *resources*, for he is a liar and the father of it. (John 8:44 NKJV)

Our default setting is sameness of desire with others, resulting in interdividual identity, along with a deeply felt sense of our own lack and/or the threat of villainy. That basic disposition of human beings is the dark fertile bed out of which grows the world's pattern of scandal, striving, scapegoating, satiation and segregation, time and time again. Uniquely, we found in the Gospel accounts that Jesus' default setting is not sameness of desire with others. Rather, His identity is distinctive, He is unique, and is not afflicted by an everpresent sense of lack or villainy. From the LORD Jesus' healthy distinctive soil grows the divine pattern of diffusion, deference, deliverance, dispersion and deification in interaction with myth-cultural others.

It has been argued here that all the pericopae of Mark's account of the Gospel contain within them the thematic motifs and episodic concepts of both this world's mythological pattern as well as a unique, transcendent pattern in Jesus. And remarkably, both patterns proceed simultaneously. The proposal made at the outset has been supported by the study that follows.

A perceived weakness or limitation of this approach to the structure of the Gospels may be that in applying the combat myth pattern to the Gospel account, an inappropriate association has been made between pagan myths and ancient Israel and Judaism. However, as indicated in the introduction, at least two factors make such a comparison appropriate: (1) The religio-political leaders of Israel, as well as the Jewish people, are clearly presented as thinking and living in conformity with the myth-culture, and even the combat myth pattern, just as all other tribes, despite their distinctive heritage in the Scriptures. Their expectations for the Messiah's behavior support this view. Despite the Scriptural prophecies that Mark's account cites as fulfilled in Jesus' coming to suffer, atone for sin with His death, and rise from the dead, the people of Israel who hold to these Scriptures seem generally to have a messianic expectation very different from the sort that Jesus turns out to be, and more in keeping with expectations typical of combat mythology. (2) In the AD first century, Judea and all Israel are inundated with Greco-Roman culture and ruled by the Roman Caesar, all of which is firmly and explicitly rooted in combat mythology. This context appears to have had considerable influence on the perceptions and values of the Jewish people.

The foregoing narratological and social-scientific analysis of the Gospel account supports the proposal that there are two opposing patterns structuring the Gospel. Evidently, the complete pattern of myth-culture is found in the account, but it is in the opponents of Jesus, both spiritual (Satan, demons and unclean spirits) and physical (religio-political leaders of Israel and Rome, the cosmic crowd, and even the disciples themselves). At the same time, Jesus evidently conforms to a pattern throughout the account, but one that systematically opposes the pattern of myth-culture. The evident reality of a complete pattern of myth-culture in the Gospel account, manifested in those opposed to Jesus rather than Jesus Himself, does not vindicate those who view the Gospels as mythological to whatever extent. This pattern of myth-culture is typical of all times and places, including all humanity today.

It is startling to find, at the end of this study, that it is everyone else (including all of us) who is mythological, while the LORD Jesus alone of all human beings is not mythological. There is clearly a mythological pattern throughout the Gospel account, though it never appears in Jesus. Jesus' pattern does, however, possess enough seeming similarities to the pattern of myth-culture, "at first glance," to explain the prevailing confusion. This confusion was already being addressed, evidently, by the apostles in their New Testament writings (e.g., 2 Pet 1:16) and Early Church Fathers (e.g., Justin Martyr), as noted in the introduction.

The proposal made of the presence of a chiastic bi-pattern structure to the Gospel accounts, that I term the biblical chiasm genre, has been strongly confirmed by the reading of René Girard incorporated here, and more thoroughly by the analysis of Mark's account conducted here. Bruce J. Malina's reading incorporated here, while not supportive of the presence of both patterns, is clearly beneficial to this study for affirming and elucidating the presence of the myth-culture's pattern in the Gospel account. The strained manner of Malina's myth-cultural reading, when applied to Jesus, was also beneficial for supporting the argument that there are in fact two opposing patterns in the Gospel account, Jesus and myth-culture. Just as for Malina, when attempts are made at applying the pattern of myth-culture to Jesus, it is evidently inconsistent with text and context, and so ultimately unconvincing.

The relation between the pattern of myth (of combat myth and myth-culture), and the pattern encountered in the LORD Jesus Christ in the Gospel account, is one of account-level antithetical chiastic parallelism. Therefore, the Gospel's structure and genre can be systematically described in the following way:

In the first episode of the Gospel account, (F1) Jesus' distinction subverts (A) sameness and inverts (F) segregation (figure 1). The rivalry between two entities, each attempting to make gods of themselves (sameness) is subverted by the coming of the one truly distinctive God. Jesus is perceived to be a contender according to the cultural expectations of myth, but in fact is declared to be eternally sovereign before the contention begins. When He declares that His kingdom has come for the liberation of Israel, and through Israel all nations, from the very system that oppresses them, and which they ignorantly fight to defend, He inverts segregation.

In the second episode of the Gospel account, (E1) Jesus' diffusion subverts (B) scandal and inverts (E) satiation. The scandalizing of rival entities by impeding each other's claims to authority is subverted by the genuine Authority's diffusion of scandal, making room for the contentious other. The true Authority is perceived to be envious and scandalized, according to the cultural expectations of myth, but in fact He who alone has a right to be offended is gracious to those at enmity with Him. When that Authority miraculously feeds the great cosmic crowd that is scandalized by Him, He inverts satiation.

In the third episode of the Gospel account, (D1) Jesus' deference subverts (C) snare of striving and inverts (D) scapegoating. The accumulation of scandal into rivals striving to ensnare the other, and being caught up and carried away by such bitter striving, seeking for means and opportunity to destroy the other, is subverted by real deference to the other. Jesus battles striving itself, deferring to the will and desire of the Father God and teaching the other to do the same. He is perceived to be striving according to the cultural expectations of myth, but in fact He who alone could justly destroy the other loves His enemy. When Jesus willingly journeys to and arrives in Jerusalem, the cosmic center of power where His persecutors await Him, He inverts scapegoating.

In the fourth episode of the Gospel account, (C1) Jesus' deliverance subverts (D) scapegoating and inverts (C) snare of striving (figure 1). The leadership of the mythological mob successfully purchasing their Passover sacrifice, their scapegoat, is subverted by Jesus' revealing the nature of the coming of the Deliverer and the method of His deliverance, and instituting the commemoration of it in advance. Jesus is perceived to be threatening a worldly coup according to the cultural expectations of myth, but in fact He is preparing to deliver humanity from this very mythological system to which their sin has enslaved them. When He allows the mythological mob that comes for Him in the garden to take Him to the cosmic powers, He inverts the snare of striving.

In the fifth episode of the Gospel account, (B1) Jesus' dispersive display subverts (E) satiation and inverts (B) scandal. The mythological powers sating themselves upon their scapegoat through abuses manifold and grotesque is subverted by God's dispersive display of the light of truth, the Seed of the Word, that puts evil on display, summable as the sign of the Cross. While Jesus graciously lays down His life for the world at enmity with Him, who deserve precisely the opposite treatment, He is perceived to be justly condemned according to the illogical cultural expectations of myth. When Jesus forgives His lost and (seemingly) hopelessly inured creatures from the Cross, and dies, He inverts the scandal of humanity. There is darkness in the afternoon, an earthquake, and the curtain of the Temple is torn in two. Sin is conquered, its curse is lifted, and the apparatus of sacrifice to control its effects is crippled. Humanity has access to God not through Temple sacrifice or sacrifice of others, but through Jesus Christ's shed blood for many.

In the sixth episode of the Gospel account, (A1) Jesus' deification of believers subverts (F) segregation and inverts (A) sameness. The attempts of the cosmic leadership to effect the re-segregation of their cultural hierarchy by sealing the cave that holds God's body and posting guards, along with the disciples' unbelieving and despondent retreat back into their proper subjugated places in the mythological world, are subverted by Jesus' resurrection from the dead on the third day and His deification of the disciples. Jesus deifies those who believe in Him, resulting in "eternal salvation," and He commands them to share that saving faith with the entire world. All the while, Jesus is perceived to be dead by the cosmic leadership, a supposedly just victim of a supposedly just system. However, the disciple and the reader know that He is innocent, and that He lives. When Jesus ascends back to the Father God in heaven, He inverts sameness. With sameness—the fundamental deception of the myth-culture—fully exposed as a great delusion, the believer is freed to move out of the cycle of the pattern of myth-culture into the pattern of Jesus Christ, by believing in Him, and so receiving the gift of distinction in Him. This new Foundation is the basis of living the new pattern like Jesus, in Jesus, in His Spirit.

Regarding these two antithetical patterns, while discussing the rehabilitation of a theological anthropology, James Alison writes:

> So the same anthropological understanding is found to be present both in the teaching and activity of Christ, as witnessed to by the writers of the Gospel. . . . This anthropological understanding links an understanding of the mimetic nature of desire with an understanding of the violent nature of desire, the resolution of that violence in a form of victimage, and, eventually, the overcoming of the pattern of desire in question by a pattern of desire that is a rupture from, and yet in continuity with, the old pattern.[1]

That is, the state of sameness, in which humanity was inured, occasioned runaway violence that was only expiated *via* scapegoating. "Eventually," as in when the Christ appeared as a man, a "rupture" was made from that pattern of myth-culture. In particular, that rupture is the event of the Cross, as the key part of the pattern of Jesus,

---

1. Alison, *Joy*, 27.

a parallel yet antithetical pattern to the "old pattern." René Girard has also discussed these two opposing patterns: "Behind a superficial appearance of recounting fabulous events, the Gospels are always giving us a message exactly opposite to the one conveyed by mythology: the message of a non-violent deity, who has nothing in common with the epiphanies of the sacred."[2] As the Apostle Paul writes:

> Look out, lest anyone capture you through philosophy and meaningless wandering, according to the tradition of men, according to the pattern of the world, and not according to *the pattern of* Christ. (Col 2:8)[3]

The demonstration of the presence of the two patterns in the Gospel account conducted in this study makes, I trust, a meaningful contribution to the search for the structuring principal of the Gospel accounts. I conclude that the Gospels' genre is "the biblical chiasm," consisting of the chiastic bi-pattern. As noted in the introduction, the search for the Gospels' genre has preoccupied a great many. I do not view the structure identified as the only organizing principle of the Gospel. However, it is evidently a genuine and significant structure in the account, and surely contributes to a more complete understanding of Gospel genre.

Certainly, a number of future directions of study are now available as a result of this study. Firstly, only Mark's account of the Gospel was thoroughly analyzed for the chiastic bi-pattern here. Matthew, Luke and John's Gospel accounts should also be studied thoroughly to verify that the structure holds true for all four canonical Gospels. I have made preliminary progress on this, which is seen in the proposed transitions between episodes provided in tables and notes in this study. I am confident that the other three Gospel accounts are also structured in this way.

Additionally, I believe various accounts in the Hebrew Bible (Old Testament) also possess the chiastic bi-pattern (e.g., the accounts of Abraham and Joseph in Genesis; the account of David; etc.). These accounts would be fruitfully studied using this approach. As also briefly mentioned, post-Biblical Christian literature, including modern works, appear to be structured using the chiastic bi-pattern. That is, the Gospels' chiastic bi-pattern is the mother of many literary children. These would be interesting to investigate for the continued presence and influence of the biblical chiasm genre.

2. Girard, *Things Hidden*, 220.
3. Author's translation.

12

Application
Imitate Paul, as He Imitates Christ

"Brethren, join in following my example,

and note those who so walk,

as you have us for a pattern.

For many walk, of whom I have told you often,

and now tell you even weeping,

that they are the enemies of the cross of Christ."

(PHIL 3:17–18)

The Gospel of the kingdom, ministered by the LORD Jesus Christ and His twelve apostles, would ultimately be rejected by Israel within just a few years of Jesus' ascension, as prophesied by Jesus Himself (Matt 12:32; 23:37—24:2). The record of this failure is found in the first portion of the sequel book to Luke's Gospel account, the book of Acts (Acts 1–9). The failure of the leadership of Israel to receive the Gospel of the kingdom, through the ministry of the Holy Spirit in the Twelve, culminates in the leadership of Israel's rejection of the Holy Spirit at the stoning of Stephen (Acts 7:51–53).[1] When the Holy Spirit's ministry to Israel was rejected at Stephen's stoning,

---

1. I am thankful for the work of Justin Johnson (www.graceambassadors.com), which has informed this chapter.

rejecting the Gospel of the kingdom according to prophecy (Acts 3:17–21), the Lord hardened Israel in unbelief for a season (Rom 11:25).

Then the Lord Jesus chose an Israelite named Saul, a chief persecutor of believers, who participated in the stoning of Stephen. He chose Saul and saved him by grace through faith (Gal 1:15–16), and he dispensed to Saul the mystery of the Gospel of grace that had been hidden from the foundation of the world (Eph 3:9; Col 1:26; 1 Cor 2:7), to minister the Gospel of grace according to the mystery of the new creature, the Body of Christ, to all nations.

The Lord Jesus revealed to Saul this mystery of a previously hidden dispensation, which would be administered not through Israel, nor covenant, nor law, nor prophecy, but according to the mystery Body of Christ, and directly to all nations (Rom 16:25). In this new age there is no distinction between Jew/Israel and Gentile/nations (Gal 3:28), but a new third entity, the new creature in Christ (Eph 2:13–16). From the perspective of Israel and prophecy, this age of grace, of the Church, the Body of Christ (Rom 12:5; 1 Cor 12:27), comprises an interim period in the Lord's sovereign plan of redemption of this world, until the time when He will indeed give the kingdom of God to Israel (Rom 11:26–27), just as He promised according to the Gospel of the kingdom (Acts 1:6–7).

I note all of this because it is necessary in order to make application of the two patterns, Jesus and myth-culture, to ourselves today. Through His Apostle Paul, the Lord's special minister of the Gospel of grace (Col 1:24–26), the Lord calls on members of the mystery Body of Christ, who are redeemed by His grace through faith in Christ and His Cross (Eph 2:1–22), and given His indwelling Spirit as the inseparable seal of salvation (Eph 1:13), to "put off" the old man of sin and "put on" Christ (Eph 4:20–24). That is, we are to keep in step with His Spirit (Gal 5:24–26), and walk in the way of the cross (Gal 6:14) with "the world . . . crucified to me, and I to the world," the pattern of Jesus Christ left us in the Gospel account.

However, most critically, walking in the pattern of Jesus, by the power of the Spirit at work in the regenerate Christian, has no bearing on the salvation of the Christian. That is, unlike for the believers in the Gospel of the kingdom, walking in Jesus' pattern is not a condition that must be met in order to secure or ensure one's salvation (e.g., contrast Matt 25:32–46 with 2 Cor 9:7; Jas 2:24 with Rom 4:5; and Matt 24:13 with Rom 5:1). For those in Christ, His grace is sufficient (2 Cor 12:9). Not only should the Christian believe that Jesus' Cross is all-sufficient for his salvation, but also that there is nothing he must do to secure it or ensure it. All such attempts diminish the finished work of Christ on the Cross. A Christian is motivated by God's grace in Jesus to respond by walking in His Spirit in Jesus' pattern, but does *not* walk in Jesus' pattern under compulsion to keep a command (contrast 2 Cor 5:14–15 with 1 John 2:3).

Thereby, the Christian is an ambassador of the grace of God in Jesus (2 Cor 5:17–21). In fact, Apostle Paul calls upon Christians to imitate him just as he imitates Christ in this (1 Cor 4:16; 11:1). So, with the pause of the Gospel of the kingdom according to prophecy through the Twelve, and instead the ministry of the Gospel of grace according to the mystery through Apostle Paul, there are elements of the message and the ministry of the Gospel of the kingdom that are not a part of that pattern of Jesus that we are to imitate, we whose message and ministry is the Gospel of grace. That is, we are to imitate Paul's imitation of Jesus, because there are some critical differences between Jesus' expectations for Jewish and Gentile believers in the Gospel of the kingdom, versus Jesus' expectations for Christian believers, neither Jew nor Gentile, in the Gospel of grace (e.g., Phil 3:17–18; 1 Tim 1:16).

So, there exists a critical change from faith in Jesus for salvation that *must* be accompanied by good works (e.g., Jas 2:24), to faith in Jesus for salvation that must *not* be understood as necessitating good works to ensure it (e.g., Rom 4:5). A case in point is the question of whether a Christian must forgive others in order to be forgiven, or not. According to the Gospel of the kingdom, God will only forgive believers if they first forgive others (e.g., Matt 6:14–15). However, according to the Gospel of grace, the Christian is forgiven without condition, independent of his forgiveness of others (e.g., Eph 4:32; 2 Cor 5:19). Rather, God has already forgiven the Christian for Christ's sake, which should inspire his forgiveness of others, in response to Jesus' free gift (Rom 5:15) of grace apart from works (Rom 3:28; Eph 2:8–9).

So, the pattern that Jesus lived, as we have explored in the Gospel account, is to be followed, but it is to be followed as Apostle Paul follows the LORD Jesus' pattern. Our pattern is Apostle Paul's distinct identity in Jesus, and his thought, word, and behavior in Jesus. Good practical examples (*inter alia*) of Apostle Paul modelling the pattern of Jesus are recorded in the book of Acts (e.g., Acts 16:11–40; 17:1–10). There, Paul practices the six episodes of Jesus' pattern, while those around him are exhibiting the pattern of myth-culture. In fact, it is for this reason that Apostle Paul's typical departure from a city to which he ministered was the result of his scapegoating by the local myth-culture. And yet, this event was also the city's deliverance, in that it would result in the founding of a local church of those saved through Apostle Paul's preaching of the Gospel of grace.

For this reason, it was necessary for me to add this step for those who would walk in Jesus' pattern, to know that His pattern is to be followed as Apostle Paul follows it. Rightly dividing between prophecy and mystery, Israel and Church, law and grace, is important in order to be able to keep in step with the Spirit of Jesus (Gal 5:24–6), walking in the pattern of Jesus Christ, according to the mystery of the Gospel of grace, as taught and modelled by the LORD Jesus' Apostle Paul.

According to the Gospel of grace, for those who have received the free gift of salvation in Christ (Rom 5:15–18), by grace through faith (Eph 2:8), apart from works of the law (Rom 3:20–22), the Christian is freely given an eternal position in Christ (2 Cor 5:17; Eph 2:6), despite his condition not fully reflecting that position (e.g., 1 Cor 3:1–3). This is a key difference from the Gospel of the kingdom, which required keeping the law of Moses in addition to faith in Jesus (Matt 5:18–20; 28:20), as confirmation of salvation. But for the Christian, saved by grace apart from works of the law, nothing can separate the Christian from the love of God in Christ Jesus (Rom 8:38–9). Even so, increasingly day by day, those who have experienced regeneration, by Jesus' Spirit's baptism into the new creature, are progressively rejecting the world's pattern of myth-culture, and walking instead in the LORD Jesus' pattern, like Apostle Paul. The Christian's position in Jesus is a "positional truth," the reality that the Christian is no longer standing in Adam, and in the old pattern of this world's myth-culture, but is standing in Jesus Christ, in grace, and in His new pattern.

Justification before God is based upon what Christ has done, having fully atoned for sin at the Cross by His blood (Eph 1:7), and freely offered salvation by grace apart from works of the Law. It is entirely Jesus' achievement, His victory, not the Christian's. But the Christian, the believer who is *in Jesus*, participates in His death and resurrection, in His victory. Thereafter, day by day, the indwelling Spirit of Christ leads (1 Cor 3:16) as he walks in the freely given newness of life, being sanctified, washed in the water of the Word (Eph 5:26). The Christian is changed more and more from his condition in the flesh to his position in the Spirit, a position already freely given by grace to the believer in Christ (Phil 3:16). And the believer who now lives in Christ, in response to Jesus' love, sees his thoughts, words and deeds become more and more in conformity with Jesus Christ by His Spirit's work in him, conforming him to His pattern that He perfectly lived (Rom 12:2), as preserved for us in Scripture, in the Gospel accounts. And this pattern is modelled by God's grace at work in Apostle Paul, which is at work in him mightily (Col 1:29), as recorded in the Acts and his letters.

But the pattern of this world, of myth-culture, the pattern of the sin position in Adam, the old man of sin, continues to tempt the new creature in Christ. Regenerate Christians are no longer in that position, but stand in grace (Rom 5:2), in the new position in the Last Adam, in the new man, Jesus Christ. However, in our condition of this mortal body, we often continue in or revert to the identity, thinking, speaking and behavior characteristic of the first position in Adam and its pattern, the pattern of the old man of sin. We still dwell in these sin-cursed bodies (Gal 5:16–18), and in this sin-cursed world, of which Satan is yet the ruler (2 Cor 4:4). Therefore, the flesh, the world, and Satan, are at war with the Spirit (Gal 5:16–18), who indwells us, until the LORD Jesus comes to glorify our bodies at the resurrection and rapture of His Church, the Body of Christ (1 Cor 15:50–58; 1 Thess 1:10, 4:13–18). Jesus alone has saved, is sanctifying, and will glorify the Christian. Praise the LORD!

Appendix 1

THE GOSPEL ACCORDING TO MARK (NASB)

Text in roman identifies the LORD Jesus' unique, divine pattern in the account, while text in italics identifies the pattern of myth-culture, of the world.

The account is divided into the twelve motifs of the combat myth as inverted and subverted by Jesus.

Mark 1:1–12: Jesus' "Heroic Emergence"

$1^{:1}$ The beginning of the gospel of Jesus Christ, the Son of God.
^{2} As it is written in Isaiah the prophet:
> "Behold, I send My messenger ahead of You,
> Who will prepare Your way;[Mal 3:1]
> ^{3} The voice of one crying in the wilderness,
> 'Make ready the way of the LORD,
> Make His paths straight.'"[Isa 40:3]

^{4} John the Baptist appeared in the wilderness preaching a baptism of repentance for the forgiveness of sins. ^{5} And all the country of Judea was going out to him, and all the people of Jerusalem; and they were being baptized by him in the Jordan River, confessing their sins. ^{6} John was clothed with camel's hair and *wore* a leather belt around his waist, and his diet was locusts and wild honey. ^{7} And he was preaching, and saying, "After me One is coming who is mightier than I, and I am not fit to stoop down and untie the thong of His sandals. ^{8} I baptized you with water; but He will baptize you with the Holy Spirit."

9 In those days Jesus came from Nazareth in Galilee and was baptized by John in the Jordan. 10 Immediately coming up out of the water, He saw the heavens opening, and the Spirit like a dove descending upon Him; 11 and a voice came out of the heavens: "You are My beloved Son, in You I am well-pleased."

12 Immediately the Spirit *impelled Him *to go* out into the wilderness.

Mark 1:13–15: Jesus' "Lack/Villainy"

13 *And He was in the wilderness forty days being tempted by Satan;* and He was with the wild beasts, and the angels were ministering to Him.

14 *Now after John had been taken into custody*, Jesus came into Galilee, preaching the gospel of God, 15 and saying, "The time is fulfilled, and the kingdom of God is at hand; repent and believe in the gospel."

Mark 1:16—3:6: Jesus' "Journey"

1:16 As He was going along by the Sea of Galilee, He saw Simon and Andrew, the brother of Simon, casting a net in the sea; for they were fishermen. 17 And Jesus said to them, "Follow Me, and I will make you become fishers of men." 18 Immediately they left their nets and followed Him. 19 Going on a little farther, He saw James [Jacob] the son of Zebedee, and John his brother, who were also in the boat mending the nets. 20 Immediately He called them; and they left their father Zebedee in the boat with the hired servants, and went away to follow Him.

21 They *went into Capernaum; and immediately on the Sabbath He entered the synagogue and *began* to teach. 22 They were amazed at His teaching; for He was teaching them as *one* having authority, and not as the scribes. 23 Just then there was a man in their synagogue with an unclean spirit; and he cried out, 24 *saying, "What business do we have with each other, Jesus of Nazareth? Have You come to destroy us? I know who You are—the Holy One of God!"* 25 And Jesus rebuked him, saying, "Be quiet, and come out of him!" 26 Throwing him into convulsions, the unclean spirit cried out with a loud voice and came out of him. 27 They were all amazed, so that they debated among themselves, saying, "What is this? A new teaching with authority! He commands even the unclean spirits, and they obey Him." 28 Immediately the news about Him spread everywhere into all the surrounding district of Galilee.

29 And immediately after they came out of the synagogue, they came into the house of Simon and Andrew, with James [Jacob] and John. 30 Now Simon's mother-in-law was lying sick with a fever; and immediately they *spoke to Jesus about her. 31 And He came to her and raised her up, taking her by the hand, and the fever left her, and she waited on them.

32 When evening came, after the sun had set, they *began* bringing to Him all who were ill and those who were demon-possessed. 33 And the whole city had gathered at the door.

³⁴ And He healed many who were ill with various diseases, and cast out many demons; and He was not permitting the demons to speak, because they knew who He was.

³⁵ In the early morning, while it was still dark, Jesus got up, left *the house*, and went away to a secluded place, and was praying there. ³⁶ Simon and his companions searched for Him; ³⁷ they found Him, and *said to Him, "Everyone is looking for You." ³⁸ He *said to them, "Let us go somewhere else to the towns nearby, so that I may preach there also; for that is what I came for." ³⁹ And He went into their synagogues throughout all Galilee, preaching and casting out the demons.

⁴⁰ And a leper *came to Jesus, beseeching Him and falling on his knees before Him, and saying, "If You are willing, You can make me clean." ⁴¹ Moved with compassion, Jesus stretched out His hand and touched him, and *said to him, "I am willing; be cleansed." ⁴² Immediately the leprosy left him and he was cleansed. ⁴³ And He sternly warned him and immediately sent him away, ⁴⁴ and He *said to him, "See that you say nothing to anyone; but go, show yourself to the priest and offer for your cleansing what Moses commanded, as a testimony to them." ⁴⁵ But he went out and began to proclaim it freely and to spread the news around, to such an extent that Jesus could no longer publicly enter a city, but stayed out in unpopulated areas; and they were coming to Him from everywhere.

2:¹ When He had come back to Capernaum several days afterward, it was heard that He was at home. ² And many were gathered together, so that there was no longer room, not even near the door; and He was speaking the word to them. ³ And they *came, bringing to Him a paralytic, carried by four men. ⁴ Being unable to get to Him because of the crowd, they removed the roof above Him; and when they had dug an opening, they let down the pallet on which the paralytic was lying. ⁵ And Jesus seeing their faith *said to the paralytic, "Son, your sins are forgiven." ⁶ *But some of the scribes were sitting there and reasoning in their hearts,* ⁷ *"Why does this man speak that way? He is blaspheming; who can forgive sins but God alone?"* ⁸ Immediately Jesus, aware in His spirit that they were reasoning that way within themselves, *said to them, "Why are you reasoning about these things in your hearts? ⁹ Which is easier, to say to the paralytic, 'Your sins are forgiven'; or to say, 'Get up, and pick up your pallet and walk'? ¹⁰ But so that you may know that the Son of Man has authority on earth to forgive sins"—He *said to the paralytic, ¹¹ "I say to you, get up, pick up your pallet and go home." ¹² And he got up and immediately picked up the pallet and went out in the sight of everyone, so that they were all amazed and were glorifying God, saying, "We have never seen anything like this."

¹³ And He went out again by the seashore; and all the people were coming to Him, and He was teaching them.

¹⁴ As He passed by, He saw Levi the *son* of Alphaeus sitting in the tax booth, and He *said to him, "Follow Me!" And he got up and followed Him. ¹⁵ And it *happened that He was reclining *at the table* in his house, and many tax collectors and sinners were dining with Jesus and His disciples; for there were many of them, and they were

following Him.[16] When the scribes of the Pharisees saw that He was eating with the sinners and tax collectors, they said to His disciples, "Why is He eating and drinking with tax collectors and sinners?"[17] And hearing *this*, Jesus *said to them, "*It is* not those who are healthy who need a physician, but those who are sick; I did not come to call the righteous, but sinners."[18] John's disciples and the Pharisees were fasting; and they *came and *said to Him, "Why do John's disciples and the disciples of the Pharisees fast, but Your disciples do not fast?"[19] And Jesus said to them, "While the bridegroom is with them, the attendants of the bridegroom cannot fast, can they? So long as they have the bridegroom with them, they cannot fast.[20] But the days will come when the bridegroom is taken away from them, and then they will fast in that day.[21] "No one sews a patch of unshrunk cloth on an old garment; otherwise the patch pulls away from it, the new from the old, and a worse tear results.[22] No one puts new wine into old wineskins; otherwise the wine will burst the skins, and the wine is lost and the skins *as well*; but *one puts* new wine into fresh wineskins."

[23] And it happened that He was passing through the grainfields on the Sabbath, and His disciples began to make their way along while picking the heads *of grain*.[24] The Pharisees were saying to Him, "Look, why are they doing what is not lawful on the Sabbath?"[25] And He *said to them, "Have you never read what David did when he was in need and he and his companions became hungry;[26] how he entered the house of God in the time of Abiathar*the* high priest, and ate the consecrated bread, which is not lawful for *anyone* to eat except the priests, and he also gave it to those who were with him?"[27] Jesus said to them, "The Sabbath was made for man, and not man for the Sabbath.[28] So the Son of Man is Lord even of the Sabbath."

3:[1]He entered again into a synagogue; and a man was there whose hand was withered. [2] *They were watching Him to see if He would heal him on the Sabbath, so that they might accuse Him.* [3] He *said to the man with the withered hand, "Get up and come forward!" [4] And He *said to them, "Is it lawful to do good or to do harm on the Sabbath, to save a life or to kill?" But they kept silent. [5] After looking around at them with anger, grieved at their hardness of heart, He *said to the man, "Stretch out your hand." And he stretched it out, and his hand was restored.[6] *And the Pharisees went out and immediately began taking counsel with the Herodians against Him, as to how they might destroy Him.*

Mark 3:7—8:26: Jesus' "Donations/Counsel"

3:[7] Jesus withdrew to the sea with His disciples; and a great multitude from Galilee followed; and *also* from Judea, [8] and from Jerusalem, and from Idumea, and beyond the Jordan, and the vicinity of Tyre and Sidon, a great number of people heard of all that He was doing and came to Him. [9] And He told His disciples that a boat should stand ready for Him because of the crowd, so that they would not crowd Him; [10] for He had healed many, with the result that all those who had afflictions pressed around Him in order to touch Him. [11] *Whenever the unclean spirits saw Him, they would fall down before Him and shout, "You are the Son of God!"* [12] And He earnestly warned them not to tell who He was.

[13] And He *went up on the mountain and *summoned those whom He Himself wanted, and they came to Him. [14] And He appointed twelve, so that they would be with Him and that He *could* send them out to preach, [15] and to have authority to cast out the demons. [16] And He appointed the twelve: Simon (to whom He gave the name Peter), [17] and James [Jacob], the *son* of Zebedee, and John the brother of James (to them He gave the name Boanerges, which means, "Sons of Thunder"); [18] and Andrew, and Philip, and Bartholomew, and Matthew, and Thomas, and James [Jacob] the son of Alphaeus, and Thaddaeus, and Simon the Zealot; [19] and Judas Iscariot, who betrayed Him.

[20] And He *came home, and the crowd *gathered again, to such an extent that they could not even eat a meal. [21] *When His own people heard of this, they went out to take custody of Him; for they were saying, "He has lost His senses." [22] The scribes who came down from Jerusalem were saying, "He is possessed byBeelzebul," and "He casts out the demons by the ruler of the demons."*[23] And He called them to Himself and began speaking to them in parables, "How can Satan cast out Satan? [24] If a kingdom is divided against itself, that kingdom cannot stand. [25] If a house is divided against itself, that house will not be able to stand. [26] If Satan has risen up against himself and is divided, he cannot stand, but he is finished! [27] But no one can enter the strong man's house and plunder his property unless he first binds the strong man, and then he will plunder his house.

[28] "Truly I say to you, all sins shall be forgiven the sons of men, and whatever blasphemies they utter; [29] but whoever blasphemes against the Holy Spirit never has forgiveness, but is guilty of an eternal sin"—[30] because they were saying, "He has an unclean spirit."

[31] *Then His mother and His brothers *arrived, and standing outside they sent word to Him and called Him. [32] A crowd was sitting around Him, and they *said to Him, "Behold, Your mother and Your brothers are outside looking for You."*[33] Answering them, He *said, "Who are My mother and My brothers?" [34] Looking about at those who were sitting around Him, He *said, "Behold My mother and My brothers! [35] For whoever does the will of God, he is My brother and sister and mother."

[4:1] He began to teach again by the sea. And such a very large crowd gathered to Him that He got into a boat in the sea and sat down; and the whole crowd was by the sea on the land. [2] And He was teaching them many things in parables, and was saying to them in His teaching, [3] "Listen *to this*! Behold, the sower went out to sow; [4] *as he was sowing, some seed fell beside the road, and the birds came and ate it up. [5] Other seed fell on the rocky ground where it did not have much soil; and immediately it sprang up because it had no depth of soil. [6] And after the sun had risen, it was scorched; and because it had no root, it withered away. [7] Other seed fell among the thorns, and the thorns came up and choked it, and it yielded no crop. [8] Other seeds* fell into the good soil, and as they grew up and increased, they yielded a crop and produced thirty, sixty, and a hundredfold." [9] And He was saying, "He who has ears to hear, let him hear."

¹⁰ As soon as He was alone, His followers, along with the twelve, *began* asking Him *about* the parables. ¹¹ And He was saying to them, "To you has been given the mystery of the kingdom of God, but those who are outside get everything in parables, ¹² so that

'while seeing, they may see and not perceive,

and while hearing, they may hear and not understand,

otherwise they might return and be forgiven.'"

¹³ And He *said to them, "Do you not understand this parable? How will you understand all the parables? ¹⁴ The sower sows the word. ¹⁵ These are the ones who are beside the road where the word is sown; and when they hear, immediately Satan comes and takes away the word which has been sown in them. ¹⁶ In a similar way these are the ones on whom seed was sown on the rocky *places*, who, when they hear the word, immediately receive it with joy; ¹⁷ and they have no *firm* root in themselves, but are *only* temporary; then, when affliction or persecution arises because of the word, immediately they fall away. ¹⁸ And others are the ones on whom seed was sown among the thorns; these are the ones who have heard the word, ¹⁹ but the worries of the world, and the deceitfulness of riches, and the desires for other things enter in and choke the word, and it becomes unfruitful. ²⁰ And those are the ones on whom seed was sown on the good soil; and they hear the word and accept it and bear fruit, thirty, sixty, and a hundredfold."

²¹ And He was saying to them, "A lamp is not brought to be put under a basket, is it, or under a bed? Is it not *brought* to be put on the lampstand? ²² For nothing is hidden, except to be revealed; nor has *anything* been secret, but that it would come to light. ²³ If anyone has ears to hear, let him hear." ²⁴ And He was saying to them, "Take care what you listen to. By your standard of measure it will be measured to you; and more will be given you besides. ²⁵ For whoever has, to him *more* shall be given; and whoever does not have, even what he has shall be taken away from him."

²⁶ And He was saying, "The kingdom of God is like a man who casts seed upon the soil; ²⁷ and he goes to bed at night and gets up by day, and the seed sprouts and grows—how, he himself does not know. ²⁸ The soil produces crops by itself; first the blade, then the head, then the mature grain in the head. ²⁹ But when the crop permits, he immediately puts in the sickle, because the harvest has come."

³⁰ And He said, "How shall we picture the kingdom of God, or by what parable shall we present it? ³¹ *It is* like a mustard seed, which, when sown upon the soil, though it is smaller than all the seeds that are upon the soil, ³² yet when it is sown, it grows up and becomes larger than all the garden plants and forms large branches; so that

'the birds of the air *can* nest under its shade.'"

³³ With many such parables He was speaking the word to them, so far as they were able to hear it; ³⁴ and He did not speak to them without a parable; but He was explaining everything privately to His own disciples.

³⁵ On that day, when evening came, He *said to them, "Let us go over to the other side." ³⁶ Leaving the crowd, they *took Him along with them in the boat, just as He

was; and other boats were with Him. [37] And there *arose a fierce gale of wind, and the waves were breaking over the boat so much that the boat was already filling up. [38] Jesus Himself was in the stern, asleep on the cushion; *and they *woke Him and *said to Him, "Teacher, do You not care that we are perishing?"* [39] And He got up and rebuked the wind and said to the sea, "Hush, be still." And the wind died down and it became perfectly calm. [40] And He said to them, "Why are you afraid? Do you still have no faith?" [41] *They became very much afraid and said to one another, "Who then is this, that even the wind and the sea obey Him?"*

5:[1] *They came to the other side of the sea, into the country of the Gerasenes.* [2] *When He got out of the boat, immediately a man from the tombs with an unclean spirit met Him,* [3] *and he had his dwelling among the tombs. And no one was able to bind him anymore, even with a chain;* [4] *because he had often been bound with shackles and chains, and the chains had been torn apart by him and the shackles broken in pieces, and no one was strong enough to subdue him.* [5] *Constantly, night and day, he was screaming among the tombs and in the mountains, and gashing himself with stones.* [6] *Seeing Jesus from a distance, he ran up and bowed down before Him;* [7] *and shouting with a loud voice, he *said, "What business do we have with each other, Jesus, Son of the Most High God? I implore You by God, do not torment me!"* [8] For He had been saying to him, "Come out of the man, you unclean spirit!"* [9] And He was asking him, "What is your name?" And he *said to Him, "My name is Legion; for we are many."* [10] And he *began* to implore Him earnestly not to send them out of the country. [11] Now there was a large herd of swine feeding nearby on the mountain. [12] *The demons* implored Him, saying, "Send us into the swine so that we may enter them."* [13] Jesus gave them permission. And coming out, the unclean spirits entered the swine; and the herd rushed down the steep bank into the sea, about two thousand *of them*; and they were drowned in the sea.

[14] *Their herdsmen ran away and reported it in the city and in the country. And the people came to see what it was that had happened.* [15] *They *came to Jesus and *observed the man who had been demon-possessed sitting down, clothed and in his right mind, the very man who had had the "legion"; and they became frightened.* [16] *Those who had seen it described to them how it had happened to the demon-possessed man, and all about the swine.* [17] *And they began to implore Him to leave their region.* [18] As He was getting into the boat, the man who had been demon-possessed was imploring Him that he might accompany Him. [19] And He did not let him, but He *said to him, "Go home to your people and report to them what great things the LORD has done for you, and *how* He had mercy on you."* [20] And he went away and began to proclaim in Decapolis what great things Jesus had done for him; and everyone was amazed.

[21] When Jesus had crossed over again in the boat to the other side, a large crowd gathered around Him; and so He stayed by the seashore. [22] One of the synagogue officials named Jairus *came up, and on seeing Him, *fell at His feet [23] and *implored Him earnestly, saying, "My little daughter is at the point of death; *please* come and lay Your

hands on her, so that she will get well and live."[24] And He went off with him; and a large crowd was following Him and pressing in on Him.

[25] A woman who had had a hemorrhage for twelve years,[26] and had endured much at the hands of many physicians, and had spent all that she had and was not helped at all, but rather had grown worse—[27] after hearing about Jesus, she came up in the crowd behind *Him* and touched His cloak.[28] For she thought, "If I just touch His garments, I will get well."[29] Immediately the flow of her blood was dried up; and she felt in her body that she was healed of her affliction.[30] Immediately Jesus, perceiving in Himself that the power *proceeding* from Him had gone forth, turned around in the crowd and said, "Who touched My garments?"[31] And His disciples said to Him, "You see the crowd pressing in on You, and You say, 'Who touched Me?'"[32] And He looked around to see the woman who had done this.[33] But the woman fearing and trembling, aware of what had happened to her, came and fell down before Him and told Him the whole truth.[34] And He said to her, "Daughter, your faith has made you well; go in peace and be healed of your affliction."

[35] *While He was still speaking, they* *came from the house of the synagogue official, saying, "Your daughter has died; why trouble the Teacher anymore?"*[36] But Jesus, overhearing what was being spoken, *said to the synagogue official, "Do not be afraid *any longer*, only believe."[37] And He allowed no one to accompany Him, except Peter and James [Jacob] and John the brother of James.[38] They *came to the house of the synagogue official; and He *saw a commotion, and *people* loudly weeping and wailing.[39] And entering in, He *said to them, "Why make a commotion and weep? The child has not died, but is asleep."[40] *They began laughing at Him.* But putting them all out, He *took along the child's father and mother and His own companions, and *entered *the room* where the child was.[41] Taking the child by the hand, He *said to her, "Talitha kum!" (which translated means, "Little girl, I say to you, get up!").[42] Immediately the girl got up and *began* to walk, for she was twelve years old. And immediately they were completely astounded.[43] And He gave them strict orders that no one should know about this, and He said that *something* should be given her to eat.

[6:1] Jesus went out from there and *came into His hometown; and His disciples *followed Him.[2] When the Sabbath came, He began to teach in the synagogue; *and the many listeners were astonished, saying, "Where did this man get these things, and what is this wisdom given to Him, and such miracles as these performed by His hands?*[3] *Is not this the carpenter, the son of Mary, and brother of James [Jacob] and Joses and Judas and Simon? Are not His sisters here with us?" And they took offense at Him.*[4] Jesus said to them, "A prophet is not without honor except in his hometown and among his *own* relatives and in his *own* household."[5] And He could do no miracle there except that He laid His hands on a few sick people and healed them.[6] And He wondered at their unbelief. And He was going around the villages teaching.

[7] And He *summoned the twelve and began to send them out in pairs, and gave them authority over the unclean spirits;[8] and He instructed them that they should take

nothing for *their* journey, except a mere staff—no bread, no bag, no money in their belt—⁹ but *to* wear sandals; and *He added,* "Do not put on two tunics."¹⁰ And He said to them, "Wherever you enter a house, stay there until you leave town.¹¹ Any place that does not receive you or listen to you, as you go out from there, shake the dust off the soles of your feet for a testimony against them."¹² They went out and preached that *men* should repent.¹³ And they were casting out many demons and were anointing with oil many sick people and healing them.

¹⁴ *And King Herod heard of it, for His name had become well known; and people were saying, "John the Baptist has risen from the dead, and that is why these miraculous powers are at work in Him."*¹⁵ *But others were saying, "He is Elijah." And others were saying, "He is a prophet, like one of the prophets of old."*¹⁶ *But when Herod heard of it, he kept saying, "John, whom I beheaded, has risen!"*

¹⁷ *For Herod himself had sent and had John arrested and bound in prison on account of Herodias, the wife of his brother Philip, because he had married her.*¹⁸ *For John had been saying to Herod, "It is not lawful for you to have your brother's wife."*¹⁹ *Herodias had a grudge against him and wanted to put him to death and could not do so;*²⁰ *for Herod was afraid of John, knowing that he was a righteous and holy man, and he kept him safe. And when he heard him, he was very perplexed; but he used to enjoy listening to him.*²¹ *A strategic day came when Herod on his birthday gave a banquet for his lords and military commanders and the leading men of Galilee;*²² *and when the daughter of Herodias herself came in and danced, she pleased Herod and his dinner guests; and the king said to the girl, "Ask me for whatever you want and I will give it to you."*²³ *And he swore to her, "Whatever you ask of me, I will give it to you; up to half of my kingdom."*²⁴ *And she went out and said to her mother, "What shall I ask for?" And she said, "The head of John the Baptist."*²⁵ *Immediately she came in a hurry to the king and asked, saying, "I want you to give me at once the head of John the Baptist on a platter."*²⁶ *And although the king was very sorry, yet because of his oaths and because of his dinner guests, he was unwilling to refuse her.*²⁷ *Immediately the king sent an executioner and commanded him to bring back his head. And he went and had him beheaded in the prison,*²⁸ *and brought his head on a platter, and gave it to the girl; and the girl gave it to her mother.*²⁹ When his disciples heard *about this,* they came and took away his body and laid it in a tomb.

³⁰ The apostles *gathered together with Jesus; and they reported to Him all that they had done and taught.³¹ And He *said to them, "Come away by yourselves to a secluded place and rest a while." (For there were many *people* coming and going, and they did not even have time to eat.)³² They went away in the boat to a secluded place by themselves.

³³ *The people* saw them going, and many recognized *them* and ran there together on foot from all the cities, and got there ahead of them.³⁴ When Jesus went ashore, He saw a large crowd, and He felt compassion for them because they were like sheep without a shepherd; and He began to teach them many things.³⁵ When it was already quite late, His disciples came to Him and said, "This place is desolate and it is already

quite late;[36] send them away so that they may go into the surrounding countryside and villages and buy themselves something to eat."[37] But He answered them, "You give them *something* to eat!" *And they *said to Him, "Shall we go and spend two hundred denarii on bread and give them something to eat?"*[38] And He *said to them, "How many loaves do you have? Go look!" And when they found out, they *said, "Five, and two fish."[39] And He commanded them all to sit down by groups on the green grass.[40] They sat down in groups of hundreds and of fifties.[41] And He took the five loaves and the two fish, and looking up toward heaven, He blessed *the food* and broke the loaves and He kept giving *them* to the disciples to set before them; and He divided up the two fish among them all.[42] They all ate and were satisfied,[43] and they picked up twelve full baskets of the broken pieces, and also of the fish.[44] There were five thousand men who ate the loaves.

[45] Immediately Jesus made His disciples get into the boat and go ahead of *Him* to the other side to Bethsaida, while He Himself was sending the crowd away.[46] After bidding them farewell, He left for the mountain to pray.

[47] When it was evening, the boat was in the middle of the sea, and He was alone on the land.[48] Seeing them straining at the oars, for the wind was against them, at about the fourth watch of the night He *came to them, walking on the sea; and He intended to pass by them.*[49] But when they saw Him walking on the sea, they supposed that it was a ghost, and cried out;*[50] for they all saw Him and were terrified. But immediately He spoke with them and *said to them, "Take courage; it is I, do not be afraid."[51] Then He got into the boat with them, and the wind stopped; *and they were utterly astonished,*[52] *for they had not gained any insight from the incident of the loaves, but their heart was hardened.*

[53] When they had crossed over they came to land at Gennesaret, and moored to the shore.[54] When they got out of the boat, immediately *the people* recognized Him,[55] and ran about that whole country and began to carry here and there on their pallets those who were sick, to the place they heard He was.[56] Wherever He entered villages, or cities, or countryside, they were laying the sick in the market places, and imploring Him that they might just touch the fringe of His cloak; and as many as touched it were being cured.

[7:1] The Pharisees and some of the scribes gathered around Him when they had come from Jerusalem,[2] *and had seen that some of His disciples were eating their bread with impure hands, that is, unwashed.*[3] *(For the Pharisees and all the Jews do not eat unless they carefully wash their hands, thus observing the traditions of the elders;*[4] *and when they come from the market place, they do not eat unless they cleanse themselves; and there are many other things which they have received in order to observe, such as the washing of cups and pitchers and copper pots.)*[5] *The Pharisees and the scribes *asked Him, "Why do Your disciples not walk according to the tradition of the elders, but eat their bread with impure hands?"*[6] And He said to them, "Rightly did Isaiah prophesy of you hypocrites, as it is written:

'This people honors me with their lips,

But their heart is far away from me.

[7] 'But in vain do they worship me,

Teaching as doctrines the precepts of men.'

[8] Neglecting the commandment of God, you hold to the tradition of men."

[9] He was also saying to them, "You are experts at setting aside the commandment of God in order to keep your tradition. [10] For Moses said,

'Honor you father and your mother';

and,

'He who speaks evil of father or mother, is to be put to death';

[11] but you say, 'If a man says to *his* father or *his* mother, whatever I have that would help you is Corban (that is to say, given *to God*),' [12] you no longer permit him to do anything for *his* father or *his* mother; [13] *thus* invalidating the word of God by your tradition which you have handed down; and you do many things such as that."

[14] After He called the crowd to Him again, He *began* saying to them, "Listen to Me, all of you, and understand: [15] there is nothing outside the man which can defile him if it goes into him; but the things which proceed out of the man are what defile the man. [16] [If anyone has ears to hear, let him hear."]

[17] When he had left the crowd *and* entered the house, His disciples questioned Him about the parable. [18] And He *said to them, "Are you so lacking in understanding also? Do you not understand that whatever goes into the man from outside cannot defile him, [19] because it does not go into his heart, but into his stomach, and is eliminated?" (*Thus He* declared all foods clean.) [20] And He was saying, "That which proceeds out of the man, that is what defiles the man. [21] For from within, out of the heart of men, proceed the evil thoughts, fornications, thefts, murders, adulteries, [22] deeds of coveting *and* wickedness, *as well as* deceit, sensuality, envy, slander, pride *and* foolishness. [23] All these evil things proceed from within and defile the man."

[24] Jesus got up and went away from there to the region of Tyre. And when He had entered a house, He wanted no one to know *of it*; yet He could not escape notice. [25] But after hearing of Him, a woman whose little daughter had an unclean spirit immediately came and fell at His feet. [26] Now the woman was a Gentile, of the Syrophoenician race. And she kept asking Him to cast the demon out of her daughter. [27] And He was saying to her, "Let the children be satisfied first, for it is not good to take the children's bread and throw it to the dogs." [28] But she answered and *said to Him, "Yes, Lord, *but* even the dogs under the table feed on the children's crumbs." [29] And He said to her, "Because of this answer go; the demon has gone out of your daughter." [30] And going back to her home, she found the child lying on the bed, the demon having left.

[31] Again He went out from the region of Tyre, and came through Sidon to the Sea of Galilee, within the region of Decapolis. [32] They *brought to Him one who was deaf and spoke with difficulty, and they *implored Him to lay His hand on him. [33] Jesus took him aside from the crowd, by himself, and put His fingers into his ears, and after

spitting, He touched his tongue *with the saliva;*[34] and looking up to heaven with a deep sigh, He *said to him, "Ephphatha!" that is, "Be opened!"[35] And his ears were opened, and the impediment of his tongue was removed, and he *began* speaking plainly.[36] And He gave them orders not to tell anyone; but the more He ordered them, the more widely they continued to proclaim it.[37] They were utterly astonished, saying, "He has done all things well; He makes even the deaf to hear and the mute to speak."

[8:1] In those days, when there was again a large crowd and they had nothing to eat, Jesus called His disciples and *said to them,[2] "I feel compassion for the people because they have remained with Me now three days and have nothing to eat.[3] If I send them away hungry to their homes, they will faint on the way; and some of them have come from a great distance."[4] *And His disciples answered Him, "Where will anyone be able to find enough bread here in this desolate place to satisfy these people?"*[5] And He was asking them, "How many loaves do you have?" And they said, "Seven."[6] And He *directed the people to sit down on the ground; and taking the seven loaves, He gave thanks and broke them, and started giving them to His disciples to serve to them, and they served them to the people.[7] They also had a few small fish; and after He had blessed them, He ordered these to be served as well.[8] And they ate and were satisfied; and they picked up seven large baskets full of what was left over of the broken pieces.[9] About four thousand were *there*; and He sent them away.[10] And immediately He entered the boat with His disciples and came to the district of Dalmanutha.

[11] *The Pharisees came out and began to argue with Him, seeking from Him a sign from heaven, to test Him.*[12] Sighing deeply in His spirit, He *said, "Why does this generation seek for a sign? Truly I say to you, no sign will be given to this generation."[13] Leaving them, He again embarked and went away to the other side.

[14] And they had forgotten to take bread, and did not have more than one loaf in the boat with them.[15] And He was giving orders to them, saying, "Watch out! Beware of the leaven of the Pharisees and the leaven of Herod."[16] *They began to discuss with one another the fact that they had no bread.*[17] And Jesus, aware of this, *said to them, "Why do you discuss *the fact* that you have no bread? Do you not yet see or understand? Do you have a hardened heart?

[18] 'Having eyes, do you not see? And Having ears, do you not hear?'

And do you not remember,[19] when I broke the five loaves for the five thousand, how many baskets full of broken pieces you picked up?" They *said to Him, "Twelve."[20] "When *I broke* the seven for the four thousand, how many large baskets full of broken pieces did you pick up?" And they *said to Him, "Seven."[21] And He was saying to them, "Do you not yet understand?"

[22] And they *came to Bethsaida. And they *brought a blind man to Jesus and *implored Him to touch him.[23] Taking the blind man by the hand, He brought him out of the village; and after spitting on his eyes and laying His hands on him, He asked him, "Do you see anything?"[24] And he looked up and said, "I see men, for I see *them* like trees, walking around."[25] Then again He laid His hands on his eyes; and he looked

intently and was restored, and *began* to see everything clearly.[26] And He sent him to his home, saying, "Do not even enter the village."

Mark 8:27—10:45: Jesus' "Defeat"

8:27 *Jesus went out, along with His disciples, to the villages of Caesarea Philippi; and on the way He questioned His disciples, saying to them, "Who do people say that I am?"*[28] *They told Him, saying, "John the Baptist; and others say Elijah; but others, one of the prophets."*[29] And He *continued* by questioning them, "But who do you say that I am?" Peter *answered and *said to Him, "You are the Christ [the Messiah]."[30] And He warned [strictly admonished] them to tell no one about Him.

[31] And He began to teach them that the Son of Man must suffer many things and be rejected by the elders and the chief priests and the scribes, and be killed, and after three days rise again.[32] And He was stating the matter plainly. And Peter took Him aside and began to rebuke Him.[33] But turning around and seeing His disciples, He rebuked Peter and *said, "Get behind Me, Satan; for you are not setting your mind on God's interests [the things of God], but man's."

[34] And He summoned the crowd with His disciples, and said to them, "If anyone wishes to come after Me, he must deny himself, and take up his cross and follow Me.[35] For whoever wishes to save his life [soul-life] will lose it, but whoever loses his life [soul-life] for My sake and the gospel's will save it.[36] For what does it profit a man to gain the whole world, and forfeit his soul [soul-life]?[37] For what will a man give in exchange for his soul [soul-life]?[38] For whoever is ashamed of Me and My words in this adulterous and sinful generation, the Son of Man will also be ashamed of him when He comes in the glory of His Father with the holy angels."

9:1 And Jesus was saying to them, "Truly I say to you, there are some of those who are standing here who will not taste death until they see the kingdom of God after it has come with power."

[2] Six days later, Jesus *took with Him Peter and James [Jacob] and John, and *brought them up on a high mountain by themselves. And He was transfigured before them;[3] and His garments became radiant and exceedingly white, as no launderer on earth can whiten them.[4] Elijah appeared to them along with Moses; and they were talking with Jesus.[5] *Peter *said to Jesus, "Rabbi, it is good for us to be here; let us make three tabernacles [sacred tents], one for You, and one for Moses, and one for Elijah."*[6] *For he did not know what to answer; for they became terrified.*[7] Then a cloud formed [occurred], overshadowing them, and a voice came out [occurred] of the cloud, "This is My beloved Son, listen [give constant heed] to Him!"[8] All at once they looked around and saw no one with them anymore, except Jesus alone.

[9] As they were coming down from the mountain, He gave them orders not to relate to anyone what they had seen, until [except when] the Son of Man rose from the dead.[10] *They seized upon [kept to themselves] that statement, discussing with one another*

what rising from the dead meant.[11] *They asked Him, saying, "Why is it that the scribes say that Elijah must come first?"*[12] And He said to them, "Elijah does first come and restore all things. And *yet* how is it written of the Son of Man that He will suffer many things and be treated with contempt?[13] But I say to you that Elijah has indeed [also] come, and they did to him whatever they wished, just as it is written of him."

[14] *When they came back to the disciples, they saw a large crowd around them, and some scribes arguing with them.*[15] *Immediately, when the entire crowd saw Him, they were amazed and began running up to greet Him.*[16] *And He asked them, "What are you discussing with them?"*[17] *And one of the crowd answered Him, "Teacher, I brought You my son, possessed with a spirit which makes him mute;*[18] *and whenever it seizes him, it slams him to the ground and he foams at the mouth, and grinds his teeth and stiffens out. I told Your disciples to cast it out, and they could not do it."*[19] And He *answered them and *said, "O unbelieving generation, how long shall I be with you? How long shall I put up with you? Bring him to Me!"[20] They brought the boy to Him. When he saw Him, immediately the spirit threw him into a convulsion, and falling to the ground, he *began* rolling around and foaming *at the mouth.*[21] And He asked his father, "How long has this been happening to him?" And he said, "From childhood.[22] It has often thrown him both into the fire and into the water to destroy him. But if You can do anything, take pity on us and help us!"[23] And Jesus said to him, "'If You can?' All things are possible to him who believes."[24] Immediately the boy's father cried out and said, "I do believe; help my unbelief."[25] When Jesus saw that a crowd was rapidly gathering, He rebuked the unclean spirit, saying to it, "You deaf and mute spirit, I [myself] command you, come out of him and do not enter him again."[26] After crying out and throwing him into terrible convulsions, it came out; and *the boy* became so much like a corpse that most *of them* said, "He is dead!"[27] But Jesus took him by the hand and raised him; and he got up.[28] When He came into *the* house, His disciples *began* questioning Him privately, "Why could we not drive it out?"[29] And He said to them, "This kind cannot come out by anything but prayer."

[30] From there they went out and *began* to go through Galilee, and He did not want anyone to know *about it.*[31] For He was teaching His disciples and telling them, "The Son of Man is to be delivered [betrayed] into the hands of men, and they will kill Him; and when He has been killed, He will rise three days later."[32] *But they did not understand this statement, and they were afraid to ask Him.*

[33] *They came to Capernaum; and when He was in the house, He began to question them, "What were you discussing on the way?"*[34] *But they kept silent, for on the way they had discussed with one another which of them was the greatest.*[35] Sitting down, He called the twelve and *said to them, "If anyone wants to be first, he shall be [let him be] last of all and servant of all."[36] Taking a child, He set him before them, and taking him in His arms, He said to them,[37] "Whoever receives one child like this in My name receives Me; and whoever receives Me does not receive Me, but Him who sent Me."

[38] *John said to Him, "Teacher, we saw someone casting out demons in Your name, and we tried to prevent him because he was not following us."*[39] But Jesus said, "Do not hinder him, for there is no one who will perform a miracle in My name, and be able soon afterward to speak evil of Me.[40] For he who is not against us is for us [on our side].[41] For whoever gives you a cup of water to drink because of your name as *followers* of Christ, truly I say to you, he will not lose his reward.

[42] "Whoever causes one of these little ones who believe to stumble, it would be better for him if, with a heavy millstone hung around his neck, he had been cast into the sea.[43] If your hand causes you to stumble, cut it off; it is better for you to enter life crippled, than, having your two hands, to go into hell [Gehenna], into the unquenchable fire,[44] (where 'their worm does not die, and the fire is not quenched'.)[45] If your foot causes you to stumble, cut it off; it is better for you to enter life lame, than, having your two feet, to be cast into hell,[46] (where 'their worm does not die, and the fire is not quenched'.)[47] If your eye causes you to stumble, throw it out; it is better for you to enter the kingdom of God with one eye, than, having two eyes, to be cast into hell [Gehenna],[48] where 'their worm does not die, and the fire is not quenched' [Isa 66:24]. [49] "For everyone will be salted with fire.[50] Salt is good; but if the salt becomes unsalty, with what will you make it salty *again*? Have salt in yourselves, and be at peace with one another."

10:1 Getting up, He *went from there to the region of Judea and beyond the Jordan; crowds *gathered around Him again, and, according to His custom, He once more *began* to teach them.

[2] *Some Pharisees came up to Jesus, testing Him, and began to question Him whether it was lawful for a man to divorce a wife.*[3] And He answered and said to them, "What did Moses command you?"[4] They said, "Moses permitted *a man* 'to write a certificate of divorce and send *her* away' [Deut 24:1, 3].[5] But Jesus said to them, "Because of your hardness of heart he wrote you this commandment.[6] But from the beginning of creation, 'God made them male and female' [Gen 1:27; 5:2].[7] 'For this reason a man shall leave his father and mother [and shall cleave to his wife],[8] and the two shall become one flesh' [Gen 2:24]; so they are no longer two, but one flesh.[9] What therefore God has joined together, let no man separate."

[10] In the house the disciples *began* questioning Him about this again.[11] And He *said to them, "Whoever divorces his wife and marries another woman commits adultery against her;[12] and if she herself divorces her husband and marries another man, she is committing adultery."

[13] *And they were bringing children to Him so that He might touch them; but the disciples rebuked them.*[14] But when Jesus saw this, He was indignant and said to them, "Permit the children to come to Me; do not hinder them; for the kingdom of God belongs to such as these.[15] Truly I say to you, whoever does not receive the kingdom of God like a child will not enter it *at all*."[16] And He took them in His arms and *began* blessing them, laying His hands on them.

¹⁷ As He was setting out on a journey, a man ran up to Him and knelt before Him, and asked Him, "Good Teacher, what shall I do to inherit eternal life?"¹⁸ And Jesus said to him, "Why do you call Me good? No one is good except God alone.¹⁹ You know the commandments, 'Do not murder, Do not commit adultery, Do not steal, Do not bear false witness,' Do not defraud, 'Honor your father and mother'" [Exod 20:12–16; Deut 5:16–20].²⁰ And he said to Him, "Teacher, I have kept all these things from my youth up."²¹ Looking at him, Jesus felt a love for him and said to him, "One thing you lack: go and sell all you possess and give to the poor, and you will have treasure in heaven; and come, follow Me."²² *But at these words he was saddened, and he went away grieving, for he was one who owned much property.*

²³ *And Jesus, looking around, *said to His disciples, "How hard it will be for those who are wealthy to enter the kingdom of God!"²⁴ The disciples were amazed at His words. But Jesus *answered again and *said to them, "Children, how hard it is to enter the kingdom of God!²⁵ It is easier for a camel to go through the eye of a needle than for a rich man to enter the kingdom of God."²⁶ They were even more astonished and said to Him, "Then who can be saved?"²⁷* Looking at them, Jesus *said, "With people it is impossible, but not with God; for all things are possible with God."

²⁸ Peter began to say to Him, "Behold, we have left everything and followed You."²⁹ Jesus said, "Truly I say to you, there is no one who has left house or brothers or sisters or mother or father or children or farms, for My sake and for the gospel's sake,³⁰ but that he will receive a hundred times as much now in the present age, houses and brothers and sisters and mothers and children and farms, along with persecutions; and in the age to come, eternal life.³¹ But many *who are* first will be last, and the last, first."

³² They were on the road going up to Jerusalem, and Jesus was walking on ahead of them; *and they were amazed, and those who followed were fearful.* And again He took the twelve aside and began to tell them what was going to happen to Him,³³ *saying,* "Behold, we are going up to Jerusalem, and the Son of Man will be delivered [betrayed] to the chief priests and the scribes; and they will condemn Him to death and will hand Him over to the Gentiles.³⁴ They will mock Him and spit on Him, and scourge Him and kill *Him*, and three days later He will rise again."

³⁵ *James [Jacob] and John, the two sons of Zebedee, *came up to Jesus, saying, "Teacher, we want You to do for us whatever we ask of You."³⁶ And He said to them, "What do you want Me to do for you?"³⁷ They said to Him, "Grant that we may sit, one on Your right and one on Your left, in Your glory."³⁸* But Jesus said to them, "You do not know what you are asking. Are you able to drink the cup that I drink, or to be baptized with the baptism with which I am baptized?"³⁹ They said to Him, "We are able." And Jesus said to them, "The cup that I drink you shall drink; and you shall be baptized with the baptism with which I am baptized.⁴⁰ But to sit on My right or on *My* left, this is not Mine to give; but it is for those for whom it has been prepared."

⁴¹ *Hearing this, the ten began to feel indignant with James [Jacob] and John.⁴²* Calling them to Himself, Jesus *said to them, "You know that those who are recognized as

rulers of the Gentiles lord it over them; and their great men exercise authority over them.[43] But it is not this way among you, but whoever wishes to become great among you shall be your servant;[44] and whoever wishes to be first among you shall be slave of all.[45] For even the Son of Man did not come to be served, but to serve, and to give His life [soul-life] a ransom for many."

Mark 10:46—11:33: Jesus' "Battle"

10:46 Then they *came to Jericho. And as He was leaving Jericho with His disciples and a large crowd, a blind beggar *named* Bartimaeus, the son of Timaeus, was sitting by the road.[47] When he heard that it was Jesus the Nazarene, he began to cry out and say, "Jesus, Son of David, have mercy on me!"[48] *Many were sternly telling him to be quiet,*but he kept crying out all the more, "Son of David, have mercy on me!"[49] And Jesus stopped and said, "Call him *here.*" So they *called the blind man, saying to him, "Take courage, stand up! He is calling for you."[50] Throwing aside his cloak, he jumped up and came to Jesus.[51] And answering him, Jesus said, "What do you want Me to do for you?" And the blind man said to Him, "Rabboni [My Master], *I want* to regain my sight!"[52] And Jesus said to him, "Go; your faith has saved you." Immediately he regained his sight and *began* following Him on the road.

11:1 As they *approached Jerusalem, at Bethphage and Bethany, near the Mount of Olives, He *sent two of His disciples,[2] and *said to them, "Go into the village opposite you, and immediately as you enter it, you will find a colt tied *there*, on which no one yet has ever sat; untie it and bring it *here.*[3] If anyone says to you, 'Why are you doing this?' you say, 'The LORD has need of it'; and immediately he will send it back here."[4] They went away and found a colt tied at the door, outside in the street; and they *untied it.[5] *Some of the bystanders were saying to them, "What are you doing, untying the colt?"*[6] They spoke to them just as Jesus had told *them*, and they gave them permission.[7] They *brought the colt to Jesus and put their coats on it; and He sat on it.[8] And many spread their coats in the road, and others *spread* leafy branches which they had cut from the fields.[9] Those who went in front and those who followed were shouting:

"Hosanna [Save Now]!

'Blessed is he who comes in the name of the LORD' [Ps 118:25–26];

[10] Blessed *is* the coming kingdom of our father David;

Hosanna in the highest!"

[11] Jesus entered Jerusalem *and came* into the temple; and after looking around at everything, He left for Bethany with the twelve, since it was already late.

[12] On the next day, when they had left Bethany, He became hungry.[13] Seeing at a distance a fig tree in leaf, He went *to see* if perhaps He would find anything on it; and when He came to it, He found nothing but leaves, for it was not the season for figs.[14] He said to it, "May no one ever eat fruit from you again!" And His disciples were listening.

¹⁵ Then they *came to Jerusalem. And He entered the temple and began to drive out those who were buying and selling in the temple, and overturned the tables of the money changers and the seats of those who were selling the doves;¹⁶ and He would not permit anyone to carry merchandise [a vessel] through the temple.¹⁷ And He *began* to teach and say to them, "Is it not written, 'My house shall be called a house of prayer for all the nations'? [Isa 56:7] But you have made it a 'robbers' den' [Jer 7:11]"¹⁸ *The chief priests and the scribes heard this, and began seeking how to destroy Him; for they were afraid of Him, for the whole crowd was astonished at His teaching.*

¹⁹ When evening came, they would go out of the city.

²⁰ As they were passing by in the morning, they saw the fig tree withered from the roots up.²¹ Being reminded, Peter *said to Him, "Rabbi, look, the fig tree which You cursed has withered."²² And Jesus *answered saying to them, "Have faith in God.²³ Truly I say to you, whoever says to this mountain, 'Be taken up and cast into the sea,' and does not doubt in his heart, but believes that what he says is going to happen, it will be *granted* him.²⁴ Therefore I say to you, all things for which you pray and ask, believe that you have received them, and they will be *granted* you.²⁵ Whenever you stand praying, forgive, if you have anything against anyone, so that your Father who is in heaven will also forgive you your transgressions.²⁶ [But if you do not forgive, neither will your Father who is in heaven forgive your transgressions."]

²⁷ *They *came again to Jerusalem. And as He was walking in the temple, the chief priests and the scribes and the elders *came to Him,²⁸ and began saying to Him, "By what authority are You doing these things, or who gave You this authority to do these things?"²⁹* And Jesus said to them, "I will ask you one question, and you answer Me, and *then* I will tell you by what authority I do these things.³⁰ Was the baptism of John from heaven, or from men? Answer Me."³¹ *They began reasoning among themselves, saying, "If we say, 'From heaven,' He will say, 'Then why did you not believe him?'³² But shall we say, 'From men'?"—they were afraid of the people, for everyone considered John to have been a real prophet.³³ Answering Jesus, they *said, "We do not know." And Jesus *said to them, "Nor will I tell you by what authority I do these things."*

Mark 12:1–44: Jesus' "Hero's Recovery"

12:1 And He began to speak to them in parables: "A man 'planted a vineyard and put a wall around it, and dug a vat under the wine press and built a tower' [Isa 5:2], and rented it out to vine-growers [tenant farmers] and went on a journey.² At the *harvest* time he sent a slave to the vine-growers, in order to receive *some* of the produce of the vineyard from the vine-growers.³ *They took him, and beat him and sent him away empty-handed.⁴ Again he sent them another slave, and they wounded him in the head, and treated him shamefully.⁵ And he sent another, and that one they killed; and so with many others, beating some and killing others.⁶* He had one more *to send*, a beloved son; he sent him last *of all* to them, saying, 'They will respect my son.'⁷ *But those vine-growers* said to one another, 'This is the heir; come, let us kill him, and the inheritance will be ours!'⁸ They took him, and killed him and threw him out of the vineyard.⁹ What will the owner [lord] of the vineyard do? He will come and destroy the vine-growers, and will give the vineyard to others.¹⁰ Have you not even read this Scripture:

'The stone which the builders rejected,

This became the chief corner *stone*;

¹¹This came about from the LORD,

And it is marvelous in our eyes'? [Ps 118:22–23]

¹² And they were seeking to seize Him, and *yet they feared the people [crowd], for they understood that He spoke the parable against them. And so they left Him and went away.*
¹³ *Then they *sent some of the Pharisees and Herodians to Him in order to trap Him in a statement.*
¹⁴ *They *came and *said to Him, "Teacher, we know that You are truthful and defer to no one [court no man's favor]; for You are not partial to any, but teach the way of God in truth. Is it lawful [permissible] to pay a poll-tax to Caesar, or not?¹⁵ Shall we pay or shall we not pay?"*But He, knowing their hypocrisy, said to them, "Why are you testing Me? Bring Me a denarius to look at."¹⁶ They brought *one.* And He *said to them, "Whose likeness and inscription is this?" And they said to Him, "Caesar's."¹⁷ And Jesus said to them, "Render to Caesar the things that are Caesar's, and to God the things that are God's." And they were amazed at Him.

¹⁸ *Some Sadducees (who say that there is no resurrection) *came to Jesus, and began questioning Him, saying,¹⁹ "Teacher, Moses wrote for us that 'If a man's brother dies' and leaves behind a wife 'and leaves no child, his brother should marry the wife and raise up children to his brother' [Deut 25:5]. ²⁰ There were seven brothers; and the first took a wife, and died leaving no children.²¹ The second one married her, and died leaving behind no children; and the third likewise;²² and so all seven left no children. Last of all the woman died also.²³ In the resurrection, when they rise again, which one's wife will she be? For all seven had married her."²⁴* Jesus said to them, "Is this not the reason you are mistaken, that you do not understand [know] the Scriptures or the power of God?²⁵ For when they rise from the dead, they neither marry nor are given in marriage, but are like angels in heaven.²⁶ But regarding the fact that the dead rise again, have you not read in the book of Moses, in the *passage* about *the burning* bush, how God spoke to him, saying, 'I am the God of Abraham, and the God of Isaac, and the God of Jacob'? [Exod 3:6] ²⁷ He is not the God of the dead [corpses], but of the living; you are greatly mistaken."

²⁸ *One of the scribes came and heard them arguing, and recognizing that He had answered them well, asked Him, "What commandment is the foremost of all?"²⁹* Jesus answered, "The foremost is, 'Hear, O Israel! The LORD our God is one Lord;³⁰ And you shall love the LORD your God with all your heart, and with all your soul, and with all your mind, and with all your strength' [Deut 6:4–5]. ³¹ The second is this, 'You shall love your neighbor as yourself' [Lev 19:18]. There is no other commandment greater

than these."[32] The scribe said to Him, "Right, Teacher; You have truly stated that 'He is one, and there is no one else besides Him' [Deut 4:35]; [33] 'And to love Him with all the heart and with all the understanding and with all the strength, and to love one's neighbor as himself' [Deut 6:5; Lev 19:18], is much more than all burnt offerings and sacrifices" [1 Sam 15:22; Hos 6:6; Mic 6:6–8].[34] When Jesus saw that he had answered intelligently, He said to him, "You are not far from the kingdom of God." After that, no one would venture to ask Him any more questions.

[35] And Jesus *began* to say, as He taught in the temple, "How *is it that* the scribes say that the Christ [the Messiah] is the son of David?[36] David himself said in [by] the Holy Spirit,

'The LORD said to my Lord,

'Sit at My right hand,

Until I put Your enemies beneath Your feet." [Ps 110:1]

[37] David himself calls Him 'Lord'; so in what sense is He his son?" And the large crowd enjoyed listening to Him.

[38] In His teaching He was saying: "Beware of the scribes who like to walk around in long robes, and *like* respectful greetings in the market places,[39] and chief seats in the synagogues and places of honor at banquets,[40] who devour widows' houses, and for appearance's sake offer long prayers; these will receive greater condemnation."

[41] And He sat down opposite the treasury, and *began* observing how the people were putting money into the treasury; and many rich people were putting in large sums.[42] A poor widow came and put in two small copper coins [lepta], which amount to a cent [quadrans].[43] Calling His disciples to Him, He said to them, "Truly I say to you, this poor widow put in more than all the contributors to the treasury;[44] for they all put in out of their surplus [abundance], but she, out of her poverty, put in all she owned, all she had to live on [her whole livelihood]."

Mark 13:1—14:52: Jesus' "Enemy Ascendant"

13[:1] As He was going out of the temple, one of His disciples *said to Him, "Teacher, behold what wonderful [how great the] stones and what wonderful [how great the] buildings!" [2] And Jesus said to him, "Do you see these great buildings? Not one stone will be left upon another which will not be torn down."

[3] As He was sitting on the Mount of Olives opposite the temple, Peter and James [Jacob] and John and Andrew were questioning Him privately, [4] "Tell us, when will these things be, and what *will be* the sign [attesting miracle] when all these things are going to be fulfilled?" [5] And Jesus began to say to them, "See to it that no one misleads you. [6] Many will come in My name, saying, 'I am *He!*' and will mislead many. [7] When you hear of wars and rumors of wars, do not be frightened; *those things* must take place; but *that is* not yet the end. [8] For nation will rise up against nation, and kingdom against

kingdom; there will be earthquakes in various places; there will *also* be famines. These things are *merely* the beginning of birth pangs.

[9] "But be on your guard [look to yourselves]; for they will deliver you to *the* courts [Sanhedrin/council], and you will be flogged in *the* synagogues, and you will stand before governors and kings for My sake, as a testimony to them. [10] The gospel must first be preached to all the nations. [11] When they arrest [lead] you and hand you over, do not worry beforehand about what you are to say, but say whatever is given you in that hour; for it is not you who speak, but *it is* the Holy Spirit. [12] Brother will betray brother to death, and a father *his* child; and children will rise up against parents and have them put to death [put them to death]. [13] You will be hated by all because of My name, but the one who endures to the end, he will be saved.

[14] "But when you see the 'Abomination of Desolation' [Dan 9:27; 11:31; 12:11] standing where it should not be (let the reader understand), then those who are in Judea must flee to the mountains. [15] The one who is on the housetop must not go down, or go in to get anything out of his house; [16] and the one who is in the field must not turn back to get his coat. [17] But woe to those who are pregnant and to those who are nursing babies in those days! [18] But pray that it may not happen in the winter. [19] For those days will be a *time of* tribulation such as has not occurred since the beginning of the creation which God created until now, and never will. [20] Unless the LORD had shortened *those* days, no life [flesh] would have been saved; but for the sake of the elect [chosen ones], whom He chose, He shortened the days. [21] And then if anyone says to you, 'Behold, here is the Christ [Messiah]'; or, 'Behold, *He is* there'; do not believe *him*; [22] for false Christs and false prophets will arise, and will show signs [attesting miracles] and wonders, in order to lead astray, if possible, the elect. [23] But take heed; behold, I have told you everything in advance.

[24] "But in those days, after that tribulation, 'The sun will be darkened and the moon will not give its light' [Isa 13:10], [25] 'and the stars will be falling' [Isaiah 34:4] from heaven, and the powers that are in the heavens [heaven] will be shaken. [26] Then they will see 'the Son of Man coming in clouds' [Dan 7:13] with great power and glory. [27] And then He will send forth the angels, and will gather together His elect [chosen ones] from the four winds, from the farthest end of the earth to the farthest end of heaven.

[28] "Now learn the parable from the fig tree: when its branch has already become tender and puts forth its leaves, you know that summer is near. [29] Even so, you too, when you see these things happening, recognize [know] that He [it] is near, *right* at the door[s]. [30] Truly I say to you, this generationwill not pass away until all these things take place. [31] Heaven and earth will pass away, but My words will not pass away. [32] But of that day or hour no one knows, not even the angels in heaven, nor the Son, but the Father *alone*.

[33] "Take heed, keep on the alert; for you do not know when the *appointed* time will come. [34] *It is* like a man away on a journey, *who* upon leaving his house and putting

his slaves in charge, *assigning* to each one his task, also commanded the doorkeeper to stay on the alert. [35] Therefore, be on the alert—for you do not know when the master [lord] of the house is coming, whether in the evening, at midnight, or when the rooster crows, or in the morning—[36] in case he should come suddenly and find you asleep. [37] What I say to you I say to all, 'Be on the alert!'"

14:[1] Now the Passover and Unleavened Bread were two days away; and the chief priests and the scribes were seeking how to seize Him by stealth and kill *Him;* [2] *for they were saying, "Not during the festival, otherwise there might be a riot of the people."*

[3] While He was in Bethany at the home of Simon the leper, and reclining *at the table,* there came a woman with an alabaster vial of very costly perfume of pure nard; *and* she broke the vial and poured it over His head. [4] *But some were indignantly remarking to one another, "Why has this perfume been wasted?* [5] *For this perfume might have been sold for over three hundred denarii [a year's wages], and the money given to the poor." And they were scolding her.* [6] But Jesus said, "Let her alone; why do you bother her? She has done a good deed to Me. [7] For you always have the poor with you, and whenever you wish you can do good to them; but you do not always have Me. [8] She has done what she could; she has anointed My body beforehand for the burial. [9] Truly I say to you, wherever the gospel is preached in the whole world, what this woman has done will also be spoken of in memory of her."

[10] *Then Judas Iscariot, who was one of the twelve, went off to the chief priests in order to betray Him [deliver Him up] to them.* [11] *They were glad when they heard this, and promised to give him money. And he began seeking how to betray Him at an opportune time.*

[12] On the first day of Unleavened Bread, when the Passover *lamb* was being sacrificed, His disciples *said to Him, "Where do You want us to go and prepare for You to eat the Passover?" [13] And He *sent two of His disciples and *said to them, "Go into the city, and a man will meet you carrying a pitcher of water; follow him; [14] and wherever he enters, say to the owner of the house, 'The Teacher says, "Where is My guest room in which I may eat the Passover with My disciples?"' [15] And he himself will show you a large upper room furnished *and* ready; prepare for us there." [16] The disciples went out and came to the city, and found *it* just as He had told them; and they prepared the Passover.

[17] When it was evening He *came with the twelve. [18] As they were reclining *at the table* and eating, Jesus said, "Truly I say to you that one of you will betray Me—one who is eating with Me." [19] They began to be grieved and to say to Him one by one, "Surely not I?" [20] And He said to them, "*It is* one of the twelve, one who dips with Me in the bowl. [21] For the Son of Man *is to* go just as it is written of Him; but woe to that man by [through] whom the Son of Man is betrayed! *It would have been* good for that man if he had not been born."

[22] While they were eating, He took *some* bread, and after a blessing [having blessed] He broke *it,* and gave *it* to them, and said, "Take *it*; this is My body." [23] And when He had taken a cup *and* given thanks, He gave *it* to them, and they all drank from it. [24] And He

said to them, "This is My blood of the covenant, which is poured out for many. ²⁵ Truly I say to you, I will never again drink of the fruit of the vine until that day when I drink it new in the kingdom of God."

²⁶ After singing a hymn, they went out to the Mount of Olives.

²⁷ And Jesus *said to them, "You will all fall away [stumble, be scandalized], because it is written, 'I will strike down the shepherd, and the sheep shall be scattered' [Zech 13:7].²⁸ But after I have been raised, I will go ahead of you to Galilee." ²⁹ But Peter said to Him, "*Even* though all may fall away [stumble, be scandalized], yet I will not." ³⁰ And Jesus *said to him, "Truly I say to you, that this very night [today, on this night], before a rooster crows twice, you yourself will deny Me three times." ³¹ But *Peter* kept saying insistently, "*Even* if I have to die with You, I will not deny You!" And they all were saying the same thing also.

³² They *came to a place named Gethsemane; and He *said to His disciples, "Sit here until I have prayed." ³³ And He *took with Him Peter and James [Jacob] and John, and began to be very distressed and troubled. ³⁴ And He *said to them, "My soul is deeply grieved to the point of death; remain here and keep watch." ³⁵ And He went a little beyond *them*, and fell [was falling] to the ground and *began* to pray that if it were possible, the hour might pass Him by. ³⁶ And He was saying, "Abba! Father! All things are possible for You; remove this cup from Me; yet not what I will, but what You will." ³⁷ And He *came and *found them sleeping, and *said to Peter, "Simon, are you asleep? Could you not keep watch for one hour? ³⁸ Keep watching and praying that you may not come into temptation; the spirit is willing, but the flesh is weak." ³⁹ Again He went away and prayed, saying the same words [word]. ⁴⁰ And again He came and found them sleeping, for their eyes were very heavy; and they did not know what to answer Him. ⁴¹ And He *came the third time, and *said to them, "Are you still sleeping and resting? It is enough; the hour has come; behold, the Son of Man is being betrayed [delivered up] into the hands of sinners. ⁴² Get up, let us be going; behold, the one who betrays Me is at hand!"

⁴³ *Immediately while He was still speaking, Judas, one of the twelve, *came up accompanied by a crowd with swords and clubs, who were from the chief priests and the scribes and the elders. ⁴⁴ Now he who was betraying Him had given them a signal, saying, "Whomever I kiss, He is the one; seize Him and lead Him away under guard [safely]." ⁴⁵ After coming, Judas immediately went to Him, saying, "Rabbi!" and kissed Him. ⁴⁶ They laid hands on Him and seized Him. ⁴⁷ But one of those who stood by drew his sword, and struck the slave of the high priest and cut off [took off] his ear. ⁴⁸* And Jesus said to them, "Have you come out with swords and clubs to arrest Me, as *you would* against a robber? ⁴⁹ Every day I was with you in the temple teaching, and you did not seize Me; but *this has taken place* to fulfill the Scriptures." ⁵⁰ *And they all left Him and fled.*

⁵¹ *A young man was following Him, wearing nothing but a linen sheet over his naked body; and they *seized him. ⁵² But he pulled free of the linen sheet and escaped naked.*

Mark 14:53—15:14: Jesus' "Victory"

14:⁵³ They led Jesus away to the high priest; and all the chief priests and the elders and the scribes *gathered together.⁵⁴ Peter had followed Him at a distance, right into the courtyard of the high priest; and he was sitting with the officers [servants] and warming himself at the fire [light].⁵⁵ *Now the chief priests and the whole Council [Sanhedrin] kept trying to obtain testimony against Jesus to put Him to death,*and they were not finding any.⁵⁶ For many were giving false testimony against Him, but their testimony was not consistent.⁵⁷ Some stood up and *began* to give false testimony against Him, saying,⁵⁸ "We heard Him say, 'I will destroy this temple [sanctuary] made with hands, and in three days I will build another made without hands.'"⁵⁹ Not even in this respect was their testimony consistent.⁶⁰ The high priest stood up *and came forward and questioned Jesus, saying, "Do You not answer? What is it that these men are testifying against You?"*⁶¹ But He kept silent and did not answer. Again the high priest was questioning Him, and saying [says] to Him, "Are You the Christ [Messiah], the Son of the Blessed One?"⁶² And Jesus said, "I am; and you shall see 'the Son of Man sitting at the right hand of Power' [Ps 110:1], and 'Coming with the clouds of heaven' [Dan 7:13]."⁶³ Tearing his clothes, the high priest *said, "What further need do we have of witnesses?⁶⁴ You have heard the blasphemy; how does it seem to you?" And they all condemned Him to be deserving of death.⁶⁵ Some began to spit at Him, and to blindfold Him [cover his face], and to beat Him with their fists, and to say to Him, "Prophesy!" And the officers received [treated] Him with slaps [blows with rods] *in the face.*

⁶⁶ As Peter was below in the courtyard, one of the servant-girls of the high priest *came,⁶⁷ and seeing Peter warming himself, she looked at him and *said, "You also were with Jesus the Nazarene."⁶⁸ But he denied *it, saying, "I neither know nor understand what you are talking about." And he went out onto the porch [forecourt/gateway] (and a rooster crowed).*⁶⁹ The servant-girl saw him, and began once more to say to the *bystanders, "This is one of them!"*⁷⁰ But again he denied it. And after a little while the bystanders were again saying to Peter, "Surely you are *one of them, for you are a Galilean too."*⁷¹ But he began to curse [put himself under a curse] and swear, "I do not know this man you are talking about!"⁷² Immediately a rooster crowed a second time. And Peter remembered how Jesus had made the remark to him, *"Before a rooster crows twice, you will deny Me three times."* And he began to weep.

15:¹ *Early in the morning the chief priests with the elders and scribes and the whole Council [Sanhedrin], immediately held a consultation; and binding Jesus, they led Him away and delivered Him to Pilate.*² Pilate questioned Him, "Are You the King of the Jews?" And He *answered him, "It is as you say."*³ The chief priests *began to accuse Him harshly [of many things].*⁴ Then Pilate questioned Him again, saying, "Do You not answer? See how many charges they bring against You!"⁵ But Jesus made no further answer; so Pilate was amazed.

[6] Now at *the* feast he used to release for them *any* one prisoner whom they request-ed.[7] The man named Barabbas had been imprisoned with the insurrectionists who had committed murder in the insurrection.[8] The crowd went up and began asking him *to do* as he had been accustomed to do for them.[9] Pilate answered them, saying, "Do you want me to release for you the King of the Jews?"[10] For he was aware that the chief priests had handed Him over because of envy.[11] But the chief priests stirred up the crowd *to ask him to release Barabbas for them instead.*[12] Answering again, Pilate said to them, "Then what shall I do with Him whom you call the King of the Jews?"[13] They shouted back [again], "Crucify Him!"[14] But Pilate said to them, "Why, what evil has He done?" *But they shouted all the more, "Crucify Him!"*

Mark 15:15–41: Jesus' "Battle Rejoined"

15:[15] *Wishing to satisfy the crowd, Pilate released Barabbas for them, and after having Jesus scourged, he handed Him over to be crucified.*
[16] *The soldiers took Him away into the palace (that is, the Praetorium), and they *called together the whole Roman cohort [battalion].[17] They *dressed Him up in purple, and after twisting a crown of thorns, they put it on Him;[18] and they began to acclaim Him,* "Hail, King of the Jews!"[19] *They kept beating His head with a reed [staff], and spitting on Him, and kneeling and bowing before Him.[20] After they had mocked Him, they took the purple robe off Him and put His own garments on Him. And they *led Him out to crucify Him.*
[21] *They *pressed into service a passer-by coming from the country, Simon of Cyrene (the father of Alexander and Rufus), to bear His cross.*
[22] *Then they *brought Him to the place Golgotha, which is translated, Place of a Skull.[23] They tried to give Him wine mixed with myrrh; but He did not take it.[24] And they *crucified Him, and *divided up His garments among themselves, casting lots for them to decide what each man should take.[25] It was the third hour [9 a.m.] when they crucified Him.[26] The inscription of the charge against Him read [had been inscribed],* "THE KING OF THE JEWS."
[27] *They *crucified two robbers with Him, one on His right and one on His left.[28] [And the Scripture was fulfilled which says, "And He was numbered with transgressors." (Isa 53:12)][29] Those passing by were hurling abuse [blaspheming] at Him, 'wagging their heads' [Ps 22:7], and saying, "Ha! You who are going to destroy the temple and rebuild it in three days,[30] save Yourself, and come down from the cross!"[31] In the same way the chief priests also, along with the scribes, were mocking Him among themselves and saying, "He saved others; He cannot save Himself [can He not save Himself?].[32] Let this Christ, the King of Israel, now come down from the cross, so that we may see and believe!" Those who were crucified with Him were also insulting Him.*
[33] *When the sixth hour [noon] came, darkness fell [occurred] over the whole land until the ninth hour [3 p.m.].[34] At the ninth hour Jesus cried out with a loud voice,*

"Eloi, Eloi, Lama Sabachthani?" which is translated, "My God, My God, why have You forsaken Me?" [Ps 22:1a]³⁵ When some of the bystanders heard it, they *began saying, "Behold, He is calling for Elijah."*³⁶ Someone ran and filled a sponge with sour wine, put it on a reed, and gave Him a drink, saying, "Let us see whether Elijah will come to take Him down."³⁷ And Jesus uttered a loud cry, and breathed His last.³⁸ And the veil of the temple was torn in two from top to bottom.³⁹ When the centurion, who was standing right in front of [opposite] Him, saw the way He breathed His last, he said, "Truly this man was the Son of God!"

⁴⁰ There were also *some* women looking on from a distance, among whom *were* Mary Magdalene, and Mary the mother of James [Jacob] the Less [Little] and Joses, and Salome.⁴¹ When He was in Galilee, they used to follow Him and minister to [wait on] Him; and *there were* many other women who came up with Him to Jerusalem.

Mark 15:42—16:8: Jesus' "Triumph"

15:⁴² *When evening had already come, because it was the preparation day, that is, the day before the Sabbath,* ⁴³ *Joseph of Arimathea came, a prominent member of the Council, who himself was waiting for the kingdom of God; and he gathered up courage and went in before Pilate, and asked for the body of Jesus.* ⁴⁴ *Pilate wondered if He was dead by this time, and summoning the centurion, he questioned him as to whether He was already dead.* ⁴⁵ *And ascertaining this from the centurion, he granted the body to Joseph.* ⁴⁶ *Joseph bought a linen cloth, took Him down, wrapped Him in the linen cloth and laid Him in a tomb which had been hewn out in the rock; and he rolled a stone against the entrance of the tomb.*⁴⁷ Mary Magdalene and Mary the *mother* of Joses were looking on *to see* where He was laid.

16:¹ When the Sabbath was over, Mary Magdalene, and Mary the *mother* of James [Jacob], and Salome, bought spices, so that they might come and anoint Him. ² Very early on the first day of the week, they *came to the tomb when the sun had risen. ³ They were saying to one another, "Who will roll away the stone for us from the entrance of the tomb?" ⁴ Looking up, they *saw that the stone had been rolled away, although [for] it was extremely large. ⁵ Entering the tomb, they saw a young man sitting at the right, wearing a white robe; and they were amazed. ⁶ And he *said to them, "Do not be amazed; you are looking for Jesus the Nazarene, who has been crucified. He has risen; He is not here; behold, *here is* the place where they laid Him. ⁷ But go, tell His disciples and Peter, 'He is going ahead of you to Galilee; there you will see Him, just as He told you.'" ⁸ They went out and fled from the tomb, for trembling and astonishment had gripped them; *and they said nothing to anyone, for they were afraid.*

Mark 16:9–20: Jesus' "Enemy Punished"

16:9 [1Now after He had risen early on the first day of the week, He first appeared to Mary Magdalene, from whom He had cast out seven demons.10 She went and reported to those who had been with Him, *while they were mourning and weeping.*11 When they heard that He was alive and had been seen by her, they refused to believe it.

12 After that, He appeared in a different form to two of them while they were walking along on their way to the country.13 They went away and reported it to the others,*but they did not believe them either.*

14 Afterward He appeared to the eleven themselves as they were reclining *at the table*; and He reproached them for their unbelief and hardness of heart, because they had not believed those who had seen Him after He had risen.15 And He said to them, "Go into all the world and preach the gospel to all creation.16 He who has believed and has been baptized shall be saved; but he who has disbelieved shall be condemned.17 These signs [attesting miracles] will accompany those who have believed: in My name they will cast out demons, they will speak with new tongues;18 they will pick up serpents, and if they drink any deadly *poison*, it will not hurt them; they will lay hands on the sick, and they will recover."

19 So then, when the LORD Jesus had spoken to them, He was received up into heaven and 'sat down at the right hand of God' [Ps 110:1].20 And they went out and preached everywhere, while the LORD worked with them, and confirmed the word by the signs [attesting miracles] that followed.]

[2*And they promptly reported all these instructions to Peter and his companions. And after that, Jesus Himself sent out through them from east to west the sacred and imperishable proclamation of eternal salvation.*]

---

1 The NASB notes that some manuscripts do not contain verses 9–20 of this last chapter of the Gospel according to Mark.

2 The NASB notes that a few late manuscripts contain this verse, either at the end as here, or after verse 8.

Appendix 2

THE AUTHENTICITY OF MARK 16:9–20

First, the charge against the authenticity of Mark 16:9–20 should be stated: In the nineteenth century, the 'higher' critics began to claim that the final twelve verses of Mark's Gospel are unoriginal, having been added after the fact.[1] Their basis for this claim is that two manuscripts, codices Sinai (ℵ) and Vatican (B), both dating as early as the AD fourth century, demonstrate this. However, it is not difficult to show that despite these verses' absence from those two early manuscripts (assuming they are indeed early[2]), there is abundant earlier evidence of Mark 16:9–20 being clearly present in Mark's account, and therefore original. That evidence is principally found in allusions to and quotations of the final twelve verses of Mark in the writings of the early Church fathers.

Burgon identified nineteen patristic witnesses to the originality of these twelve verses.[3] I note four of the earliest of these witnesses here, which all clearly predate codices Sinai (ℵ) and Vatican (B), assuming those codices do indeed date as early as the AD fourth century:

(1) Papias of Hierapolis alludes to Mark 16:18, the clauses, "and when they drink deadly poison, it will not hurt them at all." Eusebius records that Papias heard from

---

1 This claim was first made by Johann J. Griesbach (Burgon, *Last Twelve Verses*, 20).

2 Cooper lays out the case that both codex Sinaiticus(ℵ) and codex Vaticanus (B) should actually be rejected as having been tampered with by a forger (Cooper, *Forging*, 57–66). Constantine von Tischendorf purportedly "discovered" Sinaiticus and advocated for Vaticanus to be included in the text of the New Testament (Cooper, *Forging*, 9–11). And yet, Tischendorf himself asserted that one and the same scribe clearly omitted the last twelve verses from both of these codices (Tischendorf, *Vaticanum*, xxi–xxiii; Harris, *Stichometry*, 73–74).

3 Burgon, *Last Twelve Verses*, 35.

the daughters of Apostle Philip of this apostolic sign gift occurring for an apostle (though not one of the Twelve) named in Acts 1:23, who is Joseph Barsabas Justus. This man was shortlisted as one of two disciples considered to replace Judas Iscariot as the twelfth apostle, though Matthias was chosen instead. Papias' description of the event is, "that after drinking noxious poison, through the Lord's grace he experienced no evil consequence."[4] Papias lived and wrote about AD 100[5] (more broadly, his years are ca. AD 60–130), which is over two hundred years before codices Vatican and Sinai are supposed to have been transcribed. How could Papias allude to a verse that did not exist?

Without Mark 16:18, the promise there from the LORD Jesus to give His apostles such miraculous authority that they would be able to drink deadly poison and yet be unharmedwould have no textual basis. Papias clearly alludes to Mark 16:18, then, that this sign gift was just one of many confirmations of the Gospel of the kingdom preached by the apostles. Critically, this miraculous sign that is to accompany and confirm the apostolic ministry of the Gospel of the kingdom is only laid out by Jesus here in Mark's account alone. If these verses were removed, we would not have this basis for what follows in the Acts of the Apostles, and extra-biblical witnesses, in terms of the apostles' message of the Gospel of the kingdom being affirmed by these Pentecostal powers—these special, miraculous sign gifts of the Spirit.

(2) Justin Martyr of Neapolis (Nablus) quotes Mark 16:20. When discussing the LORD Jesus' ascension and the actions of the apostles afterward, he writes the clause, "ἐξελθόντες πανταχοῦ ἐκήρυξεν"; "having moved out, they preached everywhere."[6] This clause is a direct quotation of 16:20.[7] As with the portion alluded to by Papias, it does not occur anywhere else in the New Testament. Justin Martyr could only have read it here in Mark 16:20. He wrote his *First Apology* in AD 151, about two hundred years before (the supposed dates of) MSS Vatican and Sinai. How could Justin Martyr quote this verse if it did not exist when he quoted from it?

(3) Irenaeus of Lyon quotes and discusses Mark 16:19 (ca. AD 180):[8] "So then, after the Lord Jesus [*sic*] had spoken to them, He was received up into Heaven, and sitteth [*sic*] on the right hand of God."[9] The final two clauses of this verse occur with this very wording (barring the addition of 'Jesus' and the tense of 'sits' instead of 'sat') only in Mark 16:19, and altogether occur only in Mark 16:19. Irenaeus' quotation of Mark 16:19 occurred over one hundred years before Vatican and Sinai were purportedly copied. Once again, if Mark 16:9–20 is not original, and did not exist, then how could Irenaeus have quoted from it?

4 Eusebius, *Ecclesiastical History* 3.39; Burgon, *Last Twelve Verses*, 39.

5 Burgon, *Last Twelve Verses*, 40.

6 Justin Martyr, *First Apology*, 1:45.

7 Burgon, *Last Twelve Verses*, 40.

8 Irenaeus, *Against Heresies* 3.10, 5; Burgon, *Last Twelve Verses*, 40.

9 Roberts et al., *Ante-Nicene Fathers*, 1:426.

(4) Hippolytus of Portus quotes Mark 16:17–18,[10] as recorded in the *Apostolic Constitutions:*[11] "Now these signs shall follow them that have believed in my name: they shall cast out devils; they shall speak with new tongues; they shall take up serpents; and if they drink any deadly thing, it shall by no means hurt them: they shall lay their hands on the sick, and they shall recover."Hippolytus was a contemporary of Irenaeus, writing ca. AD 190–227. So once again we ask, how could he have quoted Mark 16:17–18 if it is not original, and so did not exist at the time?

In light of this evidence, which is only a sampling, how can it be claimed that the absence of Mark 16:9–20 from the much later manuscripts, codices ℵ and B, should cause us to view these twelve verses as inauthentic? Such is an irrational and baseless claim.

---

10 Burgon, *Last Twelve Verses*, 40.

11 Hippolytus, *Apostolic Constitutions* 3.1.1; Roberts et al., *Ante-Nicene Fathers*, 7:479.

Appendix 3

ARE MIRACLES MYTHOLOGICAL?

As mentioned in the introduction, the miraculousness of Jesus and the Gospel accounts is not germane to the question of whether Jesus and the Gospels are mythological. However, it is important to briefly explain why. In order to understand miracles, we must return to the beginning.

The Bible states that the LORD God is the Creator of this universe (Gen 1–2). In fact, we are told that the LORD Jesus was the One through whom all things were created (e.g., John 1:1–3; Col 1:16). He miraculously created the universe out of nothing, simply by His spoken Word (e.g., Ps 33:6, 9; Heb 11:3). Since the beginning of time, which He created (Gen 1:1, 5, 14; Ps 104:19), and of which He has maintained a record in Scripture (e.g., Gen 5; 11), the LORD Jesus has been miraculously upholding and sustaining His universe (Jer 33:19–21; Col 1:17; Heb 1:3). That is, both the creation itself, and the daily sustained order and operation of this universe, which is called providence, are miracles of God in Jesus.[1]

This assertion of Scripture may at first seem preposterous, and yet, while the Bible clearly provides this explanation for the uniform natural laws of this universe, as well as additional, apparently miraculous (seemingly supernatural) events, as by the LORD Jesus' miraculous power, "the secular worldview cannot account for either of these things. In the secular [evolutionary] worldview there is no reason at all to expect the universe to be law-like. . . . Ironically, in the secular worldview, every time we are able to make a successful prediction about the future . . . it is a sort of 'miracle' because

---

1 See also Morris's discussion of miracles in his *Biblical Basis*, 63–86.

the secular worldview has absolutely no logical reason whatsoever for the uniformity of nature, and thus the success of science."[2]

This biblical understanding of the miraculous puts the matter of the LORD Jesus' miracles as recorded in the Gospel accounts into contextual light. It is the Bible that provides the explanation for the origin of this universe, for its sustained existence and order, and for the preconditions necessary to conduct scientific inquiry. Without the biblical Creator God—the LORD Jesus' creation and sustenance of this universe—humanity has no explanation for the present existence of the tools that must already be in place in order to engage in scientific investigation. These tools being: (1) the prior existence of the laws of nature, (2) the prior existence of the laws of logic, (3) the prior existence of laws of morality, and (4) the prior existence of the reliability of human senses and memory.[3] The Bible alone explains these realities, and the explanation is the prior existence, and miraculous power and work, of the biblical Creator God; Father, Son, and Holy Spirit.

How different, then, are Jesus' miracles in the Gospel accounts from the everyday providential miracles that are the basis of existence and our ability to conduct scientific investigation, all of which we all take for granted? Lisle offers the following comment:

> All of Christ's miracles were beyond our ordinary, everyday experiences. They were unusual and were designed to accomplish a specific purpose. Christ healed the sick because He had compassion on them, but these miracles also confirmed Christ's deity. This is what makes a miracle different from ordinary providence. A miracle is an extraordinary and unusual manifestation of God's power to accomplish a specific purpose.[4]

Providence itself is miraculous, but Lisle here highlights those miracles that are recognized as beyond providence. When, as recorded in the Gospel accounts, the LORD Jesus miraculously becomes a human being, and then works miracles that confirm that He is God (e.g., John 20:30–31), can we for that reason reject those accounts as mythological? Certainly not. To do so would be to reject the very miraculous reason that we, and all things, exist. And truly, would we expect the Creator and Sustainer God to behave any differently among us?

If the LORD did not work miracles when He became a man, would anyone believe who He claimed to be? C. S. Lewis cites John Robert Seeley's *Ecce Homo* to express this reality: "The Principle at the same moment that it explains the Rules supersedes them."[5] As Lewis concludes, "If the ultimate Fact is not an abstraction but the living God, opaque by the very fullness of His blinding actuality, then He might do things. He might work miracles."[6]

---

2 Lisle, *Ultimate Proof*, 153.

3 Lisle, *Ultimate Proof*, 45–66.

4 Lisle, *Ultimate Proof*, 152.

5. Seeley, *Ecce Homo*, 174, quoted in Lewis, *Miracles*, 385.

6 Lewis, *Miracles*, 385.

Bibliography

Alexander, Loveday. "What Is a Gospel?" In *The Cambridge Companion to the Gospels*, edited by Stephen C. Barton, 13–33. Cambridge: Cambridge University Press, 2006.

Alison, James. *The Joy of Being Wrong: Original Sin through Easter Eyes*. New York: Crossroad, 1998.

Alter, Robert, and Frank Kermode, eds. *The Literary Guide to the Bible*. Cambridge, MA: Harvard University Press, 1987.

Andersen, Francis I. *The Sentence in Biblical Hebrew*. The Hague: Mouton, 1974.

Anderson, G. W., and D. E. Anderson. *A Textual Key to the New Testament: A List of Omissions and Changes*. London: Trinitarian Bible Society, 2002.

Anderson, Paul N. *The Christology of the Fourth Gospel: Its Unity and Disunity in the Light of John 6*. Valley Forge, PA: Trinity, 1997.

Apollodorus. *Bibliotheca* [*The Library*]. Translated by James G. Frazer. 3 vols. Cambridge, MA: Harvard University Press, 1921.

Aristotle. *Poetics*. Vol. 23 of *Aristotle*. Translated by W. H. Fyfe. 23 vols. Cambridge, MA: Harvard University Press, 1932.

———. *Rhetoric*. Vol. 22 of *Aristotle*. Translated by J. H. Freese. 23 vols. Cambridge, MA: Harvard University Press, 1926.

Auffret, Pierre. *Voyez de Vos Yeux: Études Structurelle de Vingt Psaumes dont le Psaume 119*. Supplements to VT 48. Leiden: Brill, 1993.

Aune, David E. *The New Testament in its Literary Environment*. Philadelphia: Westminster, 1987.

Babylonian Talmud: Tractate Berakhot. Translated by Jacob Neusner. Chico, CA: Scholars, 1984.

Baillie, Gil. *Violence Unveiled: Humanity at the Crossroads*. New York: Crossroad, 1995.

Barber, Katherine, ed. *Canadian Oxford Dictionary*. 2nd ed. Oxford: Oxford University Press, 2004.

Barber, Peter John. "The Combat Myth and the Gospel's Apocalypse in the Harry Potter Series: Subversion of a Supposed Existential Given." *Journal of Religion and Popular Culture* 24.2 (2012) 183–200.

Barrett, C. K. *Essays on John*. London: SPCK, 1982.

Barth, Karl. *The Doctrine of the Word of God.* Vol. 1/1 of *Church Dogmatics.* Edited by G. W. Bromily and T. F. Torrance. Translated by G. W. Bromily. 2nd ed. Peabody, MA: Hendrickson, 1975.

Bateson, Gregory. "Toward a Theory of Schizophrenia." In *Steps to an Ecology of Mind,* by Gregory Bateson, 201–27. New York: Ballantine, 1972.

Bellinzoni, A. J., ed. *The Two-Source Hypothesis.* Macon, GA: Mercer University Press, 1985.

Ben-Sasson, H. H., ed. *A History of the Jewish People.* Cambridge, MA: Harvard University Press, 1976.

Berger, Peter. *The Sacred Canopy: Elements of a Sociological Theory of Religion.* Garden City, NY: Doubleday, 1967.

Berlin, Adele. *The Dynamics of Biblical Parallelism.* Bloomington: Indiana University Press, 1985.

Berthelot, Katell. "Jewish Views of Human Sacrifice in the Hellenistic and Roman Period." In *Human Sacrifice in Jewish and Christian Tradition,* edited by Karen Finsterbusch et al., 151–73. Boston: Brill, 2007.

Blomberg, Craig L. *The Historical Reliability of the Gospels.* 2nd ed. Nottingham: Apollos, 2007.

Bockmuehl, Markus. "Review of *The New Testament World: Insights from Cultural Anthropology,* 3rd ed., by Bruce J. Malina." *Bryn Mawr Classical Review,* April 19, 2002. Online. http://bmcr.brynmawr.edu/2002/2002-04-19.html.

Boehm, Omri. *The Binding of Isaac: A Religious Model of Disobedience.* New York: T&T Clark, 2007.

Bornkamm, Günther. "The Stilling of the Storm in Matthew." In *Tradition and Interpretation in Matthew,* by Günther Bornkamm et al., 30–53. London: SCM, 1963.

Breck, John. *The Shape of Biblical Language: Chiasmus in the Scriptures and Beyond.* Crestwood, NY: St. Vladimir's Seminary, 1994.

Brewer, Derek. "The Gospels and the Laws of Folktale: A Centenary Lecture." *Folklore* 90.1 (1979) 37–52.

Brown, Francis, et al. *The Brown-Driver-Briggs Hebrew and English Lexicon: With an Appendix Containing the Biblical Aramaic.* 13th printing. Peabody, MA: Hendrickson, 2010.

Brown, Raymond E. *An Introduction to the New Testament.* ABRL. New York: Doubleday, 1997.

Bullinger, Ethelbert W. *Figures of Speech Used in the Bible: Explained and Illustrated.* Grand Rapids: Baker, 1968.

Bultmann, Rudolf, and Karl Jaspers. *Myth and Christianity: An Inquiry into the Possibility of Religion Without Myth.* New York: Noonday, 1958.

Burgon, John W. *The Last Twelve Verses of the Gospel According to S. Mark: Vindicated against Recent Critical Objectors and Established.* Oxford: James Parker, 1871.

Burkardt, Hans. *The Biblical Doctrine of Regeneration.* Exeter: Paternoster, 1980.

Burridge, R. A. *What Are the Gospels? A Comparison with Graeco-Roman Biography.* Cambridge: Cambridge University Press, 1992.

Callois, Roger. *Man and the Sacred.* Translated by Meyer Barash. Glencoe, IL: Free Press, 1960.

Campbell, Joseph. *The Hero with a Thousand Faces.* 21st ed. Princeton, NJ: Princeton University Press, 1973.

Celsus. *On the True Doctrine: A Discourse Against the Christians.* Edited and translated by R. Joseph Hoffmann, New York: Oxford University Press, 1987.

Childs, Brevard S. "The Canonical Shape of the Prophetic Literature." *Interpretation* 32.1 (1978) 46–55.

———. *Myth and Reality in the Old Testament*. London: SCM, 1960.

———. *The New Testament as Canon: An Introduction*. Philadelphia: Fortress, 1984.

Chilton, Bruce. "Eucharist: Surrogate, Metaphor, Sacrament of Sacrifice." In *Sacrifice in Religious Experience*, edited by Albert I. Baumgarten, 175–88. Boston: Brill, 2002.

Clemen, Carl. *Religions of the World*. Translated by A. K. Dallas. London: George G. Harrap, 1931.

Cohn, Norman. *Cosmos, Chaos, and the World to Come*. 2nd ed. New Haven: Yale University Press, 2001.

Cooper, William R. *Acts, the Epistles, and Revelation*. Vol. 2 of *The Authenticity of the New Testament*. Portsmouth: Creation Science Movement, 2017.

———. *The Forging of Codex Sinaiticus*. Portsmouth: Creation Science Movement, 2016.

———. *The Gospels*. Vol. 1 of *The Authenticity of the New Testament*. Portsmouth: Creation Science Movement, 2013.

Culpepper, R. Alan. *Anatomy of the Fourth Gospel: A Study in Literary Design*. Philadelphia: Fortress, 1987.

Dalley, Stephanie. *Myths from Mesopotamia: Creation, Flood, Gilgamesh, and Others*. Rev. ed. Oxford: Oxford University Press, 2000.

Danby, Herbert. *The Mishnah: Translated from the Hebrew with Introduction and Brief Explanatory Notes*. London: Oxford University Press, 1938.

D'Arcy, Martin Cyril. *The Mind and Heart of Love*. Cleveland: World Meridian, 1962.

Davies, W. D., and Dale C. Allison. *A Critical and Exegetical Commentary on the Gospel According to Saint Matthew*. 3 vols. ICC. Edinburgh: T&T Clark, 1988–1997.

Delcourt, Marie. *Légendes et Cultes de Héros en Grèce*. Paris: Presses Universitaires de France, 1942.

Dibelius, Martin. *From Tradition to Gospel*. Cambridge: James Clarke, 1971.

Didache. In vol. 1 of *The Apostolic Fathers*, edited by Bart D. Erhman, 403–43. LCL. Cambridge, MA: Harvard University Press, 2003.

Diehl, Judith A. "What Is a 'Gospel'? Recent Studies in the Gospel Genre." *Currents in Biblical Research* 9.2 (2011) 171–99.

Douglas, Mary. *Purity and Danger: An Analysis of the Concepts of Pollution and Taboo*. London: Routledge, 1966.

Dostoevsky, Fyodor. *The Double*. In *Three Short Novels of Dostoevsky*, 1–150. Translated by Constance Garnett. New York: Anchor, 1960.

Dundes, Alan. "The Hero Pattern and the Life of Jesus." In *In Quest of the Hero*, edited by Robert A. Segal, 179–216. Princeton, NJ: Princeton University Press, 1990.

Durkheim, Emile. *Les Formes Élémentaires de la Vie Religeuse*. Paris: Presses Universitaires de France, 1968.

Edwards, James R. *The Gospel According to Mark*. PNTC. Grand Rapids: Eerdmans, 2002.

Eusebius of Caesarea. *Historia Eccclesiastica* [*Church History*]. In *Nicene and Post-Nicene Fathers* 1, *Second Series*, edited by Philip Schaff and Henry Wace, 73–403. Translated by A.C. McGiffert. Buffalo, NY: Christian Literature, 1890.

———. *Preparatio Evangelica* [*Preparation for the Gospel*]. Edited by Roger Pearse. Translated by E. H. Gifford. 15 vols. New York: H. Frowde, 1903.

Evans, Craig A. *Mark 8:27–16:20*. WBC 34B. Nashville: Thomas Nelson, 2001.

Finamore, Stephen. *God, Order, and Chaos: René Girard and the Apocalypse.* Paternoster Biblical Monographs. Eugene, OR: Wipf and Stock, 2009.

Fontenrose, Joseph. *Python: A Study of Delphic Myth and Its Origins.* Berkeley: University of California Press, 1980.

Forsyth, Neil. *The Old Enemy: Satan and the Combat Myth.* Princeton, NJ: Princeton University Press, 1987.

Foster, George M. "The Anatomy of Envy: A Study in Symbolic Behavior." *Current Anthropology* 13 (1972) 165–202.

———. "Peasant Society and the Image of Limited Good." *American Anthropologist.* 67 (1965) 293–315.

France, R. T. *The Gospel of Mark: A Commentary on the Greet Text.* NIGTC. Cambridge: Eerdmans, 2002.

Frazer, James G. *The Illustrated Golden Bough.* Edited by Mary Douglas. Abridged and Illustrated by Sabine MacCormack. London: MacMillan, 1978.

Fruchtenbaum, Arnold G. *The Footsteps of the Messiah: A Study of the Sequence of Prophetic Events.* Rev. ed. Tustin, CA: Ariel Ministries, 2004.

———. *Yeshua: The Life of Messiah from a Messianic Jewish Perspective.* Abridged version. San Antonio, TX: Ariel Ministries, 2018.

Frye, Northrop. *Anatomy of Criticism: Four Essays.* Princeton, NJ: Princeton University Press, 1971.

Garfinkel, Harold. "Conditions of Successful Degradation Ceremonies." *American Journal of Sociology* 61.5 (1956) 420–24.

Geden, A. S. *Mithraism.* London: MacMillan & Co., 1925.

Girard, René. "Are the Gospels Mythical?" *First Things* 62 (1996) 27–31.

———. *Battling to the End: Conversations with Benoit Chantre.* Translated by Mary Baker. Studies in Violence, Mimesis, and Culture. East Lansing: Michigan State University Press, 2010.

———. *Deceit, Desire, and the Novel: Self and Other in Literary Structure.* Translated by Yvonne Freccero. Baltimore: Johns Hopkins University Press, 1965.

———. "Disorder and Order in Mythology." In *Disorder and Order: Proceedings of the Stanford International Symposium*, edited by Paisley Livingston, 80–97. Stanford Literature Studies 1. Saratoga, CA: Anima Libri, 1984.

———. "The Evangelical Subversion of Myth." In *Politics and Apocalypse*, edited by Robert G. Hamerton-Kelly, 29–49. Studies in Violence, Mimesis, and Culture. East Lansing: Michigan State University Press, 2007.

———. *Evolution and Conversion: Dialogues on the Origins of Culture.* London: Continuum T&T Clark, 2008.

———. "The Founding Murder in the Philosophy of Nietzsche." In *Violence and Truth: On the Word of René Girard*, edited by Paul Dumouchel, 227–46. London: Athlone, 1988.

———. *I See Satan Fall Like Lightning.* Translated by James G. Williams. Maryknoll, NY: Orbis, 2001.

———. *Oedipus Unbound: Selected Writings on Rivalry and Desire.* Edited by Mark R. Anspach. Stanford, CA: Standford University Press, 2004.

———. *The One by Whom Scandal Comes.* Translated by M. B. DeBevoise. East Lansing: Michigan State University Press, 2014.

———. "The Plague in Literature and Myth." In *To Double Business Bound: Essays on Literature, Mimesis, and Anthropology*, by René Girard, 136–54. Baltimore: Johns Hopkins University Press, 1988.

———. "René Girard—Generative Scapegoating." In *Violent Origins: Walter Burkert, René Girard, and Jonathan Z. Smith on Ritual Killing and Cultural Formation*, edited by Robert Hamerton-Kelly, 73–145. Stanford, CA: Stanford University Press, 1987.

———. *The Scapegoat*. Translated by Yvonne Freccero. Baltimore: Johns Hopkins University Press, 1986.

———. "The Scapegoat: René Girard's Anthropology of Violence and Religion." Radio interview and transcript by David Cayley. Toronto: Canadian Broadcasting Corporation, 2001. Online. http://www.cbc.ca/radio/ideas/the-scapegoat-the-ideas-of-ren%C3%A9-girard-part-1-1.3474195

———. *Things Hidden Since the Foundation of the World*. Translated by Stephen Bann and Michael Metteer. Stanford, CA: Stanford University Press, 1987.

———. *Violence and the Sacred*. Translated by Patrick Gregory. Baltimore: Johns Hopkins University Press, 1979.

———. "Violence Renounced: Response by René Girard." In *Violence Renounced: René Girard, Biblical Studies, and Peacemaking*, edited by Willard M. Swartley, 308–20. Telford, PA: Pandora, 2000.

———. *When These Things Begin: Conversations with Michel Treguer*. Translated by Trevor Cribben Merrill. East Lansing: Michigan State University Press, 2014.

Golsan, Richard. *René Girard and Myth: An Introduction*. New York: Routledge, 2002.

Guelich, Robert A. *Mark 1–8:26*. WBC 34A. Nashville: Thomas Nelson, 1989.

Gundry, R. H. *Mark: A Commentary on His Apology for the Cross*. Grand Rapids: Eerdmans, 1993.

Gunkel, Hermann. *Schoepfung und Chaos in Urzeit und Endzeit: Eine Religionsgeschichtliche Untersuchung Liber Gen 1 und Ap Joh 12*. Goettingen: Vandenhoeck und Ruprecht, 1895.

Gregory, J. R. "Image of Limited Good, or Expectation of Reciprocity?" *Current Anthropology* 16 (1975) 73–92.

Hagedorn, Anselm C., and Jerome H. Neyrey. "'It Was Out of Envy That They Handed Jesus Over' (Mark 15:10): The Anatomy of Envy and the Gospel of Mark." *Journal for the Study of the New Testament* 69 (1998) 15–56.

Hamerton-Kelly, Robert G. *The Gospel and the Sacred: Poetics of Violence in Mark*. Minneapolis: Fortress, 1994.

———. *Sacred Violence: Paul's Hermeneutic of the Cross*. Minneapolis: Augsburg Fortress, 1992.

Harper, Douglas. "Criss-Cross." *Online Etymology Dictionary*. 2010. Online. http://www.etymonline.com/index.php?term=crisscross&allowed_in_frame=0.

Harrill, J. Albert. "Cannibalistic Language in the Fourth Gospel and Greco-Roman Polemics of Factionalism (John 6:52–66)." *Journal of Biblical Literature* 127.1 (2008) 133–58.

Harris, James Rendell. *Stichometry*. Charleston, SC: Sagwan, 2015.

Heussi, Karl. *Kompendium der Kirchengeschichte*. Tubingen: Mohr, 1957.

Holladay, William L. *A Concise Hebrew and Aramaic Lexicon of the Old Testament*. Grand Rapids: Eerdmans, 1988.

Horrell, David G. "Social Sciences Studying Formative Christian Phenomena: A Creative Movement." In the *Handbook of Early Christianity: Social Science Approaches*, edited by Anthony J. Blasi et al., 3–28. Walnut Creek, CA: AltaMira, 2002.

———. "Social-Scientific Interpretation of the New Testament: Retrospect and Prospect." In *Social-Scientific Approaches to New Testament Interpretation*, edited by David G. Horrell, 3–27. Edinburgh: T&T Clark, 1999.

House, H. Wayne. "Tongues and the Mystery Religions of Corinth." *Bibliotheca Sacra* 110.558 (1983) 134–48.

Hubert, Henri, and Marcel Mauss. *Sacrifice: Its Nature and Function*. Translated by W. D. Halls. Chicago: University of Chicago Press, 1964.

Humphreys, Colin J., and W. G. Waddington. "The Date of the Crucifixion." *Journal of the American Scientific Affiliation* 37 (1985) 2–10.

Inwood, Brad. *The Poem of Empedocles: A Text and Translation with Introduction*. Rev. ed. Toronto: University of Toronto Press, 2001.

Irenaeus. *Against Heresies*. In vol. 1 of *The Ante-Nicene Fathers* 1, edited by Alexander Roberts et al., 309–567. Reprint, Grand Rapids: Eerdmans, 1987.

Jackson, H. M. "The Death of Jesus in Mark and the Miracle from the Cross." *NTS* 33 (1987) 16–37.

Jeremias, Joachim. *Jerusalem in the Times of Jesus: An Investigation into Economic and Social Conditions During the New Testament Period*. Translated by Freda Helen Cave and Cyril Hayward Cave. Philadelphia: Fortress, 1969.

Johnson, Justin. "What Is Mid-Acts Dispensational Right Division?" Online. https://graceambassadors.com/what-is-mid-acts-pauline-dispensational-right-division.

Johnson, Samuel. *Dictionary of the English Language*. 3rd ed. Dublin: Jones & Ewing, 1768.

Josephus, Titus Flavius. *The Antiquities of the Jews*. In *Josephus: The Complete Works*, edited by William Whiston, 33–650. Nashville: Thomas Nelson, 1998.

———. *The Jewish War*. In *Josephus: The Complete Works*, edited by William Whiston, 667–930. Nashville: Thomas Nelson, 1998.

Juel, Donald. *Messiah and Temple: The Trial of Jesus in the Gospel of Mark*. SBLDS 31. Missoula, MT: Scholars, 1977.

Justin Martyr. *First Apology*. In vol. 1 of *The Ante-Nicene Fathers*, edited by Alexander Roberts et al., 159–87. Reprint, Grand Rapids: Eerdmans, 1987.

Kittel, Rudolf, ed. *Biblia Hebraica Stuttgartensia*. 5th ed. Stuttgart: Deutsche Bibelgesellschaft, 1997.

Kloppenborg, John S. *The Formation of Q*. Philadelphia: Fortress, 1987.

Klostermaier, Klaus K. *A Survey of Hinduism*. 3rd ed. Albany: State University of New York Press, 2007.

Kugel, James L. *The Idea of Biblical Poetry: Parallelism and its History*. New Haven: Yale University Press, 1981.

Kümmel, Werner Georg. *Introduction to the New Testament*. Translated by Howard Clark Kee. Nashville: Abingdon, 1975.

Lang, Bernhard. "This Is My Body: Sacrificial Presentation and the Origins of Christian Ritual." In *Sacrifice in Religious Experience*, edited by Albert I. Baumgarten, 189–205. Boston, MA: Brill, 2002.

Levenson, Jon D. *The Death and Resurrection of the Beloved Son: The Transformation of Child Sacrifice in Judaism and Christianity*. New Haven: Yale University Press, 1993.

Lévi-Strauss, Claude. *Anthropologie Structurale*. Paris: Plon, 1958.

———. *Structural Anthropology*. Translated by Jacobson and Schoepf. London: Penguin, 1973.

———. *Totemism*. Translated by Rodney Needham. London: Merlin, 1963.

Lewin, Ariel. *The Archaeology of Ancient Judea and Palestine*. Los Angeles: Getty, 2005.

Lewis, C. S. *God in the Dock: Essays on Theology and Ethics*. Grand Rapids: Eerdmans, 1972.

———. *Miracles*. In *The Complete CS Lewis Signature Classics*, by C. S. Lewis, 297–462. New York: HarperCollins, 2002.

Liddel, H. G., and Robert Scott. *An Intermediate Greek-English Lexicon*. 7th ed. Oxford: Clarendon, 1889.

Lienhardt, R. Godfrey. *Divinity and Experience: The Religion of the Dinka*. Rev. ed. Oxford: Oxford University Press, 1987.

Lightfoot, R. H. *St. John's Gospel: A Commentary*. Edited by C. F. Evans. London: Oxford University Press, 1969.

Livingston, David. "Who Was Nimrod?" *Bible and Spade* 14.3 (2001) 67–72.

Lisle, Jason. *The Ultimate Proof of Creation: Resolving the Origins Debate*. Green Forest, AR: Master, 2009.

Lowth, Robert. *Isaiah: A New Translation with a Preliminary Dissertation and Notes*. London: Tegg, 1848.

———. *Lectures on the Sacred Poetry of the Hebrews*. London: Tegg and Son, 1835.

Lund, Nils W. *Chiasmus in the New Testament: A Study in the Form and Function of Chiastic Structures*. Boston, MA: Hendrickson, 1992.

Luter, A. Boyd, and Michelle V. Lee. "Philippians as Chiasmus: Key to the Structure, Unity, and Theme Questions." *New Testament Studies* 41.1 (1995) 89–101.

MacDonald, Dennis R. *Mythologizing Jesus: From Jewish Hero to Epic Teacher*. Lanham, MD: Rowman & Littlefield, 2015.

Malina, Bruce J. *Christian Origins and Cultural Anthropology*. Atlanta: John Knox, 1986.

———. "Limited Good and the Social World of Early Christianity." *Biblical Theology Bulletin* 8 (1979) 162–76.

———. "Mediterranean Sacrifice: Dimensions of Domestic and Political Religion." *Biblical Theology Bulletin* 26 (1996) 26–44.

———. "The Mediterranean Self: A Social Psychological Model." In *The Social World of Jesus and the Gospels*, by Bruce J. Malina, 67–96. London: Routledge and Kegan Paul, 1996.

———. *The New Testament World: Insights from Cultural Anthropology*. 3rd ed. Louisville, KY: Westminster John Knox, 2001.

Malina, Bruce J., and Jerome H. Neyrey. *Calling Jesus Names: The Social Value of Labels in Matthew*. Sonoma, CA: Polebridge, 1988.

———. *Social-Science Commentary on the Synoptic Gospels*. Minneapolis: Fortress, 1992.

Malina, Bruce J., and Richard L. Rohrbaugh. *Social-Science Commentary on the Gospel of John*. Minneapolis: Fortress, 1998.

Marcus, Joel. *Mark 1–8: A New Translation with Introduction and Commentary*. AB 27. Toronto: Doubleday, 2005.

———. *Mark 8–16: A New Translation with Introduction and Commentary*. AYB 27A. London: Yale University Press, 2009.

Martin, Ernest L. *Secrets of Golgotha*. Alhambra, CA: ASK, 1988.

———. *The Temples that Jerusalem Forgot*. Portland, OR: ASK, 2000.

McKane, W. *A Critical and Exegetical Commentary on Jeremiah*. ICC. Edinburgh: T&T Clark, 1986.

McRay, John. *Archaeology and the New Testament*. Grand Rapids: Baker, 1991.

McVann, Mark S. "Rituals of Status Transformation in Luke-Acts: The Case of Jesus the Prophet." In *The Social World of Luke-Acts: Models for Interpretation*, edited by Jerome H. Neyrey, 333–60. Peabody, MA: Hendrickson, 1991.

Metzger, Bruce M. "Methodology in the Study of Mystery Religions and Early Christianity." In *Historical and Literary Studies: Pagan, Jewish, and Christian*, by Bruce M. Metzger, 1–24. New Testament Tools, Studies, and Documents 8. Leiden: Brill, 1968.

Milbank, John. *Theology & Social Theory: Beyond Secular Reason*. Oxford: Blackwell, 1990.

Morris, Henry M. *The Biblical Basis for Modern Science*. Rev. ed. Green Forest, AR: Master, 2002.

———. *Creation and the Second Coming*. Green Forest, AR: Master, 1991.

———. *The Genesis Record: A Scientific and Devotional Commentary on the Book of Beginnings*. Grand Rapids: Baker, 1976.

———. *The Long War Against God: The History and Impact of the Creation/Evolution Conflict*. Green Forest, AR: Master, 2000.

———. *The Revelation Record: A Scientific and Devotional Commentary on the Prophetic Book of the End Times*. Carol Stream, IL: Tyndale, 1983.

Novum Testamentum Graece [*Greek New Testament*]. 27th ed. Edited by Erwin Nestle et al. Stuttgart: Deutsche Bibelgesellschaft, 2001.

Neyrey, Jerome H. "Clean/Unclean, Pure/Polluted, and Holy/Profane: The Idea and the System of Purity." In *The Social-Sciences and New Testament Interpretation*, edited by Richard L. Rohrbaugh, 80–104. Peabody, MA: Hendrickson, 1996.

———, ed. *The World of Luke-Acts: Models for Interpretation*. Peabody, MA: Hendrickson, 1991.

Niditch, Susan. *Ancient Israelite Religion*. Oxford: Oxford University Press, 1997.

Nietzsche, Friedrich. *The Gay Science: With a Prelude in German Rhymes and an Appendix of Songs*. Edited by Bernard Williams. Translated by Josefine Nauckhoff. Cambridge: Cambridge University Press, 2001.

———. *The Will to Power*. Translated by Kaufmann and Hollingdale. New York: Columbia University Press, 1983.

Nordhofen, Jacob. *Durch Das Opfer Erloest? Die Bedeutung der Rede vom Opfer Jesu Christi in der Bibel und bei René Girard*. Wien: Lit Verlag, 2008.

Nygren, Anders. *Agape and Eros*. Translated by Philip S. Watson. 3 vols. New York: Harper & Row, 1969.

O'Callaghan, José. *Los Papiros Griegos de la Cueva 7 de Qumran*. Madrid: Biblioteca de Autores Cristianos, 1974.

Origen. *Origen Against Celsus*. In vol. 4 of *The Ante-Nicene Fathers 4*, edited by Alexander Roberts et al., 395–669. Reprint, Grand Rapids: Eerdmans, 1987.

Oswalt, John N. *The Bible Among the Myths: Unique Revelation or Just Ancient Literature?* Grand Rapids: Zondervan, 2009.

Oughourlian, Jean-Michel. *The Genesis of Desire*. Translated by Eugene Webb. East Lansing: Michigan State University Press, 2010.

———. *The Mimetic Brain*. Translated by Trevor Cribben Merrill. East Lansing: Michigan State University Press, 2016.

Pahl, P. D. "The Mystery Religions." *Australian Theological Review* 20 (1949) 20.

Philo of Alexandria. *Special Laws*. In *The Works of Philo: Complete and Unabridged*, edited by C. D. Yonge, 534–639. Peabody, MA: Hendrickson, 1993.

Pierce, Claude Anthony. *Conscience in the New Testament: A Study of Syneidesis in the New Testament.* Studies in Biblical Theology 15. London: SCM, 1955.

Pixner, Bargil. *Paths of the Messiah: Sites of the Early Church from Galilee to Jerusalem.* San Francisco: Ignatius, 2010.

Plutarch. *On Envy and Hate.* In *Plutarch's Morals,* edited by William W. Goodwin, 95–99. Cambridge, MA: John Wilson and Son, 1874.

Prince, Gerald. "Narratology." In the *Johns Hopkins Guide to Literary Theory and Criticism,* edited by Michael Groden and Martin Kreiswirth, 524. Baltimore: Johns Hopkins University Press, 1994.

Porpora, Douglas V. "Methodological Atheism, Methodological Agnosticism and Religious Experience." *Journal of the Theory of Social Behaviour* 36.1 (2006) 57–75.

Propp, Vladimir. *Morphology of the Folktale.* Edited by Louis W. Wagner. Translated by Laurence Scott. 2nd ed. Austin: University of Texas Press, 1971.

Raglan, FitzRoy Richard Somerset. *The Hero: A Study in Tradition, Myth, and Drama.* Mineola, NY: Dover, 2011.

Rank, Otto. *The Myth of the Birth of the Hero: A Psychological Exploration of Myth.* Translated by Gregory C. Richter and E. James Lieberman. Expanded and updated ed. Baltimore: Johns Hopkins University Press, 2004.

Reimarus, Hermann Samuel. *Apologie oder Schutzschrift für die vernünftigen Verehrer Gottes.* 1768. Unpublished.

"Reimarus, Hermann Samuel." In *New International Encyclopedia,* edited by Daniel Coit Gilman et al. 1st ed. New York: Dodd, Mead, 1905.

Rhoads, David, et al. *Mark as Story: An Introduction to the Narrative of a Gospel.* 3rd ed. Minneapolis: Fortress, 2012.

Robinson, John A. T. *Redating the New Testament.* London: SCM, 1976.

Rousseau, John J., and Rami Arav. *Jesus and His World: An Archaeological and Cultural Dictionary.* Minneapolis: Fortress, 1995.

Ryrie, Charles C. *Basic Theology: A Popular Systematic Guide to Understanding Biblical Truth.* Chicago: Moody, 1999.

Schmithals, Walter. *Wunder und Glaube; eine auslegung von Markus 4:35–6:6a.* Neukirchen-Vluyn, Germany: Neukirchener Verlag, 1970.

Schwager, Raymund. *Must There Be Scapegoats? Violence and Redemption in the Bible.* Translated by Maria L. Assad. 2nd ed. Leominster: Gracewing and Crossroad, 2000.

Schweitzer, Albert. *Paul and His Interpreters.* Translated by G. W. Montgomery. New York: MacMillann, 1950.

———. *The Quest of the Historical Jesus.* Translated by G. W. Montgomery et al. Minneapolis: Fortress, 2001.

Seeley, John Robert. *Ecce Homo: A Survey of the Life and Work of Jesus Christ.* 12th ed. London: MacMillan and Co., 1874.

Segal, Robert A., ed. *In Quest of the Hero.* Princeton, NJ: Princeton University Press, 1990.

———. *Myth: A Very Short Introduction.* Oxford: Oxford University Press, 2004.

Seltzer, Robert M. *Jewish People, Jewish Thought: The Jewish Experience in History.* New York: MacMillan, 1980.

Sergeant, J. *Lion Let Loose: The Structure and Meaning of St. Mark's Gospel.* Exeter: Paternoster, 1988.

Shakespeare, William. *Macbeth.* Edited by Kenneth Muir. London: Methuen, 1984.

Sharma, Arvind. *Religious Studies and Comparative Methodology: The Case for Reciprocal Illumination*. Albany, NY: State University of New York Press, 2005.

Stanton, Graham. *The Gospels and Jesus*. 2nd ed. Oxford: Oxford University Press, 2002.

Starobinski, Jean. "La Démoniaque de Gérasa." In *Analyse Structurale et Exégèse Biblique*, 63–94. Neuchatel, Switzerland: Labor Fides, 1971.

Stein, Robert H. *Mark*. BECNT. Grand Rapids: Baker Academic, 2008.

Suggs, M. Jack. "The Christian Two Ways Tradition: Its Antiquity, Form, and Function." In *Studies in New Testament and Early Christian Literature*, edited by D. E. Aune, 60–74. NTSupp 33. Leiden: Brill, 1972.

Tatian. *Diatessaron*. In vol. 10 of *The Ante-Nicene Fathers*, edited by Alexander Roberts et al., 35–138. Reprint, Grand Rapids: Eerdmans, 1987.

Taylor, Vincent. *The Formation of the Gospel Tradition*. London: MacMillan, 1953.

Theissen, Gerd. "A Theory of Primitive Christian Religion." *Ciberteologia: Journal of Theology & Culture* 4.17 (2008) 47–64.

Thérèse, Sandrine, and Brian Martin. "Shame, Scientist! Degradation Rituals in Science." *Prometheus* 28.2 (2010) 97–110.

Thiede, Carsten Peter. *The Earliest Gospel Manuscript? The Qumran Fragment 7Q5 and Its Significance for New Testament Studies*. Torquay: Paternoster, 1992.

Tischendorf, Constantine von. *Novum Testamentum Vaticanum. Post Angeli Maii Aloirumque Imperfectos Labores ex ipso Codice*. Charleston, SC: Nabu, 2012.

Tocqueville, Alexis de. *Democracy in America*. Edited by Eduardo Nolla. Translated by James T. Schleifer. Indianapolis: Liberty Fund, 2010.

Todd, Emmanuel. *The Explanation of Ideology: Family Structures and Social Systems*. Oxford: Blackwell, 1985.

Todorov, Tzvetan. *Grammaire du Décaméron*. Paris: Mouton, 1969.

Trebilco, Paul. *The Early Christians in Ephesus from Paul to Ignatius*. Tuebingen: Mohr Siebeck, 2004.

Trépanier, Simon. *Empedocles: An Interpretation*. Studies in Classics 2. New York: Routledge, 2004.

Triandis, Harry C. "Cross-Cultural Studies in Individualism and Collectivism." In *Nebraska Symposium on Motivation 1989*, edited by John J. Berman and Richard Dienstbier, 41–133. Lincoln: University of Nebraska Press, 1990.

Tsumura, David. *Creation and Destruction: A Reappraisal of the Chaoskampf Theory in the Old Testament*. Winona Lake, IN: Eisenbrauns, 2005.

———. *The Earth and the Waters in Genesis 1 and 2: A Linguistic Investigation*. Sheffield: JSOT, 1989.

Tuckett, Christopher M. "The Present Son of Man." *Journal for the Study of the New Testament* 14 (1982) 58–81.

Urbach, Ephraim E. *The Sages: Their Concepts and Beliefs*. Translated by Israel Abrahams. Cambridge, MA: Harvard University Press, 1987.

VanVoorst, Robert. *Jesus Outside the New Testament*. Grand Rapids: Eerdmans, 2000.

Verhoeven, Martin J. "Buddhism and Science: Probing the Boundaries of Faith and Reason." *Religion East and West* 1 (2001) 77–97.

Vos, Johannes Geerhardus. *The Self-Disclosure of Jesus: The Modern Debate about the Messianic Consciousness*. 2nd ed. Philipsburg, NJ: P & R, 2002.

Walcott, Peter. *Envy and the Greeks: A Study in Human Behavior*. Warminster: Ares & Phillips, 1978.

————. *Hesiod and the Near East.* Cardiff: University of Wales Press, 1966.

Walton, John H. *The Lost World of Genesis One.* Downers Grove, IL: IVP Academic, 2009.

Watts, Malcolm H. *The LORD Gave the Word: A Study in the History of the Biblical Text.* London: Trinitarian Bible Society, 1998.

Welch, John W., and Daniel B. McKinlay, eds. *Chiasmus Bibliography.* Provo, UT: Research, 1999.

Wenham, David. *Did St. Paul Get Jesus Right?: The Gospel According to Paul.* Oxford: Lion Hudson, 2010.

Wenham, David, and Steve Walton. *A Guide to the Gospels & Acts.* Vol. 1 of *Exploring the New Testament.* 2nd ed. Downers Grove, IL: IVP Academic, 2011.

Wenham, Gordon J. "The Coherence of the Flood Narrative." *Vetus Testamentum* 28.3 (1978) 336–48.

————. *Genesis 1–15.* Word Biblical Commentary 1. Waco, TX: Word, 1987.

West, M. L. *Hesiod: Theogony and Works and Days.* Oxford: Oxford University Press, 1988.

Williams, James G. "Foreword." In *I See Satan Fall Like Lightning,* by René Girard, ix–xxiv. Maryknoll, NY: Orbis, 2001.

————, ed. *The Girard Reader.* New York, NY: Crossroad Herder, 1996.

Wilson, Ellen Judy, and Peter Hanns Reill. *Encyclopedia of the Enlightenment.* Rev. ed. New York: Facts on File, 2004.

Witherington, Ben, III. *The Gospel of Mark: A Socio-Rhetorical Commentary.* Grand Rapids: Eerdmans, 2001.

Wright, N. T. *Jesus and the Victory of God.* Vol. 2 of *Christian Origins and the Question of God.* Minneapolis: Augsburg Fortress, 1996.

————. *The Resurrection of the Son God.* Vol. 3 of *Christian Origins and the Question of God* Minneapolis: Augsburg Fortress, 2003.

Yarbro Collins, Adela. *The Combat Myth in the Book of Revelation.* Missoula: Scholars, 1976.

————. *Mark: A Commentary.* Edited by Harold W. Attridge. Hermeneia. Minneapolis: Fortress, 2007.

Young, Bruce W. "Lewis on the Gospels as True Myth." *Inklings Forever* 4.1 (2004). Online. https://pillars.taylor.edu/inklings_forever/vol4/iss1/26.

Zakovitz, Yair. "Reflection Story—Another Dimension of the Evaluation of Characters in Biblical Narrative." *Tarbitz* 54.2 (1985) 165–76.

Subject Index

Abomination of Desolation, 209–11
acquisitive mimesis, 31, 33–34
Adam, 46, 164–66, 217, 219, 224, 255, 273
adversary, 54, 109
Aesculapius, 6
agonism, 37, 86–89
Alison, James, 268
all-against-one, 58, 63–64
angel(s), 197, 211–12, 253, 256
anti-myth-culture, 81, 101, 123, 126
anti-mythological, 110, 113, 130, 204, 221, 230,
    241, 243, 257
anti-sameness, 51, 116, 255, 261
anti-satiation, 128, 157
anti-scandal, 238, 246
anti-scapegoating, 179, 188
anti-segregation, 110, 116
anti-snare of striving, 201, 224
Apsu, 38–41
arch-myth-type, 11
Arch of Titus, 186
Aristotle, 17, 24, 29, 83, 84
ascension, 76, 91, 96, 199, 248, 304
authority (Jesus'), 189, 194
autolapidation, 141

Babylon (Babel), 37, 41
Babylonian Cosmogony, 37, 41, 53
Bacchus, 6
baptism, 74, 96, 106–11, 178, 189, 259–62, 273
    of repentance, 107
Barth, Karl, 10
Bartimaeus, 182–83, 188

battle (motif), 15, 25–26, 39–40, 59–62, 69,
    71–72, 87, 100, 108, 159–65, 168–69,
    170–89, 212, 291
battle rejoined (motif), 15, 25–26, 40, 69, 72,
    93–94, 100, 230–37, 240–47, 299
Beelzebub (Beelzebul), 54, 63, 134–35
Bellerophon, 6
Bel-Marduk (see Marduk and Nimrod), 25,
    37–41, 111, 249
Bethlehem, 49
betrayal, 217–19, 220–2, 226, 235
biblical chiasm genre, 17, 19, 23–24, 42–45,
    266, 269
    in the *Harry Potter* series, 24
biblical prophecy, 16, 22, 43, 106, 108, 113, 173,
    183, 189, 192, 195, 209–10, 213, 220–21,
    233, 235–36, 239, 244, 271–72
blasphemy, 84–85, 124–25, 135, 142, 187–89,
    230, 234, 238–39, 243, 246, 251, 255,
    263
Blomberg, Craig, 18
blood, 40–41, 64, 67–70, 73, 219, 226, 229, 254,
    273
Bockmuehl, Markus, 21
Body of Christ, 135, 271–73
Boehm, Omri, 16, 18–19, 24
Burgon, John, 257–58, 303–5

Caesar, 163, 195–96, 202, 266
cannibalism, 36, 68
Cayley, David, 17, 48, 53, 58–59, 62, 71, 75
Celsus, 5–6, 252
centurion, 230, 245, 247, 252, 300

Ancient Document Index

Luke

John